Explorations of the Psychoanalytic Mystics

Contemporary Psychoanalytic Studies
11

Contemporary Psychoanalytic Studies (*CPS*) is an international scholarly book series devoted to all aspects of psychoanalytic inquiry in theoretical, philosophical, applied, and clinical psychoanalysis. Its aims are broadly academic, interdisciplinary, and pluralistic, emphasizing secularism and tolerance across the psychoanalytic domain. CPS aims to promote open and inclusive dialogue among the humanities and the social-behavioral sciences including such disciplines as philosophy, anthropology, history, literature, religion, cultural studies, sociology, feminism, gender studies, political thought, moral psychology, art, drama, and film, biography, law, economics, biology, and cognitive-neuroscience.

Explorations of the Psychoanalytic Mystics

Dan Merkur

Rodopi

Amsterdam - New York, NY 2010

Cover Design: Studio Pollmann

The paper on which this book is printed meets the requirements of "ISO 9706:1994, Information and documentation - Paper for documents - Requirements for permanence".

ISBN: 978-90-420-2859-3
E-Book ISBN: 978-90-420-2860-9

Printed in the Netherlands

Contents

Preface

Because most psychoanalysts scorn and ignore mysticism, the mystical character of the writings of clinical psychoanalysts who were or are mystics has rarely been recognized. Little appreciated and badly understood by their fellow clinicians, the psychoanalytic mystics have almost entirely escaped attention outside the profession. The roster of psychoanalyst mystics nevertheless includes eminent analysts from several major schools within psychoanalysis: Otto Rank (1884-1939), Erich Fromm (1900-1980), Marion Milner (1900-1998), D. W. Winnicott (1896-1971), Heinz Kohut (1913-1981), Hans W. Loewald (1906-1993), Wilfred R. Bion (1897-1979), and, among living writers, James S. Grotstein, Neville Symington, and Michael Eigen. In this volume, I have examined both their explicit remarks about mysticism and whatever in their thinking is implicitly informed by their psychoanalytic orientations to mysticism. What emerges is a sea change in the understanding and practice of both psychoanalysis and mysticism.

In retrospect, I have come to wish that I had written this book prior to composing *Mystical Moments and Unitive Thinking* (Merkur, 1999); but neither I nor any of its readers conceptualized the current project at the time. After twenty years as an academic student of religion who was interested in applied psychoanalysis, I trained as a clinician in 2000-2005. One result of entering clinical practice has been a radical re-orientation to psychoanalytic literature. As an academic I appreciated the literature as a body of theories. Now I read the same texts as efforts to verbalize clinical observations that anyone may confirm (or disconfirm) independently. I no longer read psychoanalytic theorists only for their internal coherence. I now read them also for their correspondence to my experiences with my patients. My re-orientation has made for a great deal of re-reading familiar authors with new eyes, finding self-evident all manner of things whose presence I had never suspected. The current project began to take shape when I found myself appreciating the relevance to mysticism of a considerable body of psychoanalytic writings that are not conventionally read in such a manner. Where, for example, I had long prized a few passages where Winnicott discussed mysticism explicitly, I now appreciate the place of those passages in his clinical thinking and, conversely, the relevance to mysticism of his thought as a whole. Conversations with friends and colleagues made it obvious to me that the readings that I have been making are also of keen interest to others. This book is the result.

Previous studies of psychoanalytic mystics are limited, to my knowledge, to Michael Eigen's (1998a) discussion of several psychoanalytic mystics (Milner, Winnicott, Bion) who influenced his own thinking, Joan and Neville Symington's (1996) and James S. Grotstein's (2007) books on Bion, articles on Winnicott and Loewald and a few pages on Kohut by my friend James W. Jones (1992, 2001, 2002), and chapters on Fromm, Milner, Winnicott, and Bion that are addressed to a popular audience in Janet Sayers' (2003) survey of "love, psychology, mysticism, and religion" in psychotherapy. Of these writers, Jones alone has "dual competence" (Devereux, 1957) in both the academic study of religion and clinical psychotherapy.

Bion (1970, p. 89) hoped that psychoanalysis would become "a science of at-one-ment," but the psychoanalytic mystics have not formed a research tradition among themselves. They have not engaged each other in debate, nor even refined their ideas and practices through the give-and-take of open discussions. Some had contacts with a few others, but the views of several were lonely monologues. In undertaking a critical history of research, I have sought to present the individual points of view while noting, as occasions warrant, both untenable speculations and valuable contributions to the theory and practice of psychoanalysis. It has been my hope to facilitate the emergence of a conversation.

I owe thanks of various kinds in connection with this project. All creativity is intersubjective. I want to begin by thanking my supervisors and teachers at the Toronto Institute for Contemporary Psychoanalysis. I am particularly grateful for the comparative-integrative approach to psychoanalysis that Brent Willock (2007) has advocated. I wish also to remember the late George Awad, who one night asserted to my third year class that he was a physician and did not trouble himself about whether an intervention that worked was psychoanalytic or not. Working through George's disclosure cured me of an incipient "psychoanalytic superego," which I now conceptualize as a group hysteria that is cultivated at most psychoanalytic institutes. For me, psychoanalysis is, as Freud (1914b) allowed, any practice of psychotherapy that uproots transference and resistance; all else, including mysticism, is negotiable.

While I was a candidate, my interest in psychoanalytic mysticism and, more generally, spirituality was encouraged by guest lectures and workshops that Gerald J. Gargiulo, James S. Grotstein, and Adam Phillips gave. I also received much appreciated confirmation from members of the Platonism and Neoplatonism Group of the American Academy of Religion, to whose annual meeting in November 2005 I delivered a paper entitled "Wilfred R. Bion: Psychoanalysis as a Practice of Neoplatonic Mysticism." The conference paper has been expanded to become Chapter Nine. I owe a different debt to Thomas M. Brod of the New Center of Psychoanalysis in Los Angeles. It was while brainstorming with Tom in October 2006 that I decided to adopt Loewald's perspective on psychic integration as the organizing principle of this book. I thank Michael Eigen for his generous correspondence as I worked my way through his oeuvre and also for reading and commenting on the chapter about his work. James S. Grotstein and Neville Symington have similarly read and responded helpfully to the chapters on their work. Thank you both. Lastly, I dedicate this book to J. Gail White, my conversation partner and muse.

Acknowledgments

Thanks are due to the following authors, publishers, and publications for permission to reprint materials from the following publications.

Excerpts from "Dealing with the unconscious in psychotherapeutic practice: 3 lectures 1959," by Erich Fromm. *International Forum for Psychoanalysis* 9:3-4 (2000): 167-86. Copyright 1992, Estate of Erich Fromm. Used with permission of the Estate of Erich Fromm and Tayor and Francis UK, a division of Informa UK Limited.

Excerpts from "Psychoanalysis and Zen Buddhism," by Erich Fromm. In D. T. Suzuki, Erich Fromm, and Richard De Martino, *Zen Buddhism and Psychoanalysis*. New York: Harper & Brothers, 1960. Copyright 1960, Erich Fromm and 1996, Estate of Erich Fromm. Used with permission of the Estate of Erich Fromm.

Excerpts from *Emotion and Spirit: Questioning the Claims of Psychoanalysis and Religion*, by Neville Symington. London: Cassell, 1994. Copyright 1994, Neville Symington. Used with permission of Neville Symington and Karnac Books Ltd.

Excerpts from *An Experiment in Leisure*, by Joanna Field. London: Chatto & Windus, 1937. Copyright 2009, Estate of Marion Milner. Used with permission of Paterson Marsh Ltd on behalf of the Estate of Marion Milner.

Excerpts from *The Spirit of Sanity*, by Neville Symington. London: Karnac, 2001. Copyright 2001, Neville Symington. Used with permission of Neville Symington and Karnac Books Ltd.

Excerpts from *The Psychoanalytic Mystic*, by Michael Eigen. London: Free Association Books, 1998. Copyright 1998, Michael Eigen. Used with permission of Michael Eigen and Free Association Books.

Excerpts from *Who Is the Dreamer Who Dreams the Dream? A Study of Psychic Presences*, by James S. Grotstein. Hillsdale, NJ: Analytic Press, 2000. Copyright 2000, The Analytic Press. Used with permission of Taylor and Francis Group, LLC, a division of Informa plc., and James S. Grotstein.

One

The Oceanic Feeling

During most of the history of psychoanalysis, academic students of mysticism shared the unearned and, as we now know, mistaken assumption that mystical experiences were all one and the same. William James (1902) had proposed six invariants of mystical experiences: a sense of union (p. 321); a "consciousness of illumination"; and the subsidiary features of ineffability, noetic character, transiency, and passivity (pp. 292-94). In another influential formulation, Evelyn Underhill (1910) had suggested that "mysticism, in its pure form, is...the science of union with the Absolute, and nothing else, and...the mystic is the person who attains this union" (p. 72). These and similar definitions were taken for granted by Freud and almost all psychoanalytic writers; but we now know them to have been errors. The world's religions do not have a common core in mystical experiences that are everywhere one and the same (Katz, 1978, 1983; Almond, 1982). Mystical experiences do not provide a transcendent unity for global spirituality. The experiences are as individual as the dreams of sleep; their contents are shaped both by the particulars of individual mystics' lives and by shared cultural materials (Pike, 1965, pp. 147-48; Garside, 1972, pp. 101-2; Almond, 1982, pp. 162, 173-74).

The failure of the common core hypothesis has led some scholars to abandon the concept of "mysticism" as a mistaken scholarly construct. The popular use of the term is not as easily corrected, however; and ecumenically minded scholars continue to see the value of comparative studies of religious experiences. Recent cross-cultural studies count as mystical not only the unitive and nothingness experiences of Christian contemplatives, Jewish Kabbalists, Muslim Sufis, Hindu yogins, and Buddhist meditators, but also the interior dialogues of prophets, the visionary states of vision questers, shamans, Taoists, and others, and the motor compulsions of spirit mediums and the possessed. To reflect the current trend in comparative surveys, mysticism may be defined as a practice of religious ecstasies (that is, of religious experiences during alternate states of consciousness), together with whatever ideologies, ethics, rites, myths, legends, magics, and so forth, are related to the ecstasies (Merkur, 2002, 2009).

Many mystical traditions regard mystical experiences as transformative, but they refer to changes that are metaphysical. A mystical experience may be thought to integrate the mystic within God, the Way, or another metaphysical reality, or to confer magical or theurgical powers, salvation, justification, liberation, perfection, or another metaphysical attainment. Mystical transformations presumably boost self-esteem and possibly facilitate success in coping with stressful realities (Pargament, 1997). Mystical experiences may happen spontaneously or be cultivated through prayer, meditation, rituals, and/or psychoactive drugs. Importantly, mystical experiences are neither rare nor abnormal. In repeated surveys of adults in Britain, Australia, and America, one-third or more reported one or more experiences that were variously called mystical, spiritual, transcendent, or numinous (Spilka et al., 2003, p. 311). In double-blind experiments, mystical experiences were induced with 99% probability in normals, using a combination of the psychedelic drug psilocybin, positive expectations, and a supportive environment (Pahnke, 1966; Doblin, 1991; Griffiths et al., 2008). The uses of prayer and meditation to induce mystical states are, by contrast, more arduous and less reliable. They are nevertheless more accessible and effective than is often supposed (Deikman, 1963). In some religious traditions, a person is expected to pursue ethical and moral excellence in advance of mystical experience. Where meditation is performed, the procedures must be learned and practiced. Meditation is a generic term for thousands of different mental disciplines that manipulate attention and thinking, each to its own distinctive end. Because success in meditation requires the cultivation of a cognitive skill set (Brown, 1977), it neither requires nor causes character development (Brown & Engler, 1984). Richard Sterba (1968, p. 79) noted, however, that "every mystic experience of lasting effect is a...*tour-de-force* conflict solution." Like dreams, free associations, and some styles of meditation, mystical experiences are psychological events that can be conducive to the attainment and manifestation of conflict solutions; but they are by no means intrinsically or necessarily therapeutic.

The world's religions regularly consider mystical experiences discontinuous with normal waking sobriety. They are sacred moments, lasting seconds, minutes, or hours, that interrupt otherwise secular experiences of reality. Mystical experiences provide transient glimpses of ordinarily imperceptible spiritual phenomena. The sense of the discontinuity with the commonplace is often heightened by highly positive emotions that may attend mystical experiences: bliss, ecstasy, euphoria, love, innocence, absolution, esteem. Horrific, nightmarish episodes also occur. The psychoanalytic mainstream has regularly secularized this understanding of mysticism, but it has otherwise left the traditional religious paradigm unchallenged. Mystical experiences are called regressive episodes rather than sacred moments, but they are nevertheless allocated to a special category of anomalous experience that is theoretically split-off from the remainder of the mystical experiences are seen as encapsulated interludes that coincide with a personality style that can be discussed satisfactorily without reference to the mysticism. When clients report mystical experiences, the events are regularly treated as incidental and adventitious. They are not discussed, for example, as unconscious productions whose interest and therapeutic potential is equivalent to dreams. Mystical experiences are known to occur in a variety of circumstances; but almost all psychoanalysts think it appropriate to discuss schizophrenia, mania, hysteria, hypnosis, psychoactive drug use, and euphoric states during waking sobriety without reference to their mystical components.

FREUD AND HIS CONTEMPORARIES

Freud initiated the mainstream approach to the psychoanalysis of mysticism; but as Freud once quipped to Theodor Reik (1948, p. 513), "Moi, je ne suis pas un Freudiste." Freud had studied hypnotherapy in Paris with Jean-Marie Charcot, whose controversial diagnosis of Roman Catholic saints as hysterics had been responsible for reviving theological interest in mysticism among both Catholic and Anglican apologists (Knowles, 1967). Freud's lifelong opposition to animism, magic, ritual, and religion continued Charcot's anti-clerical project. Psychoanalysis's proximity to mysticism was nevertheless self-evident. In the early years when psychoanalysis was little known, Freud (1904) had occasion to remark, "To many physicians, even to-day, psychotherapy seems to be a product of modern mysticism" (pp. 157-58). What did Freud understand of mysticism in 1904? Bruno Goetz reported the following intervention during a consultation with Freud in that year. Goetz remembered Freud as having said:

> A clear, sparkling intelligence is one of the greatest gifts. The poet of the Bhagavad Gita would be the first to affirm that very thing....The Bhagavad Gita is a great and profound poem with awful depths. "And still it lay beneath me hidden deep in purple darkness there", says Schiller's diver, who never returns from his second brave attempt. If, however, without the aid of a clear intellect you become immersed in the world of the Bhagavad Gita, where nothing seems constant and where everything melts into everything else, then you are suddenly confronted by nothingness. Do you know what it means to be confronted by nothingness? Do you know what that means? And yet this very nothingness is simply a European misconception: the Hindu Nirvana

> is not nothingness, it is that which transcends all contradictions. It is not, as Europeans commonly take it to be, a sensual enjoyment, but the ultimate in superhuman understanding, an ice-cold, all-comprehending yet scarcely comprehensible insight. Or, if misunderstood, it is madness. What do these European would-be mystics know about the profundity of the East? They rave on, but they know nothing. And then they are surprised when they lose their heads and are not infrequently driven mad by it--literally driven out of their minds. (Goetz, 1975, p. 141)

If Goetz's memory is to be trusted, Freud began by contrasting "a clear intellect," implicitly referring to the secondary process of the system *Perception-Consciousness* (*Pcpt.-Cs.*), with a world "where nothing seems constant and where everything melts into everything else." This formulation anticipated Freud's (1933) description of the unconscious as "a chaos, a cauldron full of seething excitations" (p. 73). Freud went on to explain that this chaos suddenly gives way to a confrontation by a nothingness that "transcends all contradictions." Unlike the unconscious, Nirvana is not at all "a sensual enjoyment," but is instead "an ice-cold, all-comprehending yet scarcely comprehensible insight." Freud's distinction between the chaos of the Gita's mythology and the clarity of Nirvana onto which it gives way accurately summarized the doctrine of the *Yoga Aphorisms* of Patanjali (Merkur, 1999, pp. 18-21).

At a scientific meeting of the Vienna Psychoanalytic Society that was held on March 20, 1907, Häutler presented a paper on "Mysticism and Comprehension of Nature." He argued that a "*feeling* of unity is...projected onto nature and transformed into the understanding of nature" in both mysticism and science. Häutler further maintained that "when the mystic awakes from his blissful mood and returns to sober reality," he "construct[s] a world on the basis of two contrasting sensations" that reflect the "contrast" between the mystic state and sobriety. A third point of contact between mysticism and science was the concept of the infinite. Häutler ended his presentation with the observation that "since mysticism originates only in an abnormally intensified emotional life, the development of the [scientific] intellect must be viewed as a pathological symptom" (Nunberg & Federn, 1962, pp. 146-48). In the course of the ensuing discussion, Freud remarked that "in metaphysics, we are dealing with a projection of so-called endopsychic perceptions...the dim perception of his own psychic processes." Scientists engage in realistic perceptions of limited aspects of the outside world but otherwise fall back on anthropomorphic projections for the bulk of their thinking (Nunberg & Federn, 1962, p. 149).

In a paper that he delivered to the American Psychoanalytic Association in 1913, Trigant Burrow proposed that the neonate has no experience of anything existing but self. This speculation was the first psychoanalytic theory that the worldview of the newborn is solipsistic. Burrow (1914) stated:

> In the original social relationship, which is exemplified in that of mother and offspring, the relationship is not, for the primary, infantile psyche, truly social in the sense of being objective, as it comes to be later, but there is originally an identification of the object (the mother) with the primary ego; later, as was said, a differentiation takes place through the gradual entrance of obstacles which tend to emphasize more and more the other self or the non-ego and the derivative self or the secondary ego, and so is introduced the objective factor of experience, constitutive of the social relation, a relation which is thus not less social in respect to the self than in respect to others. (p. 123)

Burrow (1917) introduced the term "primary identification" in a further paper that he delivered in 1914. He continued to contrast the undifferentiated consciousness of the newborn with its differentiation; but by 1916 he was discussing the solipsistic phase as "preconscious." He attributed consciousness only to the subsequent stage, when self and its objects are differentiated.

> Before it may be said to experience satisfaction in any conscious sense, the organism does at least embody satisfaction as a condition of being. It is this state of tranquil quiescence, representative of the infant's existence prior to the inception of cognition, that I call the *preconscious*. It is thus a pre-judicial, a pre-conative, a pre-covetous phase of consciousness--a phase of consciousness which precedes the desire or the sexual phase. (Burrow 1917-18b, p. 164)

"There is as yet no cognition, no objectivation, no contrasting of the ego with the outer world, of the self with other selves--no *consciousness* in the habitual sense" (Burrow, 1918, p. 246). "Existing without object, it is, so to speak, one with life, like the course of the planets or the growth of trees. Being preconscious, it is in the truest sense unconscious" (ibid.). Burrow's denial of sexuality to the mystical preconscious phase was an attempt to reconcile the libido theories of Freud and Jung.

Burrow did not acknowledge sources for his ideas; but his theory of the end of the "mental oneness of the infant with the maternal organism" (p. 245) through the origin of consciousness blended Søren Kierkegaard's (1980) exegesis of the biblical Fall of Adam with Nietzsche's concept of primal unity (*Ur-Eine*), the mystical, Dionysian source of all existence (Danto, 2005, pp. 79, 98). Kierkegaard had imagined that every child replicates Adam's transition from unconscious, instinctive, amoral fellowship with animal life, to consciousness of self as a human being who makes choices between good and evil. Burrow (1958, p. 221) later reminisced that he had been much taken with Nietzsche's philosophy during his student years; his familiarity with Kierkegaard's thought may possibly have been at second hand. The phenomenological psychiatrist Karl Jaspers (1963) drew on both Nietzsche and Kierkegaard in his encyclopedic *Allgemeine Psychopathologie*, which he first published in 1913. In all events, Burrow, who was one of the eight founders of the American Psychoanalytic Association and served as its president in 1926 (Oberndorf, 1950), is to be credited with the first recognition that mystical experiences have implications for the psychoanalytic theory of child development.

Freud presented his own version of the same developmental process only months later. Freud wrote his essay "On Narcissism" in the early months of 1914 and published his text before Burrow's conference papers of 1913 saw print. In keeping with his lifelong habit of never citing any psychoanalytic writing to which he could not give unqualified endorsement, Freud made no mention of Burrow's contributions. Because Freud (1900, p. 574) conceptualized consciousness as "a sense organ for the apprehension of psychical qualities," he could not agree with Burrow that neonatal experience could involve percepts and affects without involving consciousness. Physiological sensations cannot be perceived mentally in the absence of consciousness. At the same time, Freud endorsed the postulated developmental transition from neonatal solipsism to realistic objectivity. To account for the transition, Freud postulated a distinction between "ego-libido" and "object-libido." Freud (1914a) explained that "a differentiation of libido into a kind which is proper to the ego and one which is attached to objects is an unavoidable corollary to an original hypothesis which distinguished between sexual instincts and ego-instincts" (p. 77). In this model, the unconscious furnishes libido, and consciousness supplies libido with a target. The initial target is the sensorium, which the infant naively treats as its ego. As the sensorium comes to be differentiated by means of reality testing into self and its objects, the libidinizing of the sensorium becomes differentiated too. "Thus we form the idea of there being an original libidinal cathexis of the ego, from which some is later given off to objects, but which fundamentally persists and is related to the object-cathexis much as the body of an amoeba is related to the pseudopodia which it puts out" (p. 75). Freud's technical term "primary narcissism" avoided the logical inconsistency in Burrow's term "primary identification," which had implied that a separate identity is known to be such, for only then could it be identified with. At the same time, Freud agreed with Burrow's idea that morality has its lifelong basis in neonatal solipsism. He differed only in minor details, again for the sake of precision, when he introduced his concept of the ego ideal and traced its origin to primary narcissism. "What he projects before him as his ideal is the substitute for the lost narcissism of his childhood in which he was his own ideal" (p. 94).

Other features in Freud's paper "On Narcissism" may be treated as unacknowledged responses to Herbert Silberer's *Problems of Mysticism and Its Symbolism* (1914), the first book-length psychoanalytic study of mysticism. Silberer claimed that mysticism accomplished a therapeutic resolution of the Oedipus complex by integrating conscience within consciousness. Freud published two articles the same year that implicitly distanced psychoanalysis from mysticism as Silberer had portrayed it. In "On Narcissism," Freud (1914a) attributed the judgments of conscience to a psychical agency whose values varied from person to person. The values were the individual ego's ideals. They were not shared ideals that were biologically determined; much less were they objective truths, as religious conceptions of conscience commonly alleged. The objectivity that Silberer had claimed for mysticism was consequently untenable. Freud also put into print a definition of psychoanalysis that he had previously voiced in 1911 in criticism of the Zurich school, led by Jung, at the Fourth Psychoanalytic Congress held at Nuremberg: "It is not the discovery and counting and tabulating of complexes that is the object of psychoanalysis, but the sole object of psychoanalysis is the overcoming of a patient's resistances" (Burrow, 1917-18a, p. 61). In "On the History of the Psychoanalytic Movement," which criticized the views of both Adler and Jung, Freud (1914b) famously defined psychoanalysis in terms of "the facts of transference and resistance. Any line of investigation which recognizes these two facts and takes them as the starting-point of its work has a right to call itself psycho-analysis" (p. 16). Mysticism, as discussed by Silberer, fell short of Freud's definition. It reconciled the ego with its conscience, but it did not engage in the special province of psychoanalysis: the address of resistance (including transference-resistance), which Freud attributed *ex hypothesi* to repression.

In 1919 (English translation, 1933), Sandor Ferenczi proposed the theory that genitality, the adult drive to coitus, is symbolically a return to the condition of the fetus in the womb. The concept of intrauterine regression was promptly taken up by psychoanalytic writers on mysticism. Cavendish Moxon (1920), whom Otto Rank had analyzed (Lieberman, 1985, p. 207), initiated the line of theoretic speculation when he described mystical experience as an "introversion" that involved a "lack of interest in reality" (p. 329). Moxon characterized the positive content of mysticism as autoerotic and narcissistic, meaning that it was both libidinal and devoted to the sense of self. He suggested that the content of the experience was "nothing less than a return to the intra-uterine condition," whose inclusion of a concept of God involved an additional "regression to the mother" (p. 330). "Mystical states of ecstasy" were hysterical in nature, and "mystics...are a sub-class of hysterics" (pp. 331, 334). Moxon summarized: "We may therefore posit in the mystics as well as in the hysterics a primary auto-erotic or narcissistic activity, a secondary repression, and a final return of the repressed activity in the sublimated or spiritualised form of a religious experience or a mystic ecstasy" (p. 335).

In a widely praised Berlin congress paper in 1922, Franz Alexander (1931) drew on Friedrich Heiler's (1932) discussion of comparative mysticism and suggested that both Hindu yogins and Buddhist meditators aspire to artificial catatonias--yogins by means of autohypnosis--that constitute "a regression to the condition before birth, immobility, being folded together, without breathing, lying in the mother" (p. 136). Theodore Schroeder (1922) agreed, and Alfred Carver (1924) similarly explained mystical experiences as regressions "to the undifferentiated subjective phase, which obtains *in utero* when there is complete organic harmony and union with the universe as then experienced, namely the mother" (p. 113).

Rank integrated the emerging consensus within his *Trauma of Birth* (1929b), whose first German edition appeared in 1924. Rank discussed hysterical dream states as "reproductions of the intrauterine state, or of birth....Withdrawal from the outer world is represented by psychical isolation" (p. 50). After noting that similar symbolism was "materialized in psychoses" (pp. 50-51), Rank remarked: "How near these states approach to mystical ecstasies and inner meditations is well known, although their origin is not understood" (pp. 50-51). Combining and extending the formulations of Freud and Alexander, Rank added: "The Hindu Yoga practice through mystical meditation likewise enables *each individual himself to become God*--that is, by entering the womb, by being transformed back into the embryo, he participates in the god-like omnipotence" (p. 130; Rank's italics).

Rank partly left and partly was expelled from the psychoanalytic movement over the reception of his *Trauma of Birth*. The book was methodologically consistent with Freud's work, and its thesis enlarged on an idea that Freud had twice presented in passing (Roazen, 1975, p. 400). Freud was initially extremely enthusiastic. He wrote Abraham: "When Rank first told me about his findings, I said jokingly: 'With an idea like that anyone else would set up on his own'" (Freud & Abraham, 1965, p. 352). On a walk with Ferenczi, Freud remarked: "I don't know if 33 or 66% of it is true, in any case, this is the most significant advance since the discovery of psychoanalysis" (Freud & Ferenczi, 2000, p. 131). Freud did not initially regard Rank's departures from his views as a threat to psychoanalysis. He wrote Abraham:

> Let us assume the most extreme case, and suppose that Ferenczi and Rank came right out with the view that we were wrong to stop at the Oedipus complex, and that the really decisive factor was the birth trauma, and that those who did not overcome this later broke down also on the Oedipus complex....We could remain under the same roof with the greatest equanimity, and after a few years' work it would become plain whether one side had exaggerated a useful finding or the other had underrated it. (Freud & Abraham, 1965, pp. 352-53)

Freud's expectations proved correct, but only when the importance of the pre-Oedipal period was proposed anew by later generations of analysts: Melanie Klein, Bertram D. Lewin, Margaret S. Mahler, and others.

The problem with Rank's book was the timing of its publication. Freud had recently been diagnosed with cancer and did not expect to survive. Rank was not only Freud's closest co-worker and most intimate friend; but Ferenczi and Rank had recently co-authored *The Development of Psychoanalysis* (1923), whose technical innovations established them as Freud's intellectual heirs apparent (Roazen, 1975, p. 397). Karl Abraham and Ernest Jones, presumably motivated by jealousy, poisoned Freud against Rank (Roazen, 1975, p. 401) by construing Rank's challenge to the privileging of the Oedipus complex as a challenge to the cause of psychoanalysis. Once panicked, Freud deployed his formidable skills to protect his legacy, and Rank's reputation was irreparably damaged. For his part Rank was deeply disturbed by Freud's ill health--Jones (1955, pp. 160, 187) called him hysterical--and over-reacted by rejecting not only Abraham and Jones, but also Freud and psychoanalysis. Abraham died soon afterward at the age of 48. Ferenczi abandoned Rank and recanted their work together in order to stay on good terms with Freud (Lieberman, 1985, pp. 211-260, 267; see also Ferenczi, 1927). Ferenczi nevertheless fell out with Freud again shortly before his own death in 1933.

A variety of theoretic and technical issues were disputed at the time, but it is always a mistake in intellectual history to misrepresent personality conflicts through "secondary revision" that rationalizes irrational behavior. Here it suffices to note that the consensus interpretation of mystical ecstasy as an intrauterine regression, which Rank had endorsed, abruptly disappeared from the psychoanalytic literature. The hegemony of the Oedipus complex was preserved against Rank's prioritizing of the pre-Oedipal relation to the mother, and politically correct theories of mysticism were proposed. In a frequently cited article that was originally published in 1927, Helene Deutsch (1989) discussed mystical ecstasy in terms of Freud's (1923a) structural hypothesis, which divided the psyche among the id, ego, and superego. Deutsch described mystical experience as "the feeling that the ego experiences a fusion of the spiritual part of the soul with God, and the sense of self disappears in favour of a higher, divine consciousness" (p. 719). Interpreting God as a symbol of the father representation that the superego internalized, Deutsch explained mystical experience as an identification of the ego with its superego.

> In the ecstatic experience the self fades away and God moves into its place, but this God is neither a loving nor a punishing personality but is the experience itself, the attainment of a new consciousness, that of one's own divinity through disappearance of the frontier between the self and God. In the state of ecstasy the idea of God that was projected outside is taken back into the ego again, but there is no conflict between ego and superego or between self and God, because self and God are both self. (Deutsch, 1989, p. 719)

Deutsch's discussion pertained to theistic mystical experiences in which a sense of the presence of God replaces the mystic's self-awareness. Its application to other varieties of mystical experience remained an open question.

During a scientific meeting of the Vienna Psychoanalytic Society in 1928 that discussed Freud's *Future of an Illusion* (1927a), Freud remarked in passing on "the mystic Weltanschauung."

> A great many cultured people who liberated themselves from religion adhere to this mystic Weltanschauung. Its essence is the high esteem of the irrational. The mystic Weltanschauung is the Weltanschauung of the future. Scholars, artists, scientists, embrace it and feel they have the right to look down on other Weltanschauungen....In contrast...the scientific Weltanschauung is

> honest, it has nothing to give, and even that nothing is uncertain. (Sterba, 1978, p. 179)

Freud's remarks on "the mystic Weltanschauung" agreed with the views that he had expressed in response to Häutler's paper two decades earlier.

The novelist Romain Rolland responded to Freud's *Future of an Illusion* with a personal letter in which he reported "a sensation of 'eternity', a feeling as of something limitless, unbounded--as it were, 'oceanic'....a feeling of an indissoluble bond, of being one with the external world as a whole" (pp. 64-65; see also Fisher, 1976; Parsons, 1999). Freud began the first chapter of *Civilization and Its Discontents* (1930) with a discussion of Rolland's experience. Implicitly because the self-report involved sense perception of external reality, Freud rejected previous formulations of mystical experiences as regressions to intrauterine experiences of the fetus. Also implicitly, because Rolland's self-report did not contain any theistic content, Freud discussed the "oceanic feeling" as a regression to a *neonatal* "ego-feeling," without reference to the superego whose origin he attributed to the resolution of the Oedipus complex around age five and a half. Freud (1930) wrote:

> An infant at the breast does not as yet distinguish his ego from the external world as the source of the sensations flowing in upon him. He gradually learns to do so, in response to various promptings.....originally the ego includes everything, later it separates off an external world from itself. Our present ego-feeling is, therefore, only a shrunken residue of a much more inclusive--indeed, an all-embracing--feeling which corresponded to a more intimate bond between the ego and the world about it (pp. 66-8).

Freud's description of the oceanic feeling as a regression to neonatal solipsism agreed with his formulation of 1914, where he had described neonatal solipsism in libidinal terms as "primary narcissism." Unlike intrauterine regression, neonatal solipsism was independent of the mother and so posed no threat to Freud's prioritizing of the father in the Oedipus complex. Freud accounted for theistic mystical experiences by speculating that "the oceanic feeling became connected with religion later on" (p. 72).

Following the several paragraphs that Freud devoted to Rolland's oceanic feeling, Freud added a further paragraph that has not enjoyed the attention that it deserves. Freud (1930) wrote:

> Another friend of mine, whose insatiable craving for knowledge has led him to make the most unusual experiments and has ended by giving him encyclopaedic knowledge, has assured me that through the practices of Yoga, by withdrawing from the world, by fixing the attention on bodily functions and by peculiar methods of breathing, one can in fact evoke new sensations and coenaesthesias in oneself, which he regards as regressions to primordial states of mind which have long ago been overlaid. He sees in them a physiological basis, as it were, of much of the wisdom of mysticism. It would not be hard to find connections here with a number of obscure modifications of mental life, such as trances and ecstasies. (pp. 72-73)

Anna Freud identified her father's anonymous friend as Friedrich Eckstein (c. 1860-1939). Freud knew Eckstein by 1894, when Freud arranged for his friend Wilhelm Fliess to operate on the nose of Eckstein's sister Emma (Masson, 1984, p. 233; Eckstein, 1936, p. 304). Eckstein was a minor celebrity in Vienna, publicly as an opera singer, and privately as Austria's leading occultist. Eckstein first became interested in mysticism as a teenager, turned to spiritualism around 1880, and soon joined the Theosophical Society. After corresponding with Theosophists internationally and visiting Theosophists in England, Eckstein helped found the Vienna Theosophical Society (J. Webb, 1976, pp. 42-44). Remembered as a powerful lecturer, Eckstein endorsed the traditional secrecy of the occult and wrote comparatively little. Both his knowledge of esotericism and his personal influences were nevertheless extensive. For example, Eckstein introduced Rudolf Steiner, then an academic specialist on Goethe, to alchemy, Rosicrucianism, and Theosophy (Leijenhorst, 2005, p. 1085). Freud's understanding of nirvana and his scorn of "European would-be mystics" presumably benefited from his friendship with Eckstein.

Following the paragraph in *Civilization and Its Discontents* on Eckstein's views, Freud concluded his chapter on the oceanic feeling with a quotation from Friedrich von Schiller's poem, "The Diver." Immediately following the words, "It would not be hard to find connections here with a number of obscure modifications of mental life, such as trances and ecstasies," Freud (1930) wrote:

> But I am moved to exclaim in the words of Schiller's diver:--
> '...Es freue sich,
> Wer da atmet im rosigten Licht.' (p. 73)

Strachey translated the poetry, "Let him rejoice who breathes up here in the roseate light!" (p. 73 n. 1). Contrary to what Freud is widely assumed to have thought about mysticism (for example, Leavy, 1995, p. 367), we here see him explicitly rejecting reductive discussions of trances and ecstasies in favor of a Romantic approach to the mystical.

Schiller's poem, which Freud had mentioned to Goetz over a quarter century earlier, tells of a king who threw a golden cup into a whirlpool and offered it to anyone who would dive to the sea bottom to fetch it up. When the diver, with cup in hand, broke the water surface, breathing air once again, he spoke the lines that Freud quoted. The poem goes on with the king proposing to throw a golden ring into the sea as a second challenge to the diver. When the king's daughter objected to placing the diver at renewed risk, the king announced that if the diver instead fetched the cup from the deep a second time, he would give him his daughter to marry. The diver accepted the conditions, but never returned from the sea (Schiller, 1844, pp. 125-31). The poem is possibly to be read as an early Romantic allegory of the soul's descent into the body, its return to the spiritual realm, and its subsequent reversion to the body and loss of immortality. More esoterically, the poem likely pertains to the initiation of a Freemason, whose third degree replicates the murder of Hiram Abiff and the raising of his corpse, but explicitly does not include his resurrection (Waite, 1916, p. 19). Like the diver, a masonic candidate descends but does not rise. By Freud's time, the multi-level allegory also supported reinterpretation in Nietzsche's terms of Apollonian order and Dionysian chaos.

Freud's quotation added a further level to the poem. Because Freud psychologized the Romantic categories (Merkur, 1993), we may read the diver in search of the cup as an analysand descending to the depths of the unconscious, negotiating its terrors, and returning successfully to the primacy of consciousness. In his second dive, however, the diver succumbed to the unconscious, like the "European would-be mystics" who--Freud had told Goetz--"know nothing. And then...are surprised when they lose their heads and are not infrequently driven mad." Even as Freud turned Schiller's poem to a psychoanalytic account, Schiller's intended reading would not have been lost on him. For Freud, the lines that he quoted from Schiller referred simultaneously, in Schiller's sense, to mystical death and ascension, and in Freud's, to a successful psychoanalysis.

Paul Federn may have influenced Freud's endorsement of the oceanic feeling. Vice-President of the Vienna Psychoanalytic Society at the time, Federn had been with Freud for a quarter century. At the scientific meeting in Vienna in 1907 when Häutler had spoken on mysticism, Federn had voiced his suspicion that "states of ecstasy" were not unknown to Häutler. Intimating that he was himself no stranger to ecstasy, Federn further remarked that he understood the opposition of those unfamiliar with the experiences. Federn stated:

> Knowledge, which seems so self-evident to us today, was once gained laboriously.
>
> Ecstasy seems to be the condition in which the great discoveries were made. The narrowing of the ideational field, combined with the feeling of pleasure, induced by ecstasy, causes the ecstatic individual to experience a totally different ego; hence his feeling of oneness with God. (Nunberg & Federn, 1962, p. 151)

Federn, we may infer, is to be counted among the psychoanalytic mystics.

An early contributor to ego psychology, Federn (1926) introduced the psychoanalytic concept of ego-feeling, contrasted mental ego-feeling with body ego-feeling, and suggested that mental ego-feeling has developmental priority. Federn suggested that mental ego-feeling alone "accompanies states of ecstasy and is responsible for the self-evident dualistic conviction of the separate existence of body and soul" (p. 437). Federn was also responsible for conceptualizing ecstasy as a mental orgasm. "Whenever a person tells us of an ecstatic, mystic, or artistic exaltation of libidinal satisfaction to an orgasm-like state, we usually learn of simultaneous autoerotic end-pleasure. It is not impossible, of course, that processes similar to end-pleasure and orgasm exist in the mental field also" (Federn, 1952, p. 353). Federn favored the term "ecstasy" in preference to "mysticism" because he followed popular usage (and Freud) in speaking of mysticism as an irrational *Weltanschauung*. Federn wrote, for example, that "Mysticism...would say that the mind leaves the body during sleep and returns to it on waking" (Federn, 1952, p. 74).

In a 1928 paper that he delivered to the Vienna Psychoanalytic Society, Federn suggested that primary narcissism persists and undergoes maturation unconsciously, after its conscious, infantile original has been superseded developmentally.

> Clandestinely, as it were, the narcissistic cathexes with ego feeling of many representations of the external world persist, they change and develop, they are given up and again are newly invested. Most deeply hidden, even from one's own consciousness, the entire world of primary narcissism remains extant, as dreams and psychosis reveal; for, the primary narcissistic ego (which

> comprised external world and individual) is repressed and becomes unconscious in its totality. (Federn, 1952, p. 302)

Federn named the "unconscious continuation" of primary narcissism as "the ego-cosmic ego" and suggested that its repression is lifted partially in dreams and psychoses (pp. 303, 305). The theory rephrased Rank's ideas about the persistence of intrauterine solipsism as an unconscious influence on later development in terms that were acceptable to Freud.

In a review of Freud's *Civilization and Its Discontent*, Federn (1932) presupposed his theory of the unconscious "ego-cosmic ego" when he criticized Freud's discussion of the oceanic feeling. In Federn's view, the oceanic feeling was not a direct and uncomplicated regression to primary narcissism. It was developmentally more advanced than primary narcissism--indeed, so markedly advanced that it was integrally connected with religion.

> I am not wholly of Freud's opinion when he thinks the religious feeling to be a restitution of the old narcistic [sic] primitive ego. There are two arguments against this. In the first place one would have to suppose that the child has a feeling something like the religious or oceanic, when it is still in the narcistic period of comprehension of the universe, when outer world and ego are not yet discerned in the ego-feeling. In the second place we always find the narcistic comprehension of the universe to be very uncertain like at psychosis and mystic trance, where the narcistic attitude towards the world has penetrated into later life. Religious feeling on the contrary makes man's attitude towards the world peaceful and secure. To my opinion the oceanic feeling does not restore the primitive ego. It appears when the normal limits of the ego are extended to the human, earthly and cosmic surrounding world with strong narcistic accentuation. Excessive narcistic occupation of the ego seems like any other excessive narcistic accentuation always to produce discomfort by excessive isolation. It is a fact that religious need makes man feel lonely and he is then oppressed by the narcistic isolation of his ego. The extension of the ego's limits to the universe are felt as pleasurable relaxation, then self-abandonment with more or less masochistic gratification and union producing normal libidinal gratification may give rise to high mental raptures. The extent of the narcistic occupation of the ego-limits is thus enlarged by the religious-oceanic feeling while its intensity is diminished. This theory which is only very slightly different from Freud's is supported by

> the fact that the oceanic feeling has the character of love for many people, as Freud shows with Franciscus of Assisi, and also by the fact that the religious is possible without any relation to God. On the other hand every analysis of "strictly" religious people can show us that the relation to God is possible alone with very little oceanic feeling. (Federn, 1932, pp. 134-35)

Freud did not respond directly to Federn's criticism, but his final contributions on the topic of mysticism tacitly conceded Federn's point that mysticism is not necessarily immature. In *New Introductory Lectures on Psycho-Analysis*, Freud (1933) acknowledged the affinity of psychoanalysis with a naturalistic understanding of the psychological effects of mysticism.

> It is easy to imagine...that certain mystical practices may succeed in upsetting the normal relations between the different regions of the mind, so that, for instance, perception may be able to grasp happenings in the depths of the ego and in the id which were otherwise inaccessible to it. It may safely be doubted, however, whether this road will lead us to the ultimate truths from which salvation is to be expected. Nevertheless it may be admitted that the therapeutic efforts of psycho-analysis have chosen a similar line of approach. Its intention is, indeed, to strengthen the ego, to make it more independent of the super-ego, to widen its field of perception and enlarge its organization, so that it can appropriate fresh portions of the id. Where id was, there ego shall be. It is a work of culture--not unlike the draining of the Zuider Zee. (pp. 79-80)

Freud denied that metaphysical truth and salvation may be attained through mysticism, because mysticism, like psychoanalysis, was "a work of culture." Freud acknowledged, however, that psychoanalysis and mysticism have similar effects on the ego, strengthening it, increasing its independence, widening its perception and enlarging its organization. In *Moses and Monotheism*, Freud (1939) asserted: "A child's emotional impulses are intensely and inexhaustibly deep to a degree quite other than those of an adult; only religious ecstasy can bring them back" (p. 134). Freud (1941) expressed the same concept differently at the very end of his life when he wrote: "Mysticism is the obscure self-perception of the realm outside the ego, of the id" (p. 300).

LATER CONTRIBUTIONS ON THE OCEANIC FEELING

Psychoanalytic orthodoxy treated Freud's theory of the oceanic feeling as a definitive formulation, ignored all else that he had written of mysticism, and added almost nothing new until the 1950s. At that time, several ego psychologists interpreted mystical experiences as regressions to falling asleep after satiated nursing (Lewin, 1951; Greenacre, 1958; Linn & Schwarz, 1958). Mystical experiences were regularly regarded as pathological regressions to infancy (Ostow & Scharfstein, 1954; Furst et al. 1976); but as large numbers of youths began to report mystical experiences in the 1960s, psychoanalysts began to speak of regression in the service of the ego, which is considered wholesome (Deikman, 1966a, 1966b; Prince & Savage, 1966; Allison, 1968; Fauteux, 1994, 1997; Meissner, 1999). In the 1980s, when direct infant observation by both psychoanalysts and cognitive scientists established that newborns communicate with their mothers (Gaensbauer, 1982; Lichtenberg, 1983; Stern, 1983, 1985; Bråten, 1988; Murray, 1991; Neisser, 1993; Murray & Andrews, 2000; Nagy & Molnar, 2004), the theory of neonatal solipsism was falsified (Kernberg, 1991). Theories that were predicated on the assumption of neonatal solipsism, such as Freud's account of the oceanic feeling, became equally untenable (Harrison, 1986).

Following the discovery of neonatal communication, Fred Pine attempted to rescue the separation-individuation theories of Margaret S. Mahler, which had argued that children normally spend the first two years of their lives emerging from neonatal solipsism. As a corollary to his defense of separation-individuation, Pine also reformulated the traditional claim that the oceanic feeling was an infantile regression. To do so, he replaced Freud's theory of neonatal solipsism with Jacobson's theory of toddler's fantasies of mother-child merger (Pine, 1981; 1986; 1990; Harrison, 1986; Meissner, 1992; Modell, 1993, pp. 106-7). Jacobson (1954, 1964) had originally advanced her theory of infantile merger fantasies in connection with the maternal roots of the ego ideal (see also Nunberg, 1955). Jacobson's theory was cited widely if not always accurately, and for two decades it articulated the consensus among ego psychologists concerning the origin of the ego ideal (Novey, 1955; Kramer, 1958; Spitz, 1958; Bing, McLaughlin & Marburg, 1959; Ottenheimer, 1959; Reich, 1960; Ritvo & Solnit, 1960; Hammerman, 1965; Esman, 1972; Kernberg, 1976). Many readers seem not to have noticed that Jacobson had relocated subject-object nondifferentiation from the infantile ego feeling postulated by Freud to the content of an infantile fantasy. In Jacobson's formulation, merger was not a sense perception that was produced through naive reality-testing in the neonatal period. Merger originated in a later period as a wish-fulfillment, a mental image or fantasy, in response to disappointment with a realistic perception of discreteness. Because merger was not an ego feeling but was instead separate from the ego, it was available for developmental elaboration into the ego ideal. Pine valued Jacobson's distinction and proposed that merger fantasies provide emotional consolation for the separateness that infants and toddlers realistically know.

The question must be asked, however, whether mysticism is a regression in any sense whatever. No mystical experience is a simple or direct *fantasy* of merger with the mother. Unlike the Isakower phenomenon (Isakower, 1938; Heilbrunn, 1953; Finn, 1955; Garma, 1955; Socarides, 1955; Fink, 1967; Easson, 1973; Blaustein, 1975), unitive experiences include no imagery that manifestly portrays the breast or any other part or whole of the mother's body. Werman (1986, p. 136) remarked: "although the relative absence of boundaries in the infant may be the *prototype* for the oceanic experience...these experiences are not simple regressions to an infantile level" (see also Hood, 1976; Merkur, 1998, 1999). A decade ago, I advanced the suggestion that mystical experiences are *sublimations* of merger fantasies (Merkur, 1999, 2001); but in retrospect I find the proposal unsatisfactory. It may be true; but even if it is, its explanatory power does not begin to do justice to the variety and complexity of unitive experiences.

UNITIVE MODES OF EXPERIENCE

In *The Creative Imagination* (Merkur, 1998, pp. 148-53), I developed a typology of unitive experiences on the evidence of psychedelic experiences in both Western and Native American populations; and in *Mystical Moments and Unitive Thinking* (Merkur, 1999), I demonstrated the same typology on the evidence of spontaneous "peak" experiences and mystical experiences that had been attained through meditation. I constructed the categories on phenomenological criteria appropriate to the academic study of religion that would simultaneously be meaningful psychoanalytically in terms of their latent unconscious determinants. My single most important finding, however, was an unanticipated generalization concerning unitive experiences as a group.

In each instance, a unitive experience consists, above all, of a mode of conceptualizing unity that is superimposed on the sense perception of reality and/or the internal perception of the mind. Consider some everyday examples. When you are naked, your sense of the extent of your self concerns your body. When you are dreaming or in the process of beginning to awaken, your sense of self is instead limited to your mind and does not necessarily include your body. When you are clothed, however, anyone making contact with so little as the hem of your garment is touching "you"; and when you are driving a car, the domain of "you" extends to the outer edge of the vehicle's bumper. The plasticity or fluidity of the sense of self in its individuality is also present in interpersonal relations, where, for example, harm done to parents, to a spouse or significant other, or to children, is consciously experienced as harm done to you. Not only your loved ones, but in some way you yourself are violated when your loved ones are harmed. The enlargement of the self may similarly extend to friends, distant relations, a neighborhood, hometown, ethnic group, nation, or humanity as a whole. The emotion that accompanies the enlargement of the sense of self in interpersonal relations may be loving and affectionate; it may in more remote relations instead be moral. People may also have strong feelings of identity with the non-human environment--land that they own or have grown up on, the country or other place of their origin. In rare instances, the sense of identity extends to the universe as a whole, or to God; but the commonplace instances, which everyone experiences in the course of every day, are equally mystical. Phenomenologically, we each of us experience the self to be highly variable, as to what it does and does not include. Much of what the self includes--family, nation, humanity, country--is not the self at all; and words are inadequate to express the paradox. Self is bound up in not-self, as though not-self were rooted in and part of self. Identity, identicality is involved; it is not simply a question of attachment to what is other. Moreover, there are no phenomenological grounds for privileging one sense of self over another. Our senses of ourselves shift automatically from context to context in predictable but mysterious ways. It is only in theory, as distinct from experience, that we can treat one sense of self (the mental self, or the bodily self, or the cosmic self, depending on one's belief-system) as true, and the others as illusory variations that are produced *ex hypothesi* through identification, projection, or some other psychological process.

A review of mystical experiences discloses a series of discrete modes of experiencing the self that function simultaneously to impose the unity of the self on whatever the self is bound up with. Other mystical experiences are similarly unitive, but attribute selfhood externally through projection, or construct objectivity by compromising introjection and projection. A *mode* of unitive experience might equally appropriately be called a schema, Gestalt, or "procedural memory"; but these are all technical terms that I learned after I settled on the term "mode" while writing my MA thesis in 1982. I chose the term "mode" because I was inspired by and hoped eventually to harmonize my typology with Erik Erikson's (1963) concept of psychosocial modes that could be linked to the epigenetic sexual development of the ego. Because a few of the unitive modes are identical with functions that are ordinarily attributed to the superego, I have speculated that their entire developmental series may prove to be modes of superego function. For the present I think it best, however, to remain close to the phenomenological data. All unitive modes involve extremely intense affects that accompany ideation. The affects are so powerful that their affirmation of the unitive ideas produces involuntary conviction in the ideas for the duration of the unitive experiences, much as a child at play is persuaded of the subjective reality of the play's contents for the duration of the play. At the same time, unitive modes are analogous to colored filters that each admit only a certain color of light and register others only as darkness and brightness. They selectively interfere with the perception of reality in fashions similar to the projection of transferences--highlighting, skewing, and repressing different aspects of reality, all at the same time.

Unitive modes vary in their relation to reality. Most of the world's mystical traditions use "concentrative meditations" (Goleman, 1977) or self-hypnotic techniques in their pursuit of mystical experiences. The resultant experiences occur during trances or other dissociated states that cause unitive experiences to undergo reification. Owing to their dissociation, the manifestations of unitive modes are not integrated into the general sense of reality. They instead acquire a sense of reality of their own (Shor, 1959). In place of a unitive appreciation of the perceptible world, dissociated unitive experiencing proceeds *despite* the perceptible world. The unitive ideas are not treated reflectively as metaphors that concern the world. Unavailable for reflective integration with the general reality sense, the ideas become transcendent, world-denying truths. In this manner, reification converts imaginations into delusions and is among the vicissitudes of unitive modes that Haartman (2001) has termed "unitive distortions." The negative reputation that mysticism has acquired since the Enlightenment owes, I suggest, to the dissociation from reality that reification induces. The world's mystical traditions frequently extend the reification beyond the moments of unitive experiencing, into a mystical theology or philosophy that derogates physical reality to lesser or greater extents.

When, however, unitive experiences are not complicated by trance or another dissociative state, the unitive ideas are spontaneously and effortlessly integrated with the general sense of reality. David Bakan (1966) suggested the term "rational mysticism" to discuss the historically rare phenomenon of mysticism that has been rational and realistic; but the relation of mystical experiences to elaborated mystical philosophies is not always immediate. Even when unitive experiences retain their harmlessly metaphoric character, they continue to relate variously to reality. Each mode of union emphasizes certain aspects of the normal apperception of reality. It also censors or, at least, diminishes the importance of other aspects. Each mode also contains an element of fantasy or imagination concerning the unity or unification of the realities whose existence it acknowledges. Some modes are more fantastic. Others are more realistic. Modes may be developmentally progressive even when they are fantastic, because cognitive development always proceeds through a dialectic of assimilation and accommodation, in Piaget's (1954, pp. 92-96) sense of the terms.

Consider a representative selection of unitive modes. The *solitary mode* presents the self as a passive subject amid an affect of serenity, tranquility, peace, and comfort. These several ideas and affects are logically tenable. However, the further modes also include the elements of being timeless, boundless, and the only existent thing. Consider the following self-report.

> Usually I direct my steps toward a certain part of the nearby river, where it meanders among lush meadows with herds of content brown and white cattle, quietly browsing. There is a rookery nearby, and the only sounds which break the silence are the cawing of the rooks as they wheel among the elms. The all pervading sense of peace which I always experience when I stand there, makes me forget all sense of time, and any worry or anxiety which I had before seems to float away. I do not think I commune with nature, I merely forget myself and everything about me! I just have a sense that the world is standing still and everything, except the rooks, is at rest. (Paffard, 1973, p. 191)

The *self-transcendent mode* adopts the perspective of the not-self, from which to view the self as an object. Since no one can ever be other than subjective, the seemingly objective perspective of the mode is imaginary. It is not inherently fantastic, however. It is a realistic speculation regarding the perspective on self of a not-self.

> I looked round me at the moor stretching for seemingly endless miles. Stretch after stretch of purple and brown until the end of the moor was lost in the beginning of the sky. I looked and felt exhilarated, alive, and in that moment I knew that life was indeed worth living and, in the realisation of this, all earthly attachments vanished. I felt as though I only existed spiritually; my body was no use. (Paffard, 1973, pp. 179-80)

The *incorporation mode* presents a self-image that encompasses the whole of reality. Having a bodily self-image is realistic, but the incorporation of all reality within it is fantastic. The fantasy may be seen, however, as a compromise that partly admits and partly denies the knowledge that reality consists of a great many different phenomena.

> The only way I can described it is as being at one with the music and not only with the music but with the people, concert hall, etc. It was as if it were inside me. I can't remember any feeling but a sort of crazy joy. What happened afterwards, I don't remember. Quietly happy. It had no effect except that I was in a good mood--contented. (Panzarella, 1980, p. 77)

The *inclusion mode* is realistic in its presentation of a self-image that is limited to the bodily self. It locates the bodily self within a unified cosmos, which it discovers to be a positive, hospitable place. These features are potentially realistic. The optimism is tenable but indemonstrable: an imagination whose validity can be neither refuted nor proved.

> It was ten o'clock of a beautiful spring evening and I was walking along a country road. I was alone and thinking of nothing in particular. Then suddenly I felt hypertensive. I could hear the animals in the bushes. I saw a petal on the ground and all at once I began to feel ecstatic. It was as though my heart was opening up and then filling with joy. I felt a part of everything. It was an enchanted place. (Prince, 1979-80, p. 172)

The *identification mode* presents external phenomena--people, animals, and things--as identical with the bodily self. The equation of self with other both knows and denies the otherness of others. The logical impossibility of the compromise, which represents the bodily self as other than itself, isolates or abstracts the aspect of another self that can realistically be adopted as one's own, namely, an identity. The mode can be realistic in its appraisal of the identities of the external phenomena; it can also be fantastic in anthropomorphizing or personifying non-human phenomena that have no identities. Invariably fantastic is the self's borrowing of other identities.

> I was sitting on a lawn after dinner with three colleagues, two women and one man. We liked each other well enough but were certainly not intimate friends, nor had any one of us a sexual interest in another. Incidentally, we had not drunk any alcohol. We were talking casually about everyday matters when, quite suddenly and unexpectedly, something happened. I felt myself

> invaded by a power which, though I consented to it, was irresistible and certainly not mine. For the first time in my life I knew exactly--because, thanks to the power, I was doing it--what it means to love one's neighbour as oneself. I was also certain, though the conversation continued to be perfectly ordinary, that my three colleagues were having the same experience. (In the case of one of them, I was able later to confirm this.) My personal feelings toward them were unchanged--they were still colleagues, not intimate friends--but I felt their existence as themselves to be of infinite value and rejoiced in it.
>
> I recalled with shame the many occasions on which I had been spiteful, snobbish, selfish, but the immediate joy was greater than the shame, for I knew that, so long as I was possessed by this spirit, it would be literally impossible for me deliberately to injure another human being. I also knew that the power would, of course, be withdrawn sooner or later and that, when it did, my reeds and self-regard would return. The experience lasted at its full intensity for about two hours when we said good-night to each other and went to bed. When I awoke the next morning, it was still present, though weaker, and it did not vanish completely for two days or so. (Freemantle, 1964, pp. 30-31)

The *relational mode* presents the self in relationship to external phenomena. The relationship may be based specifically on the common possession of life, or of beauty. The mode is capable of being completely realistic. Its optimism is tenable but indemonstrable.

> One afternoon I was lying down resting after a long walk on the Plain...The grass was hot and I was on an eye level with insects moving about. Everything was warm, busy and occupied with living. I was relaxed but extraneous to the scene.
>
> Then it happened: a sensation of bliss. No loss of consciousness, but increased consciousness...I could feel the earth under me right down to the centre of the earth, and I belonged to it and it belonged to me. I also felt that the insects were my brothers and sisters, and all that was alive was related to me, because we were all living matter that died to make way for the next generation...And I felt and experienced everything that existed, even sounds and colours and tastes, all at once, and it was blissful...I had a conviction that a most important truth had been enunciated: that we are all related--animal, vegetable and mineral--so no

> one is alone. I have never forgotten this experience. (Cohen & Phipps, 1992, p. 87)

The *chronological mode* presents external phenomena as having unilinear temporal extensions, commencing in the past and, in some cases, extending also into the future. The idea that phenomena have temporal extensions is realistic, but the specific ideas and visual fantasies of particular experiences are typically imaginative.

> One day in the 1950s, a warm, soggy, sullen afternoon in autumn, I happened to be standing in the quadrangle of an Oxford college. I was in the middle of a busy day, and my thoughts were of work and sociability, of books, ideas, and people. Suddenly, looking up, I saw a swan flying in a leisurely, deliberate straight line right over my head, just above the level of the rooftops; in that marshy air, its broad heavy wings flapping quite slowly, it seemed almost to be swimming rather than flying. A few strong, purposeful wingbeats and it was gone; but in an instant I had realised, and with a sharp physical intensity, the fact that all my scurrying to and fro, talking, comparing ideas, gossipping, discussing personalities, was limited, contained, held in and at the same time supported by the green earth, the grey stones, the stretches of water and weed. I suddenly saw beyond the libraries, the lectures, the talk, to what underlay them: the fact that men had come to a meadowy river-bank under a grey and white sky, and had decided on it as the site of a town, and reared those stone walls and towers. And centuries later, here I stood, and the rushes still grew on the banks, and the air still lay as heavily as water, and above my head the great kingly bird flapped, from one stretch of the river to another, as it had done a thousand years ago--and we were all, the bird and I and the men who had hewn the stones, and the other men who had written the books on the library shelves, and the earth-worms in the soil, the fish in the river, and the dogs running about the streets, all living together in one eternity, here and now on this earth; the eternity of nature. (Wain, 1962, pp. 35-36; as cited in Paffard, 1976, p. 108)

The *propriety mode* presents temporally present phenomena as right, proper, harmonious, utilitarian, functional, and perfect, in and of themselves. In other words, the mode presents the idea that their function in relation to each other causes things to be as they should be. The mode is potentially completely realistic. Its optimism is as irrefutable as it is unprovable.

> In 1945 I was in Chemistry class. We were being introduced to the Table of Elements. It was a sunny day. Then the light seemed to flood into me--I was it and it was me. I never lost the view of being in the class, but suddenly I understood everything, how the world was made, how terribly important it was for the sciences to join together, that biology would have to involve chemistry and physics in order to be completely studied (these were just fragments of thoughts coming out of the experience). The feeling was of looking on at the ecstasy of those worshipping God. I seemed to be at once amongst them and yet a long distance away. While I was in this state I had a feeling of wholeness, and of sympathy and love for everyone in the room, and afterwards this feeling lingered. (Prince, 1979-80, p. 173)

> I was a girl of 15 or 16, I was in the kitchen toasting bread for tea and suddenly on a dark November afternoon the whole place was flooded with light, and for a minute by clock time I was immersed in this, and I had a sense that in some unutterable way the universe was all right. This has affected me for the rest of my life, I have lost all fear of death, I have a passion for light, but I am in no way afraid of death, because this light experience has been a kind of conviction to me that everything *is* all right in some way. (Huxley, 1961, p. 49)

The *energic mode* presents all phenomena as manifestations of a universal energy. In its imagination of matter as energy, the mode is inherently fantastic. However, when treated as a metaphor, it is potentially completely realistic.

> One day, when I was four, I found myself standing at the beach, alone. The sea touched the sky. Breathing with the waves, I entered their rhythm. Suddenly there was a channeling of energy: the sun, the wind, the sea were going right through me.

> A door opened, and I *became* the sun, the wind, and the sea. There was no 'I' anymore. 'I' had merged with everything else. All sensory perceptions had become one. Sound, smell, taste, touch, shape--all melted into a brilliant light. The pulsating energy went right through me, and I was part of this energy. (Hoffman, 1992, pp. 38-39)

The *vitality mode* presents external phenomena as infused with a transcendent but immanent vitality. In its reification of vitality, the mode is inherently fantastic. However, when treated as a metaphor, it is potentially completely realistic.

> I was lying in bed and trying to imagine the end of life: of not being alive. Is it nothingness, and if so, what is nothingness? It was impossible to image, and also frightening. So then I tried to imagine living forever...life as never ending. This was also impossible to image, but I was still attempting to 'experience' it in my mind.
>
> Suddenly, with a sort of burst of inner light, I felt life to be God and myself to be connected to God. It was a silent explosion. I understood that I was part of something loving and much, much greater than myself. It was not a thought but an ecstatically intense feeling. (Hoffman, 1992, p. 123)

The *loving mode* imagines self as the recipient of love's loving presence. In its reification of love, the mode is inherently fantastic. However, when treated as a metaphor, it is potentially completely realistic.

> I am specially affected by the calmness of a summer evening; when the day has been busy, as it usually is, I get an urge to be alone, in the peaceful surroundings of the countryside where I love to watch the varied changes in the sky, as the day draws to its close. I feel a sense of freedom at such times, yet I feel closer to God, and more conscious of his love. Whenever I have the opportunity, I leave all my friends behind, and go alone to a small hill near my home, where solitude means peace. (Paffard, 1973, p. 188)

The *omniscient mode* presents self as identical with an intelligent and emotional personality whose knowledge and range of concerns are universal. Because the intelligence is universal in scope, it is one in number.

Due to the transcendence of the omniscient personality, the mode is neither provable nor refutable. It is beyond the capacity for reality-testing to evaluate.

> On the following Sunday my husband and I were driving along a country road...We were talking sorrowfully of our dear friend [who had died], when suddenly I knew that his spirit lived and was as close to me that moment as it had ever been in life. When I say I knew, words are inadequate to convey the experience. This was 'knowing' more vivid and real than anything I have ever experienced in the literal sense. It was as if for a moment one had known reality and in comparison the world of the senses was the dream. I was filled with an unutterable joy, which I shall never be able to describe. I seemed to apprehend, in a measure, the inexhaustible love of God for us, which envelops the universe and everything in it. Above all, I understood beyond all questioning that nothing in life, however seemingly insignificant, is ever lost or purposeless, but all tends towards the fulfilment of a design which one day will be made clear to us...,
>
> From the day of what I can only consider my rebirth, my neurotic difficulties disappeared and have never since returned. (Cohen & Phipps, 1992, pp. 77-78)

The *omnipresent mode* presents external reality as the location of an omnipresent, divine, or holy power. Due to the transcendence of the omnipresent power, the mode is neither provable nor refutable. It is beyond the capacity for reality-testing to evaluate.

> It was as if the cocoon had burst and my eyes were opened and I saw.
>
> The world was infinitely beautiful, full of light as if from an inner radiance. Everything was alive and God was present in all things; in fact, the earth, all plants and animals and people seemed to be made of God. All things were one, and I was one with all creation and held safe within a deep love. I was filled with peace and joy and with deep humility, and could only bow down in the holiness of the presence of God...if anyone had brought news that any member of my family had died, I should have laughed and said 'There is no death'. It was as if scales had fallen from my eyes and I saw the world as it truly was. How had I lived for thirty-three years and been so blind? This was the

> secret of the world, yet it all seemed so obvious and natural that I had no idea that I should not always see it so. I felt like going round and telling everyone that all things were one and that knowledge of this would cure all ills. (Cohen & Phipps, 1992, pp. 20-21)

The *mode of interior dialogue* involves intrapsychic affects and thoughts that seem subjectively to communicate the feelings and ideas of a personality other than the ego. The intrapsychic experience is subjectively recognized as an imagination. Due to the transcendence of the (alleged) personality whose feelings and ideas are communicated, the validity of the mode is neither provable nor refutable. Within these limits, the dialogue may potentially be completely realistic.

> God is quite real to me. I talk to him and often get answers. Thoughts sudden and distinct from any I have been entertaining come to my mind after asking God for his direction. Something over a year ago I was for some weeks in the direct perplexity. When the trouble first appeared before me I was dazed, but before long (two or three hours) I could hear distinctly a passage of Scripture: 'My grace is sufficient for thee.' Every time my thoughts turned to the trouble I could hear this quotation. I don't think I ever doubted the existence of God, or had him drop out of my consciousness. God has frequently stepped into my affairs very perceptibly, and I feel that he directs many little details all the time. But on two or three occasions he has ordered ways for me very contrary to my ambitions and plans. (James, 1902, pp. 70-71)

These several examples of unitive experiences amply illustrate their diversity and complexity. They are experiences of apperceiving reality in different, unitive ways. The concept of unitive modes refers *ex hypothesi* to unconscious functions that produce unitive experiences by processing the apperception of reality each in its own distinctive way. The modes are not at all pschologically naive or primitive but, to the contrary, intellectually sophisticated. They are modes of comprehension or understanding. They are conceptual as distinct from sensory. At the same time, modes are invariably imaginative. They range from realistic wishful thinking to fantastic impossibilities, but they are never simply empirical. They add a unitive overlay to whatever perceptible realities they apperceive.

THE SYSTEMATIZING FUNCTION

The sheer variety of unitive experiences puts paid to all psychoanalytic theories of mysticism that concern only the oceanic feeling; and their intellectual character makes it highly improbable that regression has much, if anything, to do with them. The mainstream approach is wrong and should unhesitatingly be abandoned. In *Mystical Moments and Unitive Thinking*, I postulated that unitive experiences are manifestations of an unconscious process of unitive thinking that is latent in a good deal of conscious thought (Merkur, 1999). I have since noticed a few sentences in *Totem and Taboo* where Freud (1913) wrote of unconscious unitive thinking from his own theoretical perspective. The sentences digressed from the topic of the systematizing nature of magic to the topic of systematization in dreams. Freud wrote:

> The secondary revision of the product of the dream-work is an admirable example of the nature and pretensions of a system. There is an intellectual function in us which demands unity, connection and intelligibility from any material, whether of perception or thought, that comes within its grasp; and if, as a result of special circumstances, it is unable to establish a true connection, it does not hesitate to fabricate a false one. Systems constructed in this way are known to us not only from dreams, but also from phobias, from obsessive thinking and from delusions. The construction of systems is seen most strikingly in delusional disorders (in paranoia), where it dominates the symptomatic picture; but its occurrence in other forms of neuro-psychosis must not be overlooked. (Freud, 1913, p. 95)

Freud did not publicly announce that the existence of this "intellectual function" was inconsistent with his topographic hypothesis of the systems *Pcpt.-Cs.* and *Ucs.* (Freud, 1900), but he evidently thought so. In the paragraph prior to the sentences quoted above, Freud had contrasted secondary revision with the dreamwork as though the processes were mutually exclusive; and elsewhere in *Totem and Taboo* where he provided a general introduction to the dreamwork, he mentioned only condensation, displacement, and representability (pp. 170-71). Freud implicitly recognized that the intellectuality of a systematizing function was inconsistent with his concept of the primary process. Secondary revision, which he had earlier considered part of the dreamwork, had now to be exempted. At the same time, Freud's emphasis of the systematizing function's influences on dreams, phobias, obsessive thinking, and delusions, amply indicated the unconsciousness of its operation. Freud was discussing a function that was intellectual, as *Pcpt.-Cs.* was, yet was also both unconscious and unitive, as *Pcpt.-Cs.* was not. The systematizing function--or as I term it, unconscious unitive thinking--was inconsistent with Freud's model of the psyche, and he knew it.

Two

The Psyche's Unitive Trends

Freud took up the problem of the "function in us which demands unity" in *Beyond the Pleasure Principle* (1920a), when he revised his theory of drives. From 1900 onward, he had opposed unconscious sexual drives to conscious self-preservative drives; beginning in 1920, he counted sexual and self-preservative drives together under the concept of Eros, a drive to unity, to which he opposed aggressive drives (Freud, 1920a). As is widely recognized, Freud's concept of "Eros, the drive which strives for ever closer union" (Freud, 1926b, p. 265) was metaphysical rather than psychological. Freud trumpeted his own awareness of the metaphysical character of his thinking about Eros by the wordplay in his title, *Jenseits des Lustprinzips*. The word *Jenseits*, which literally means "the other side" rather than "beyond," was also a colloquial expression for the other world and life after death (Curran, 1963, p. 73). Ernest Jones stated that Freud jokingly referred to *Beyond the Pleasure Principle* as "The Hereafter" (Freud, 1920a, p. 54). The pun implicitly disclaimed scientific ambition for the book's ideas. Freud wrote of Eros as a drive to unity in inorganic physics (Freud, 1937, p. 246), the adhesion of cell walls (Freud, 1920a, pp. 60-61, n. 1), sex cell conjugation (Freud, 1921, p. 92; 1930, p. 108) and, more generally, the ever-increasing complexity of organization that constitutes life (Freud, 1920a, pp. 42-43; 1923c, p. 258). In addition to its inorganic and physiological manifestations, Eros also acted psychologically in both personal (Freud, 1920a, p. 59; 1925, p. 239; 1926a, p. 122) and group psychology (Freud, 1930, p. 122). For psychological purposes, Eros was a superordinate drive, mysteriously at work throughout the psyche in a way that Freud could not explain. Freud (1933) candidly acknowledged the inadequacy of his concept. "The theory of the drives is so to say our mythology. Drives are mythical entities, magnificent in their indefiniteness. In our work we cannot for a moment disregard them, yet we are never sure that we are seeing them clearly" (p. 95).

Most psychoanalysts have always reacted to Freud's concept of Eros by ignoring it. The term persists as a metaphoric way of speaking of the sexual drives of the id (Reisner, 1992, pp. 286-87); but it would be better appreciated, I suggest, as the expression of a vague awareness or hunch that Freud had about a superordinate tendency to unity that is shared by the id, ego, and superego. Eros was, in short, a radically novel appreciation of the mystical, a metaphor that concerned unitive trends throughout the psyche. As Lacan (1982) remarked:

> This *There is something of One* is not simple--to say the least. In psychoanalysis, or more precisely in the discourse of Freud, it is set forth in the concept of Eros, defined as a fusion making one out of two, that is, of Eros seen as the gradual tendency to make one out of a vast multitude....
>
> We can, however, comfort ourselves that there is unquestionably much less of the biological metaphor here than elsewhere. If the unconscious is indeed what I say it is, as being structured like a language, then it is on the level of language that we must interrogate this One. This One has resounded endlessly across the centuries. Need I bother to evoke here the neo-platonists?...
>
> We must start on the basis that this *There is something of One* is to be taken with the stress that there is One alone....
>
> The mystical is by no means that which is not political. It is something serious, which a few people teach us about, and most often women or highly gifted people like Saint John of the Cross....they sense that there must be a *jouissance* which goes beyond. That is what we call a mystic....It is clear that the essential testimony of the mystics is that they are experiencing it but know nothing about it. (Lacan, 1982, pp. 138-39, 146-47)

Lacan's concept of "a *jouissance* which goes beyond" referred to transcendence of the linguistic structure of the unconscious. It did not refer to metaphysical transcendence of the physical. Lacan explicitly denied belief in God. He instead affirmed his belief in "the *jouissance* of the woman in so far as it is something more" (p. 147), referring in his idiosyncratic way to sublimation of love for the mother. For Lacan this *jouissance* was simultaneously the conscious experience of the psychological manifestation of Freud's Eros. It is joy, bliss, ecstasy; and it is, Lacan claimed, what the mystics meant by their "mystical ejaculations" about God (p. 147).

Let me underscore Lacan's basic observation. Freud's concept of Eros, a metaphysical drive to unity, was an original and innovative way of discussing the mystical. It was an attempt to address what mystics mean by the mystical, that Freud detached from both the word "mystical" and all discussions of mystical experiences. It was not a successful formulation. Freud attempted to claim the mystical for science but could not free the concept of its traditional metaphysical baggage. As a result, he failed to meet his own methodological demand "to transform *metaphysics* into *metapsychology*" (Freud, 1901, pp. 258-59). Because Lacan routinely misappropriated Freud by converting Freud's philosophical realism into a postmodernism that Lacan limited to discourse, he completed Freud's move from metaphysics into metapsychology. He did so, however, at the price of disallowing the relevance of his discourse to the real. Physical reality plays no part in Lacan's use of psychoanalysis because the real is wholly and permanently outside the self-referentiality of discourse. No less than Freud, but for entirely different reasons, Lacan was unable to formulate a detailed psychological theory to replace summary and euphemistic references to Eros.

It is a mistake, however, to retreat from the concept of Eros to the concept of sexual drives as the psychoanalytic mainstream has done. We need a detailed depth psychology of the mystical; and the concept of Eros is, as Lacan appreciated, the appropriate place in Freud's discourse to commence its discussion. Freud laid the foundations for a satisfactory theory in the structural hypothesis. Had he not already embarked on the metaphysical extravagance of Eros, he might have recognized that his discussions of the id, ego, and superego (Freud, 1923a) could accommodate the systematizing function of *Totem and Taboo* without any need for alterations. When Freud introduced his concept of the superego, he described it as "a precipitate in the ego" that "confronts the other contents of the ego as an ego ideal or super-ego" (Freud, 1923a, p. 34). Not only was it fully as intellectual as the remainder of the ego, but its three major functions--self-observation, conscience, and ego ideal (Freud, 1914a, 1921, 1933)--made it responsible for "the higher, moral, supra-personal side of human nature" (Freud, 1923a, p. 35). At the same time, the superego differed from the remainder of the ego in having unparalleled access to the unconscious. "The super-ego is always close to the id....It reaches deep down into the id and for that reason is farther from consciousness than the ego is" (pp. 48-49). Expanding his theory of the dream in perspective of the structural hypothesis, Freud (1923b) accounted for the occasional evidence of higher mental functions in dreams by postulating the category of dreams "from above" that the superego shaped, which were to be contrasted with dreams "from below" that were shaped by the unconscious drives of the id. Freud further implicated the superego in the dreamwork when he identified it as the psychical agency that he had earlier called the dream censorship (Freud, 1923b, 262; 1933, pp. 27-28; see also: 1914a, p. 97; 1916-17, p. 429). "The psychical agency which otherwise operates only as a censorship plays a *habitual* part in the construction of dreams....There can be no doubt that the censoring agency, whose influence we have...recognized in limitations and omissions in the dream-content, is also responsible for interpolations and additions in it" (Freud, 1900, p. 489). "The dream-censorship itself is the originator, or one of the originators, of the dream-distortion" (Freud, 1916-17, p. 140; see also: pp. 168, 233, 429).

Freud never appreciated that his theory of the superego provided a thoroughly psychological account of Eros that made his indulgence in metaphysics superfluous. Condensation, the first and foremost operation of the dreamwork, routinely condenses mental representations. It always makes a minimum of two into one. Its conceptually maximal operation presumably makes all into one, producing the unitive component of the simplest or least intellectual unitive experiences. Adding intellectual content of differing sorts will account for the full variety of unitive experiences. They are waking analogs of dreams from above. They acquire their unitive component from the dreamwork, their intellectual component from the superego, and their unconscious origin from both.

THE COMPROMISE FUNCTION OF THE UNCONSCIOUS

Most of Freud's discussions of Eros referred to the id, a topic too extensive to be discussed adequately in these pages. Space permits only a few basic remarks. Freud's extension of the concept of sexuality is, in my experience, undeniably valid clinically. At the same time, his concepts of "psychic energy" and "libido" were metaphors that glossed over much that deserves to be conceptualized in careful detail. Freud usefully articulated the ordinarily unformulated details in a passing remark that he offered in support of his claim that there are no conflicts in the unconscious. Freud (1915b) asserted: "When two wishful impulses whose aims must appear to us incompatible become simultaneously active, the two impulses do not diminish each other or cancel each other out, but combine to form an intermediate aim, a compromise" (p. 186). In this sentence, Freud distinguished two unconscious processes: (i) a function that is responsible for wishful impulses becoming active, and (ii) a compromising function that is able to combine separate impulses to pursue a common aim. Freud's subdivision of the system *Ucs.* into two distinct functions is, to my thought, logically necessary. It would implicitly be the first of the two functions, the wish-activating function, that operates "on the frontier between the mental and the somatic, as the psychical representative of the stimuli originating from within the organism and reaching the mind" (Freud, 1915a, p. 122). As for the compromising function, it assuredly is or involves condensation, the first of the four functions that comprise the dreamwork (Freud, 1900). Condensation, by which two or more mental representations are combined into one, invariably effects compromises.

Freud's distinction between wish-activating and wish-compromising removes much of the mystery of the id. What crosses over from the body into the mind is not some vaguely perceived and scientifically indemonstrable quiddity to be called "drive" or "instinctual drive" or "psychic energy" or "libido" or any other metaphysical substance. Psychoanalysis has no need to depart from neurology and academic psychology on this issue. The frontier function is no other than the group of processes that are well known under the collective name "proprioception," the mind's perception of bodily sensation, on which we have a host of established scientific data. Proprioception accomplishes the transition from the body to the mind by representing the body's impulses within the mind, that is, by creating mental representations of the body's impulses. Proprioceptions sometimes reach consciousness, as for example, hunger, thirst, needs to urinate and defecate, sexual excitement, and so forth. All of these proprioceptive arousals may also be inhibited, for example, when we are pre-occupied with other matters and do not attend to bodily sensations until our tasks are completed, or the arousal reaches sufficient intensity to intrude on the focus of attention. Whether proprioceptions become conscious or are inhibited, the process of the initial conversion of bodily sensation into proprioception is always unconscious and constitutes the "frontier" function that Freud allocated to the system *Ucs.* and its successor, the id.

Freud presumably saw the compromise function at work in the synthesis of the sexual instincts. He asserted, for example, that "the sexual instincts....are numerous, emanate from a great variety of organic sources, act in the first instance independently of one another and only achieve a more or less complete synthesis at a late stage" (Freud, 1915a, p. 125). Freud's extension of the concept of sexuality also meant that in some manner that Freud never explained, proprioceptions that do not initially have anything to do with sexuality nevertheless come unconsciously to be imbued with sexual meanings. The sexualization of unconscious thought is coherent, I suggest, as an effect of the compromise function. Wishes that are not sexual are reconciled with wishes that are sexual through the unconscious formulation of compromises. This process of sexualization includes object relations. If "the ultimate goal of libido is the object" (Fairbairn, 1941, p. 31), so that "libido is not primarily pleasure-seeking, but object-seeking" (Fairbairn, 1946, p. 30), then the converse is also true. The same compromise function that directs sexuality toward objects, also invests object relations with sexual meanings (Reisner, 1992, p. 302).

Whether unconscious compromises are complete, so that the whole of unconscious thinking is sexualized, or merely extensive, so that large parts of unconscious thinking are sexualized, is, in my view, an empirical question that should optimally be resolved experimentally. Certainly my own expectation would be that the extent of unconscious compromise will prove to have a developmental history and be subject to vicissitudes. For clinical purposes, it will suffice for the present to assert that remarkably large parts of unconscious thinking are sexualized. It may be the case, however, that as Freud implied in 1905, there is no non-sexuality in the unconscious. All mental representations of physiological impulses--including aggression (Fromm, 1973)--may routinely be sexualized through the unconscious operation of the compromise function.

The unconscious compromises by which wishes come to be invested with sexual meanings are correctly appreciated as mystical. They are mystical historically, in the sense that the universality of sexuality is a central doctrine of three of the great mystical traditions of the world, the Hindu and Buddhist tantras of South Asia and the Jewish Kabbalah. They are also mystical psychologically, in that the extended sexuality of the unconscious is an instance of the inherently mystical or unitive character of the psyche. All that is at stake empirically is whether the psyche is completely or only extensively mystical, and by what developmental stages.

Unlike Freud's claims about Eros, psychic energy, and libido, there is nothing metaphysical in my assertions regarding the mysticism of the psyche. Unconscious unitive thinking is a secular process of the mind, a collaboration of condensation with the intellectual and unitive functions of the unconscious superego. This collaboration is as true for unconscious psychosexuality as for mystical experiences. Religious mystics who have depended heavily on dissociated and reified mystical experiencing have often grossly overvalued and considerably distorted the natural mysticism of the psyche (Ostow & Scharfstein, 1953; Furst et al., 1976); but their misrepresentations of the psyche's unifying, integrative, and unitive trends should not divert us from a naturalistic appreciation of the psyche's mysticality. Mysticism is not metaphysical and transcendent; it is inborn.

The type of condensation that is responsible for extending sexuality is of a high order. Modell (2003) persuasively suggested that "what Freud attributes to libidinal continuity...is made possible by means of an unconscious metaphoric process that interprets and transforms sensations" (p. 89). The sexual zones of the body inspire symbols that have all-purpose use in thought. The investment of nonsexual proprioceptions with sexual meanings depends not on synecdoche (part for the whole), nor usually on metonymy (symbolic association by juxtaposition), but most frequently on metaphor, a knowing substitution of the signified by a signifier that may otherwise be completely unrelated and arbitrary. Because metaphors are a category of symbols that are known to be such, I infer that reflexive thinking, which Freud called self-observation and credited to the superego, must combine with condensation in order to produce the extended sexuality of the unconscious.

THE SYNTHETIC FUNCTION OF THE EGO

In 1919, Freud added to his repeated assertion that "the sole object of psychoanalysis is the overcoming of a patient's resistances" (Burrow, 1917-18a, p. 61), the explanation that the synthetic function of the ego accomplishes the further aspect of healing spontaneously.

> As we analyse it [the mind] and remove the resistances, it grows together; the great unity which we call his ego fits into itself all the instinctual impulses which before had been split off and held apart from it. The psychosynthesis is thus achieved during analytic treatment without our intervention, automatically and inevitably. We have created the conditions for it by breaking up the symptoms into their elements and by removing the resistances. (Freud, 1919, p. 161)

In 1920, when Freud introduced the concept of Eros, he maintained that Eros was active not only as unconscious sexual drives but also as self-preservative drives that were conscious and belonged to the ego. "It would still retain the main purpose of Eros--that of uniting and binding--in so far as it helps towards establishing the unity, or tendency to unity, which is particularly characteristic of the ego" (Freud, 1923a, p. 45). He further suggested that it is the ego's failure to synthesize that obliges it to split off the repressed.

> In the course of things it happens again and again that individual instincts or parts of instincts turn out to be incompatible in their aims or demands with the remaining ones, which are able to combine into the inclusive unity of the ego. The former are then split off from this unity by the process of repression, held back at lower levels of psychical development and cut off, to begin with, from the possibility of satisfaction. (Freud, 1920a, p. 11)

Freud here divided the ego and the repressed on structural criteria. The ego included what it could synthesize. What it could not synthesize remained outside its structure and was repressed.

The ego's need to impose repression on selected instincts was due, in this formulation, to a failure of the ego's synthetic function. It was a failure, in other words, precisely of the mystical. Freud retained the same formulation after 1923, when he began referring to the repressed as a portion of the id.

> In repression the ego....[has] permanently narrowed its sphere of influence. The repressed instinctual impulse is now isolated, left to itself, inaccessible, but also uninfluenceable. It goes its own way. Even later, as a rule, when the ego has grown stronger, it still cannot lift the repression; its synthesis is impaired, a part of the id remains forbidden ground to the ego. (Freud, 1926c, p. 203)

In 1926, when Freud reorganized his theories of defense, he attributed a further activity to the ego's synthetic function. He credited it with the stabilization of *ad hoc* symbol formations into long-term structures that integrated the pathological symptoms within the ego's structure as defense mechanisms.

> The ego is an organization. It is based on the maintenance of free intercourse and of the possibility of reciprocal influence between all its parts. Its desexualized energy still shows traces of its origin in its impulsion to bind together and unify, and this necessity to synthesize grows stronger in proportion as the strength of the ego increases. It is therefore only natural that the ego should try to prevent symptoms from remaining isolated and alien by using every possible method to bind them to itself in one way or another, and to incorporate them into its organization by means of those bonds. As we know, a tendency of this kind is already operative in the very act of forming a symptom. (Freud, 1926a, p. 98)

At the same time, Freud (1926c) contrasted the repressed drives of the id with the systematic approach of the ego. "The ego is an organization characterized by a very remarkable trend towards unification, towards synthesis. This characteristic is lacking in the id; it is, as we might say, 'all to pieces'; its different urges pursue their own purposes independently and regardless of one another" (p. 196). "What distinguishes the ego from the id quite especially is a tendency to synthesis in its contents, to a combination and unification in its mental processes which are totally lacking in the id" (Freud, 1933, p. 76). Freud's remarks presupposed that the ego accomplishes sense perception that obliges its drive to unity to compromise with external reality. Because the laws of nature impose a logic of cause-and-effect on external reality, the ego's reality-testing of its representations of the external world imposes logic and system on the psyche. Constrained by reality, the ego never pursues unity as mystical experiences do, by going so far as to reduce all to one. The ego's synthetic function instead coordinates unity with the logicality that reality-testing discloses. The result is a tendency toward systematic organization, which is all that Freud meant by the ego's synthetic function.

Nunberg's classical essay, "The Synthetic Function of the Ego," was originally delivered as a conference paper in 1929. It began with a prefatory summary of Freud's position.

> According to the hypothesis of Freud the ego is a part of the id, the surface of which has become modified. In the id there are accumulated various trends which, when directed towards objects in the outside world, lead to a union between these and the subject, thereby bringing into existence a new living being These libidinal trends are ascribed by us to Eros, in the Freudian sense of the term. Our daily experience teaches us that in the ego also there resides a force which similarly binds and unites, although it is of a somewhat different nature. For its task is to act as an intermediary between the inner and the outer worlds and to adjust the opposing elements within the personality. It achieves a certain agreement between the trends of the id and those of the ego, an agreement which produces a harmonious co-operation of all the psychic energies. (Nunberg, 1931, p. 123)

Nunberg's original contributions included the idea that Eros and the synthetic function work together to accomplish the psyche's integration.

> The tendency constantly to bring about a reunion between the ego and the id or to preserve their unity never wholly dies out, though in individual cases it may suffer disturbance. In this self-sufficient unity the id finds in the ego the gratification of its narcissism. An unmistakeable effort is made to cancel the differen-

> tiation between the ego and the id and to reunite and fuse the diverging psychic forces. (p. 124)

Nunberg credited the synthetic function with the ego's identification with its sexual objects, assimilating the parents to itself in the formation of the superego (pp. 124-25). "The synthetic capacity of the ego...assimilates alien elements (both from within and from without), and it mediates between opposing elements and even reconciles opposites and sets mental productivity in train" (p. 125). The ego's infusion with Eros is the vehicle of the psyche's union: "It is through this alone that free intercourse between all three systems becomes possible, that is to say, that connection, union, reconciliation and adjustment of opposites can take place amongst the psychic trends themselves and between them and the ego" (p. 138). Freud (1926, p. 98) had referred to "free intercourse" within the ego; Nunberg used the phrase to refer instead to intersystemic cooperation among the id, ego, and superego. Building on Freud's idea that repression impairs the synthetic function, Nunberg described therapy as a synthetic activity. "Repression depends on the ego's synthetic capacities being temporarily inadequate. Ultimately, then, the process of cure becomes a process of assimilation of those psychic trends which the defence-mechanisms have rendered alien to the ego and in this way it seems to ensure *the continuity of the personality*" (p. 139).

Subsequent discussions of the ego's synthetic function sometimes repeated Freud and Nunberg but more frequently pertained to phenomena inconsistent with Freud's concept. When Anna Freud (1966) credited the ego with irreducible antagonism to the id, she made it impossible for ego psychologists to follow Freud and Nunberg in conceptualizing Eros and the synthetic function in harmony with each other. Further diverting ego psychology from Freud, Hartmann (1958) introduced the idea that synthesis is not limited to the organization of the ego, but includes all manner of "adaptation and fitting together" (p. 40). Hartmann's formulation was one of his many aggrandizements of the ego at the expense of the id and superego. Freud had conceptualized consciousness in a consistent way throughout his life. In the topographic hypothesis, he famously described consciousness as "a sense-organ for the perception of psychical qualities" (Freud, 1900, p. 615). He expressed the same concept in a slightly different way in the structural hypothesis when he stated that "the ego represents what may be called reason and common sense" (Freud, 1923a, p. 25). Like the system *Pcpt.-Cs.* which it replaced, the ego "observes the external world with the help of its sense-organ, the system of consciousness" (Freud, 1926c, p. 201). Hartmann was presumably unaware that Freud's description of consciousness as a sense-organ invoked Avicenna's concept of common sense. Aristotle had suggested that the psyche is able to perceive the data of the five senses simultaneously because the senses are brought together into a common sense. Avicenna, writing in the eleventh century, argued that the common sense was a discrete mental process, that involved more than a mere aggregation of the individual senses, because the very bringing together of the senses into a common perception was the condition of consciousness (Wolfson, 1935; Harvey, 1975). Any single sense may both sense and initiate corresponding actions unconsciously as a reflex. Decision-making or judgment that can evaluate data from all of the senses simultaneously requires knowledge, which is to say, consciousness of all of the senses simultaneously. Freud's (1923a) definition of the ego as "reason and common sense" summarized Avicenna's concept of the relation between judgment and consciousness. Reason, as distinct from reflex, and common sense, as distinct from unconsciousness are necessarily functions of a single agency. Freud's agreement with Avicenna should not be thought coincidental. Freud studied philosophy as a young man in the mid 1870s with Franz Brentano (Merlan, 1945, 1949), who had discussed Avicenna's views in his book *The Psychology of Aristotle* (Brentano, 1977), which he first published in German in 1867.

Freud's concept of the ego's synthetic function is properly understood, I suggest, as the synthetic function that consciousness intrinsically is, that the ego cannot do other than to perform. The types of syntheses that the common sense produces involve associations by juxtaposition, which is a type of symbolic relationship that is termed "metonymy" in literary contexts (Merkur, 2001). The most famous example of metonymy in psychology is Pavlovian conditioning: the salivation of a dog at the sound of a bell that had come through habituation to be associated with the arrival of food to eat. For the dog, the sound of the bell was a metonym that signified food. Because consciousness perceives reality, its unifications of sense data conform with the reality principle. Metonyms are incapable of the kind of free and capricious synthesis that Freud credited to unconscious compromise formation. The bringing together of the individual senses in the common sense which is consciousness is the prototypical synthetic function of the ego. Association by metonymy is also to be seen in all of Freud's specific examples of the synthetic function: (i) secondary revisions of dreams, which work metonymously with dream's manifest contents in uncomprehension of their symbolic meaning; (ii) the automatic integration of formerly repressed materials, once they have emerged from repression and entered consciousness; and (iii) the arbitrary and irrational appropriation of unconsciously originating symptoms, as habitual or chronic defensive operations of the preconscious ego. Freud's references to the ego's synthetic function nowhere departed from a carefully Avicennan conceptualization of the common sense.

Nunberg's original contributions pertained to intersystemic collaborations and consequently included types of integration that exceeded the reach of the ego alone: (i) superego introjection; (ii) the "free intercourse" of id, ego, and superego; and (iii) the therapeutic process.

MULTIPLE FUNCTION

Nunberg's treatment of both ego functions and id-ego collaborations under the phrase "synthetic function" was taken for granted in Robert Wälder's classical article, "The Principle of Multiple Function" (1936), which was first published in German in 1930. The paper's subtitle, "Observations on Over-Determination" referred to Freud's concept that condensation has the by-product of investing single manifest contents with multiple meanings, so that their meaning may be said to be over-determined. Wälder suggested that "the principle of multiple function" provided an explanation for several phenomena. He began with the id:

> Pansexualism... [is] the propensity of psychoanalysis to look for a sexual meaning in all matters even when its realistic interpretation yielded a complete meaning. Inasmuch as each psychic act has a multiple function and therefore a multiple meaning and since one of these functions and meanings will refer to the problem of instinctual gratification (furthermore, the instinctual life of man is never entirely dormant), obviously everything that man does, all his purposeful action directed toward reality, must contain the elements of instinctual gratification. (p. 52)

Wälder's paper was principally concerned, however, with the implications of multiple function for the psychology of the ego. Wälder saw the ego as responding to the demands of the id, implicitly including the complexities of condensations. "The ego always faces problems and seeks to find their solution....Even in the extreme case of an action carried out under the pressure of impulse which may seem at first to be driven purely by the instincts, the ego contributes its part; the imperatively appearing demand for satisfaction is that problem proposed to the ego, the resulting action is the means to the solution of that problem" (p. 46). Wälder credited the ego with a "central steering" function that allowed it to work with the id. His initial example alluded to Freud's (1926a) idea that the ego incorporates symptoms into its organization and so transforms them into defenses.

> In its contact with the instinctual life there exists from the very beginning this trend to coördinate itself with its central steering–a fact which seems to be proven in that the ego experiences each excessive *crescendo* of the instinctual forces as danger for itself and independently of any consequences menacing from the outside, a danger to be destroyed and its organization overwhelmed. Evidently, the ego has then also an active trend toward the instinctual life, a disposition to dominate or, more correctly, to incorporate it into its organization. (Wälder, 1936, pp. 47-48)

Wälder's phrasing did not specifically mention defenses but instead generalized about id-ego relations. He referred specifically to healthy processes when he counted sublimation as a further example of multiple function. "Sublimations, for example, can definitely be termed such successful solutions of the problem of adaptation to the outer world or of mastering the outer world, as simultaneously and in accordance with another meaning which they carry, they represent successful gratifications of strong impulses" (p. 53). Although the theory of sublimation remains a controversial topic in psychoanalysis, Wälder accepted Freud's view that the superego is implicated in the process; and he advanced an account of superego function that merits consideration in the present context.

> The superego is the domain of the human being; it is that element through which man in his experience steps beyond himself and looks at himself as the object--be it in a way aggressively penalizing, tenderly cherishing, or dispassionately neutral--as, for instance, in the case of self-observation and the ability of abstracting one's self from one's own point of view.
>
> Here belongs the ability to see a garden as a garden regardless of the place of observation, or the ability not only to experience the world in its momentary instinctual and interest phases but also to recognize that the individual is independent of his own ego and that this independence outlives his own ego. In this sense it is a function of the superego when man as the only living entity makes his will. The thesis that it is in his possession of the superego that man is distinguished from animal is proven by everything we know of animal psychology....There is always the possibility of transcending the instinct and interest foundation in a given situation, of stepping beyond thinking, experi-

> ence, acting--in short, of placing one's self in the realm of the superego. (Wälder, 1936, pp. 61-62)

The devising of viable compromises among the id, ego, and superego is a reflective function, a product of the psyche's knowledge of itself, very much in keeping with Wälder's portrait of the superego. Wälder's formulation echoed and updated Aristotle's assertion that the possession of *nous*, "mind"--which accomplishes reflective awareness (Lear, 1988, p. 131)--is the distinguishing feature and *telos* of the human species. Freud (1927b) believed that the concept of the superego warranted further investigation: "If it is really the super-ego which, in humour, speaks such kindly words of comfort to the intimidated ego, this will teach us that we have still a great deal to learn about the nature of the super-ego" (p. 166). Freud's superego concept was rapidly abandoned, however, by Franz Alexander (1929a, 1929b), Melanie Klein (1933, 1935), and, most influentially, Heinz Hartmann and his co-authors (Hartmann, Kris, & Loewenstein, 1946; Hartmann & Loewenstein, 1962), all of whose theories were based one-sidedly on clinical evidence of masochistic self-criticism, psychosomatic symptoms, and self-sabotaging behavior. With the pathologizing of the superego concept, efforts to widen the scope of psychoanalysis to include higher mental functions ceased to make use of the superego concept. When, for example, Erich Fromm (1947) reverted to Freud's concept he termed it "conscience" and contrasted it with "superego," by which he meant Hartmann's pathological mechanism.

Having failed to grasp Freud's concept of the ego, Hartmann failed also to distinguish (i) the specific and limited type of synthesis that Freud had attributed to the ego, (ii) the id-ego collaborations that Nunberg had added to the discussion, and (iii) the more complex id-ego-superego interactions on which Wälder had remarked. Hartmann (1947) referred summarily to the ego's "coordinating tendencies" and he proposed that the term "synthetic function" be replaced with the term "organizing function," among other reasons, "because in the concept of organization we include elements of differentiation as well as of integration" (p. 62). Hartmann (1947) wrote of "a strengthening of the ego and a widening of its field of action" through psychoanalysis, that led to its acquisition of "directing tendencies" (p. 58) and "the control of instinctual drives (Hartmann, 1959, p. 202). Hartmann (1956) explicitly placed the ego in *control* of the psyche: "The recognition of the synthetic function (not exclusive of, but in addition to, other regulations) made the ego, which had always been considered an organization, now also an organizer of the three systems of personality. This has rightly been compared with Cannon's concept of homeostasis, or described as one level of it" (p. 291). Thomas M. French (1941) wrote of ego activity similarly: "the capacity of a goal-directed striving to maintain its dominance depends first of all upon the ability of its cognitive field to inhibit and regulate the tendency of its own underlying tension to seek discharge in diffuse motor activity. This ability to withstand tension we may designate quantitatively as the integrative capacity of a goal-directed striving" (p. 175). Heinz Kohut's (1971) concept of the cohesion of the nuclear self, and its fragmentation or disintegration, echoed French's discussion of ego strength in terms of the integration and disintegration of the ego. Ego psychology's concept of the ego as a central authority that integrates through mastery (see also: Grotjahn, 1941, pp. 393-94; Murphy, 1959, p. 531; Peto, 1960; Weiss, 1967, p. 520) was inconsistent, I suggest, with Nunberg's idea of "free intercourse" among the id, ego, and superego. It was equally irreconcilable with both the leading function that Wälder attributed to the superego and Marion Milner's concept of artists' "creative surrender," the conscious giving over of control to the unconscious creative process (Field, 1957).

PSYCHIC INTEGRATION

Freud's treatment of the synthetic function as a technical term, with a specific and limited meaning, has meant that psychoanalysts have used other terms in other contexts. In addition to its use as a synonym for the synthetic function, "integration" has been a term of choice both for general or non-specific purposes and for discussions specifically of the concept of the "free intercourse" of the id, ego, and superego. Analysts then talk of the integration of the psyche, or of the total personality. Carl G. Jung famously used the term in the latter sense in a 1938 book, titled *The Integration of the Personality*; but psychoanalysts had begun using the term in the same way some years earlier (for example, Brierley, 1932). Both the synthetic function and multiple-function integration are presumably at work in the ego's structure. Glover (1932) proposed that "ego organization...as an organized system of psychic impressions ultimately expressed in terms of memory-traces" (p. 166) commences as clusters of memory that form ego-nuclei that come to be organized into a cohesive system only through development. "The earliest ego tendencies are derived from numerous scattered instincts and *converge* gradually until, probably about the age of two, a coherent anal-sadistic organization is established" (p. 169; see also Glover, 1938, 1943, 1968). The synthetic function acting on its own may account for the ego nuclei or, at least, their initial memory-traces; but the coordination of ego nuclei with sexual development involves intersystemic integration. Commenting further on ego development, Hendricks (1942, p. 44) noted that "mature behavior is a synthesis of abilities which are first developed in little pieces during infancy" (p. 44). The ego commences with reflexes, moves through a learning phase when the same activities are practiced independently of stimuli, and arrives at maturity, when the function is available for use at will, in service of the total personality. Michaels (1945) suggested that the developmental co-ordination of the different sexual drives--oral, anal, Oedipal, and coital--as proposed by Freud (1905) and extended by Abraham (1924), had always implicitly been a concept of developmental integration; and he cited Wälder (1936) to support his case: "The whole phenomenon of the multiple functions and of the multiple meaning of each psychic act, then, is not--in analogy to the older neurology--to be understood through any sort of conception of a summation of stimuli and threshold values, but parallel to the concepts of newer neurology and biology--is to be understood as the expression of the collective function of the total organism."

Brierley (1951) contributed a major theoretic statement on the topic of the integration of the id, ego, and superego. She began by emphasizing the complexity of the phenomenon. The real phenomenon is not an ideal, all-or-nothing category, but a process that varies from person to person and moment to moment in a person's life. "Integration is always relative, never absolute, and organization varies both in stability and in adaptive efficiency" (p. 114). Integration of the psyche is a different phenomenon than the synthetic function of the ego, but nevertheless bears a role in the construction and maintenance of identity.

> Integration of the personality as a whole is not to be confused with integration of the reality-ego alone since this is only one of the major systems. Integration of the personality implies a degree of harmonization between super-ego-, ego- and id-drives which amounts to some degree of integration of the total psyche. Experience leads to the assumption that a sufficient number of closely knit process-systems are so regularly integrated with the major ego-organizations in the same functional pattern that they enable the ordinary person to retain his identity. (Brierley, 1951, p. 114)

In Brierley's (1951) view, an integrated psyche is the optimal outcome of psychoanalytic treatment. "There...exists for psycho-analysts a useful, though perforce still relative standard for mental health, namely, the standard of personal integrity" (p. 186).

> The term 'integration' may easily become something of a catchword, but it conveys perhaps better than any other term the sense of wholeness resulting from the organization of dynamic components, a living unity engendered by the harmonious patterning of variety. Integration, in its application to personality, is a strictly relative term. Individuals react at any given moment as functional wholes, but these functional wholes are more or less temporary and vary, according to psycho-social circumstances, within limits imposed by the total personality. Applied to the living but more permanent total pattern of mental organization, the term integration conveys the meaning of a stable and unified personality, a microcosm of harmoniously interrelated systems, as contrasted with a schizoid micro-chaos of mutually discordant sub-organizations....Integrative living is a continual resolution of conflict, and integration is a constant, creative transcendence of disintegrative trends. Therapeutic success and failure both point to the difficulty of such transcendence, but indicate the possibility that human beings might achieve more satisfactory degrees of personal integrity than are common to-day if they could overcome their profound dread of understanding and accepting themselves, and develop a more enlightened psychological reality-sense. (Brierley, 1951, pp. 180-81)

After introducing the general concept of psychic integration, Brierley attempted to address specifics by turning to traditional cultural data that were pertinent to her topic. Brierley (1951) remarked that "religions offer plans or methods of integration and ethics purport to supply the rules of integrative living" (p. 181). At the same time, she cautioned that "the psycho-analytic conception of integration as a threefold working harmonization of the total personality must be distinguished....from a series of partial integrations, for example, from the ego super-ego alliance against the id favoured by traditional inhibitory morality and Puritanism" (p. 187). Allowing "for the probability that there may be more than one type of adequate integration" (p. 188), Brierley contrasted partial integrations with the example of Christian sainthood. She suggested that the integration of the ego and superego there coincides not with a repression of sexuality, but with its sublimation. Rather than a hypocritical hatred in the name of love, there is genuine and unconflicted love.

> What is remarkable about the integrity of the Saints is not its impairment by certain inevitable dissociations but its validity. Sanc-

> tity would appear to be a positive condition in which by far the greater part of the total personality is God-centred and effectively dominated by the love and will of God, as apprehended by the person concerned. It may not be too much to assume that sanctity is the sublimatory positive of infantile sexuality in the same way that neurosis is described as the negative of perversion. This way of thinking of it helps to explain both the rarity of its achievement and its status as a type of integration. It would seem that the price of sanctity is total sublimation of genital drives and total surrender of ego-direction to super-ego control. In the conduct of life, this surrender may take the form of obedience to spiritual and practical direction by superior ecclesiastical authority. The symbolic significance of surrendering personal initiative in order to become an instrument of the Divine Will need not be laboured here. The wholeness of the Saints is proportionate to the completeness of their sublimation and to the inclusiveness of their surrender to Supreme Reality, the incomprehensible and indescribable God who is, nevertheless, indubitably experienced as Love.
>
> Even if the unification of the Saints is to be thought of as self-cure rather than disease, the impression remains that the integration of sanctity should, nevertheless, be regarded as a striking variation rather than as the end stage of the main line of human development. The true spiritual vocation is very rare and the findings of psycho-analysis suggest, very definitely, that the high road for the majority does not lead to super-ego autocracy and selective idealization, but to a more inclusive and democratic harmonization of id, ego, and super-ego systems, to the development of more comprehensive reality-sense, and to the more enlightened ego-direction of personal life. (Brierley, 1951, pp. 228-29)

Both the strengths and limitations of Brierley's theory become evident when the sublimation of love through devotion to God and to accomplishing God's service in the world is likened to artists' sublimation of love through artistic creativity. There is merit to the thesis that sublimation and integration are being achieved, but neither sainthood nor artistic creativity is able to occupy any human being on a full time basis. People continue to need food, drink, and sleep; they also need sexual attachments and contact. The psychic integration that is possible through sainthood is compatible with a robust sexual and familial life, not only in principle but also historically, for example, in Eastern Orthodox Christianity and Jewish Kabbalah. Brierley overspoke in so far as she rationalized celibacy in the Western Christian experience. On her own admission, "Personal integrity is a libidinal end which is attained in the main only by libidinal means" (Brierley, 1951, p. 255).

Reverting to the clinical implications of her findings, Brierley (1951, p. 256) remarked that "the essential capacity which has to be encouraged to develop in the interest of personal integrity is the capacity for active loving." Brierley summarized:

> *Integrative values: total personality and mature ego standards.* It will now be evident that a 'good life' can result only in so far as the demands of instinct and of conscience can be harmonized sufficiently well to give the ego some measure of united backing in its conduct of daily life. The demand for a rational ethic of necessity is really nothing less than a demand for a third, post-moral or integrative, standard of values. (p. 279)

Brierley's concept of psychic integration was echoed, possibly independently, by the humanistic psychologist Abraham Maslow (1968), when he defined self-actualization "as a fusion of ego, id, super-ego and ego-ideal, of conscious, preconscious and unconscious, of primary and secondary processes, a synthesizing of pleasure principle with reality principle, a healthy regression without fear in the service of the greatest maturity, a true integration of the person at all levels" (p. 96; italics deleted).

UNFINISHED BUSINESS

Existing psychoanalytic discussions of the unconscious systematizing function, the unconscious compromise function, the synthetic function of the ego, and the integration of the total personality provide a coherent but partial account of the psyche's unitive processes. Freud attributed these processes to Eros, a mysterious, metaphysical drive to unity at work in the cosmos. Treating Eros not as a fiction but as a metaphor, I have instead argued that well known psychological processes--condensation, the sense organ of consciousness, and unconscious superego functions--account for the unitive trends within the psyche.

The unitive tendency can also be recognized in other theories of the psychoanalytic mainstream that are presently incomplete. The theory of the ego ideal is a prominent example. When Freud (1923a) introduced his tripartite model of the mind, the structural hypothesis of the id, ego, and superego, he abandoned his theory of 1914 that morality had its basis in a psychic agency that he had called "conscience" and described as the heir to primary narcissism. In 1923, Freud proposed a revised version of his previous theory that gave pride of place not to primary narcissism but to the Oedipus complex. Morality now had its basis in a psychic agency that he called the superego and suggested to originate upon the resolution of the Oedipus complex around age six. In *Principles of Psychoanalysis* (1955), whose first German edition appeared in 1933, Herman Nunberg reconciled the two theories. He used the term "ideal ego" in reference to the neonatal circumstance (p. 126) and treated it as a developmental foundation for the superego.

> While in the ideal ego the impulses of the id are accepted without opposition and are granted satisfaction, this harmonious accord of the strivings of the ego and the id is disturbed by the formation of the superego. The superego inserts itself between the ego and the id. It ends the harmony which until then existed between them and influences the strivings of the id as well as those of the ego....The superego...develops through identifications and derives its power from the energies which belonged to the objects whose cathexes have been withdrawn. But as the source of those energies lies in the id, the superego derives its power indirectly from the id....When [Oedipal] instinct gratification is renounced out of fear of losing the love object, this object is absorbed by the ego and cathected with libido; it becomes a part of the ego. In contrast to the ideal ego, it is called ego ideal....The narcissism of the ego ideal is a *secondary* one....The predominantly maternal ego ideal starts to develop as early as the pregenital stages. (pp. 141, 142, 145-46)

Where Federn had proposed that the oceanic feeling is a developmentally advanced form of primary narcissism, Nunberg suggested that the ego ideal, and later the superego, accommodate secondary narcissism but are otherwise its developmental successors. Freud's praise of Nunberg's book as "the most complete and accurate presentation we have at this time" (in Nunberg, 1955, p. xi) indicates his approval of the idea that a developmental line (A. Freud, 1963) should be drawn from primary narcissism through the ego ideals of the pre-Oedipal period to the superego of the resolved Oedipus complex. Because direct infant observation obliges us to abandon the theory of primary narcissism in favor of the theory of primary love (Balint, 1952), we may perhaps treat neonatal awareness of the mother as the original foundation of a developmental line that proceeds through the ego ideal to the superego.

Having redefined the psychoanalysis of mysticism by shifting its topic from the oceanic feeling to plural modes of unitive experiencing, and its explanatory theory from primary narcissism to the unitive trends that Freud conceptualized inadequately under the term Eros, I anticipate that a place in mainstream psychoanalysis will also someday be found for a clinically responsible appreciation of mystical experiences.

My present ambitions are more modest, however. This chapter has addressed mainstream psychoanalytic theorizing about the psyche's unitive trends, but most of the existing literature on unitive processes stems from analysts whose formulations were more idiosyncratic. A small number of psychoanalysts who were or are mystics have repeatedly offered original contributions whose departures from the mainstream can be appreciated as partly deliberate and partly intuitive explorations of the psyche's unitive trends. The remainder of this book chronicles their original achievements.

Three

Otto Rank's Will Therapy

Rank began developing original clinical techniques as early as 1921; and *The Development of Psychoanalysis* (1923), which he co-authored with Ferenczi, published a portion of his innovations in impeccably Freudian terminology. Freud seems to have been fully abreast of Rank's innovations, unpublished as well as published, and to have considered them acceptably psychoanalytic. Following Rank's break with Freud over *The Trauma of Birth*, Rank's work was shunned by the psychoanalytic establishment. Grinker (1940, p. 183) reported, however, that in private conversation Freud "had nothing but good to say about Rank--his imagination and brilliance--but simply stated 'he was a naughty boy.'" Because Clara Thompson was indebted to Rank, and Thompson analyzed Harry Stack Sullivan, many of Rank's most important technical innovations came to be preserved by Sullivan's school of interpersonal psychiatry--even though Sullivan personally participated in Rank's expulsion from the American Psychoanalytic Association (Lieberman, 1985, pp. 236-37, 293). At the same time, American ego psychologists called the interpersonalists "Neo-Freudian," and Rank's admiration by Carl Rogers and Rollo May (pp. 396-97) did his reputation no good among self-styled Freudians. The rehabilitation of Rank's reputation and technical innovations within psychoanalysis awaited the rise in the 1980s of the American school of relational psychoanalysis.

We are here concerned, however, less with Rank's technical innovations than with original theories that he first published only after breaking with Freud. Like Burrow, Rank had come to Freud after an enthusiasm for Nietzsche, and he drew on Nietzsche as a resource for the elaboration of his own version of ego psychology. In 1935, Rank went so far as to call Nietzsche "the greatest psychologist of modern times" (Rank, 1996, p. 255). Nietzsche's metaphysics were mystical. He postulated a chaotic, ever innovative, Dionysian "Primal Unity" underlying an equally unified illusion of the Apollonian form, structure, order, and truth of phenomenal reality. The rare individual, the *Übermensch* or "superman," critiques the conscious façade and so facilitates a reconnection with primal unity; but instead of being engulfed in its oneness, expresses his own creative individuation. Rank reconceptualized Nietzsche's metaphysics in developmental terms as a progression from infantile solipsism to adult creativity. In this way, Rank conceptualized mysticism as a line of ego development that commences with primary narcissism and ends with the individuation of creative adults. Although Rank (1927b) scorned "the concept of the *Id* (Es) which...is just as mystical as the old unconscious" (p. 9), he was no more successful than Freud at eliminating metaphysics from his theories. Appropriating mystical ideas by psychologizing them reductively removes a patina of supernaturalism while leaving the interior logic of the mystical intact. Another major resource for Rank was the Christian philosophy of Søren Kierkegaard, which was then only beginning to be known outside Denmark. Rank drew selectively on Kierkegaard's (1980) ideas about the interrelation of consciousness, self, moral choice, anxiety, and guilt in order to enrich his analysis of the ego. In the process, Rank eliminated the torturous casuistry that Kierkegaard sometimes indulged in rationalization of Christian dogmas. Because Rank opened his diary for 1905 with a quotation from Kierkegaard (Lieberman, 1985, p. 34), we know that his familiarity with Kierkegaard antedated both his meeting with Freud later the same year and Jaspers's attention to Kierkegaard eight years later.

THE MYSTICAL CORE OF THE PERSONALITY

The better to distinguish his clinical approach from psychoanalysis, Rank came to call it "will therapy." Rank's innovations had their basis in several simple but far-reaching corollaries of Freud's theory. Without using Freud's term "primary narcissism," Rank invoked the theory of neonatal solipsism and concluded that a natural, biological urge to mysticism informs much of human culture.

> Already, in that earliest stage of individualization, the child is not only factually one with the mother but, beyond all that, one with the world, with a Cosmos floating in mystic vapours in which present, past, and future are dissolved. The individual urge to restore this lost unity is...an essential factor in the production of human cultural values. (Rank, 1932a, p. 113)

Rank insisted that he was not simply interpreting the biological through a mystical lens. He suggested that the psychical was incompletely understood biologically. A philosophical approach was a necessary addition (Rank, 1996, p. 228).

Rank agreed that the drives that Freud allocated to the id were "supra-individual" phenomena that were shared by the human species. Because everyone's id contains the same bisexual drives, it would be equally fair to say that we all share a single common id. Individuality resided in the ego alone. Rank (1936a) "value[d] the ego, not only as a wrestling ground of (id) impulses and (super-ego) repressions, but also as conscious bearer of a striving force, that is, as the autonomous representative of the will and ethical obligation in terms of a self constituted ideal" (pp. 11-12). Working with a theory of will and guilt that traced back through Nietzsche and Schopenhauer to Hindu philosophy (p. 37), Rank recognized the id, the ego, and the creative process of individuation as mystical phenomena. "The philosopher creates, as little as the artist or the religious believer, merely from his own personality. What manifests in all of them, although in different form, is at once something supra-individual, natural, cosmic" (p. 23). With this formulation, originally published in German in the late 1920s, Rank inaugurated a paradigm shift in the psychological understanding of mysticism. Mysticism was not a question of rare, transient experiences that were unconnected with the major trends of psychic life. The psyche was mystical from birth to adulthood.

Rank's theory gave particular attention to what, in Freud's terminology, comprised the transition between primary and secondary narcissism. How does the experience of the mystical cosmic reality come to be replaced by an experience of human individuality? For Rank, will was the differential factor. One aspect of its experience was "the subjective feeling of free will" (Rank, 1998, p. 111) but will, as Rank understood it, also entailed a good deal more.

> By the will.....I mean...an autonomous organizing force in the individual which does not represent any particular biological impulse or social drive but constitutes the creative expression of the total personality and distinguishes one individual from another. This individual will, as the united and balancing force between impulses and inhibition, is the decisive psychological factor in human behaviour. (Rank, 1941, p. 50)

Because the German word *Geist* means both "spirit" and "intellect," Rank's (1936a) description of will as "the spiritual principle" that is distinctive of humanity (p. 7) referred to the same psychological phenomenon that he elsewhere described as "the urge for abstraction, which....led beyond the purely abstract to....objectivizing and concretizing" (Rank, 1932a, p. 12). The intellectual aspect of Rank's concept of will requires its conceptualization, in conventional English terms, as intentionality or purpose. For Rank, will was neither a motor conation nor an emotional wish, but an intellectual power to decide on action. When Rank wrote of "will," he meant the power that formulates and intends intentions.

Rank's theory can be seen as a logical extension of Freud's (1920b, p. 264) claim that dreams and free associations are not meaningless but are instead psychically determined. Contrary to the popular misunderstanding, Freud's formulation of psychical determinism did not assert that dreams and free associations are necessarily determined *mechanically*. Freud claimed only that they were always meaningful. To account for meaningful intentionality on the part of the unconscious, Freud suggested that the ideas of the Oedipus complex were transmitted genetically through a Lamarckian inheritance of acquired characteristics. Even if geneticists' objection to the theory could be satisfied, the philosophical conundrum remained: how did the ideas of the Oedipus complex originate? One cannot inherit ideas if one cannot formulate them; and if one can formulate them, one has no need to inherit them (Róheim, 1925). Rank (1927b) claimed that his *Trauma of Birth* "endeavoured to replace the so-called primal phantasies by tangible, individual real experiences" (p. 17); and his theory of will similarly did without Freud's theory of inborn phantasies. Rank postulated that meaningful intentionality on the part of the unconscious arises directly from intentionality on the part of existence. The concept of the psyche's participation in the intentionality of all existence is intrinsically mystical and metaphysical.

In Rank's formulation, will constructs both the objectivity of the external world and the individuality of the self. The two constructions proceed simultaneously, as the example of psychotherapy illustrates.

> The ego needs the Thou in order to become a Self, be it on the individual plane of human relationship or on the social plane of a foreign group-ideology, or on the broadest basis of one civilization needing another one for its development and maintenance. The tragic element in this process is that the ego needs a Thou to build up an assertive self with and against this Thou.
>
> Just as in individual therapy this complementary Thou is only partly assimilated, while partly reciprocated, so all inspirational ideologies as well as cultural diffusions are in the last analysis therapeutic, that is, serve the purposes of strengthening a self--be it personal, social or national--by borrowed support from the opposite type, whether directly as borrowed strength or indirectly as strengthening the assertive forces by stimulating them antagonistically....The psychology of the Self is to be found in the Other, be that Other the individual Thou, or the inspirational

ideology of the leader, or the symbiotic diffusion of another civilization. (Rank, 1941, p. 290)

Rank agreed with Freud's concept of drive to the extent of attributing compulsion and determinism to unconscious motivation, which, however, he conceptualized in mystical terms as vitalism (Rank, 1941, p. 47; 1996, p. 270). Like Freud, Rank attributed will to the ego. In Rank's formulation, vitalism was transformed into will through the ego. His phrasing, "evolution from blind impulse through conscious will to self conscious knowledge" (Rank, 1936a, p. 24), indicates that he attributed vitalism's transformation into will to the mediation of consciousness, as distinct from self-consciousness. Consciousness involves perception and thinking with concrete ideas, which, according to Freud, intervene between drive and motor action. Abstract conceptual thinking is a precondition of self-consciousness, but not of will.

Rank differed from Freud in his understanding of the place of will in the therapeutic process. Freud described the freeing of a patient's will as an *outcome* of psychoanalysis. In making the unconscious conscious, Freud (1923a) sought "to give the patient's ego *freedom* to choose one way or the other" (p. 50). Rank instead understood the ego's conflict with the id as a conflict of will with determinism. Enhancement of will was Rank's *means of cure*, and not its consequence alone. "Beyond Psychology," the title of an early lecture that Rank's editors employed for a posthumous book (Rank, 1941), expressed Rank's belief that creativity was truly originary, truly beyond determinism. As such, it was beyond the scope of psychology. Deterministic aspects of the psyche could be studied. The circumstances surrounding creativity could be studied, but creativity exceeded the reach of science.

Rank saw the individual will originating in opposition to determinism. "The will...has a negative origin, it arises as counter force against an outer or an inner compulsion" (Rank, 1936b, p. 69). "Counter-will" was synonymous with "inhibition" (Rank, 1936a, p. 103). Spitz's (1957) studies of the toddler's discovery of the head shake and word "no," around thirteen months, may readily be co-ordinated with Rank's ideas about negative will. At the same time, Rank's categorical formulation here anticipated the equally categorical formulation of Hartmann, Kris, and Loewenstein (1949) that aggression underlies all defense.

In Rank's (1932a) view, will's negative aspect includes a controlling element that also manifests positively as creativity (p. 39). Rank's theory of individuation, from (i) unconscious drivenness, through (ii) negative will, to (iii) creative, non-reactive, innovative will, presumably named the stages of separation-individuation that he noticed clinically in the therapeutic progress of his patients. Rank discussed the stages, however, on the assumption that therapeutic progress proceeded through developmental stages of childhood that patients had failed to complete properly.

Creativity involves a complicated process of internalization, assimilation to will, and projection that alters external reality to conform with will (Rank, 1936a, pp. 7-8). Will develops beyond oppositionality and becomes creative through its formulation of ego ideals.

> The creative type...is able...to create voluntarily from the impulsive elements and moreover to develop his standards beyond the identifications of the super-ego morality to an ideal formation which consciously guides and rules this creative will....he evolves his ego ideal from himself, not merely on the ground of given but also of self-chosen factors. (Rank, 1936a, p. 9)

The difference that Rank saw between the superego, which introjected parental standards, and the ego ideal, which projected individual standards creatively, led him to claim that Freud's theories had not taken the line of autonomous development into account. Rank blamed Freud's reductionism for his oversight of the original, willful, creativity in the formulation of ideals. In treating ideals as sublimations of sexuality, Freud had overlooked their reality as ideals.

INDIVIDUATION, FEAR, AND GUILT

Rank designed his will therapy to facilitate patients' individual standards. "Real psychotherapy is not concerned primarily with adaptation to any kind of reality, but with the adjustment of the patient to himself, that is, with his acceptance of his own individuality or of that part of his personality which he has formerly denied" (Rank, 1936b, p. 149). "At the same time the love claim has to be transformed into his own ethical ideal formation which self acceptance makes possible" (p. 92).

Rank wrote approvingly of character analysis, which was then a new psychoanalytic procedure that was beginning to replace Freud's program of symptom analysis. Rank (1936b) described character analysis as the patient's "voluntary re-creation of the own self" (p. 237). Rank also valued the neutrality and abstinence of psychoanalysis' clinical procedure. "The man who suffers from...repression of will, must again learn to will, and not to force on him an alien will is...the best protection....the patient should make himself what he is, should will it and do it himself" (Rank, 1936a, p. 41).

Rank maintained that individuation was the central human problem and corresponded at a psychological level to the biological process of birth. All that Rank had written in *The Trauma of Birth* about the death symbolism surrounding the fear of psychological separation from the mother (Rank, 1927a, p. 181) appeared in his post-Freudian writings in a mystical key, as symbolism that surrounded the fear of individuation from the cosmos.

> Nature becomes even more conscious of herself in a man who at the same time with the increasing knowledge of himself which we designate as individualization, tries always to free himself further from the primitive....births, rebirths and new births...reach from the birth of the child from the mother, beyond the birth of the individual from the mass, to the birth of the creative work from the individual and finally to the birth of knowledge from the work....we find in all these phenomena, even at the highest spiritual peak, the struggle and pain of birth, the separation out of the universal. (Rank, 1936a, pp. 24-25)

What was at stake physically and spiritually for the child was, for example, not death as the existentialists held, but "the trauma of separation" (Rank, 1936b, p. 174), whose memory was repressed, unconscious, and the latent content of dreams, fantasies, and symptoms. "The fear in birth, which we have designated as fear of life, seems to me actually the fear of having to live as an isolated individual....primary fear corresponds to a fear of separation from the whole, therefore a fear of individuation" (p. 175).

In Rank's view, the fear of life--the existentialists' "problem of anxiety"--was insoluble. Every effort to overcome the fear of separation through creativity served paradoxically to promote individuation that inadvertently increased reason for fear. Not only did individuation resolve one moment's fear of separation by creating reasons for the renewal of the fear in future, but individuation brought with it an opposing fear, the fear of loneliness, "the loss of the feeling of kinship with others, finally with the ALL" (Rank, 1936b, p. 219).

Equally intractable was the ethical issue of guilt. Blending Kierkegaard with Freud, Rank (1936a) traced the origin of guilt consciousness to the achievement of self-consciousness. "Guilt consciousness is simply a consequence of consciousness, or more correctly, it is the self-consciousness of the individual as of one willing consciously. As the [biblical] Fall presents it--knowing is sin, knowledge creates guilt" (p. 64). Rank emphasized that both willing and guilt originally existed unconsciously. "Will and guilt are the two complementary sides of one and the same phenomenon" (p. 61). Guilt consciousness was not simply a burden. It had the practical advantage of motivating moral behavior. "The more we individualize ourselves--that is, remove and isolate ourselves from others--the stronger is the formation of guilt-feeling that originates from this individualization and that again in turn unites us emotionally with others. This is the psychological basis of our ethical socialization" (Rank, 1996, p. 236).

Rank (1936a, pp. 57-58) criticized mythology and religion for naively overvaluing union with nature, which leads them to condemn will--and individuation--as evil. Rank (1998) claimed that the "root problem of religion," the central problem that religions everywhere address, "is the moral stance toward will: its interpretation as evil. The issue is evil in the world, confronting us subjectively with sin and guilt as personal transgression or fault" (p. 101; italics deleted). Rank (1936a, pp. 62-63) instead averred that guilt is an unavoidable component of the human situation. Because therapy cannot resolve either the contradictory fears of unity and individuation or the inevitability of guilt through will, Rank replaced the psychoanalytic ambition to relieve guilt feelings with his own aim to promote creativity. "The essential therapeutic problem is...to enable him to bear and to accept himself instead of constantly defending himself against himself" (Rank, 1936a, pp. 115-16).

Rank followed Nietzsche in recognizing the irrationality of the unconscious as intrinsic and insurmountable.

> Nietzsche was the first to recognize, from a cultural study, the human value of irrational forces in the suppressed self, which Freud in his rationalistic system could only see as the cause for neurosis. Hence, the cure psychoanalysis had to offer the individual could not be the creative expression of those energies. Freud's therapeutic method aims at making the individual merely conscious of his irrational self, thereby convincing him that it had been rightly suppressed and should now be rationally condemned. (Rank, 1941, p. 38)

Where Freud placed his faith in a rational universe, to which all irrationality was to be reconciled, Rank envisioned a paradoxical universe whose irrationality was to be negotiated but never resolved.

HERMENEUTICS *AVANT LA LETTRE*

Rank (1936b) objected to Freud's concept of "sublimation" on the grounds that it rationalized as real what was only illusory. "The concept of sublimation includes the denial of something else, which indeed may be more primitive but perhaps stands closer to life, is more real, and so stamps sublimation as a self deception" (p. 243). Rank's formulation both endorsed Freud's extension of the concept of sexuality and declined to follow Freud in reducing everything to sexuality. Union was real, but will demanded individuation. Rank accepted the illusory nature of all that is not manifestly sexual and then proceeded to question conventional attitudes to illusions.

> All doing and feeling falling within the field of sublimation, from the purely aesthetic to the simple emotional, would be not a substitute [for sexuality]...but a self willed creation of a sphere of illusion in which a make-believe life with less expense and therefore with less fear, that is, with a pleasure gain, is possible. The therapeutic situation, according to our conception, provides such a play level. (Rank, 1936b, pp. 247-48)

Rank saw illusion as a creative achievement--and therapy as an instance of the general phenomenon of play. Rank (1936b) suggested that the patient's projection of the transference onto the therapist is an illusion that serves to identify the therapist with the projected part of the self. Through the projection--we would now say, projective identification--"the two selves become one" (p. 248) and the patient uses the enlargement of his self as a basis for creative innovation in life.

Rank found Freud's formulation unsatisfactory because speaking of sublimation left a causal factor out of account. "Psychology could not explain how from the sex-impulse there was produced, not the sex-act, but the art-work, and all the ideas called in to bridge this infinite gulf--"compensation," "sublimation," etc.--were only psychological transcriptions for the fact that we have here something different" (Rank, 1932a, p. 26). "The question as to what diverted and what directed is just being dismissed with an allusion to repression" (pp. 39-40). Rank (1936b, p. 228) concluded that what is sex at the level of the impulse life ceases to be sex at the individuated levels of the will. It is instead to be recognized as creativity. Rank's (1932a, p. 39) concept of counter-will that inhibits and constrains the impulse life allowed him to dispense with Freud's concept of aggression and reduce all motivation to the unity of the will. What for Freud were sexuality, aggression, and sublimation, was will alone for Rank.

Rank's (1932a) subscription to Nietzsche's cosmology, where all order and structure are appearances that disguise an underlying creative chaos, led him to conclude that consolation--including therapy--is intrinsically illusory (p. 100). Truth was not exempt from the generalization. Unlike external reality, which is material and leaves sense impressions, truth is an intellectual and emotional verdict that always and only refers to psychic reality. "Truth is what I believe or affirm, doubt is denial, or rejection....the reality which penetrates consciousness through our sense organs can influence us only by way of the emotional life and becomes either truth or falsehood accordingly; that is, is stamped as psychic reality or unreality" (Rank, 1936a, p. 77). Because Rank held that truth is always a subjective interpretation, a willful, creative judgment, he rejected Freud's claim that reconciling patients to truth has curative power. Rank maintained that some truths are so far from being therapeutic, that they are destructive.

> The rationalistic slogan of Socrates that virtue can be taught and that self-knowledge is healing appears revived in Freud's therapeutic conviction that truth in and by itself is curative; one of those principles the opposite of which is just as true, is borne out by Ibsen's evaluation of what he calls the individual's life-lie. It is the climax of irony that the Greek Oedipus-saga, on the interpretation of which Freud based the justification of his truth-therapy, explains the tragic failure of the hero from just this same intellectual curiosity about the truth. Not unlike Ibsen's heroes, Oedipus, too, perishes as soon as he knows the truth about himself, revealed by the historical self-analysis of his past in true Freudian fashion. (Rank, 1941, p. 279)

Rank's remarks on the illusory nature of sublimation and the unavoidable subjectivity of truth expressed a hermeneutic epistemology that was consistent with his belief in the irrationality of the unconscious. Although Freud credited the unconscious with producing irrationality, he always maintained that its process was systematic, lawful, and comprehensible. For Rank, the process of the unconscious was collective and undifferentiated, which precluded the possibility that making the unconscious conscious could result in rationality. Successful therapy had to be paradoxical, in reflection of the irrationality of the unconscious. Like the psyche, with its impulse, counter-will, will, and ideals, therapy would at best be dialectic.

THE CREATIVE SOLUTION

For Rank, the hero of legend and the artist or creative type of personality exemplified the unified psyche at which his will therapy aimed. "The...highest level of development is characterized by a unified working together of the three fully developed powers, the will, the counter-will and the ideal formation....Here the human being, the genius, is again at one with himself; what he does, he does fully and completely in harmony with all his powers and ideals" (Rank, 1936a, pp. 111).

The unconscious too was to be integrated within the creative process. Consider the following discussions of poetic activity.

> In poetic creation....language appears on the one hand as something self-creative and on the other as something created by the poet, who is thus its master. For the self-creative urge inherent in language is expressed for the poet himself in the feeling of unconscious creation; but that means the tendency of language in itself, independent of his conscious will, which threatens to carry him away again and which he can only check by linguistic means of his own, which also are special to himself.....every emotional experience forms itself for him speakably....thenceforward he has to shape consciously--that is, to bring into a form which is collectively intelligible. That is the second, conscious phase of poetic production, the real constructive process. (Rank, 1932a, p. 275)

An element of drive, impulse, and compulsion is to be recognized in the unconscious formulation of the creative expression. Counter-will, seeking to individuate from unconscious impulse, initially seeks mastery through verbal formulation. Later, having mastered impulse, conscious will takes the opportunity to elaborate originally, without need, out of freedom. The name "will therapy" is taken out of context when it is treated as a therapy of consciousness, as though Rank had abandoned the theory of the unconscious. His therapeutic concern was the integration of the whole psyche, conscious and unconscious.

Rank recognized the practical advantages of a religious approach to his therapeutic project.

> The religious solution was and still is so much the more gratifying because it admits *the Unknown*, indeed, recognizes it as the

> chief factor instead of pretending an omniscience that we do not possess. Besides, religion is also more consoling, I should like to say more therapeutic because, with the admission of the unknown and unknowable it also leaves room for all kinds of hope that it still may not be so hopeless as it seems. (Rank, 1932b, pp. 44-45)

In personal conversation, Rank referred to Rudolf Otto's (1950) concept of numinous experience "and always insisted that the 'existential' unconscious is absolutely inaccessible to any *intellectual* grasp" (Kramer, in Rank, 1996, p. 225 n. 5; Kramer's italics).

Rank conceptualized individuation through creativity as a developmental opposite to cosmic unity, but he also recognized that creativity accomplishes a spiritual union in a developmentally advanced manner.

> The artist....puts into [his art]...his being, his "soul," as we say...his essence, and with it the essence of man and of humanness in general....this very essence...is found again in the work by the enjoyer, just as the believer finds his soul in religion or in God, with whom he feels himself to be one. It is on this *identity* of the spiritual...and not on a psychological identification with the artist, that the pleasurable effect of the work of art ultimately depends....the *feeling of oneness* with the soul living in the work of art, a greater and higher entity. (Rank, 1932a, pp. 109-10)

In Rank's (1932a) view, it was not simply that the artist projects into an artwork with which the audience empathizes. The objective reality of beauty formed a third term in the process. The artist united with beauty in fashioning the artwork, and the audience united with the beauty in appreciating it (p. 110). Rank attributed the impulse to create to the urge to restore the original cosmic unity of the drives, but he credited will with directing "this human striving towards a super-individual unity and its spiritual premises" (Rank, 1932a, pp. 113-14). For Rank, creativity was intrinsically mystical.

Rank's emphasis on creativity was central to his understanding of the limitation of psychotherapy. "The therapeutic experience is...only to be understood from the creative experience because it is itself a creative experience and in truth a very special form of it" (Rank, 1936a, p. 159). Like any creative activity, individuation is time bound, limited, a single work in a lifelong series. Individuation was not to be achieved once for always. It was instead to be achieved and re-achieved time and again for as long as a person lived. An artist, for example, would begin a career by learning to create in the conventional style and only later individuate further by developing an original style. The artist experiences "creative conflict" between his "loyalty to his own self-development" and guilt over abandoning his loyalties to the prevailing conventions. "So the struggle of the artist against art is really only an ideologized continuation of the individual struggle against the collective" (Rank, 1932a, p. 372). Each and every process of individuation is unconsciously experienced as a renewal of the birth trauma, with its varied symbols of death and rebirth. "The process, though similar in principle to, is not a simple repetition of, the trauma of birth; it is, broadly, the attempt of the individual to gain a freedom from dependence of any sort upon a state from which it has grown" (Rank, 1932a, pp. 374-75).

RANK'S INNOVATIONS IN CLINICAL TECHNIQUE

Rank's clinical procedures were consistent with his views on individuation through creativity. Freud had once set a date to terminate psychoanalysis in dealing with an obsessive-compulsive personality, and Rank discovered that setting a termination date at the start of an analysis regularly provoked dreams and fantasies that were characterized by death and rebirth symbolism, much as the prospect of terminating would do toward the end of an analysis that was conducted in Freud's customary manner. Rank (1996, p. 79) found that patients of both sexes then manifested mother transferences from the beginning of their analyses. He concluded that he could abbreviate the therapeutic process by proceeding directly toward the analysis of its climactic transference.

> It is technically possible to begin with the disclosure of the primal trauma, instead of giving the patient time automatically to repeat it at the end of the analysis. By this method one is enabled to sever the Gordian knot of the primal repression with one powerful cut, instead of laboriously troubling to unknot it. (Rank, 1929b, p. 213)

Rank (1996) agreed with Freud that "the analyst can bring about a radical cure only by first rousing the repressed conflicts before setting to work to solve them" (p. 74), but he saw greater efficiency in actively setting a termination date, than in waiting patiently for the eventual development of a transference neurosis. He also saw the Oedipus complex as less pathogenic than the birth trauma, so that no analysis was complete that did not address the latter. "This technique of 'active intervention'....not only definitely shortened the treatment but is quite necessary for a correct conclusion of the analysis, for freeing of the transference, and for final healing of the patient" (pp. 78-79).

Following his break with Freud, Rank moved beyond Freud's model of reviving and resolving an infantile trauma, to address the individuation that Freud's technique left patients to achieve on their own after their analyses ended. Rank's experience with actively setting a termination date led him to appreciate that the patient's separation anxiety drew its symbolism from memories of infantile separation from the mother but was provoked by the therapist in the here-and-now of the therapeutic situation. This realization made impossible his continued subscription to Freud's theory that the transference is to be "explained historically in every single reaction...and is constantly related to the past" (Rank, 1936b, pp. 47-48). It was separation from the therapist in reality, and not merely from the mother in unconscious fantasy, that created anxiety in the patient. Rank regarded the infantile trauma as the prototype of a traumatic situation that subsequently became habitual, and whose correction concerns the present much more than the past.

> The undischarged, unreleased, or traumatic experiences are not repressed into the unconscious and there preserved, but rather are continued permanently in actual living, resisted, carried through to an ending or worked over into entirely new experiences. Here in actual experience, as in the therapeutic process, is contained not only the whole present but also the whole past, and only here in the present are psychological understanding and therapeutic effect to be attained. (Rank, 1936b, p. 40)

Rank's (1929a) emphasis on the here-and-now of the transference led him to recognize the "ethical" dimension of "Thou-Psychology" at work in the analytic situation (p. 4). He also conceptualized his "theory of cognition" as a move "beyond psychoanalysis" through "the analysis of the analytic situation" (p. 5). Rank rejected Freud's concept of the repetition-compulsion.

> Freud's analytic method...placed the emphasis upon infantile impressions and experiences...(Oedipus situation), which in later life are assumed to be merely 'repeated.' In reality, it is the *reactions* of the ego that are 'repeated'....these reactions are continually produced anew in similar situations....even when we go back to the very earliest expressions of life, in birth...we should conceive of them only as the first occasion, the first opportunities for

> manifestations of affect-reactions that will emerge again...on similar occasions. (Rank, 1996, p. 103)

In 1923, two years prior to his break with Freud, Rank had proposed that the curative component of psychoanalytic therapy was not the interpretation of the transference. What was curative was the patient's experience of the new relationship with the analyst that insight into the transference makes possible (Ferenczi & Rank, 1923). This emphasis of the post-transferential experience, as distinct from the intellectual interpretation that precipitates the therapeutic insight, sought to explain the insufficiency of merely theoretical understanding of the transference. Unless interpretation catalyzed an experience of insight that changed the patient's experience of the analyst, therapy was not accomplished. Rank concluded that the theoretical differences among Freud, Jung, Adler, and himself were incidental to the therapeutic process. Teaching theories, making interpretations, and so forth were beside the point.

> Real psychoanalysis...is a radical therapy that starts out by removing the conditions to which symptoms owe their origin. This is not possible by merely communicating analytic knowledge to the patient. An emotional re-experience is necessary. (Rank, 1996, p. 73)

Where Freud had written of the patient developing a new neurosis, the transference neurosis, that had the analyst at its center, Rank understood the patient to be engaged in a creative process of attempting to adapt to the therapeutic situation. He regarded the patient as an *artiste manqué*, a failed artist (Rank, 1996, pp. 253, 268). "The artist, through a strong will-organization, finds a way to objectify his self-creation in the work of art, whereas the neurotic remains fixed on his own ego" (Rank, 1996, p. 268). Rank (1936b) provided patients with the opportunity, as it were, to practice their art until they became better at it.

> The therapeutic experience affords to the individual a potential living out of the hitherto suppressed or denied side of his personality....While this therapeutic release of the hitherto blocked portions of the ego is used by the patient as protection against real experience, it has at the same time the value of a developmental level which no longer needs to be merely potential. (pp. 256-57)

Because the creativity of each patient in each session would be original and unpredictable, Rank's technique was fluid and versatile. "My technique consists essentially in having no technique, but in utilizing as much as possible experience and understanding that are constantly converted into skill but never crystallized into technical rules which would be applicable ideologically" (Rank, 1936b, p. 149).

THE PSYCHOANALYTIC CHARACTER OF WILL THERAPY

To what extent is Rank's will therapy compatible with psychoanalysis? Every therapeutic re-awakening of the birth trauma was, in Rank's (1929b, p. 213) view, a transference in Freud's sense of the term. His provocation of the transference by setting a termination date was no different in principle than classical psychoanalysts' provocation of a transference through the austerity, neutrality, and abstemiousness of the psychoanalytic frame (Freud, 1919, pp. 162-63; 1937, p. 232; Menaker, 1942; Alexander and French, 1946, pp. 85-130; Alexander, 1950; Macalpine, 1950; Stone, 1961). Both clinical procedures were passive aggressive and traumatogenic. They brought quiescent neuroses to florid conditions that permitted therapeutic access and intervention. Rank's recognition of the patient's response to the here-and-now reality of the therapeutic situation was preserved by Sullivan and the interpersonalists. The insight was finally accepted by ego psychologists, not without opposition, upon its independent formulation by Gill (1982).

Although Rank abandoned Freud's concept of resistance, he supplied the concept of "counter-will" in order to account for the same clinical phenomena.

> I transformed the Freudian theory of resistance to getting well into the human problem of accepting help, and the "gain through illness" into what one may call a philosophy of suffering. Independent experience taught me that the "gain" of illness....is *self-willed*, a sort of creation that can find expression only in this negative, destructive way....I assumed, from the very beginning, the existence of a *self-inhibiting* mechanism inherent in the individual. This inhibition of instinct, which operates as a self-preserving protection, I was able later on to define as the individual will....the individual not only brings about his illness but also its prerequisites, fear and guilt....instead of affirming or asserting his will, the neurotic has to find an excuse to prove to himself as

> well as to others his inability or incapability. *Instead of saying, "I don't want to do that," he says, "I cannot do it, because I am afraid or feel guilty."* (Rank, 1996, pp. 252-54)

Because Rank addressed resistance clinically under the term "counter-will," I suggest that his will therapy met Freud's criteria for psychoanalysis. Rank provided radically innovative language for his technique; but unlike Adler, Jung, and others who abandoned the treatment of "transference and resistance" (Freud, 1914b), Rank worked clinically with the particular therapeutic process that Freud discovered and designed psychoanalysis to address.

CONCLUDING REFLECTIONS

Rank's pioneering voice deserves to be heard in our on-going discussions. Rank argued that mysticism has a natural basis. In coordinating Nietzsche's dualism of Dionysian chaos and Apollonian order with Freud's theory of infantile solipsism and the development of a sense of reality, Rank created a dated and untenable framework for his clinical concerns; but the latter remain important. Every child's maturation and every patient's therapy depend on successful individuation from the unconscious, which houses both the mother-infant dyad and the Oedipus complex. In important ways, the process of individuation is simultaneously a movement beyond mechanistic determinism to the humanistic domain of voluntary action. We are not unconsciously driven automata. We individuate, achieving both autonomy and individuality by virtue of a mental function that is conventionally called will. Rank maintained that the individuation process pertains to real events in the here-and-now, but typically employs unconscious symbolism whose manifest contents derive from the trauma of separation from the mother.

Rank's distinction between counter-will and will expressed a distinction within the individuation process. Counter-will was equivalent to Freud's inhibition and resistance; its task was to restrain the unconscious, freeing consciousness from the obligations of determinism. Will, in its turn, looked forward creatively and originally. Rank attributed will to consciousness; Wälder (1934), writing a few years after Rank, instead made a case for self-consciousness. Wälder claimed that the superego's self-observing function transcends mechanical causativity and enables will to be free (see also Noy, 1979). Rank discussed the integration of counter-will, will, and ideal formation in the creative personality; his formulation anticipated Nunberg's attention to the "free intercourse" of the id, ego, and superego in wholesome personalities.

Writing in advance of the existentialists, Rank noticed that anxiety and guilt are inevitable concomitants of originality. Every creative effort is achieved at the cost of imagining resistance, jealousy, and woundedness on the part of others; and the therapist's task is to help patients find the strength to be original nonetheless.

Rank's will therapy had no place for oceanic feelings, and his reliance on Freud's theory of neonatal solipsism was mistaken. These limitations do not diminish his original achievement. His concern to extend the concept of the mystical led him to brilliant and enduring contributions on the topics of individuation and the integration of the psyche.

Four

Erich Fromm's Humanistic Psychoanalysis

Erich Fromm (1900-1980) was the most widely read psychoanalyst of his generation and had the literary gifts to contribute to psychoanalytic theory in books that were accessible to the general public. He was an original, who belonged to no school within psychoanalysis. He called his own approach humanistic psychoanalysis. He was one of the first analysts to abandon the piety toward Freud that characterized mainstream psychoanalysis, in favor of the blend of admiration and critical skepticism that is normative in academia. For his efforts, the American Psychoanalytic Association disavowed him, labelling him "Neo-Freudian" (Roazen, 2001). Fromm was widely regarded as a mystic. He practiced and recommended Buddhist meditation, openly advocated selected doctrines of the Christian mystics, and was concerned with union and unities throughout his writings.

Fromm had rabbinical ancestors on both sides of his family, was raised in a strictly orthodox, middle class German Jewish family, received an excellent education in Bible and Talmud as a child and adolescent, and remained observant after entering the University of Heidelberg in 1917. From 1919 until 1925 Fromm visited his third teacher of Talmud, Shlomo Barukh Rabinkow, almost daily. The bulk of their time together was devoted to the Talmud, but the two also discussed Maimonides' philosophical writings, the *Tanya* of Rabbi Shneur Zalman, and Weiss's Jewish history. Rabinkow (c. 1882-c. 1941) hailed from the Chabad (Lupavitch) sect of Hasidic Judaism, acquainted Fromm with the Hasidic doctrine of serving God with joy, and taught him many Hasidic songs that Fromm continued to sing informally all of his life. At the same time, Rabinkow had embraced, in Fromm's (1987) words, "the culture of protest as it was expressed by the radical Russian *intelligentzia*" (p. 105), had studied philosophy and law at Heidelberg, and was responsible for exposing Fromm to both socialism and humanism (Fromm, 1987, pp. 99, 102-3; Funk, 1982, p. 229; Burston, 1991, pp. 13-14). During his university years, Fromm emulated Rabinkow's blend of "a basically revolutionary attitude" with Judaism, in Fromm's case, by combining sociology and Marxism, on the one side, with the religious existentialism of Martin Buber and the negative theology of the medieval German mystic, Meister Eckhart, on the other. Fromm was studying with

Rabinkow at the same time that he earned his doctorate in sociology from Heidelberg with a 1923 dissertation entitled "Jewish Law, A Contribution to the Sociology of Diaspora-Judaism." Fromm reviewed the position of Jewish law in three historically unrelated Jewish sects, the Karaites, Hasidim, and Reform Jews. He argued that Jewish law functioned sociologically to provide social cohesion across the centuries and continents (Ortmeyer, 1995, p. 19; Funk, 2000, pp. 55-58).

Fromm pursued post-doctoral studies in psychology and psychiatry in 1925 and 1926 at the University of München (Landis, 1971, p. x). No longer meeting daily with Rabinkow, Fromm rapidly individuated in his attitudes toward Judaism. "When he became acquainted with Buddhism in 1926, he felt this as a kind of revelation. For the first time he saw a spiritual system, a way of life, based on pure rationality and without any irrational mystification or appeal to revelation or authority" (Landis, 1971, p. xii). Fromm considered the negative theology of the Western mystics to be equivalent to Buddhist atheism in promoting humanism, by making people responsible for their own projections. Also in 1926, Fromm abandoned his practice of Jewish religious observances. The next year, he renounced Zionism, embraced Marxism, and began his clinical practice (Burston, 1991, pp. 12-13).

Fromm's psychoanalytic training proceeded concurrently. He began analysis with Frieda Reichmann in 1925, but when they fell in love he continued with Wilhelm Wittenberg in Munich. Fromm was also analyzed for a year by Karl Landauer in Frankfurt, and then for two more years in Berlin with Hanns Sachs and Theodor Reik (Burston, 1996a, pp. 416-17). He qualified at the Psychoanalytic Institute in Berlin in 1931. He boasted of his analysis by Sachs, because Sachs was a member of Freud's inner circle; but Fromm was also deeply indebted to Reik for his ideas about "listening with the third ear." While in Berlin, the Fromms were frequent visitors to George Groddeck's establishment in Baden Baden, where they additionally befriended Karen Horney and Sandor Ferenczi, who were similarly regular visitors. Fromm credited both Groddeck and Ferenczi with formative impact on his own clinical style (Funk, 2000, p. 123).

Fromm early distinguished himself by introducing sociological perspectives within psychoanalysis, as Wilhelm Reich was also doing. Relocating in the United States in 1933, Fromm found himself outside the psychoanalytic mainstream, which was exclusively medical and socially conservative. In 1935, Fromm abandoned classical technique (Roazen, 1996, p. 438). He published an article (Fromm, 2000b) that critiqued Freud's bourgeois, capitalist assumptions and instead advocated Ferenczi's technical innovations (see also Bacciagaluppi, 1993). Fromm's (1992b) revision of psychoanalysis drew also on many further sources. Blending psychoanalysis with the variety of Marxist argumentation that was later to be designated as "ideology critique," he invented a theory of social character or social personality types (Grey, 1992; Funk, 1996; Margolies, 1996). He earned the label "Neo-Freudian" for his resultant claim that the Oedipus complex is a cultural construction that pertains above all to power relationships, and is not a biologically driven, psychosexual phase (Fromm, 1959a). Freud had allocated culture to the superego and biology to the id, combining both culture and biology in his theory of the Oedipus complex; but ego psychology had so changed superego theory that all was reduced to biology. Fromm replied with an equally one-sided privileging of social structure.

> My suggestion that the Oedipus complex be interpreted not as a result of the child's sexual rivalry with the parent of the same sex but as the child's fight with irrational authority represented by the parents does not imply, however, that the sexual factor does not play a significant role, but the emphasis is not on the incestuous wishes of the child and their necessarily tragic outcome, its original sin, but on the parents' prohibitive influence on the normal sexual activity of the child. (Fromm, 1944, p. 410; see also Fromm, 1959a)

Ego psychologists classified Fromm as a member of the "culturalist school" of psychoanalysis because he agreed with Abram Kardiner, Harry Stack Sullivan, and Karen Horney that culture functions independently of biology in its impact on the formation of personality (on Kardiner, see Merkur 2005, pp. 50-57). However, Kardiner, Sullivan, and Horney approached culture from a perspective in American cultural anthropology, where Fromm maintained a sociologist's interest in economics and politics (Fromm, 1970, p. 21, n. 1). Fromm (1959b, 1980, 1992b, 1997) was an early and persistent critic of Freud's--and classical psychoanalysis's--cultural bias against women. In psychoanalytic studies of fascism, capitalism, and communism, Fromm (1941, 1955b, 1961) maintained that truly healthy child-rearing requires reform not only of the family but of the entire social structure.

Marxist politics had not excluded other analysts, such as Géza Róheim and Otto Fenichel, from membership within the psychoanalytic establishment (Robinson, 1969). However, Fromm left the New School for Social Research and was never part of Fenichel's psychoanalytic circle, in both cases because he was too critical of Freud to suit his fellow Marxists. At the same time, Fromm's Marxism constituted a problem for psychoanalysts. Among other issues, Fromm relied extensively on a "dialectical" mode of theory-formation (Fromm, 1941, p. 30) that "calls for an understanding of psychic phenomena as the outcome of opposing forces" (Fromm, 1992b, p. 27). Most psychoanalysts have adhered to the scientific assumption of a lawful and orderly cosmos and the ideal of a single, linear, theory system. Like Hegel, whom Marx had followed (Fromm, 1959b, p. 102), Fromm instead maintained that the cosmos is intrinsically conflicted and that a dialectical process of thesis-antithesis-synthesis is unending. Nature is forever producing first one thing and then its opposite, which between them create a novelty that, in its turn, becomes the basis for a further dialectical opposition. In the dialectical model of the historical process, external reality is inherently conflicted and contradictory. It is not then possible ever to achieve a unilinear theory; but a person can navigate conflicts by aligning with the dialectical process. In Fromm's (1992b) "dialectic revision of psychoanalysis," an analysts's task is to interpret the dialectic, confronting the patient with the opportunity to make knowing choices.

Fromm's dialectical approach had more radical consequences for his theory formation than for his clinical work. Drawing additionally on the sociological methodology that was current in his time, Fromm regularly constructed and wielded Weberian "ideal types" (Fromm, 1956, p. 41; see also Weber, 1949; Hekman, 1983) which, he claimed, were in dialectical relations to each other. At his best, Fromm devised ways of contrasting wholesome and morbid character traits. In other instances, his dialectic degenerated into sweeping statements that seem doctrinaire, dogmatic and, to a psychoanalytic eye, instances of splitting in the Kleinian sense of the term.

Fromm found colleagues among the interpersonalists at the William Alanson White Institute of Psychiatry in New York, but he called his own formulations "humanistic psychoanalysis." In posthumously published works, written after humanistic psychology had come on the scene and given the word "humanism" a meaning that Fromm disliked, he renamed his approach "transtherapeutic psychoanalysis" (Fromm, 1992a, p. 55; 1992b, pp. 76-80). Fromm (1960) agreed with Freud that psychoanalysis addresses "repressedness" (pp. 139-40). He maintained, however, "that the method of uncovering the unconscious, if carried to its ultimate consequences, may be a step toward enlightenment" (p. 140). It was this additional use of the psychoanalytic process not to dissolve repressedness but to promote mysticism, that Fromm considered "humanistic" and "transtherapeutic."

FROMM'S HUMANISM

Fromm had fully developed his humanistic program by the time that he published *Escape from Freedom* (1941), which was his first book in English. Fromm (1939b) had read Rank's post-Freudian work carefully enough to publish a review that criticized the fascist implications of both its elitist view of creative artists and Rank's claims about the illusory nature of truth. Fromm later regretted the article and did not want it reprinted (Roazen, 2001, p. 17). Politics aside, Fromm often agreed closely with Rank. Consider, for example, the following summary of his views on the human.

> Man, the more he gains freedom in the sense of emerging from the original oneness with man and nature and the more he becomes an "individual," has no choice but to unite himself with the world in the spontaneity of love and productive work or else to seek a kind of security by such ties with the world as destroy his freedom and the integrity of his individual self. (Fromm, 1941, pp. 22-23)

Without referring to Kierkegaard by name, Fromm appropriated his ideas of original oneness with nature and the acquisition of freedom through individuation. At the same time, Fromm interpolated Freud's criteria for the good life, *Lieben und Arbeiten*, love and productive work. Lastly Fromm added his original contribution, that psychopathology can be understood from a humanistic perspective as conditions that damage freedom and integrity. Making the unconscious conscious was not limited to sexuality but included "the spontaneous activity of the total integrated personality" (Fromm, 1941, p. 258).

Like Burrow, Freud, and Rank, Fromm replaced Kierkegaard's idea of an original fellowship with the animals with a concept of infantile solipsism. Avoiding metaphysics, Fromm referred to Freud's theory of primary narcissism, the solipsism of the newborn (Fromm, 1941, p. 26; 1956, p. 38; 1960, pp. 89-90, 128; 1963, pp. 154-55; 1964a, pp. 63-65; 1992a, p. 117). Like Rank, Fromm followed Kierkegaard in explaining the biblical story of the Fall as an illustration of the developmental change that replaced an original naiveté with consciousness of self (Fromm, 1960, pp. 128-29; 1963, pp. 207-8). Like Rank, Fromm (1941) accepted Kierkegaard's evaluation of the human predicament. "The process of individuation is one of growing strength and integration of its individual personality, but it is at the same time a process in which the original identity with others is lost and in which the child becomes more separate from them" (p. 31). Where, however, Rank had followed Nietzsche in despairing of the masses and advocating artistic creativity for an elite, Fromm valued wholesome commonplaces of everyone's life. "This growing separation may result in an isolation that has the quality of desolation and creates intense anxiety and insecurity; it may result in a new kind of closeness and a solidarity with others if the child has been able to develop the inner strength and productivity which are the premise of this new kind of relatedness to the world" (p. 31). "Man can be free and yet not alone, critical and yet not filled with doubts, independent and yet an integral part of mankind" (p. 257).

Fromm agreed with Rank, above all, in regarding development as a continuous effort to differentiate from a neonatal mystic state and, at the same time, to achieve unity at a more advanced or higher level through individuation. Failed individuation was the essential nature of psychopathology. Under the phrase "mechanisms of escape from freedom," Fromm (1941) discussed commonplace processes of failing to individuate whose disproportionate use assumes pathological significance (p. 141). Fromm proposed three mechanisms and noted that each involved a form of union. He cited the authoritarianism of both Nazism and Stalinism as instances of his first category.

> The first mechanism...is the tendency to give up the independence of one's own individual self and to fuse one's self with somebody or something outside of oneself in order to acquire the strength which the individual self is lacking. Or, to put it in different words, to seek for new, "secondary bonds" as a substitute for the primary bonds which have been lost. (Fromm, 1941, p. 141)

Fromm considered authoritarianism from the perspectives of both those who inflict and those who suffer irrational authority, and he arrived at the term "symbiosis" to designate the process. "Symbiosis, in this psychological sense, means the union of one individual self with another self (or any other power outside of the own self) in such a way as to make each lose the integrity of its own self and to make them completely dependent on each other" (p. 158). Fromm maintained that symbiosis underlies both sadism and masochism (p. 158), but he claimed that Freud's treatment of sadomasochism was reductive. Whether the syndrome manifests in sexual behavior or otherwise, it was more fully and appropriately regarded humanistically as an unwholesome type of union that thwarted individuation.

Fromm (1941) suggested that symbiosis may "use no pressure but only mild persuasion." In this event, symbiosis occurs through "'anonymous' authority" that may be "disguised as common sense, science, psychic health, normality, public opinion" (p. 167). Fromm also drew attention to what he called a "magic helper." People "expect protection from 'him,' wish to be taken care of by 'him,' make 'him' also responsible for whatever may be the outcome of their own actions" (p. 174). Symbiosis with a magic helper can be directed toward God, a parent, spouse, or superior in a business or other organization. Fromm cautioned that falling in love is frequently a question of the reciprocal projection of magic helpers.

Fromm (1941) listed destructiveness as a second mechanism of escape from freedom. "Destructiveness...aims...at elimination of its object. But it, too, is rooted in the unbearableness of individual powerlessness and isolation" (Fromm, 1941, p. 179). He counted "automaton conformity" as a third mechanism of escape (p. 185). Fromm discussed symbiosis, destructiveness, and automaton conformity as dialectic alternatives to individuation and noted, more or less in passing, that each mechanism was a kind of union.

In *Escape from Freedom*, Fromm (1941) analyzed the pathologies of Nazism and Stalinism. He advocated "positive freedom" on humanistic criteria. "There is no higher power than this unique individual self...man is the center and purpose of his life...the growth and realization of man's individuality is an end that can never be subordinated to purposes which are supposed to have greater dignity" (p. 265). Like Kierkegaard, Rank, and the existentialists, Fromm affirmed that freedom is inextricably involved with ideals. With Freud, however, he insisted that ideals were far from self-evident. Fromm rejected the conventional association of ideals with self-sacrifice. "From this subjectivist viewpoint a Fascist, who is driven by the desire to subordinate himself to a higher power and at the same time to overpower other people, has an ideal just as much as the man who fights for human equality and freedom" (Fromm, 1944, pp. 265). For Fromm, ideals were associated with healthy growth. "All genuine ideals...express the desire for something which is not yet accomplished but which is desirable for the purposes of the growth and happiness of the individual" (pp. 265-66).

Fromm often composed sentences that adopt an individualistic perspective, consistent with Rank and the existentialists. "Positive freedom...is identical with the full realization of the individual's potentialities, together with his ability to live actively and spontaneously" (Fromm, 1941, p. 270). Because he theorized dialectically, he also expressed opposing views in other sentences. "We believe that man is *primarily* a social being, and not, as Freud assumes, primarily self-sufficient and only secondarily in need of others....In this sense, we believe that individual psychology is fundamentally social psychology or, in Sullivan's terms, the psychology of interpersonal relationships" (p. 290). The paradoxes of Fromm's dialectic instantiated the *coincidentia oppositorum* of mystical thinking.

AUTHORITARIAN AND HUMANISTIC ETHICS

Fromm took up the problem of wholesome ideals in his second English book, *Man for Himself* (1947). Having rejected the ethical relativism implied by Rank (Fromm, 1939b), Fromm (1947) asserted that "the sources of norms for ethical conduct are to be found in man's nature itself... moral norms are based upon man's inherent qualities, and...their violation results in mental and emotional disintegration" (p. 7).

Fromm (1947) contrasted two types of authority. Rational authority had its basis in competence, while irrational authority had its basis in power over people (p. 9). Fromm suggested that humanistic ethics are compatible with rational authority. Authoritarian ethics differed. They are "based not on reason and knowledge but on awe of the authority and on the subject's feeling of weakness and dependence" (p. 10). Anticipating the Kleinian distinction between persecutory and depressive guilt (Grinberg, 1964, 1992), Fromm (1947) suggested that people suffering from authoritarian conscience "do not feel *guilty* but *afraid*" (p. 144).

Fromm (1947) contrasted humanistic ethics whose "sole criterion" is human welfare (p. 13). "Good in humanistic ethics is the affirmation of life, the unfolding of man's powers. Virtue is responsibility toward his own existence. Evil constitutes the crippling of man's powers; vice is irresponsibility toward himself" (p. 20). Because Freud had regarded the superego as an internalization of parental authority, Fromm (1947) considered it an exclusively "authoritarian conscience" (p. 34) and contrasted it with conscience which formulates humanistic ethics rationally. I have elsewhere argued (Merkur, 2001) that Fromm's account of superego theory reported ego psychology's misreading of Freud. To account for the judgments of conscience, Freud (1914a, 1921, 1933) had conceptualized a unified psychic agency that engaged in self-observation, possessed ego ideals, and performed moral deliberations. Many analysts misunderstood Freud's superego concept. Most influentially, American ego psychologists insisted that the superego does not think, does not self-observe, and issues its moral judgments by rote repetition of parental examples (Hartmann, Kris, & Loewenstein 1946, p. 30; Hartmann & Loewenstein, 1962, p. 160). Where Freud's superego concept originated through the analysis of conscience, ego psychology appropriated Freud's term in order to address a different phenomenology and a different mental process. Freud conceived of a superego that was both humanistic and authoritarian by turns; ego psychology's superego is exclusively authoritarian. Fairbairn (1944) noted the discrepancy between the two superego concepts, followed Freud in attributing conscience to the superego, and allocated savage self-rebuke, self-punishment, and so forth, to a split-off portion of the ego that he called the "internal saboteur" or, in later formulations, the "anti-libidinal ego" (Fairbairn, 1963). Winnicott's (1960a, p. 470) statement, "It is in health only that the classical superego...can be observed," similarly worked with Freud's superego concept, and not ego psychology's. Fromm independently recognized the differences between conscience and its pathological displacement; but because he was misled by ego psychologists' claim that they were working with Freud's superego concept, he formulated his thinking by contrasting conscience and the superego.

For Fromm (1947), what was important was not the structure of the psyche, but the criterion by which "the normal, mature, healthy personality" (p. 83) determines good and evil. Echoing both Freud's "*Lieben und Arbeiten*" and Marx's concern with productivity, Fromm proposed the concept of a "productive character."

> The "productive orientation" of personality refers to a fundamental attitude, a *mode of relatedness* in all realms of human experience....[A person] experiences himself as the embodiment of his powers and as the "actor"...he feels himself one with his powers and at the same time that they are not masked and alienated from him. (Fromm, 1947, p. 84)

Several conditions must be met for productiveness to be possible. The individual must enjoy freedom to act, must be guided by reason, and must know the powers that are available for use (p. 84).

Applying the criterion of productivity to love, Fromm (1947) conceptualized love as an action rather than an experience. He asserted love's essential unity whether it is devoted to a child, a fellow human being, or a sexual partner (p. 98). In all cases, love was a type of union.

> The idea expressed in the Biblical "Love thy neighbor as thyself" implies that respect for one's own integrity and uniqueness, love for and understanding of one's own self, can not be separated from respect for and love and understanding of another individual....Love of others and love of ourselves are not alternatives (Fromm, 1947, p. 129; see also Fromm, 1939a)

Fromm (1947) similarly argued that hostility and destructiveness proceed simultaneously against self and others (p. 216). "Selfishness and self-love, far from being identical, are actually opposites....selfish persons are incapable of loving others, but they are not capable of loving themselves either" (p. 131). Fromm's observation follows from the fact that whenever the psyche feels any emotion, it feels the emotion toward all that it contains: mental representations of the self, other people, and the non-human environment..

Because disturbances of love have interpersonal behavioral consequences, Fromm (1947) concluded that "every neurosis represents a moral problem" (p. 224). Rational ethics traced to love. Authoritarian ethics were equally a type of union but involved a symbiosis that agreed closely with Freud's (1921) discussions of "identification" in the context of group psychology.

> [The authoritarian] has found inner security by becoming, symbiotically, part of an authority felt to be greater and more powerful than himself....His feeling of certainty and identity depends on this symbiosis; to be rejected by the authority means to be thrown into a void, to face the horror of nothingness. (Fromm, 1947, p. 146)

Fromm (1947) discussed faith as an activity that may be placed in either the rational or the irrational. "Faith...[is] a basic *attitude* of a person, a character trait which pervades all his experiences" (p. 199). Fromm defined irrational faith as "the belief in a person, idea, or symbol which does not result from one's own experience of thought or feeling, but which is based on one's emotional submission to irrational authority" (p. 201). Dialectically opposed to faith was doubt, which Fromm found pandemic in a contemporary form: "an attitude of *indifference* in which *everything is possible, nothing is certain*" (p. 200).

Fromm suggested that rational faith has its basis in productivity. A history of having been productive forms a rational basis for faith in oneself (p. 208). Moreover, the capacity to be productive produces a need to be so. "The power to act creates a need to use this power and...the failure to use it results in dysfunction and unhappiness" (p. 219). Faith in oneself--in one's identity and capacity for productivity--was a precondition of fidelity toward others. "Only the person who has faith in himself is able to be faithful to others because only he can be sure that he will be the same at a future time as he is today and, therefore, to feel and to act as he now expects to" (p. 206).

Fromm (1947) argued that "Freud overvalued the significance of sexual satisfaction" (p. 219) because people need to make productive uses of all their capacities.

> [A person] has no other way to be one with the world and at the same time to feel one with himself, to be related to others and to retain his integrity as a unique entity....If he fails to do so, he can not achieve inner harmony and integration; he is torn and split, driven to escape from himself, from the feeling[s] of powerlessness, boredom and impotence which are the necessary results of his failure. (p. 220)

Freud never claimed that sexuality is the unique motivation of humankind; but he did claim that frustration of sexuality is the universal cause of neurosis. If his claim were correct, preoccupation with sexuality would be appropriate for psychotherapeutic purposes. Fromm claimed, however, that psychoanalysis does not have to be limited, as Freud thought, to the therapeutic. The technique is also useful in addressing the transtherapeutic; and the transtherapeutic has mystical criteria of well-being.

THE PLACE OF MYSTICAL EXPERIENCE IN HUMANISTIC PSYCHOANALYSIS

In his third English language book, *Psychoanalysis and Religion* (1950), Fromm asserted the religious character of his work. Freud had referred to the Delphic Oracle's, "Know thyself!"; and Fromm cited Plato's phrase in arguing that a psychoanalyst should be a "physician of the soul" (p. 74). Fromm agreed with Freud in calling neurosis a private form of religion (p. 27) and he went on to discuss "authoritarian religion" in which "God is a symbol of power and force, He is supreme because He has supreme power, and man in juxtaposition is utterly powerless" (p. 36). Fromm discussed authoritarian religions as tyrannies run by elites. "To such ideals as 'life after death' or 'the future of mankind' the life and happiness of persons living here and now may be sacrificed; the alleged ends justify every means and become symbols in the names of which religious or secular 'elites' control the lives of their fellow men" (pp. 36-37).

Fromm (1950) argued, however, that in addition to neurosis and authoritarian religion, there also exists such a thing as humanistic religion, which has its basis in reason, self-knowledge, love, and ethics (p. 37). Humanistic religion has been best represented historically by the mystics.

> Religious experience in this kind of religion is the experience of oneness with the All, based on one's relatedness to the world as it is grasped with thought and love....Virtue is self-realization, not

> obedience....The prevailing mood is that of joy, while the prevailing mood in authoritarian religion is that of sorrow and of guilt. (Fromm, 1950, p. 37)

Fromm (1950) argued that when humanistic religion speaks of God, it knows that its view of God is an anthropomorphizing human projection. "In humanistic religion God is the image of man's higher self, a symbol of what man potentially is or ought to become" (p. 49). Later writings indicate that Fromm (1963, p. 197; 1966, p. 62; 1992b, p. 43; 1994b, pp. 117-118) had in mind the negative theology of mystics and theologians who regarded God as utterly unknowable. When they spoke of God, they were aware that everything that they said, including the noun "God" and the verb "is" ascribes to God something that is other than God.

Authoritarian religion, by contrast, reifies its projections onto God and then seeks union with them.

> When man has...projected his own most valuable powers onto God....They have become separated from him and in this process he has become *alienated* from himself....In worshiping God he tries to get in touch with that part of himself which he has lost through projection. (Fromm, 1950, p. 50)

Fromm (1950) claimed that psychoanalysis promotes a humanistic religious attitude (p. 93). Freud had defined psychoanalysis in terms of relief from repression, but a successful psychoanalysis also invariably provides relief from inauthenticity. "In the psychoanalytic process a person learns to recognize which of his ideas have an emotional matrix and which are only conventional clichés without root in his character structure" (Fromm, 1950, p. 14). Fromm considered authenticity essential to a religious attitude. Among its other functions, authenticity confronted a person with inalienable aspects of human nature.

> There are immutable laws inherent in human nature and human functioning which operate in any given culture....If someone violates his moral and intellectual integrity he weakens or even paralyzes his total personality....the problem of mental health cannot be separated from the basic...aims of human life: independence, integrity, and the ability to love. (Fromm, 1950, p. 74)

Freud (1914a) had argued that people must love to be healthy and fall ill from an inability to love. Fromm extended Freud's line of reasoning to include independence and integrity as well.

Turning to the topic of humanistic religious experience, Fromm (1950) noted "the wondering, the marveling, the becoming aware of life and of one's own existence, and of the puzzling problem of one's relatedness to the world" (p. 94). He invoked Paul Tillich's definition of religion in terms of ultimate concern (p. 94). He wrote more fully, however, of the mystical.

> Beyond the attitude of wonder and of concern there is....an attitude of oneness not only in oneself, not only with one's fellow men, but with all life and, beyond that, with the universe....The religious attitude in this sense is simultaneously the fullest experience of individuality and of its opposite; it is not so much a blending of the two as a polarity from whose tension religious experience springs. It is an attitude of pride and integrity and at the same time of a humility which stems from experiencing oneself as but a thread in the texture of the universe. (Fromm, 1950, p. 95).

Fromm's description of mystical sensibility was inconsistent with conventional discussions of the oceanic feeling and theories of infantile regression. He described a dialectical relationship between union and individuality. All is One; yet within this One, self is individual. At the same time, Fromm's description of mystical sensibility made it seem more exotic than it is. In normal waking sobriety, every person is both the center of his or her own universe and a mere speck of dust within the cosmos. This paradox is part of every sane person's continuous, lifelong experience of reality. Worldviews that are self-consistent--and both science and philosophy attempt to be self-consistent--are obliged to deny one or the other term of the paradox. Either they deny narcissism in the name of objectivity, or externality in the name of solipsism. When a mystical experience manifests the sense of union with an intellectual clarity and emotional intensity that is ordinarily unconscious, it draws attention to the common paradox of subjectivity and objectivity. The resulting sensibility, which endures long after the mystical experience has waned, finds the commonplace paradox extraordinary, and overthrows the tyranny of unilinear reasoning. The result is a mystical *Weltanschauung*.

Fromm (1950) suggested that therapeutic value is to be had from the type of access to the unconscious that religious experiences provide. "Outside the confines of the particular organization of ego are all human potentialities, in fact, the whole of humanity. When we get in touch with this disassociated part we retain the individuation of our ego structure but we experience this unique and individualized ego as only one of the infinite versions of life....one replaces the principle of repression by that of permeation and integration" (pp. 97-98).

UNIVERSAL SYMBOLS AND THE SLEEP STATE

In *The Forgotten Language*, Fromm (1951) presented his approach to the interpretation of dreams. The text was designed as a self-contained work, but it may also be read as a crucial step in Fromm's construction of humanistic psychoanalysis. Fromm advanced three major concepts in the book. He took the general position that "we are not only less reasonable and less decent in our dreams but...we are also more intelligent, wiser, and capable of better judgment when we are asleep than when we are awake" (p. 33; italics deleted). Citing explicitly sexual, violent, and other socially unacceptable behavior that dreams portray, Fromm agreed with Freud that dreams can be irrational wish-fulfilments, but he denied that they are exclusively so (p. 47). He surveyed dreams that exhibited (i) insight into other people's character that was more astute than waking though (pp. 37-38), (ii) increased capacity to make rational predictions of the likely course of future events (pp. 38-39), (iii) increased clarity on ethical issues (p. 44), and (iv) increased creativity.

> Not only do insight into our relation to others or their to us, value judgments and predictions occur in our dreams, but also intellectual operations superior to those in the waking state....There are numerous examples of people who look for solutions of a problem in mathematics, engineering, philosophy, or of practical problems, and one night they dream the solution with perfect clarity. (Fromm, 1951, p. 45)

Rejecting Jung's "assumption of a source of revelation transcending us," Fromm (1951) insisted that "what we think in our sleep is *our* thinking" (p. 97). The state of sleep permits a degree of concentration that is often impossible during wakefulness; but "there is no expression of mental activity which does not appear in the dream" (p. 25). The versatility of dreams accounts for the need to interpret "whether a dream is expressive of an irrational wish and its fulfillment, of a plain fear or anxiety, or of an insight into inner or outer forces and occurrences. Is the dream to be understood as the voice of our lower or our higher self?" (pp. 148-49).

To account for dreams' capacity for superior mental function, Fromm offered a theory of the sleep state that proceeded from the fact that sleepers who are conscious of dreaming are at the same time uninvolved in and unconscious of bodily action.

> Consciousness is the mental activity in our state of being preoccupied with external reality--with acting. The unconscious is the mental experience in a state of existence in which we have shut off communications with the outer world, are no longer preoccupied with action but with our self-experiences....
>
> The "unconscious" is the unconscious only in relation to the "normal" state of activity....the day world is as unconscious in our sleep experience as the night world is in our waking experience. (Fromm, 1951, pp. 28-29)

Fromm (1951) suggested that the sleep state's unconcern with action provided for systematic differences with waking thought. "Sleep experience is not lacking in logic but is subject to different logical rules, which are entirely valid in that particular experiential state" (p. 28). "Logical categories are employed which have reference only to my self-experience. The same holds true of feeling" (p. 30). Possibly because Fromm approached the topic as a theory of sleep, he did not connect his theory with the concept of introversion during waking life. It was only in a posthumous publication that Fromm (1992b) suggested that the conditions of the sleep state may also be achieved "more rarely, in other states such as meditation and ecstasies or states induced by drugs" (p. 57).

A third major innovation in *The Forgotten Language* was the topic announced in its title. Fromm (1951) distinguished three types of symbol. Conventional symbols are exemplified by language (p. 13). Accidental symbols arise through happenstance in a person's or a culture's life (p. 14). Fromm's original contribution pertained primarily to a third category, which he termed the universal symbol.

> The *universal* symbol is one in which there is an intrinsic relationship between the symbol and that which it represents....Take, for instance, the symbol of fire. We are fascinated by certain qualities of fire in a fireplace. First of all, by its aliveness. It changes continuously, it moves all the time, and yet there is constancy in it. It remains the same without being the same....When we use fire as a symbol, we describe the inner experience characterized by the same elements which we notice in the sensory ex-

> perience of fire; the mood of energy, lightness, movement, grace, gaiety--sometimes one, sometimes another of these elements being predominant in the feeling. (Fromm, 1951, pp. 15-16)

Fromm's term "universal symbol" can be misleading. Fromm was not claiming that single symbols have universal meanings. He noted that the sun has different symbolic meanings in the tropics and in northern latitudes (Fromm, 1951, p. 19) and that fire has different meanings depending on whether it is in a comforting fireplace or is destroying a building or a forest (p. 19). He also discussed the symbolic meanings of human creations. For example, "the sensory experience of a deserted, strange, poor environment" in "the outskirts of the city" has the capacity to evoke "a mood of lostness and anxiety" (p. 16).

What was universal in universal symbols were the inner experiences that were projected onto the symbols.

> The universal symbol....is rooted in the experience of the affinity between an emotion or thought, on the one hand, and a sensory experience, on the other. It can be called universal because it is shared by all men....The universal symbol is rooted in the properties of our body, our senses, and our mind, which are common to all men and, therefore, not restricted to individuals or to specific groups. (Fromm, 1951, pp. 17-18)

Where phenomenologists had made claims about the universal meanings of *phenomena*, Fromm psychologized their project. He offered a depth psychology of universal meanings that treated their projection onto phenomena both as constructions and as responses to external realities.

> Man....has the function of experiencing reality not in terms of what he can do with it, but as a pure subjective experience. He looks, let us say, at a tree. Now the man who owns the tree may look at it from the standpoint: "What is it worth? Should I cut it?" He looks at the tree as a tree in terms of its sale value essentially. But if I look at the world with a subjective point of view, that is to say as something I see because I have eyes to see it, to feel, to sense, I have a sense of beauty, then I experience this tree as something wonderful--just as I can experience another person or look at a person or talk to a person. (Fromm, 1994a, p. 79)

Fromm (1951) suggested that dreams and myths employ universal symbols (p. 18). The capacity of art to translate cross-culturally, when language and aesthetic conventions are set aside and shared humanity can be experienced, may also be counted as evidence in support of Fromm's contention. Of the various arts, perhaps music, mime, and silent motion pictures translate best, because they depend most directly on universal symbols.

Fromm theorized that the wisdom that dreams sometimes exhibit has its basis in the access to universal symbols that the sleep state provides. In the posthumously published extension of his thesis to meditation, autohypnosis, and psychedelic drugs, he provided an express link to mystical experiences.

IMMEDIACY, EXISTENTIALISM, AND PSYCHOANALYSIS

Fromm's theories articulated healthy norms: freedom, as against symbiosis; humanistic ethics and religion, as against authoritarian ethics and religion; and universal symbols. These formulations of humanistic standards or goals for analytic patients' aspiration eventuated in Fromm's redesign of his clinical technique. Edward S. Tauber (1959), who trained with Fromm, claimed that Fromm "experienced a change in himself since approximately 1954" (p. 1811).

> He has now a more focused and more maturely developed conviction concerning what he considers the essence of psychoanalysis--that psychoanalysis shall penetrate as deeply and as speedily as possible to the very core of the patient's life, to locate his tenaciously held, unreal, unconscious solution to his separateness, to waste no time on the consequences of his problems and on his adjustments, but to force him to face his resistances and give no quarter. This process is carried out in a setting where the analyst is his full self with the patient. The analyst is not waiting, figuring things out, cautiously weighing what the patient can tolerate because, Fromm regretfully asserts, most delays are in the service of the therapist's anxiety anyway. The therapist should reveal, by his own genuine interest, dedication, openness, and true participation, that there is an urgency to grasp life, to live, to search, and to dare uncertainty. (pp. 1811-12)

Tauber's description suggests that Fromm had abandoned the ego psychological technique of defense analysis. Benjamin Wolstein (1981), who was in supervision with Fromm in 1955, remembered that Fromm was then advocating "the classical procedure of 1915-1917" (p. 484) that Freud had devised prior to the introduction of ego psychology. Fromm's simultaneous embrace of authenticity suggests that he was starting to puzzle out what would become his own distinctive way of working.

Fromm's publications in 1955 included a short paper on free association that rejected the conventional ego psychological procedure. Fromm (1955a) wrote:

> In orthodox Freudian analysis, (not always, but in many instances), free association has become an empty ritual. The patient lies on the couch, he is instructed not to hide anything, to say everything that comes to his mind. That is fine. Let us assume that the patient does that, and is conscientious and honest, and says whatever comes to his mind. What guarantee do we have that the things that do come to his mind have any meaning in the sense of the dissociated personality? That in speaking without restriction he is saying things which are relevant? In many instances free association has deteriorated into meaningless chatter, into "free talk," into uncontrolled complaining, and sterile thinking....The original meaning of free association was to be spontaneous association; the deteriorated free association is not spontaneous at all; it is free only in the negative sense that no thought is omitted....Rather than doing this, I find it helpful to stimulate free association at various times during the session by asking the patient in a definite way: "Tell me what is in your mind *right now.*" The difference sounds small, yet it is considerable. What matters is the *now*, the urgency of the request. Usually the patient will answer this request more spontaneously than the general question, "What comes to mind?" When he has said what is in his mind, one can go on requesting further association with the ideas expressed. (pp. 2-4)

Fromm's discussion of the analyst's free associating represents an original variation on Reik's (1933, 1936, 1948) concept of "listening with the third ear."

> To understand means to respond, to answer, to be in touch. To interpret means to react with one's own imagination and free associations to the patient's utterances. It does not mean to apply the patient's associations to the theory. The analyst's function is to a large extent not thinking, but free associating, and often helping the patient in his free associations by presenting him with

> his (the analyst's) own. All this means that the analyst is, as Sullivan put it, a "participant observer," not a blank mirror, a detached observer. The process of analysis may well be described in this way. Two people communicate. The one says whatever goes through his mind. The other listens, and says what reactions (associations) the patient's utterances have produced in him. His, the analyst's, ideas are not said with the claim that they are right, but only because they indicate how one person's imagination reacts to the patient's imagination. The only claim the analyst can make is that he has been concentrating on what the patient was saying, and that his imagination is trained by experience and appropriate theoretical thoughts. The patient then reacts with new associations to the analyst's, who in turn reacts again, and so on, until some clarification and change is reached. (It must not be understood that I mean there is continuous dialogue; in my concept of analysis the patient does, quantitatively speaking, most of the talking, but what matters is that the analyst's "interpretations," when they are given, are essentially his free associations.) (Fromm, 1955a, p. 6)

Also dating to 1955 was the first of Fromm's books that made substantial use of existentialist ideas and vocabulary. Fromm had drawn on both existentialism and Marxism from the beginning of his career, but a marked increase in his use of both jargons first appeared in *The Sane Society* (1955b). In summarizing humanistic psychoanalysis in the opening portions of the book, Fromm merged Kierkegaard's theory of the Fall of Man with the biological theory of evolution.

> At a certain point of animal evolution, there occurred a unique break, comparable to the first emergence of matter, to the first emergence of life, and to the first emergence of animal existence....When the animal transcends nature, when it transcends the purely passive role of the creature...*man is born....life became aware of itself.* (Fromm, 1955b, p. 23)

Kierkegaard had suggested that the human capacity for "transcendence," the capacity to know that one knows what one knows, is essential to being human. For Kierkegaard, the existentialists, and Fromm, the capacity for transcendence--in other terminologies, the capacity for reflective thinking, or for self-observation--defined the human, much as the capacity for mind had defined the human in Aristotle's philosophy. Kierkegaard's definition of the human accommodated Christian ideas of a soul that can transcend the body at death. Freud and most psychoanalysts instead followed Aristotle in treating the soul as a group of bodily functions that live and die, grow, mature, and age, sicken and heal.

Because the soul concepts of psychoanalysis and existentialism are irreconcilable, most people opt for one or the other point of view; but Fromm was eclectic. Whatever formulations seemed good to him, he took from each point of view. He routinely placed conflicting perspectives in dialectical relationship with each other without seeking to resolve the logical inconsistencies. Fromm considered his procedure appropriately mystical. He regarded the rationalism of natural science as a false consciousness, a denial and repression of the dialectic or paradoxical logic of reality that is both mystical and integral to sanity.

> Spiritual experience, which underlies many theistic and nontheistic forms of union and at-onement, is closely related to the problem of sanity. Human existence is an absurdity; it would be impossible to experience fully the dichotomy of human existence and to remain sane. "Sanity" is "normalcy" paid for by the anesthetizing of full awareness by false consciousness, routine busyness, duty, suffering, and so on. (Fromm, 1992b, p. 77)

Fromm (1992b) conceived of the self not as a rational construct, a self-representation, but as a subjectivity, an agency that sanely engages in the dialectic of reason and paradox. "When there is no need for repression, the possibility exists for emergence of the self as the integrating subject of authentic being" (pp. 77-78).

Fromm's apology for paradox notwithstanding, the inconsistencies of his thought were more often semantic than substantive. Consider, for example, Fromm's privileging of the existential over the physiological.

> In the theory presented here, there are no corresponding *physiological* substrata to the needs for relatedness, transcendence, etc. The substratum is not a physical one, but the total human personality in its interaction with the world, nature and man; *it is the human practice of life as it results from the conditions of human existence.* (Fromm, 1955b, p. 70)

There is more rhetorical and less substantive disagreement here with mainstream psychoanalysis than might appear. Fromm was claiming that human beings are more strongly motivated by abstract concepts that are conscious psychological inventions, than we are by physiological impulses. Fromm (1973) argued, for example, that there is no such thing as a death instinct, but there is such a thing as *necrophilia*, a love of death and decay. Fromm treated necrophilia as pleasure taken in destruction that manifests in only a minority of instances in sexual activities that involve corpses. He saw necrophilia as the major source of human aggression, and considered it a desperate attempt to overcome alienation by making contact, if only in a hostile and destructive manner. Fromm took for granted, however, that his readers would appreciate that death is an existential but not a physiological phenomenon. Like life, healthy growth, sickness, and decay, death is an abstract concept that we project onto physical phenomena in arbitrary designation of certain states of chemical change. None of these concepts exists in nature; none of the states that they designate are distinguished *naturally* from each other. Chemical change is constant, but grouping years of changes together under one label, and other years of changes as another, is a human projection of value-laden ideas. Psychoanalysts have generally maintained that the unconscious does not know death. More precisely, because the concept of death requires abstract thinking, the id does not know death as death. A death wish is invariably a wish for pain to end. Fromm consequently endorsed Freud's concept of a self-preservative instinct, while objecting to its replacement by the idea of a death instinct.

In a similar way, Fromm saw love as a much more important motive than sex, and he rejected as philosophically unsound any effort to reduce the psychology of love to the biology or physiology of sex. Freud's term "sublimation" alleged that love is in some unspecified manner derived from sex, so that wherever Freud saw love, he postulated unconscious sex. At the same time, because Freud never articulated a coherent, testable theory of sublimation, his claims in its regard have always been wholly speculative. Fromm kept closer to the psychological data.

> To explain the fixation to mother on a sexual basis, or as repetition-compulsion, is to miss the true character of this answer to existence.
>
> All these considerations have led me to assume that the central issue is not really "attachment to mother" but what we might well call "paradisical existence," characterized by the attempt to avoid reaching full individuation and, instead, living in the fantasy of absolute protectedness, security, and at-homeness in the world, at the expense of individuality and freedom. This fantasy is a biologically conditioned state of normal development. But we would be thinking too much in genetic terms if we were

> to focus on the attachment to mother, rather than on the function of this experience. (Fromm, 1992b, pp. 40-41)

Freud routinely discussed sex and biology even when the evidence that he was considering concerned love and psychology. In this way, he systematically addressed existential concerns by using biological tropes in metaphoric ways. Fromm insisted instead on explicating the metaphors.

Because Fromm did not solve the puzzle of psychology's relation to human biology, his own preference for existentialist formulations sometimes led him to simplistic overstatements. If, for example, we accept from Kierkegaard that the human capacity for reflective awareness, the capacity to be conscious of being conscious, has far-reaching consequences for human experience, we can approach the capacity for reflective awareness from a psychoanalytic perspective without endorsing either Christian or existential assumptions about "transcendence." Freud routinely employed the term "self-observation" for the capacity. The term that psychoanalysts currently favor, "reflective awareness," deletes the term "self" in acknowledgement that the self-representation is a developmental construction. The contemporary psychoanalytic understanding agrees with Kierkegaard's claim that the capacity for transcendence--reflective awareness--generates the concept of self, without endorsing the metaphysics that led Kierkegaard to refer to transcendence.

The passage in *The Sane Society* that is quoted above also uses another turn of phrase that Fromm owed to existentialism. Where existentialists say that *being* becomes aware of itself, Fromm remarked that *life* did so; but both formulations reify abstractions. It is one thing to say that the human animal becomes aware of itself, and quite another to suggest that by virtue of an animal's act of self-awareness *being* or *life* becomes self-aware. Being and life are abstract concepts, particular ways of referring summarily to great quantities of sense data. The abstract concepts must be reified, personified, and treated as objectively existing external realities before they can be described as self-aware.

Fromm's explicit statements about transcendental idealism imply, however, that he treated existentialism's rhetoric as poetic metaphor. In a passage that praised Copernicus, Darwin, and Marx, Fromm (1970) went on to remark:

> Freud attacked the last fortress that had been left untouched--man's consciousness as the ultimate datum of psychic experience. He showed that most of what we are conscious of is not real and that most of what is real is not in our consciousness. Philosophi-

> cal idealism and traditional psychology were challenged head-on, and a further step was taken into the knowledge of what is "really real." (p. 5; see also Fromm, 1980, pp. 23-24)

Another passage took similar license with Heidegger's concept of being by ignoring Heidegger's concern with the metaphysics of being as such. Fromm limited discussion to the well-being of individual people.

> Well-being is the state of having arrived at the full development of reason: not in the sense of a merely intellectual judgment, but in that of grasping truth by "letting things be" (to use Heidegger's term) as they are....Well-being means to be fully born, to become what one potentially is; it means to have the full capacity for joy and for sadness....it means also to be creative...to react and to respond as the real, total man I am to the reality of everybody and everything as he or it is. (Fromm, 1960, p. 91)

Fromm referred here to the phenomenological experience that the existential psychoanalyst Medard Boss termed an encounter with *Da-sein*, "being-there." Boss (1963) wrote: "The things and fellow men which an individual encounters, appear to him--within the meaning-disclosing light of his *Dasein*--immediately (and without any subjective processes being involved) as what they are, according to the world-openness of his existence. Because it is the essence of *Dasein* to light up, illuminate, disclose, and perceive, we always find *Dasein* primordially *with* what it encounters, similar to so-called physical light" (pp. 93-94). Fromm's formulation reduced the grandiosity of *Dasein* to a realistic concern with genuine well-being.

Fromm never explicitly discussed his procedure, but he seems to have treated the abstract concepts that are existentialism's stock-in-trade in a fashion that was consistent with his theory of universal symbols. The validity of some abstractions, such as life and death (Freud, 1920a), reason, love, ethics and union, are scarcely to be challenged; and each of the abstractions arouses, or has the potential to arouse, a similar inner experience cross-culturally. Psychological distress, the sicknesses of the soul, consist, among other features, of failures of universal symbols to elicit their universal meanings. Where Freud believed that repression was devoted primarily to sexuality, Fromm (1955b, p. 274) maintained that a variety of existential concerns might be subject to repression. Inhibitions of the symbol-forming process prevent the dialectics of life and death, reason and love, and ethics and union from acquiring universal symbols; these inhibitions leave the sufferer alienated from shared human experience--from the mystical within the experience of humanity.

Fromm (1980) was discussing Freud's creativity when he wrote:

> The creative thinker must think in terms of the logic, the thought patterns, the expressible concepts of his culture. That means he has not yet the proper words to express the creative, the new, the liberating idea. He is forced to solve an insoluble problem: to express the new thought in concepts and words that do not yet exist in his language. (They may very well exist at a later time when his creative thoughts have been generally accepted.) The consequence is that the new thought as he formulated it is a blend of what is truly new and the conventional thought which it transcends. The thinker, however, is not conscious of this contradiction. (p. 3)

I suggest that this observation is equally applicable to Fromm's contributions. He was indebted to the existentialists, but he appropriated their concepts for psychoanalysis, turning reifications into metaphors. Unfortunately, the imprecisions of mythic and poetic modes of expression routinely inhibit clarity in theorizing (Langer, 1957), and some of Fromm's formulations were self-contradictory. His major existentialist works, *To Have Or To Be?* (1976) and the posthumous *On Being Human* (1994b), additionally suffered from the diminishing powers of advancing years.

IDOLATRY

In *The Sane Society*, Fromm (1955b) addressed a central existential concern, the human awareness "of his aloneness and separateness, of his powerlessness and ignorance; of the accidentalness of his birth and of his death" (p. 30). Fromm offered the mystical as the only effective solution to the existential dilemma.

> [A person] could not face this state of being for a second if he could not find new ties with his fellow man which replace the old ones, regulated by instincts. Even if all his physiological needs were satisfied, he would experience his state of aloneness and individuation as a prison....The necessity to unite with other living beings, to be related to them, is an imperative need on the fulfillment of which man's sanity depends. (Fromm, 1955b, p. 30)

Marx had followed Feuerbach's reinterpretation of Hegel's concept of "alienation"; both had referred to the divorcement of a portion of self through its projection as God (Funk, 1982, p. 73). Fromm further recognized that alienation not only projects aspects of self but does so in dialectical opposition to the experience of union. Alienation was symptomatic of resistance to union. It was a deficit of the mystical.

> By alienation is meant a mode of experience in which the person experiences himself as an alien. He has become, one might say, estranged from himself....He, like the others, are experienced as things that are experienced; with the senses and with common sense, but at the same time without being related to oneself and to the world outside productively. (Fromm, 1955b, p. 120)

Fromm (1955b) noted that Marx's use of the term referred to the alienation of human productivity from its producer, so that the product "becomes to him an alien power, standing over and against him, instead of being ruled by him." Fromm suggested that alienation, in Marx's sense of the term, was what the Old Testament prophets had called "idolatry" (p. 121).

> What is common to...the worship of idols, the idolatrous worship of God, the idolatrous love for a person, the worship of a political leader or the state, and the idolatrous worship of the externalizations of irrational passions--is the process of alienation. It is the fact that *man does not experience himself as the active bearer of his own powers and richness, but as an impoverished "thing," dependent on powers outside of himself, onto whom he has projected his living substance.* (Fromm, 1955b, p. 124)

Fromm's concept of idolatry corresponds approximately to the Kleinian concept of projective identification. In both formulations, there is an identification with an external object onto which a projection has been made.

> Man spends his energy, his artistic capacities....and this thing, having become an idol, is not experienced as a result of his own productive effort, but as something apart from himself, over and against him, which he worships and to which he submits....*The idol represents his own life-forces in an alienated form.* (Fromm, 1955b, pp. 121-22)

Unlike projective identification in Kleinian theory, idolatry is not limited to negative features. Kleinian theory typically refers to the evacuation of a portion of a person through its attribution to another person or thing. It is only what is conflicted that is disowned through evacuation. Fromm's concept of idolatry pertained instead to the abdication of parts of the self that were highly desirable, for example, the allocation of a person's better qualities, including love, generosity, and so forth.

Much of *The Sane Society* is a critique of capitalist society on the criteria of alienation, the idolatry of money, authoritarianism, conformism, and so forth. In his last book, *Greatness and Limitations of Freud's Thought* (1980), Fromm applied his theory in a different context, when he identified transference as an instance of idolatry that occurs within clinical psychoanalysis (pp. 41-43).

> If one understands idolatry as prophetic thought does, then what occurs is precisely what Freud called *transference.* In my view, transference, as we know it in psychoanalysis, is a manifestation of idolatry: A person transfers his own activities or all of what he experiences--of his power of love, of his power of thought--onto an object outside himself. The object can be a person, or a thing made of wood or of stone. As soon as a person has set up this transferential relatedness, he enters into relation with himself only by submitting to the object onto which he has transferred his own human functions. (Fromm, 1994b, p. 24; see also 1980, pp. 41-43; 1994a, pp. 118-120)

It was the erotic or irrationally positive transference that Fromm discussed as idolatry.

THE MYSTICAL NATURE OF LOVE

In *Psychoanalysis and Religion*, Fromm (1950) remarked in passing that the psychoanalytic concern with love was religious (pp. 87, 76); but he did not explain his meaning until *The Art of Loving* (1956), where he emphasized, far more than he had in the past, that the alienation that individuation causes may be overcome through the mystical. "Man--of all ages and cultures--is confronted with...the question of how to overcome separateness, how to achieve union, how to transcend one's own individual life and find at-onement" (p. 9).

Fromm suggested that there were several "ways of escaping separateness." Each was a type of union. One group of techniques commonly produced orgiastic states, sometimes involving sexual orgasm, but in other cases auto-induced trances, drugs, and/or group rituals. "In a transitory state of exaltation the world outside disappears, and with it the feeling of separateness from it" (Fromm, 1956, p. 11). Fromm referred to "primitive tribes" but his observations apply as well to the "mob psychology" at political rallies, soccer games, rock concerts, and other public events in industrialized societies. "Orgiastic union" is intense and can be violent, involves mind and body, and is transitory and periodical.

A second escape from separateness, "the union based on *conformity* with the group, its customs, practices and beliefs," was more widely employed (Fromm, 1956, p. 12); but it was not particularly satisfactory.

> Union by conformity...is calm, dictated by routine, and for this very reason often is insufficient to pacify the anxiety of separateness. The incidence of alcoholism, drug addiction, compulsive sexualism, and suicide in contemporary Western society are symptoms of this relative failure of herd conformity." (Fromm, 1956, p. 16).

Nodding in Rank's direction, Fromm (1956) discussed the union afforded by "creative activity, be it that of the artist, or of the artisan....in all types of creative work the worker and his object become one, man unites himself with the world in the process of creation" (p. 17). The unity afforded through productive work was limited in that it was not interpersonal (p. 18).

The best and most complete escape from separateness was "the achievement of interpersonal union, of fusion with another person, in *love*" (Fromm, 1956, p. 18). Like Freud, Fromm considered love to be the *sine qua non* of mental health.

> This desire for interpersonal fusion is....the most fundamental passion, it is the force which keeps the human race together, the clan, the family, society. The failure to achieve it means insanity or destruction--self-destruction or destruction of others. (Fromm, 1956, p. 18)

Fromm characterized mature love in paradoxical terms that were closely similar to his description of mystical sensibility. "Mature *love is union under the condition of preserving one's integrity*, one's individuality....In love the paradox occurs that two beings become one and yet remain two". (Fromm, 1956, pp. 20-21). In mystical experience, individuality is preserved despite union with all, in love, despite union with the beloved. "Love is active penetration of the other person, in which my desire to know is stilled by union. In the act of fusion I know you, I know myself, I know everybody--and I 'know' nothing. I know in the only way knowledge of that which is alive is possible for man--by experience of union--not by any knowledge our thought can give" (pp. 30-31).

Fromm (1956) insisted that the biological dimension of sexual desire that preoccupied Freud was no more than a component of the humanistic phenomenon of love and union that he was addressing (p. 35). Fromm suggested that religious love paralleled interpersonal love (pp. 32, 63). "It springs from the need to overcome separateness and to achieve union" (p. 63).

Because the distinction between theology and mystical experience parallels the distinction between knowing about a person and knowing a person (Fromm, 1956, p. 32), the doctrinal differences between "strict monotheism and a non-theistic ultimate concern with the spiritual reality" did not prevent the respective experiences of monotheistic and non-theistic religious love from being closely similar (p. 72).

> In all theistic systems, there is the assumption of the reality of the spiritual realm, as one transcending man, giving meaning and validity to man's spiritual powers and his striving for salvation and inner birth. In a non-theistic system...the realm of love, reason and justice exists as a reality only because, and inasmuch as, man has been able to develop these powers in himself....In this view there is no meaning to life, except the meaning man himself gives to it. (Fromm, 1956, p. 72)

Fromm distinguished his non-theism from atheism, explaining that he disbelieved in a personal God (Landis, 2009, p. 139). In both monotheism and non-theism, the experiences of love, reason, and justice impart meaning to life. A strictly held negative theology, appropriate to humanistic religion, treats all affirmations about God as anthropomorphizing projections. Negative theology differs from non-theism not in tracing meaning to projection, but in attributing the human capacity to project meaning to its creation by God.

Not only did religious love closely resemble interpersonal love, but idolatry could be found in love as well as in religion. Fromm called idolatrous love "a form of pseudo-love."

> If a person has not reached the level where he has a sense of identity, of I-ness, rooted in the productive unfolding of his own powers, he tends to "idolize" the loved person. He is alienated from his own powers and projects them into the loved person, who is worshiped as...the bearer of all love, all light, all bliss. In this process he deprives himself of all sense of strength, loses himself in the loved one. (Fromm, 1956, p. 99)

Fromm believed that Freud's program of psychoanalysis had a humanistic goal that Freud had never expressed in so many words. The title of Fromm's study of Freud, *Sigmund Freud's Mission* (1959b), expressed his belief that Freud "saw in his creation, the psychoanalytic movement, the instrument to save--and to conquer--the world for an ideal." Fromm believed that Freud had acted in "a faith" whose "content...remained always *implicit*" (p. 92). Quoting Freud's (1923a) statement, "Psychoanalysis is the instrument destined for the progressive conquest of the Id," Fromm articulated what he believed to have been Freud's faith.

> Freud expresses here a religious-ethical aim, the conquest of passion by reason. This aim has roots in Protestantism, in Enlightenment philosophy, in the philosophy of Spinoza and in the religion of Reason, but it assumed its specific form in Freud's concept. (Fromm, 1959b, p. 93; see also Fromm, 1963, pp. 142-43)

With this formulation, psychoanalytic mysticism came full circle. It was no longer an alternative to Freud's achievement, as Rank had assumed, and Fromm had initially taken for granted. It was a way of looking precisely at Freud's achievement, but in a way that Freud had never made explicit.

ANALYTIC LISTENING

Fromm's appreciation of love as a kind of mystical union had implications for his understanding of the psychoanalytic dyad. At the center of his approach was his subscription to the philosopher Martin Buber's (1958) concept of a dialogical encounter. Fromm had known Buber as a youth. In 1919, Fromm co-founded an association for the education of Jewish adults in Frankfurt am Main, that was renamed the Freie Jüdisches Lehrhaus (Free Jewish Teaching Institute) in the fall of 1920. Fromm was then in Heidelberg but occasionally visited and taught there. In the summer of 1920, the philosopher Franz Rosenzweig became program director, and Fromm became acquainted with Buber through Rosenzweig (Burston, 1991, p. 14; Funk, 2000, pp. 41, 44). Fromm had occasion to renew his acquaintance with Buber in the late 1950s. Fromm was apparently uninvolved when Leslie Farber invited Buber to lecture at the William Alanson White Institute in the spring of 1957; but Fromm spoke on the same program as Buber when "the Executive Committee of the 'American Friends' of Ihud, an Israeli organization of Zionists, held a celebration honoring Buber's eightieth birthday, also a fund-raising event, at the Community Church in New York City in the spring of 1958" (Ortmeyer, 1995, p. 26).

In lectures that Fromm gave in New York in 1959, he integrated Japanese Zen Buddhist meditation and Buber's I-Thou philosophy with the practice of analytic listening. Fromm (2000a) prefaced by defining the term "experience" in a manner that agreed with the technical significance of *Erlebnis*, "experience," in Wilhelm Dilthey's (1833-1911) hermeneutic philosophy. Dilthey proposed that "the objective value of the categories of the mind-constructed world...emerge from experience" (Mueller-Volmer, 1985, p. 149). Dilthey wrote:

> The present is the filling of a moment of time with reality; it is experience, in contrast to memory or ideas of the future occurring in wishes, expectations, hopes, fears and strivings. This filling with reality constantly exists while the content of experience constantly changes. Ideas, through which we know the past and the future, exist only for those who are alive in the present. The present is always there and nothing exists except what emerges in it. (Mueller-Volmer, 1985, p. 149)

> Experience is a temporal flow in which every state changes before it is clearly objectified because the subsequent moment always builds on the previous one and each is past before it is grasped. It then appears as a memory which is free to expand. But observation destroys the experience. (Mueller-Volmer, 1985, p. 150)

> Science, by discovering the laws of physical phenomena, unravels the conditions under which mind occurs. Among observable bodies we find that of man: experience is related to man in a way which cannot be further explained. But with experience we step from the world of physical phenomena into the realm of mental reality. This is the subject-matter of the human studies on which we must reflect: the value of knowledge in them is quite independent of the study of their physical conditions.

> Knowledge of the mind-constructed world originates from the interaction between lived experience, understanding of other people, the historical comprehension of communities as the subject of historical activity and insight into objective mind. All this ultimately presupposes experience....
>
> Experience includes elementary acts of thought....These acts occur when consciousness is intensified. A change in a state of mind thus becomes conscious of itself. We grasp an isolated aspect of what changes. Experience is followed by judgments about what has been experienced in which this becomes objectified. It is hardly necessary to describe how our knowledge of every mental fact derives entirely from experience. (Mueller-Volmer, 1985, pp. 151-52)

Dilthey's distinction between experience and thinking was expressed by William James (1890), possibly independently, as a contrast of "knowledge of" and "knowledge about." The term *Erlebnis* also had use in the mystical revival of the early twentieth century, which had introduced the idea that mystical experience (*Erlebnis*) is the ultimate and transformative achievement possible for human beings (Friedman, 1976, p. 27). Dilthey's contrast of experience and thinking, which had treated thinking as secondary and derivative mentation, was developed into a privileging of ecstatic intuitions in preference to truths expressed linguistically. Freud alluded to the mystical celebration of the personal and irrational in private correspondence with Karl Abraham (Freud & Abraham, 1965, pp. 345-46), when he discussed Ferenczi and Rank's (1923) attribution of therapeutic change not to the interpretation of the transference, but to the transformed experience of the analyst to which interpretation brings the patient. Franz Alexander and Thomas M. French (1946) later drew on the work of Ferenczi and Rank when they attributed therapeutic change to a "corrective emotional experience." Theodor Reik (1948, pp. 433, 437) contrasted "knowledge experienced" and "knowledge merely learned by rote" in reference to the difference between his own aspirations for his patients and those of New York's ego psychologists. Fromm brought the mystical and psychoanalytic developments of *Erlebnis* together when he integrated Buber, Zen, and analytic listening. Fromm (2000a) stated:

> What actually happens when we have an *experience*? Let me give an example: We have a ball and we throw the ball and the ball rolls, and we say: "The ball rolls"....we make an intellectual statement that really amounts to saying that we....know this is a

> ball and we know the law of nature that a ball rolls. But what happens to a little boy of four when the ball rolls?...he really sees the ball rolling. That is an entirely different experience; it is a beautiful experience; it is an experience--you could call it an ecstatic experience--in which the whole body participates in this beautiful thing of seeing a ball rolling....The simple act of a rolling ball usually appears boring to us after the second time....Because we feel we already know that the ball rolls. But for the little boy, it is not a matter of knowing it. For the little boy it is a matter of seeing this movement, which is a full experience. (pp. 168-69)

Fromm's concept of "experience" referred to sense perception and direct emotional and aesthetic responses to it, by contrast with verbal concepts about it. But Fromm was not simply theorizing about experience. He was defining experience in order that his audience know what he wished for them to achieve. He wanted people to be mindful of the ball rolling, as distinct from thinking conceptually about the idea of the ball rolling. Fromm's concept of "experience" was also consistent with an account of meditation that Fromm provided during a seminar in Locarno, Switzerland, in 1974.

> To feel your breathing does not mean to think about your breathing. Once you think about your breathing, you don't feel it. I say that in order to emphasize the difference between thinking and awareness...Your body is aware of your breathing. It is not a thought...And that holds true for practically all experiences. Once you think about them, you stop experiencing them...Awareness is not only a matter of the intellect, as it is the fashion to believe today. Awareness is a matter of one's whole body sensing something clearly which does not itself appear as a thought. (As cited in Burston, 1991, p. 81)

Fromm's concept of awareness corresponded to the Buddhist practice of "bare attending," the basic element of both Zen and Theravadin Buddhist mindfulness meditations. In Fromm's formulation, awareness involves an avoidance of conceptual thinking, thinking-about, while attending deliberately to perceptual thinking, thinking-of.

Later in the 1959 lecture in New York, Fromm (2000a) related experience to the Zen aspiration to empty the self.

> The one who experiences his self as an ego experiences only his package. He looks from the outside and asks...."What will be the impression this little package makes on the world...?" To that same extent, of course, I am inhibited in being, in experiencing myself as a subject of my *powers*. And on the other hand, to the same extent to which I experience myself as the subject of my powers, I do not contemplate my ego. That is actually what the New Testament means as far as I understand by "slay yourself," or what the Zen Buddhists mean when they say "empty yourself"....This slaying yourself means simply forget about your ego, because this attempt to hold onto your ego, to look at yourself from what some people call the objective standpoint, actually stands in your way. (p. 174)

The *experience* of "I" or "self" as a subjectivity, an observer, and an agency, is not to be confused with the *idea* of self as an object, a thing. It is possible to abandon thinking about self-as-object and simply proceed to the direct experiencing of self as agency (Fromm, 2000a, p. 177).

Both Fromm's explanation of "experience" and his account of meditation were in close agreement with Buber's concept of "meeting," as famously described in a reminiscence from his childhood. Buber (1973) wrote:

> When I was eleven years of age, spending the summer on my grandparents' estate, I used, as often as I could do it unobserved, to steal into the stable and gently stroke the neck of my darling, a broad dapple-gray horse. It was not a casual delight but a great, certainly friendly, but also deeply stirring happening. If I am to explain it now, beginning from the still very fresh memory of my hand, I must say that what I experienced in touch with the animal was the Other, the immense otherness of the Other, which, however, did not remain strange like the otherness of the ox and the ram, but rather let me draw near and touch it. When I stroked the mighty mane, sometimes marvellously smooth-combed, at other times just as astonishingly wild, and felt the life beneath my hand, it was as though the element of vitality itself bordered on my skin, something that was not I, was certainly not akin to me, palpably the other, not just another, really the Other itself; and yet it let me approach, confided itself to me, placed itself elementally in the relation of *Thou* and *Thou* with me. The horse, even when I had not begun by pouring oats for him into

> the manger, very gently raised his massive head, ears flicking, then snorted quietly, as a conspirator gives a signal meant to be recognizable only by his fellow-conspirator; and I was approved. But once--I do not know what came over the child, at any rate it was childlike enough--it struck me about the stroking, what fun it gave me, and suddenly I became conscious of my hand. The game went on as before, but something had changed, it was no longer the same thing. And the next day, after giving him a rich feed, when I stroked my friend's head he did not raise his head. A few years later, when I thought back to the incident, I no longer supposed that the animal had noticed my defection. But at the time I considered myself judged. (pp. 26-27)

For Buber, meeting or encounter consisted of a mutual and reciprocal sharing of experience.

The Zen objective of bare subjectivity was not only consistent with experience, as for example in the case of the ball rolling. It was also consistent with Buber's concept of "meeting" another person in a truly dialogical relationship, as Fromm's (2000a) lecture went on to explain.

> I can explain the other person as another ego, as another thing, and then look at him as I look at my car, my house, my neurosis, whatever it may be. Or I can relate to this other person in the sense of...experiencing, feeling this other person. Then I do not think about myself, then my ego does not stand in my way....There is what I call a *central relatedness* between me and him. He is not a thing over there which I look at, but he confronts me fully and I confront him fully. (p. 174)

In these sentences, Fromm made the same distinction between experience and conceptualization as it applies to relations with other people. He did not here cite Buber by name, but he was expressing Buber's basic teaching regarding the distinction between knowing a person as an It, and knowing the same person as a Thou. He acknowledged his debt to Buber in an article written for an audience familiar with Buber's name, that he published three years later.

> The situation in therapy....should be a situation of full human relatedness, between one human being and another, or to use Martin Buber's terminology, a relationship of the I to the Thou. In this relatedness which is alive and productive, the patient experi-

> ences himself, the reality of his life, perhaps for the first time in his life....we arrive at and touch reality, the human reality in the patient rather than the fictions which exist in the mind. (Fromm, 1962b, pp. 30-31)

Buber had endorsed Carl Roger's client-centered psychotherapy (Farber, 1967; Friedman, 1992). Fromm instead saw a way to re-design psychoanalytic technique to meet Buber's philosophical goals.

Fromm's 1959 lecture continued with a brief discussion of alienation. For Fromm, alienation began with the construction of self as an idea, the shift from mindfulness into having a self.

> You can see why this is alienation: As soon as I experience myself as that nice, intelligent doctor, whatever he may be, married with two kids, and so on, I do not experience anything. I put my experience in that image...Because the image is that of the kind, nice, intelligent doctor, I...[experience myself as] kind, nice and intelligent....
>
> Alienation...[is] a particular form of unconsciousness, namely the unawareness of inner experiences and the pseudo-awareness of experience in the alienated person who deceives himself about experiencing when he is actually in touch with thought, in touch with the idol, and so on. (Fromm, 2000a, p. 174)

Let me gather the ideas in Fromm's 1959 lecture together for emphasis. Experience is beautiful and, indeed, ecstatic in the mystical sense of the term. Experience of self requires what Zen calls emptying the self, an abandoning of ideas about oneself while simultaneously remaining subjectively mindful. The extension of the same attitude, of an emptied self, toward another person, so that one is mindful of the other person, was, for Fromm, precisely Buber's I-Thou, interhuman, dialogical "encounter" or "meeting." The better to express Buber's concept, Fromm supplied the terms "central relatedness" and, more informally, "a *touching* of the selves of two persons" (Spiegel, 1981, p. 438).

Fromm's approach to analytic listening was considered mystical by his contemporaries. Tauber (1959) wrote:

> Fromm's conception of the analyst's role is not something to be prescribed nor to be acquired but something *to be*. Here we are entering what has been called the mystical tradition. Admittedly,

> a simple, uncontroversial definition of mysticism is extremely difficult, because the concept refers primarily to man's way of grasping nature as a total experience. Mystical experience consists in experiencing the "here and now" in its immediacy where rational, objective, discursive elements are subordinated to intuitive, nondiscursive, nonanalytic elements. Mysticism, however, does not repudiate the unconscious cognitive components in the total perceptive encounter with reality. It is opposed to the process whereby one simply uses reason to the exclusion of the other qualities in man's total self which participate in understanding what goes on around him. Mysticism attempts to avoid duality. It seeks the experience of oneness. Mysticism is realistic, involving the totality of the person's encounter with the world, although certain traditions in mysticism are far removed from this description. These traditions advocate quietism, self-abnegation, and denial of reason and the sense. They are designed to cut one off from the world. (p. 1812)

Fromm's technique of analytic listening also had its conventional aspects. According to Rose Spiegel, Fromm's involvement in the immediacy and spontaneity of the psychoanalytic dialogue coincided with a more conventional process of theoretical formulation. At the same time, Fromm voiced his formulations with spontaneity.

> When he listened, it was total immersion, and an empathic flow back and forth. This did not preclude his formulating the inner logic of what was being said, or the line of reasoning that certain behavior or action was implementing. He stressed immediacy and spontaneity for the analyst, of voicing his or her experience with the patient, or an insightful interpretation, without a methodical waiting for the so-called "right" moment, which at that time was a favorite preoccupation of analysts (and that is still an appropriate issue to address). (Spiegel, 1981, p. 439)

Fromm explained his procedure as a matter of honest self-knowledge. It is not possible to relate better to patients than to people in general. Character defects that affect relations with people in general also limit effectiveness with patients.

> To really relate is....a faculty, it is an orientation, it is something in you, and not something in the object. If I am caught in fiction

> and unreality, as far as people in general are concerned--myself, my wife, my children, my friends, the whole world--then I am just as caught in fiction when it comes to the patient. (Fromm, 2000a, p. 180)

Here then we have a Jewish-Buddhist mystical state, to be cultivated by the analyst, at the core of Fromm's psychoanalytic technique. Fromm (2000a) valued the Buddhist component, among other reasons, for its help in overcoming judgmentalism in his own person. The result was "a sense of union, of sharing, of oneness, which is something much stronger than being kind or being nice...a feeling of human solidarity" (p. 178).

FROMM'S THERAPEUTIC PROCESS

Fromm's abandonment of the standard clinical procedures of ego psychology initially led him to fall back on Freud's technique of the late 1910s, but Fromm presently developed his own approach to the therapeutic process. From Freud, Fromm retained, above all, the theory that truth is therapeutic (Fromm, 1955b, p. 168; 1980, pp. x-xi) and the willingness to devote years to the therapy of a single individual (Fromm, 1950, p. 98; 1960, p. 83). He suggested that patients get better not because of some "mechanistic" consequence of "overcoming the resistances" (Fromm, 1991, p. 584), but due to "a built-in tendency for health and well-being--i.e., for the attainment of all those conditions that further the growth and development of the individual and the human species" (Fromm, 1992a, p. 68).

> The *fact* of suffering, whether it is conscious or unconscious, resulting from the failure of normal development, produces a dynamic *striving to overcome the suffering*, that is, *for change in the direction of health*. This striving for health in our physical as well as in our mental organism is the basis for any cure of sickness, and it is absent only in the most severe pathology. (Fromm, 1955b, p. 274)

Fromm noted that most mental illnesses "cure themselves without any kind of intervention" (Fromm, 1992a, p. 68; 1994a, p. 50); and he thought that many "light forms of neurosis" could be resolved in twenty hours, rather than two hundred as was customary (Fromm, 1991, pp. 601-2).

Fromm understood the therapeutic process to involve two major steps. The patient must first become aware of the suffering (Fromm, 1955b, p. 274) by reaching "the bottom of his suffering" (Fromm, 1991, p. 595) and acquiring an "experiential knowledge" of it (Fromm, 1960, p. 111). "The first task of analysis is...to help the patient be unhappy rather than to encourage him" (Fromm, 1991, p. 595). For Fromm, alienation was synonymous with transference in the general sense of the term. People constantly project transferences onto everyone and everything they meet and frequently alienate themselves from their projections in the process. Some clinical procedures intensify the transference, producing the transference neurosis; but both Kleinians and interpersonalists commonly work with transferences from the patient's first appearance. In Fromm's procedure, an alienated patient's inability to participate in central relatedness to the analyst constitutes the patient's transference, and the alienation can be analyzed immediately that the treatment begins. Misunderstandings of Fromm's procedure have led to incorrect statements that he failed to analyze the transference (Cortina & Maccoby, 1996, p. 8; Maccoby, 1996, p. 64). In fact, Fromm was analyzing transference whenever he analyzed a patient's alienation.

In addition, "the patient must know what he really wants" (Fromm, 1991, p. 596). The analyst's task was to present the patient with understanding of opportunities to make choices.

> All that one man can do is to show him the alternatives truthfully and lovingly, yet without any sentimentality or illusion. Confrontation with the true alternatives may awaken all the hidden energies in a person, and enable him to choose life, no one else can breathe life into him. (Fromm, 1962a, p. 176)

The second step in therapy is a behavioral implementation of the increased self-awareness. Behavior that replicates the neurotic structure must be abandoned, and more wholesome behavior acquired. Morbid relationships, work situations, and so forth must be changed or abandoned; and wholesome values and goals acquired (Fromm, 1955b, p. 274)

To promote the patient's awareness of suffering, Fromm (1955b, pp. 166-67) insisted on a return to Freud's way of working with free associations. Fromm (1994a) similarly adhered to Freud's privileging of the dream (pp. 121, 125, 143). Quite to the contrary of ego psychology's treatment of the reportage of dreams as free associations that should not be interpreted unless they can be interpreted as evidence of the patient's transference onto the analyst, Fromm maintained that dream interpretation is important in its own right. Everyone needs to be competent at interpreting symbolic language (Fromm, 1955b, p. 10).

Fromm praised Freud's rebellion against Victorian values and criticized later analysts' comfortable embrace of more recent social conventions.

> As psychoanalysis became successful and respectable it shed its core and emphasized that which is generally acceptable....To discover one's incestuous wishes, "castration fear," "penis envy," was no longer upsetting. But to discover repressed character traits such as narcissism, sadism, omnipotence, submission, alienation, indifference, the unconscious betrayal of one's integrity, the illusory nature of one's concept of reality, to discover all this in oneself, in the social fabric, in the leaders one follows--this indeed is "social dynamite." (Fromm, 1973, pp. 83-84)

Fromm objected strongly to the classical psychoanalytic situation and its infantilization of the patient (Fromm, 1992b, p. 47; 1994a, p. 29).

> The entire constellation of the silent, allegedly unknown analyst who is not even supposed to answer a question, and his position of sitting behind the analysand (turning around and having a full look at the analyst is practically taboo) actually results during the hour in the analysand's feeling like a little child. Where else is a grown-up person in such a position of complete passivity? All prerogatives are the analyst's and the analysand is obliged to utter his most intimate thoughts and feelings toward the phantom; this in terms not of a voluntary act but of a moral obligation that he accepts once he has agreed to be an analytic patient. From Freud's standpoint this infantilization of the analysand was all to the good since the main intention was to discover or reconstruct his early childhood.
>
> One major criticism of this infantilization is that if the analysand is transformed into a child during the session, the adult person is, so to speak, removed from the picture and the analysand utters all his ideas and feelings that he had as a child, but he does not concern himself with the adult person in him, which has the capacity of relating to the child person from the standpoint of the adult. In other words he feels little of the conflict between his infantile and his adult self, and it is this very conflict that is conducive to improvement or change. (Fromm, 1980, p. 40)

In Fromm's view, the infantilization of the patient produces "a dream, but in a waking state" (Fromm, 1991, p. 592), in which the patient "lack[s] the judgment and independence which he needs in order to be able to understand the meaning of what he is saying" (Fromm, 1980, p. 43). "The patient talks in an 'interpersonal vacuum,' and his thoughts often remain quite unreal to him; they gain full experiential reality only when they are truly shared with the analyst as a person, not as a shadowy phantom" (Fromm, 1992b, p. 48).

Fromm attributed severe transferences to patients' infantilization by their analysts (Fromm, 1980, pp. 41-43). He considered the exacerbation of the transference to be clinically unnecessary.

> Having analyzed people for many years in the classic manner, and then later in a face-to-face situation, I observed that, especially in the less severe forms of mental disturbance, the intensity of the transference (not its existence) depends largely on the degree of this artificial infantilization. If the psychoanalyst responds to a patient as to another adult human being, if he does not hide himself behind the mask of "the great Unknown," and if the patient is given a more active role in the process, the intensity of the transference--as well as the obstacles created by this intensity--are considerably reduced. (Fromm, 1992b, p. 47)

Moreover, the "transference is one factor conducive to the professional sickness of analysts, namely the confirmation of their narcissism by receiving the affectionate admiration of their analysands regardless of the degree to which they deserve it" (Fromm, 1980, p. 39).

Fromm also subscribed to a technical innovation that Ferenczi had introduced. "Ferenczi...in the last years of his life postulated that it was not enough for the analyst to observe and to interpret; that he had to be able to love the patient with the very love which the patient had needed as a child, yet had never experienced" (Fromm, 1960, p. 111). Fromm felt that Sullivan's technique tended in a similar direction but fell short of the mark. An analyst is not a participant observer, as Sullivan maintained, but is instead an observant participant (Fromm, 1960, p. 112). Fromm insisted on the analyst's full participation as a human being within the psychoanalytic relationship. The participation began with the ambition to empathize with the patient as fully as possible, but continued with a full meeting of two individuals. Fromm advocated empathy in the original sense of the term. "If I cannot experience in myself what it means to be schizophrenic or depressed or sadistic or narcissistic or frightened to death, even though I can experience that in smaller doses than the patient, then I just don't know what the patient is talking about" (Fromm, 1991, p. 599). Implicitly criticizing self psychology, he opposed "sentimentality" (Fromm, 1992b, p. 77). At the same time, "one is not lacking in compassion, because one has a deep feeling that nothing that happens to the patient is not also happening in oneself. There is no capacity to be judgmental or to be moralistic or to be indignant about the patient once one experiences what is happening to the patient as one's own" (Fromm, 1991, p. 600).

At the same time, Fromm implicitly opposed the adoption of an artificial, professional, couch-side manner.

> There should be something in the analytic attitude and in the analytic atmosphere by which from the very first moment the patient experiences that this is a world which is different from the one he usually experiences: it's a world of reality, and that means a world of truth, truthfulness, without sham--that's all that reality is. Secondly, he should experience that he is not supposed to talk banalities, and the analyst will call his attention to it, and that the analyst doesn't talk banalities, either. (Fromm, 1991, p. 599)

The analyst was instead to engage the patient in a conversation that involved give-and-take and sought to make progress in discovering the patient.

> This is possible only if the analyst responds to the patient, who in turn responds to the analyst's response, and so on. In this process the analyst becomes aware of experiences that at a given moment the patient may not be aware of; and by communicating what he sees, the analyst furthers new responses. The whole process leads to ever-greater clarification. (Fromm, 1992b, p. 70)

What did Fromm talk about with his patients? He claimed that he simply said what he perceived.

> I don't interpret; I don't even use the word interpretation. I say what I hear. Let us say the patient will tell me that he is afraid of me and he will tell me a particular situation, and what I "hear" is that he is terribly envious; let us say he is a oral-sadistic, exploitative character and he would really like to take everything I have. If I have the occasion to see this from a dream, from a gesture, from free associations, then I tell him: "Now, look here, I gather from this, that, and the other that you are really afraid of me be-

> cause you don't want me to know that you want to eat me up." I try to call his attention to something he is not aware of. The whole point here is that there are some analysts, Rogers most extremely so, some Freudian analysts less extremely so, who believe the patient should find it himself. But I think that prolongs the process tremendously; it is long enough and difficult enough anyway. What happened? There are certain things in the patient which he represses; and he represses it for good reasons; he doesn't want to be aware of them; he is afraid of being aware of them. If I sit there and wait for hours and months and years perhaps, until these resistances are broken through, I waste time for the patient. (Fromm, 1994a, pp. 98-99)

What Fromm heard and remarked, another analyst might call a transference, or a defense, or a parataxic distortion. For Fromm, it was a character trait or attitude that interfered with the patient's participation in the interpersonal relationship that he was inviting the patient to join.

Fromm characterized the analyst's encounter with the patient as a mystical union that was contingent on the analyst's prior resolution of his own alienation.

> The analyst must overcome the alienation from himself and from his fellow man which is prevalent in modern man.....modern man experiences himself as a *thing*, as an embodiment of energies to be invested profitably on the market. He experiences his fellow man as a thing to be used for profitable exchange. Contemporary psychology, psychiatry, and psychoanalysis are involved in this universal process of alienation. The patient is considered as a thing, as the sum of many parts. Some of these parts are defective and need to be repaired, as the parts of an automobile need to be repaired. There is a defect here and a defect there, called symptoms, and the psychiatrist considers it his function to repair or correct these various defects. He does not look at the patient as a global, unique totality which can be fully understood only in the act of full relatedness and empathy. If psychoanalysis is to fulfill its real possibilities, the analyst must overcome his own alienation, must be capable of relating himself to the patient from core to core, and in this relatedness to open the path for the patient's spontaneous experience and thus for the "understanding" of himself. He must not look on the patient as an object, or even only be a "participant observer"; he must become one with him and at

> the same time retain his separateness and objectivity, so that he can formulate what he experiences in this act of oneness. The final understanding cannot be expressed fully in words; it is not an "interpretation," which describes the patient as an object with various defects, and explains their genesis, but it is an intuitive grasp. It takes place first in the analyst and then, if the analyst is to be successful, in the patient. This grasp is sudden; it is an intuitive act which can be prepared by many cerebral insights but can never be replaced by them. (Fromm, 1963, pp. 199-200)

Fromm (1956, p. 117) asserted the analyst's function as a spiritual teacher who served as role model. "And that means periods when one finds oneself in the dark, periods where one is frightened, and yet where one has faith that there is another side of the tunnel, that there will be light" (Fromm, 1991, p. 598). In all of the roles that an analyst may fulfill for a patient, the analyst's realism requires recognition of "the patient as the hero of a drama and not...as a summation of complexes" (Fromm, 1991, p. 600). Above all, the patient is an autonomous human being whose own efforts carry the therapy. "Neither the analyst nor any man can 'save' another human being. He can act as a guide--or as a midwife; he can show the road, remove the obstacles, and sometimes lend some direct help, but he can never do for the patient what only the patient can do for himself" (Fromm, 1960, pp. 112-13).

When done correctly, the analyst's task of empathy leads on to the analyst's self-analysis, because the analyst is analyzing a patient who is responding to the analyst, and whose responses furnish evidence of unconscious aspects of the analyst. "Hence the analyst not only cures the patient, but is also cured by him. He not only understands the patient, but eventually the patient understands him. When this stage is reached, solidarity and communion are reached" (Fromm, 1960, pp. 112-13).

The termination of an analysis was appropriate, in Fromm's view, when the patient acquired the practice of self-analysis.

> Analysis is successfully ended when a person begins to analyze himself every day for the rest of his life. In this sense self-analysis is the constant active awareness of oneself throughout one's life, to be aware, to increase the awareness of oneself, of one's unconscious motivations, of everything which is significant in one's mind, of one's aims, of one's contradictions, discrepancies. I can only say personally that I analyze myself every morning--combined with concentration and meditation exercises--for an

> hour and a half, I wouldn't want to live without it. (Fromm, 1994a, p. 188)

Where Rank had modified psychoanalytic technique to cultivate creativity, including but not limited to mysticism, Fromm's redesigned the psychoanalytic situation to cultivate mysticism, including but not limited to creativity, in a manner that was mystical for both the analyst and the patient. In Fromm's humanistic psychoanalysis, the mystical was not simply the goal, it was also the psychoanalytic means to the goal.

ZEN, SATORI, AND INSIGHT

Fromm happily integrated selected practices of traditional mysticism as adjuncts to humanistic psychoanalysis. From the 1940s onward, Karen Horney (1885-1952) had recommended Zen meditation to candidates at the William Alanson White Institute, as a means to help them to learn the analytic practice of "wholehearted attention" (Horney, 1987, pp. 18-21). She met D. T. Suzuki, who was responsible for popularizing Zen Buddhism in the West, possibly as early as the late 1930s. Fromm became acquainted with Suzuki in the postwar period, when he and his wife attended Suzuki's seminars and spoke with him afterward (Landis, 1971, p. xi). Fromm felt that he only came to grasp Zen properly in late 1956, when Suzuki visited him in Cuernevaca, Mexico, and Fromm reciprocated with a visit to Suzuki in New York (Funk, 2000, p. 123). In August 1957, Fromm participated with Suzuki in seminars on Zen Buddhism and psychoanalysis that they gave Mexico (Suzuki, Fromm, & De Martino, 1960). Suzuki spent most of 1959 living in a hut on Fromm's property in Mexico. Then eighty-eight years of age, Suzuki helped Fromm with the planting and landscaping of his garden. Suzuki also taught Fromm both Buddhism and meditation (Burston, 1996a, p. 420; Funk, 2000, p. 123).

Fromm, Suzuki, and Richard de Martino, a Jungian analytic psychologist, co-authored a book, *Zen Buddhism and Psychoanalysis*, that provided Fromm with the opportunity to advance his ideas about the integration of meditation within psychoanalysis. In his contribution, Fromm articulated his concept of mysticism as a developmental line that some traditions had conceptualized theistically but others non-theistically.

> Unity is sought in all these religions--not the regressive unity found by going back to the pre-individual, preconscious harmony of paradise, but unity on a new level: that unity which can be arrived at only after man has experienced his separateness, after he

> has gone through the stage of alienation from himself and from the world, and has been fully born....There are many symbols for the new goal which lies ahead, and not in the past: Tao, Nirvana, Enlightenment, the Good, God. (Fromm, 1960, p. 94)

Fromm (1960) suggested that in contrast with "Aristotelian logic," which involves the laws of non-contradiction and the excluded middle, mysticism rests on "what one might call *paradoxical logic*," which "assumes that A and non-A do not exclude each other as predicates of X" (pp. 101-2). Fromm made his argument on behalf of non-theistic mysticism in an appropriately paradoxical manner. "To follow God's will in the sense of true surrender of egoism is best done if there is no concept of God. Paradoxically, I truly follow God's will if I forget about God. Zen's concept of emptiness implies the true meaning of giving up one's will, yet without the danger of regressing to the idolatrous concept of a helping father" (p. 95).

Having located the paradoxicality of mysticism--and implicitly dialectic!--in the unconscious, Fromm (1960) arrived at a model of the psyche that approximated Rank's appropriation of Nietzsche. "Consciousness represents social man, the accidental limitations set by the historical situation into which an individual is thrown. Unconsciousness represents universal man, the whole man, rooted in the Cosmos" (p. 106). Fromm might have been speaking of the Primal Unity of the Dionysian unconscious, by contrast with the illusory order of Apollonian consciousness.

Where Rank's will therapy had promoted creativity, Fromm's (1960) therapeutic aspiration privileged mysticism. "Making the unconscious conscious transforms the mere idea of the universality of man into the living experience of this universality; it is the experiential realization of humanism" (p. 107). Mysticism was not a regression to unconsciousness. It was instead a progression past individuation to a union with unconsciousness. The patient was to move beyond consciousness, recognize its illusory nature, and regain access to unconscious mysticism.

> Every step in this process is in the direction of understanding the fictitious, unreal character of our "normal" consciousness. To become conscious of what is unconscious and thus to enlarge one's consciousness means to get in touch with reality, and--in this sense--with truth (intellectually and affectively). To enlarge consciousness means to wake up, to lift a veil, to leave the cave, to bring light into the darkness. (Fromm, 1960, p. 109)

Fromm (1960) was not referring to mystical unity and the alleged illusory nature of the Many. He was instead using the language of mysticism to discuss the psychoanalytic commonplace that the neurotic is a "person who is not aware to what degree his perception of the world is purely mental, or parataxical" (p. 117). Because parataxical distortions or, in Freud's term, transferences are products of the defense mechanisms of the ego, they belong to consciousness. Mainstream psychoanalysis has always aimed at the emergence of unconscious insights that convey the experiential knowledge that the transferences are fallacies. In calling the insights truthful perceptions of reality, Fromm was emphasizing the mystical character of normative psychoanalysis and its compatibility with Zen (p. 121).

Fromm (1960) described the meditative practices of Zen in dialectical terms as an infantile regression that is simultaneously adult. "It is oneness, immediacy, entirety, but of the fully developed man who has become a child again, yet has outgrown being a child" (p. 129). Fromm noted that psychoanalytic insight is similarly an intuitive, experiential knowing (p. 132). Fromm (1960, p. 134) suggested that R. M. Bucke's (1901) term, "cosmic consciousness" referred to the "direct, unreflected, conscious experience" that both Zen and humanistic psychoanalysis sought to achieve. Fromm (1960) claimed that "the therapeutic aim of curing this or that symptom; or this or that neurotic character trait" (p. 135) constrains conventional psychoanalysis to make only a limited part of the unconscious conscious. Pathology is to be expected whenever mature mysticism has failed to be achieved. "Man, as long as he has not reached the creative relatedness of which *satori* is the fullest achievement, at best compensates for inherent potential depression by routine, idolatry, destructiveness, greed for property or fame, etc. When any of these compensations break down, his sanity is threatened" (p. 137).

At the same time, the compatibility of the goals of Zen and psychoanalysis did not prevent a divergence of methods; and the value of psychoanalysis to facilitate enlightenment was a working hypothesis that merited further research (Fromm, 1960, pp. 139-40).

HUMANISM DEFINED

In a journal article whose importance Rainer Funk (1982; personal communication, 2009) has emphasized, Fromm (1964b) defined humanism in terms of a multifaceted idea: "that in each individual all of humanity is contained; that each man is all men; that each individual represents all of humanity and, hence, that all men are equal, not in their gifts and talents, but in their basic human qualities" (p. 70). "Some other aspects of humanist thought....are the idea of man's dignity, strength, freedom and joy, and of love as a fundamental force of all creation" (p. 72). Fromm's definition of humanism permitted him to cite Talmudic precedents for his point of view, in the late antique rabbinical teaching that each person is an entire universe. The microcosm-macrocosm concept, that each individual replicates the cosmos, was a mystical notion that the Talmudic rabbis had absorbed from Hellenistic science; and it provided Fromm's concept of humanism with a mystical thrust that medieval, Renaissance, and modern European formulations often lacked.

The existentialist agenda of self-actualization formed an integral part of Fromm's concept of humanism at the same time.

> The humanist thinkers speak of the humanity inherent in each individual...but....Their concept of the *essence of man*, that is to say, of that by virtue of which a man is what he is--namely, human, refers not to an unalterable substance, but to the *potentialities* and *possibilities* existing in all men....It is man who, in the process of history, can and must develop this human potential by his own effort, and by his own activity. (Fromm, 1964b, p. 72)

Another component of Fromm's concept of humanism was a simple but far-reaching revision of the concept, variously expressed by Nietzsche, Freud, and Rank, of unconscious nondifferentiation and conscious individuation.

> Man, in any culture, *has all the potentialities*: he is the archaic man, the beast of prey, the cannibal, the idolater, and he is the being with the capacity for reason, for love, for justice....The unconscious is the whole man--minus that part of man which corresponds to his society. Consciousness represents the social man, the accidental limitations set by the historical situation into which an individual is thrown. Unconsciousness represents universal man, the whole man, rooted in the Cosmos. (Fromm, 1964b, p. 77)

Because the universality of the unconscious remains a source of human potential throughout life, "it always contains the basis for the different answers which man is capable of giving to the question which existence poses" (Fromm, 1964b, p. 77). Fromm suggested that Freud's theory of "the fear of the father and of his castration threat" did not account adequately for people's repression of their feelings, thoughts, and experiences. Fromm instead proposed a stronger and implicitly earlier fear.

> The fear is deeper and of a social character: man is afraid of nothing more than of being ostracized, isolated, alone....If a society lays down the law that certain experiences and thoughts must not be felt or though consciously, the average individual will follow this order because of the threat of ostracism which it implies if he does not" (p. 76).

Fromm was writing here not only of group psychology but also implicitly of the society that baby and mother together constitute. The fear that is deeper than paternal authority is the developmentally earlier fear of maternal abandonment. Group dynamics acquire their power precisely because they manipulate attachment anxiety.

Fromm's (1964b) concept of humanistic psychoanalysis followed from these considerations.

> *Making the unconscious conscious transforms the mere idea of the universality of man into the living experience of this universality; it is the experiential realization of humanity....*
>
> The experience of my unconscious is the experience of my humanity, which makes it possible for me to say to every human being "I am thou." I can understand you in all your basic qualities, in your goodness and in your evilness, and even in your craziness, precisely because all this is in me, too. (pp. 77-78)

Fromm aimed at inculcating in his patients both a capacity for empathy and an understanding of the inalienably mystical and humanistic character of empathic experience. Meditation and mystical experiences could be vehicles for cultivating the capacity for empathy; but so too could psychoanalytic progress that inculcated a capacity for Buberian encounter or meeting.

THEISM REVISITED

In *You Shall Be as Gods*, Fromm (1966) discussed aspects of the Old Testament and Judaism that were consistent with humanistic psychoanalysis. Fromm again asserted that he was not a theist (p. 7) and that he regarded religious experience "as a human experience which underlies, and is common to, certain types of theistic, as well as non-theistic, atheistic, or even antitheistic conceptualizations" (p. 57). At the same time, he saw his way clear to a positive regard for certain types of theism.

> The highest authority in the biblical system is God, who is the lawgiver and who represents conscience. In the process of the development of the human race, there was perhaps no other way to help man liberate himself from the incestuous ties to nature and clan than by requiring him to be obedient to God and his laws.....*obedience to God is also the negation of submission to man.* (Fromm, 1966, p. 73)

Citing various passages from rabbinical literature, Fromm (1966) contended that Judaism had preserved the biblical association of freedom with faith in God. "The idea of serfdom to God was, in the Jewish tradition, transformed into the basis for the freedom of man from man. *God's authority thus guarantees man's independence from human authority*" (p. 75). Fromm's reflections on the psychological function of theism led him to wonder: "What could take the place of religion in a world in which the concept of God may be dead but in which the experiential reality behind it must live?" (p. 229).

Rejecting the idea of divine intervention (Fromm, 1966, pp. 92, 115) and insisting that "man is free to choose his way and yet must accept the consequences of his choice" (p. 116), Fromm derived a theory from the biblical text regarding the pathogenic nature of evil.

> Every evil act tends to harden man's heart, that is, to deaden it. Every good act tends to soften it, to make it more alive. The more man's heart hardens, the less freedom does he have to change; the more is he determined already by previous action. But there comes a point of no return, when man's heart has become so hardened and so deadened that he has lost the possibility of freedom, when he is forced to go on and on until the unavoidable end which is, in the last analysis, his own physical or spiritual destruction. (Fromm, 1966, p. 101)

Maimonides (1912) had proposed this theory in his psychological treatise, *Shemoneh Perakim*, "Eight Chapters," the most widely published and easily accessed of his writings.

Also presumably owed to familiarity with Maimonides' *Shemoneh Perakim* was Fromm's implication of imagination in the human experience of good and evil.

> The term *yetzer* thus means "imaginings" (evil or good). It corresponds to what we would call "drive." The significant point is that the Hebrew word indicates the important fact that evil (or good) impulses are possibly only on the basis of that which is specifically human: imagination. For this very reason, only man--and not animals--can be evil or good. An animal can act in a manner which appears to us cruel (for instance, a cat playing with a mouse), but there is no evil in this play, since it is nothing but the manifestation of the animal's instinct. The problem of good and evil arises only when there is imagination. Furthermore, man can become more evil and more good because he feeds his imagination with thoughts of either evil or good. What he feeds, grows; and hence, evil and good grow or decrease. They grow precisely because of that specifically human quality--imagination. (Fromm, 1966, pp. 160-61)

PSYCHEDELIC MYSTICISM

In *The Anatomy of Human Destructiveness*, Fromm (1973) referred in passing to the psychedelic mysticism of the era. His comments constituted a significant revision of his previous interpretation of drug-induced orgiastic states of fusion as a way of escaping separateness (Fromm, 1956, p. 11). Fromm did not consider psychedelic mysticism pathological, but the psychedelic subculture provided him with sociological evidence that advanced his understanding of the mystical.

> Many users of drugs, especially among young people who have a genuine longing for a deeper and more genuine experience of life --indeed, many of them are distinguished by their life affirmation, honesty, adventurousness, and independence--claim that the use of drugs "turns them on" and widens their horizon of experience. I do not question this claim. But the taking of drugs does not change their character and, hence, does not eliminate the permanent roots of their boredom. It does not promote a higher state of development; this can be achieved only by taking the path of patient, effortful work within oneself, by acquiring insight and learning how to be concentrated and disciplined. Drugs are in no way conducive to "instant enlightenment." (pp. 247-48)

Fromm recognized the mystical nature of the drug experiences. At the same time, he appreciated, as he had not previously done, that the occurrence of mystical experiences is no guarantee of the characterological change with which he associated enlightenment. "'Instant enlightenment' with the aid of drugs...is no substitute for a radical change of personality" (Fromm, 1994b, p. 80). Fromm had repeatedly discussed mystical experiences as the culmination, the crowning achievement, of humanistic psychoanalysis. But he had been arguing from a minute data base that proved to have been skewed through self-selection. The psychedelic counter-culture established what might have been predicted from psychoanalytic experience: that even mystical insights must be worked through, repeatedly and in detail, before the experiential understanding can be expected to lead to long term character change.

Fromm expressed equally judicious caution, again in passing, in *The Revision of Psychoanalysis* (1994b), where he contrasted narcissistic types of mysticism with the non-narcissistic type that he recommended.

> Descending into the labyrinth...., in whatever way it is produced --for example, through meditation, autosuggestion, or drugs--can lead to a state of narcissism in which nobody and nothing else exist outside of the expanded self. This state of mind is egoless inasmuch as the person has lost his ego as something to hold onto; but it can nevertheless be a state of intense narcissism in which there is no relatedness to anyone, inasmuch as there is no one, outside of the extended self. This type of mystical experience has been misunderstood by Freud and many others as representing mystical experience as such (the "Oceanic feeling") and has been interpreted by Freud as regression to primary narcissism.
>
> But there is another type of mystical experience that is not narcissistic, which is found in Buddhist, Christian, Jewish, and Muslim mysticism. (pp. 78-79)

Fromm listed "meditation, autosuggestion, or drugs" as means to attain mystical experiences. What mattered to Fromm was not how the experiences were produced, but whether or not they were narcissistic in content.

MEDITATION AND SELF-ANALYSIS

In *The Art of Listening*, a posthumous publication, Fromm augmented his previous recommendation of Zen with a discussion of Buddhist mindfulness meditation, a South-East Asian practice that became popular in the United

States in the 1980s. Fromm had practiced both concentrative and mindfulness meditation for an hour daily under the direction of Nayanaponika Mahathera in Lucarno, Switzerland, in the early 1970s (Funk, 2000, p. 162). Fromm (1994a) stated: "Mindfulness means awareness: I am fully aware at every moment of my body, including my posture, anything that goes on in my body, and I am fully aware of my thoughts, of what I think; I am fully concentrated--is precisely this full awareness" (p. 180). *The Art of Being* (1992a) similarly includes instructions regarding Buddhist meditation (Fromm, 1992a, pp. 46-54). It employed the term "transtherapeutic" in replacement of "humanistic" (pp. 55-57, 63-64), and raised the question "whether a person can analyze himself as part of his meditation practice" (p. 66). Fromm suggested that a brief psychoanalysis that was aimed at teaching self-analysis would be appropriate (pp. 66-67). Fromm cautioned that self-analysis is difficult, because resistances and rationalizations may cause reasoning to become circular. However, he stated that he found the practice congenial and recommended it to others who similarly found it useful (pp. 81-82).

CONCLUDING REFLECTIONS

In *Civilization and Its Discontents* (1930), Freud had concluded "may we not be justified in reaching the diagnosis that, under the influence of cultural urges, some civilizations, or some epochs of civilization--possibly the whole of mankind--have become 'neurotic'?" (p. 144). Under the circumstances, a person who had been psychoanalyzed successfully arrived at sufficient mental health to be able to recognize the sickness of our culture. Freud felt that the task of psychoanalysis was done at this point. A healthy person in a sick society must inevitably be conflicted, and Freud left his patients to work out their own solutions to the problem of life after therapy. He candidly admitted, "I have not the courage to rise up before my fellow-men as a prophet, and I bow to their reproach that I can offer then no consolation" (p. 145).

Less courageous than Freud, the psychoanalytic mainstream retreated even from the clarity of the predicament that Freud articulated. Both before and after the Hitlerian war, the psychoanalytic mainstream opted for compromise, accommodation, and adaptation to sick societies. Rank and Fromm both claimed, however, that psychoanalysis could and should do more. Each was convinced that psychoanalysis has extraordinary power to promote the mystical, and each was sustained by his faith to conceptualize a social location for the mystical in the world. Rank proposed the Romantic model of the artist, the self-realized eccentric who maintains a personal standard of values and creates a personal culture. Fromm, fortified as much by the Old Testament prophets as by his Marxist convictions, was a Utopian thinker. He believed in the revolutionary task of imagining, creating, and implementing a humanistic culture that, in its entirety, would be sane--and by sane he meant paradoxically mystical.

Five

The Mystical in Art and Culture

Milner, Winnicott, and Ehrenzweig

Exclusion from the psychoanalytic establishment may have played an important role in freeing Rank and Fromm to articulate and explore their mystical interests. Following their important and, in some respects, still unequalled contributions, others psychoanalysts began to assert their mysticism in limited ways while retaining their membership within the psychoanalytic establishment.

THE JOANNA FIELD BOOKS

Perhaps the first was Marion Milner, a founding member of the British Middle School or Independents, who had been a mystically inclined painter and author before she trained as a psychoanalyst. She published three books under the pseudonym Joanna Field in which she explored her discoveries of the creative process and its relation to the mystical. The first Joanna Field book, *A Life of One's Own* (1934), was based on a diary that Milner had kept in which she recorded self-observations of the workings of her own mind. Midway through the book, she reported her discovery of what for her was a new way to manage her thoughts.

> Every one of the gestures I had discovered involved a kind of mental *activity*. Whether it was the feeling of listening through the soles of my feet, or perhaps putting into words what I was seeing, each gesture was a deliberate mental act which arrested the casual drift of my thought, with results as certain as though I had laid my hand on the idly swinging tiller of a boat. It seemed to me now that it was perhaps not *what* I did with my thought that brought the results, but the fact that I did anything at all. Yet this activity was as different from my usual attempts to take control of my thoughts as steering a boat is from trying to push it....I must neither push my thought nor let it drift. I must simply make an internal gesture of standing back and watching, for it was a state in which my will played policeman to the crowd of

> my thoughts, its business being to stand there and watch that the road might be kept free for whatever was coming. Why had no one told me that the function of will might be to stand back, to wait, not to push? (pp. 101-2)

Although she did not recognize it at the time, Milner had discovered how to enter a state of reverie, the alternate state that characterizes the creative process.

Also in her first book, Milner reported several unitive experiences. She wrote:

> Once when I was lying, weary and bored with myself, on a cliff looking over the Mediterranean, I had said, 'I want nothing', and immediately the landscape dropped its picture-postcard garishness and shone with a gleam from the first day of creation, even the dusty weeds by the roadside....once when ill in bed, so fretting with unfulfilled purposes that I could not at all enjoy the luxury of enforced idleness, I had found myself staring vacantly at a faded cyclamen and had happened to remember to say to myself, 'I want nothing'. Immediately I was so flooded with the crimson of the petals that I thought I had never before known what colour was. (Field, 1934, p. 107)

> I came to the Beach feeling sick and cold...then slowly the waves became a delight, white reflexions on the wet sand, the rhythm with which they follow each other and seep back, the seethe and crispness that I taste on my tongue. So--I inherit the earth...then I let the sun and sky and waves possess me and emerged feeling they were part of my being...'conceived by the Holy Ghost'...isn't something born of this? Then, coming home through the vineyards to the village, the air full of the smell of grape pulp, breathing it, tasting it, I remembered the Eucharist....One does want to swallow and be swallowed by one's love.
>
> I came to the conclusion then that 'continual mindfulness' could certainly not mean that my little conscious self should be entirely responsible for marshalling and arranging all my thoughts, for it simply did not know enough. (pp. 188-89)

In an "Afterword" dated 1986, Milner stated that she had been surprised when the book came out and one or two reviewers had called her experiences "mystical." In her final book, *Eternity's Sunrise* (Milner, 1987a), she reminisced:

> I think again of that strange moment described near the end of my 1927 diary, the entry that made one reviewer say that the diary had culminated in a mystical experience. The important thing now seems to be the feeling I had then of not knowing whether they were his eyes or mind. But now I can add, what's been emerging again and again–the answer is, 'It's both.' Which of course, isn't commonsense, but I do believe that 'I yet not I' is the basic fundamental contradiction....Some people seem to talk about moments of bliss, high points of experience, as if the experience, 'I', disappeared altogether. But if so, how does one know it was bliss? (pp. 128-29)

Another reviewer of her first book commented on her "slow recognition of the power of the unconscious in affecting thought and behaviour." The remark led her to think, "Yes, and not just its power in stupid ways, stupid mistakes, but also in ways that showed it knew better than I did where I had to go" (Field, 1934, p. 220).

Milner's second book, *An Experiment in Leisure* (Field, 1937), reported the consolidation of her growing ability to access her unconscious powers. At one point, she became aware that religious symbols were frequently appearing in her thought, and she began to formulate a theory of symbolism. Because she was dissatisfied with religion as she had been taught it (p. 142), her spontaneous recourse to religious symbols suggested an "underlying need" to address "the creative spirit of man, with man's capacity to find expression for, and so lay hold upon, the truth of his experience" (pp. 143-46).

Milner now turned to Silberer's *Problems of Mysticism and Its Symbolism* (1914). Its account of mysticism reminded her of "moments of perception that I had sometimes known when the whole world seemed new created" (Field, 1937, p. 155). Her reflections led her to question the adequacy of Freud's reductionism. In addition to "the instinctive life," account had to be taken of "the inner attitudes and movements of the spirit" (p. 167). Milner was grappling at the time with inhibitions of her own sexuality. She was reading Jung and wondering whether to admire Christian mystics' rejections of the physical when she had a mystical experience that addressed the topic.

> I still remembered what at the time I would not admit--the spreading fields had seemed to burn with more than the light of sunset, as if the glowing fires of earth had been laid bare by the cutting of the corn: in those miles of flat rich cornland under the still sky, I had felt the earth as a living thing--and for an instant, had felt as though my own body were the earth. (p. 176)

The mystical union of her body with the earth attested to the spirituality of the physical and resolved Milner's doctrinal dilemma.

Milner soon developed what she regarded at the time as a spirituality that differed from mysticism.

> If each of...these sudden feelings of immense importance...is the first intimation of something I am going to find in myself, in my own personal experience, in day to day living with others, then I am sure I must not stop at mystery or mysticism, it is everyday human experience that comes first and last and all the time....spiritual things are not remote things, but vital things. (p. 176)

Milner retained a similar perspective to the end of her life. In *Eternity's Sunrise*, she revisited her experience of cosmic extension only to discount its importance.

> There is certainly this bigger self, not only this body that is a great sagacity, as Nietzsche said, but also this self that is not tied to the body, that can expand and include everything, like that time when I felt for an instant that I was the cornfield, consciously aware of such a feeling for the first time? Like what Freud called the oceanic feeling, becoming everything? But of course it was only a flash of feeling. I did not stay expanded. (Milner, 1987a, p. 120)

Not only did the transcience of Milner's unitive experience lead her to disparage it, but she recognized that her experiences were insufficiently otherworldly to be counted as mystical.

> Surely I'm no mystic. I just want to realise the mystery that just living is, even that just thinking is. Yes, it's obvious I'm no mystic, I love the created world too much to turn away from it--for more than a little time. Probably I'm not even religious, what-

> ever that means. But to perceive the created world aright one does have to relate to the inner private sea, just as Traherne said.
>
> Facing the mysteriousness that's at the ground of one's existing at all, why so seeming dangerous? Is it really that one has recurrently to turn inwards, away from the world, away from the shared commonsense world into a private one, where one might not be able to get back, like my fear of the Kashmiri music, which I suppose would mean becoming mad.
>
> Yes, I must be no mystic because I don't feel I want to give up everything for union with God. I'm really only interested in finding more and more ways of saying what I feel about the extraordinariness of the world and of being alive in it. Looking always for language. A language of love? What about hate then? But I do know that to find the language, gestural, verbal or pictorial, one has recurrently to let everything go, all thoughts of what one loves, all images, and attend to the nothingness, seemingly nothing there--silence. Is this mysticism? Also this does seem to mean going through all the agonies of 'Why has thou forsaken me?' some time or other. Yes, surely it can be said that my beds have been leading me to questions of how to relate oneself to the background of one's experience? Which can be seen as relating oneself to the nothing, the no-thing, the silence, to what seems like emptiness. Or to the un-conscious, to what we are not aware of, except as nothing there. (Milner, 1987a, pp. 113-14)

Milner articulated the distinctive point of view that most psychoanalytic mystics share. Hers was not an interior mysticism, wholly caught up in the radical transcendence of God, who remained detached from human society and the environment. Milner knew extrovertive mystical experiences that perceived unity in the environment (Stace, 1960), and her experiences led her to formulate an embodied mysticism in the world of everyday experience.

Having decided that she both was and was not a mystic, Milner developed a distinctive awareness of her unconscious. Like Fromm, she found that it might be both better and worse than her consciousness. "The mysterious force by which one is lived, the 'not-self', which was yet also in me...seemed sometimes like a beast within, sometimes like a god" (Field, 1937, p. 179). Milner gradually became aware that it "could be a guiding force in one's life" (p. 185). At the same time, Milner appreciated that she could place no conditions on it. "The price of being able to find this 'other' as a living wisdom within myself, had been that I must want nothing from it, I must turn to it with complete acceptance of what is, expecting nothing, wanting to change nothing; and it was only then that I had received those illuminating flashes which had been most important in shaping my life" (pp. 185-86).

Influenced by the clinical procedure of free association, Milner had previously done some "free writing"; but now she experimented with "free drawings" (p. 180). After drawing without preconceptions, Milner would try to understand the images. She found that they contained ideas of which she had been unaware while she was drawing. Her analyses of the meanings of her drawings deepened her convictions regarding the wisdom of the unconscious.

Milner's reflections on her free drawings increased her appreciation of both the strengths and limitations of psychoanalysis. Psychoanalysis had devoted itself to "storm-giving images, and others...that brought sudden panics and confusions." Milner was also interested in "peace-giving images, which seemed to be no less powerful" (Field, 1937, p. 192).

Milner soon arrived at the realization that her pursuit of her art demanded of her that she subordinate herself to her unconscious. "I must learn to trust it completely" (Field, 1937, p. 196).

> The moment of blankness and extinction was the moment of incipient fruitfulness....the person who is by nature dominated by the subjective factor is committed to a life of faith whether he likes it or not, since all his important mental processes are unconscious. (pp. 205-6)

"The internal gesture of submission" that was necessary to artistic creativity provided escape from the egocentricity of consciousness (p. 207).

Once Milner had come to trust to the wisdom of her unconscious, she found that she could dependably express "the movement of life" in the imagery of her thoughts and art. "This process, rather than logic and reasoning,...made it more possible for me to live reasonably" (p. 222). Milner had become persuaded of a basic psychoanalytic truth. "I had learned that in these images unrecognized desires expressed themselves, that when people purported to be talking of external facts, but talked with extreme enthusiasm or extreme hatred, then what they said had less reference to the facts than to their own inner needs" (p. 223). Milner (Field, 1957, p. 158) later remarked that in 1937 she had used the word "image" in ignorance of psychoanalytic usage and had not appreciated "that a mental image is a symbol."

In March 1938, Dr. Colin Campbell, a friend of Milner who had been training with Rank, wrote her a lengthy letter that summarized his experiences. Campbell died later that year (Lieberman, 1985, pp. 383-84). What further familiarity Milner may have had with Rank's work is unclear. After a degree in psychology and physiology at University College London, she worked in industrial psychology and, beginning in 1933, educational psychology, which brought her into contact with Susan Isaacs, who was a Kleinian analyst as well as an educational psychologist. In the late 1930s, Milner began part-time psychoanalysis with Sylvia Payne, a founder of the Middle School of British psychoanalysis. Soon afterward, Milner heard a public lecture by D. W. Winnicott and began attending a Saturday morning clinic for mothers and babies that Winnicott gave at Paddington Green Children's Hospital. Milner and Winnicott became friends, and in 1940 Milner was accepted for training as a psychoanalyst (Milner, 1987b, pp. 2-4, 6, 9, 248). Following supervision by Ella Freeman Sharpe, Joan Riviere, and Melanie Klein, Milner qualified as an analyst in 1943.

Milner's third Joanna Field book, *On Not Being Able to Paint*, was published in 1950. The text concerns her efforts to overcome her inhibitions about painting and, with the exception of an appendix that she added for the second edition of 1957, the prose avoids psychoanalytic jargon. Milner once again asserted her conviction that her drawings both confirmed psychoanalytic views about the unconscious and manifested a wholesome creativity to which Freud's theories were unequal. "They were a form of visual reflection on the basic problems of living--and of education...they were intimately connected...with the problems of creativity and creative process" (Field, 1957, p. xviii). Milner's speculation led her to conceptualize art as "the transfiguration of the external world." "The bit of oneself that one could give to the outside world was of the stuff of one's dreams, the stored memories of one's past, but refashioned internally to make one's hopes and longings for the future" (p. 26). From the Hindu philosopher Santayana, Milner derived the idea that "our inner dream and outer perception both spring from a common source or primary phase of experience in which the two are not distinguished, a primary 'madness' which all of us have lived through and to which at times we can return" (p. 28). These conclusions led Milner to fundamental insights regarding the nature of perception.

> They threw light, for instance, on the persistent feeling about parts of the country that I loved most, that these were haunts of the gods, places where indefinable presences were about. They threw light on the conflict between common sense which said

> these presences were something I was endowing the place with, out of fancy, imagination, and another sense which was intensely aware of the value of the experience and loath to believe it was 'only imagination'. (Field, 1957, p. 28)

Milner recognized that projections might be distressing as well as pleasing (Field, 1957, p. 38). Her musings on the projection of subjectivity in moments of intense experience of the environment led her to speculate on the experience of external reality more generally. "They are the actual moments when the forms of imagination...happily grow significant and without which, somewhere in our lives, we should have no drive to see permanent objectives in the external world" (p. 29). Milner's conclusion is a necessary corollary of Freud's epistemology. If oral, anal, phallic (Oedipal), and genital (coital) psychosexuality are epigenetically constituted categories of unconscious thought, they--and not Kant's categories--are the ultimate building blocks of everyone's worldview (Erikson, 1963); and there is no appreciation of external reality, no organization of sense data into coherent perceptions, that lack sexual contents. Milner remarked explicitly on the implication of Freud's epistemology for object relations theory. The sexuality that is projected onto the world consists of attitudes and expectations that ultimately concern the mother. "The relationship of oneself to the external world is basically and originally a relationship of one person to another....in the beginning one's mother is, literally, the whole world" (Field, 1957, p. 116).

At this juncture, Milner conceptualized the projective process "in terms of illusion" and associated it with the production of art. "By finding a bit of the outside world, whether in chalk or paper, or in one's analyst, that was willing temporarily to fit in with one's dreams, a moment of illusion was made possible, a moment in which inner and outer seemed to coincide....and...one could seek to rebuild, restore, re-create what one loved, in actual achievement" (Field, 1957, p. 119). Milner's theory of the illusion that facilitates creativity was indebted to Winnicott (1945, 1948a) concept of "illusion" as the application of subjective fantasy to external reality. Winnicott had been thinking of the circumstance of the infant; Milner applied his concept to artists and their art.

Milner suggested that maturation ordinarily involves a renunciation of illusion. The renunciation may be considered excessive whenever creativity is inhibited as a consequence (Field, 1957, pp. 133-34). Artistic creativity restores the illusory unity of inner and outer (p. 131). The same process is also involved, however, in the creation of every worldview. "Awareness of the external world is itself a creative process, an immensely complex...alternation of fusing and separating" (pp. 146-47). Science investigates only what has first been conceptualized through creative illusion. "The poet and artist in us, by their...capacity for seeing the world in terms of metaphor, do in fact create the world for the scientist in us to be curious about and seek to understand" (pp. 138-39).

Milner recognized that her theory of creative illusion might reasonably be regarded as a theory of contemplation, providing only that contemplation were redefined in a manner that eliminated the unearned assumption of passivity. "The mistake...lay in thinking of contemplation as essentially involving sitting still....What the method of the free drawings had embodied was something that could be called 'contemplative action'" (Field, 1957, p. 140). In Milner's formulation, creativity is intrinsically mystical, but the secularism of our culture keeps it from being described as such.

In a psychoanalytic article that Milner published in her own name in 1952, she reported unitive experiences during creative activity.

> There comes a moment, when painting some object from the outer world, when the excitement about whatever it was made you want to paint it and the immensely complicated practical problems of how to represent that feeling in colour, shape, texture, and so on, all disappear as conscious problems. One becomes lost in a moment of intense activity in which awareness of self and awareness of the object are somehow fused, and one emerges to separateness again to find that there is some new entity on the paper. (Milner, 1987b, p. 80)

Rank had similarly discussed the artist's sense of union with the art during the creative moment. Milner (1987b) went further. She recognized that the art exhibited a unity in its own right. She often found the results startling because they showed "a rhythm and pattern and integrated wholeness far beyond anything I had ever achieved by a deliberate plan" (p. 80). She attributed the integrative process to her unconscious. "Under these conditions of spontaneous action in a limited field with a malleable bit of the outside world it seemed that an inner organizing pattern-making force other than willed planning seemed to be freed, an inner urge to pattern and wholeness which had then become externally embodied in the product there for all to see" (p. 80). In order to allow for the emergence of unconscious integration, Milner began to approach creative work by beginning with "a blank space, a framed gap" (p. 80). A search for knowledge could be facilitated similarly by articulating the question; the development of an invention, or a new procedure, could be cultivated by conceptualizing the need that the innovation was to meet (Field, 1957, p. 104).

Winnicott (1945, 1948a) had initially developed the concept of "illusion" in reference to infants. Milner had applied Winnicott's idea extensively to artists, but she also mentioned inventors in passing. In a review of Milner's *On Not Being Able to Paint*, Winnicott (1951) unpacked the implication of Milner's contribution for a psychoanalytic audience.

> Psycho-analysts are accustomed to thinking of the arts as wish-fulfilling escapes from the knowledge of this discrepancy between inner and outer, wish and reality. It may come as a bit of a shock to some of them to find a psycho-analyst drawing the conclusion, after careful study, that this wish-fulfilling illusion may be the essential basis for all true objectivity. If these moments of fusion of subject and object, inner and outer, are indeed more than islands of peace, then this fact has very great importance for education. For what is illusion when seen from outside is not best described as illusion when seen from inside; for that fusion which occurs when the object is felt to be one with the dream, as in falling in love with someone or something, is, when seen from inside, a psychic reality for which the word illusion is inappropriate. For this is the process by which the inner becomes actualised in external form and as such becomes the basis, not only of internal perception, but also of all true perception of environment. Thus perception itself is seen as a creative process. (pp. 391-92)

Milner had written of creativity in art and technological invention. Winnicott generously credited Milner with the idea that objectivity and the perception of the environment depend on the same creative processes of projection. Perhaps she had expressed the idea to him in private conversation.

Milner took up Winnicott's idea in "The role of illusion in symbol formation," which phrased some of the ideas in *On Not Being Able to Paint* for a psychoanalytic audience. Citing a roster of orthodox theorists, Milner noted that creativity in science and invention involves generalization, which is a "failure to discriminate." It also occurs in the form of a metaphor. Primary process and realistic perception were not mutually exclusive. Milner (1987b) inferred that "some form of artistic ecstasy may be an essential phase in adaptation to reality" (p. 85). Two variables were involved: "the emotional state of the person experiencing this fusion" and the "conditions in the environment [that]...facilitate or interfere with it" that together "make it possible to find the familiar in the unfamiliar" (pp. 86-87). As an example of creative illusion, she cited the transference in a clinical analysis, whose existence is made possible by the psychoanalytic frame (p. 87).

Milner attributed therapeutic change to an integration of the ideal and the actual that a patient may achieve when being conscious of the two simultaneously.

> The change in character and growth in stature...seems to have as its starting-point those moments when the patient is able to look at his sins, defects, weakness, without either trying to whitewash them nor trying to alter them in order that they themselves may become more admirable people. They are in fact moments in which hopelessness about oneself is accepted....when one can just look at the gap between the ideal...and the failure to live up to it in one moment of vision,...the ideal and the actuality seem to enter into relation with each other and produce something new. (p. 187)

Having reviewed instances of scientific discovery and the psychoanalytic process to augment the evidence of artistic creativity, Milner arrived at her thesis: that creativity is intrinsically mystical.

> These are moments when there is a temporary fusion of inner and outer, an undoing of the split between self and not-self, seer and seen...these are the crucial moments which initiate the growth of new enthusiasms, the finding of new loves, moments when what Blake calls each man's poetic genius 'creates' the world for us, by finding the familiar in the unfamiliar, moments when imagination catches fire and lights up a whole new vista of possibilities of relationship with the outside world. Thus they are moments of falling in love, which need not only be with a person, but can be also with a skill or a subject or a medium, with words or clay or sounds or stone. They are moments when the 'Spirit bloweth where it listeth'. (p. 190)

THE TRANSITIONAL OBJECT

Winnicott took the shared concept of creative illusion in directions of his own. He had originally formulated his theory on the basis of Freud's (1900) speculations about the infant's first encounter with the breast. Freud suggested that when an infant, who has previously experienced nursing, becomes hungry, he hallucinates nursing at the breast in fulfillment of his wish to satiate his hunger. Only when hallucination fails to satiate does the infant seek the reality of the breast. Klein had developed her notion of unconscious phantasy, that phantasy is the mental representative of instinct (Isaacs, 1948), as a direct corollary, a rephrasing, of Freud's speculation. Winnicott (1945) instead proposed a modification of Freud's speculation. He suggested that if hallucination and reality "overlap there is a moment of *illusion*--a bit of experience which the infant can take as *either* his hallucination *or* a thing belonging to external reality....the infant comes to the breast when excited, and ready to hallucinate something fit to be attacked. At that moment the actual nipple appears and he is able to feel it was that nipple that he hallucinated" (p. 152).

Later in the same article, as Winnicott struggled to clarify the multiple senses in which he was using the words "fantasy" and "illusion," he arrived at a formulation in terms of subjectivity and objective reality.

> In fantasy things work by magic: there are no brakes on fantasy, and love and hate cause alarming effects. External reality has brakes on it, and can be studied and known, and, in fact, fantasy is only tolerable at full blast when objective reality is appreciated well. The subjective has tremendous value but is so alarming and magical that it cannot be enjoyed except as a parallel to the objective.
>
> It will be seen that fantasy is not something the individual creates to deal with external reality's frustrations. This is only true of fantasying. Fantasy is more primary than reality, and the enrichment of fantasy with the world's riches depends on the experience of illusion. (Winnicott, 1945, p. 153)

Winnicott (1945) imagined a developmental phase "prior to a true relation to external reality" (p. 155) when "the object behaves according to magical laws, i.e. it exists when desired, it approaches when approached, it hurts when hurt" (p. 153). A few years later, Winnicott (1948a) improved his formulation by interpolating the mother's point of view. "By fitting in with the infant's impulse the mother allows the baby the *illusion* that what is there is the thing created by the baby; as a result there is not only the physical experience of instinctual satisfaction, but also an emotional union, and the beginning of a belief in reality as something about which one can have illusions" (p. 163). Winnicott's use of the term "illusion" here became stable. For the remainder of his life, "illusion" described a state where subjective fantasy is applied to external reality.

In *On Not Being Able to Paint*, Milner applied Winnicott's ideas about creative illusions to the cases of art and invention; and in a review of her book, Winnicott (1951) extended the discussion to the illusory nature of the perception of reality. In a follow-up article, "Transitional objects and transitional phenomena" (1953), Winnicott discussed the teddy bear as the paradigmatic example of creative illusion. The substitution of the teddy bear for the maternal breast permitted Winnicott to avoid issues, unrelated to his theory, that involved the breast as part of the mother, the mother as a person in her own right, and so forth. Readers who had been confused by his discussions of the breast grasped his concept when he wrote of the teddy bear. In later writings, he explicitly described the mother whom an infant creates as a transitional object: "The essential feature in the concept of transitional objects and phenomena (according to my presentation of the subject) is *the paradox, and the acceptance of the paradox*: the baby creates the object, but the object was there waiting to be created and to become a cathected object" (Winnicott, 1969b, p. 104). However, the paradigmatic example of the teddy bear simplified explanation of his concept.

Winnicott took for granted the theory of infantile solipsism when he chose the term "transitional object" in order to refer to the infant's special attachment to its "first not-me possession," a cloth, teddy bear, or doll that the infant cannot bear to be without. Winnicott intended the term "transitional" developmentally, as intermediate between the stages of infantile solipsism and the infant's later senses of self and others as whole individual persons. The term "transitional" was simultaneously coherent phenomenologically in reference to a discrete type of object that is neither exclusively solipsistic and subjective nor exclusively external and objective. A teddy bear is a real physical object, but an infant regards it subjectively as a beloved companion and not realistically as an inanimate thing. Its importance for the infant is accepted by the family, given social validation through tolerant regard, and surrounded with appropriate ritualized behaviors.

Winnicott (1953) was talking not only of the teddy bear, but of a considerable variety of phenomena, all of which were neither purely subjective nor purely objective. "My subject widens out into that of play, and of artistic creativity and appreciation, and of religious feeling, and of dreaming, and also of fetishism, lying and stealing, the origin and loss of affectionate feeling, drug addiction, the talisman of obsessional rituals, etc." (p. 233). He emphasized that all of these many transitional objects and phenomena bear a single discrete relation to subjectivity and objective reality. "The transitional object is never under magical control like the internal object, nor is it outside control as the real mother is" (p. 237).

> My claim is that...there is the third part of the life of a human being....an intermediate area of *experiencing*, to which inner reality and external life both contribute. It is an area which is not challenged, because no claim is made on its behalf except that it shall exist as a resting-place for the individual engaged in the perpetual human task of keeping inner and outer reality separate yet interrelated.
>
> It is usual to refer to 'reality-testing', and to make a clear distinction between apperception and perception. I am here staking a claim for an intermediate state between a baby's inability and growing ability to recognize and accept reality. I am therefore studying the substance of *illusion*, that which is allowed to the infant, and which in adult life is inherent in art and religion. We can share a respect for *illusory experience*, and if we wish we may collect together and form a group on the basis of the similarity of our illusory experiences. This is a natural root of grouping among human beings. Yet it is a hall-mark of madness when an adult puts too powerful a claim on the credulity of others, forcing them to acknowledge a sharing of illusion that is not their own. (Winnicott, 1953, pp. 230-31)

As previously, Winnicott deployed Freud's (1927a) term "illusion" to designate the distinctive character of transitional objects.

> From birth, ...the human being is concerned with the problem of the relationship between what is objectively perceived and what is subjectively conceived of....*The intermediate area to which I am referring is the area that is allowed to the infant between primary creativity and objective perception based on reality-testing.* The transitional phenomena represent the early stages of the use of illusion, without which there is no meaning for the human being. (Winnicott, 1953, p. 238; Winnicott's italics).

External realities are endowed with meanings through the illusions that are projected on them.

Winnicott (1953) recognized that his concept of the transitional object involved an unresolved logical problem.

> *Of the transitional object it can be said that it is a matter of agreement between us and the baby that we will never ask the question 'Did you conceive of this or was it presented to you from with-*

> *out?'....The question is not to be formulated.* (pp. 239-40; Winnicott's italics)

In another phrasing, Winnicott attributed the irresolution of his concept to a paradox that was intrinsic to transitional objects and phenomena.

> I....ask for a paradox to be accepted and tolerated and respected, and for it not to be resolved. By flight to split-off intellectual functioning it is possible to resolve the paradox, but the price of this is the loss of the value of the paradox itself. (Winnicott, 1971, p. xii)

Winnicott's phrasing played on Freud's term "flight from reality," which has diagnostic significance. In asserting that recourse to the conventional dichotomy of fantasy and reality entails a flight from the value of illusory experience, Winnicott questioned the adequacy of psychoanalysis' exclusively empirical, scientific orientation.

It is conventional to treat Winnicott's ideas about the infant's creation of reality in a manner that brings him to agree with Klein's ideas about phantasy. However much he may have been inspired by Klein's work, the theory at which he arrived bears a family resemblance to the cognitive psychologist Jean Piaget's (1954, pp. 92-96) ideas about assimilation and accommodation. In Piaget's model, every new phenomenon is initially appreciated unrealistically through the application of existing concepts (Gestalts, schemata) to its appreciation. Due to the novelty of the phenomenon, the existing concepts are necessarily inadequate, and the phenomenon's assimilation to them distorts its understanding. If, to Piaget's model, we add Freud's qualification that every infant's initial fund of ideas are fantasies that are based on the erogenous zones of the body, we arrive at Winnicott's view, that the application of fantasy to objective reality produces an illusion --in Piaget's term, an assimilation--that brings the objective reality within the scope of subjective fantasy. The achievement of the illusion is a necessary prelude to reality testing. Until the illusion is achieved, it is not possible to readjust it in order to improve its coordination with reality, in the manner that Piaget termed accommodation. Winnicott went a step further than Piaget, however, when he emphasized that the arrival is finally not at an objective knowledge of reality, but only and always at a creative illusion concerning it. "In health *the object is created, not found*" (Winnicott, 1963a, p. 181; Winnicott's italics).

EHRENZWEIG'S THEORY OF DEPTH PERCEPTION

Anton Ehrenzweig, a university level art teacher in London who was deeply engaged in Kleinian object relations theory, was a friend of Milner whose thinking influenced the subsequent course of her work. Ehrenzweig (1948-49, 1949) published two articles that he expanded into a book entitled *The Psychoanalysis of Artistic Vision and Hearing* (1953). His theories were premised on the well-known distinction in perception psychology between the figure and ground of attention. To this concept, Gestalt psychologists had added that the perception of the figure projects an unconscious gestalt onto the sense data, where the form, structure, or pattern is recognized. To these findings, Ehrenzweig (1948-49) added a psychoanalytic perspective. He argued "that there must be an unconscious perception which is not bound by the conscious gestalt (the surface gestalt) and which perceives competing form-combinations"; and he cited psychoanalysis as witness that "depth perception is not only free from the surface gestalt but follows a different form-principle altogether" (p. 189). Ehrenzweig next offered an original theory of depth perception.

> When we turn our eye inwards, as in play, art, day-dreaming or in the deep dreams of our sleep...our vision loses its sharp and well-defined edge, the forms perceived become more fluid and intermingle and separate in a continuous flux....So dream visions do not tend to precision, simplicity and unambiguity, but on the contrary to vagueness, diffusion, and ambiguity. (p. 189)

Further to prove the incoherence of dream imagery, Ehrenzweig cited Freud's concept of the "secondary revision" of dreams.

To account for the ambiguity of unconscious perception, Ehrenzweig appealed to the theory of early cognitive development.

> Child psychologists conclude from the ways in which the child takes notice of his surroundings that to him the things of the world appear much less *differentiated* than to the grown-up. For the very young child there exists only one single thing filling the universe; it is the *Ego* of the child himself which he has not yet learned to differentiate from the other world. His mother would belong to him like a limb of his own body. Later the child learns to single out a few broad classes of things which in a chaotic medley contain things which to a grown-up would appear totally different. The child-things are 'too general'; all male persons are

> 'papa'; a thing called 'It burns' might comprise such different objects as hot soup, the candle flame, the heat in the garden, etc. (p. 190)

Ehrenzweig suggested that the comparatively nondifferentiated perception of infancy and early childhood persists unconsciously throughout life and is applied at all times in unconscious perception of reality. Consciousness is peripherally aware of the unconscious modes of perception, but experiences them as chaotic.

> Only from the height of the surface mind does the infantile technique of perception persisting in the depth mind seem chaotic and totally undifferentiated, because the Gestalt Technique of the surface mind cannot grasp any other structure than gestalt on its own particular level of differentiation. The difference between surface and depth perception is not the extreme contrast which it appears to be to the surface mind--one precise and differentiated, the other chaotic and undifferentiated--but it is a difference of gradual transition from a low primitive stage of differentiation up to the highest gestalt level.
>
> ...the description of depth vision as gestalt-free, chaotic, undifferentiated, vague, superimposed fits only the naïve impression of our surface mind. (p. 191)

In this formulation, primary narcissism furnishes the deepest level of unconscious perception, and all developmentally more advanced gestalts presuppose it.

Ehrenzweig (1953) suggested that creative and mystical experiences differed chiefly in the duration of the conscious experience of depth perception. Creative experiences involved a brief exposure to depth perception that permitted its integration within surface reality, where mystical experiences were more prolonged and isolated.

> We distinguished between these *transitive* depth perceptions which lead back to articulate surface perceptions and the inert *static* depth perceptions which lacked the dynamic tension leading back to the restoration of surface perception. Such static depth perceptions are the visions of dreams, day-dreams or the mystic orison in which the mystic may remain for indefinite periods....these static depth perceptions...appear as mere 'gaps' be-

> cause no translation into more articulate structures takes place. (p. 18)

Ehrenzweig's misunderstanding of the phenomenology of mystical experience promptly led him into a substantial theoretic error.

> The mystic returns to surface consciousness with the memory of deeply significant visions without a trace of any definite image. Just because the *static* mystic orison is so far removed from ordinary consciousness so that every attempt at a secondary gestalt elaboration must fail, the mystic has a truer memory of inarticulate perceptions than more 'scientific' minds. (p. 19)

This claim has no basis in mystics' self-reports. It is premised on Ehrenzweig's (1953, p. 19) acceptance of William James' (1902) famous claim that mystical experiences are "ineffable." James had failed to appreciate, however, that *all experiences are ineffable*. Words can refer to experiences that two people both know experientially, but words cannot convey any touch, taste, sight, sound, or smell to a person who has never known it. Words are at best knowledge-about; they can never be knowledge-of, never *Erlebnis*. Moreover, James and Ehrenzweig notwithstanding, mystics have written an enormous literature in which they project all manner of gestalts onto their experiences.

Ehrenzweig carefully argued that developmentally early, childlike, but otherwise coherent gestalts persist unconsciously, but are wrongly perceived by consciousness as incoherent and chaotic. However, his endorsement of James on the ineffability of mystical experience was the first of a series of remarks to a considerably different effect. For example, he psychoanalyzed Nietzsche's aesthetic categories as follows:

> His Dionysian art principle, both chaotic and destructive, corresponds to the unconscious form play of the depth mind; his Apollinian form principle which moulds the Dionysian break-through into the images of dreams and art corresponds to the gestalt function which articulates the chaotic break-through of the depth mind....Apollo and Dionysos in this sense are the structural principles of differentiation and of chaos underlying all manifestations of life. (pp. 47-58)

Psychologizing Nietzsche's metaphysics, Freud (1933) had called the id "a chaos, a cauldron," but Ehrenzweig's phrasing tended to reify the alchemical metaphor.

As Ehrenzweig addressed the topic of abstract art, he no longer qualified unconscious perception as comparatively less differentiated than consciousness. He referred without qualification to its undifferentiation.

> Every act of creative thinking involves the disintegration of 'concrete' thing perception into the 'abstract' images or ideas of creative thought....the first phase in creating the 'abstract' thought is a return to the undifferentiated thing perception of the child or to the lack of thing differentiation in primitive thought. The second phase 'reifies' this undifferentiated perception into a new concept of external reality, i.e. an 'abstract' thing. The act of creative thinking may perhaps be conceived as repeating the primordial obliteration of all thing differentiation and the slow reintegration of the thing categories in the internal world of thought. (p. 168)

Explicit statements toward the end of Ehrenzweig's book preclude any non-literal interpretation of "undifferentiation." He insisted that sense data can be experienced in the absence of any gestalt. "Thing perception is bare of a definite form experience" (p. 217). Abstract art, he claimed, was even less differentiated, being both "gestalt-free" and "thing-free" (p. 255). These formulations suggest that Ehrenzweig postulated a complete undifferentiation, lacking even the gestalt of primary narcissism.

Ehrenzweig added a complex Kleinian theory of differing levels of psychosexuality that different aspects of creativity involved. For present purposes, a single, explicitly mystical example suffices.

> 'Abstraction' in artistic and scientific perception involves a libidinous withdrawal from external reality which permits the individualized thing perception to disintegrate (as far as this individuality is at all achieved). The retrogression can be considerable, reaching down to that infantile 'oceanic' state when the child cannot even differentiate his own ego from the external world. (p. 170)

All in all, Ehrenzweig's theory of the mystical in art closely resembled Milner's approach. Milner emphasized the union of subjective experience with external reality that united the artist with the artwork during the creative process and permanently imparted a mysticism or spirituality to the art product. Ehrenzweig agreed, and he emphasized the developmental and topographic aspects of the perception and projection of union.

> Freud showed us that the mystic in his 'oceanic' feeling of union with the Universe contemplates an infantile state of consciousness before the formation of a separate ego....even creative thinking can reach these deepest layers of consciousness when the human mind has not recognized the separateness of the external world; a more 'thing-free' state of perception cannot be conceived. While the mystic, however, remains *statically* in his calm religious rapture, the creative mind is able to reify *transitively* the thing-free vision into a rationally comprehensible idea or image....the 'abstraction' of the creative vision...represents a disintegration of adult thing differentiation into the more fluid and flexible 'abstract' vision of the child under the influence of a parallel disintegration of the object libido. (Ehrenzweig, 1953, pp. 171)

In an article entitled "The Creative Surrender," Ehrenzweig (1957) suggested that "creative sterility may be the result of ego rigidity impeding the free flow of mental imagery" (p. 193). "Normal surface consciousness with its precise, narrow focus cannot surrender to such undifferentiated fantasy, and the fear of self-destruction adhering to the phantasy is partly explained by its threat to the surface functions" (p. 198). "In the creative surrender the undifferentiated low-level imagery overwhelms the articulate surface imagery" (p. 200).

> The creative use of imagery, then, depends on the free flexible ego rhythm swinging out between widely distant levels. Images will be constantly immersed into oceanic undifferentiation and brought up again to the surface in a newly articulated shape, a new symbol for a cluster of unconscious images with which it was brought into contact....When this surface ego is abandoned, the way to oceanic undifferentiation is open. The imagery sinks to a lower structural level where it loses its precise definition and sharp boundaries, and merges with other images into new symbolic equations; then as the ego rhythm rebounds, the melted image recrystallizes and reassumes an independent existence, while, on the lower level, it still remains equated with, or diffused into, the other images which it now merely 'symbolizes'. (pp. 202-3)

MILNER'S RECEPTION

In 1955, an article by Milner was published in *New Directions in Psycho-Analysis*, which Melanie Klein, Paula Heimann, and Roger E. Money-Kyrle edited. Two years later, the second edition of Joanna Field's *On Not Being Able to Paint* (1957), which identified Field as Milner's pseudonym, included a foreword that Anna Freud penned. Anna Freud compared the creative process that Milner described with the psychoanalytic process that analysands undergo. "The amateur painter, who first puts pencil or brush to paper, seems to be in much the same mood as the patient during his initial period on the analytic couch. Both ventures, the analytic as well as the creative one, seem to demand similar external and internal conditions" (A. Freud, 1957, p. xiii). Although Anna Freud did not refer to Milner's discussion of the mystical in art, her endorsement of the book spoke to Milner's membership at the center of the psychoanalytic establishment. It also caused difficulties in Milner's relationship with Melanie Klein (Parsons, 2001, p. 610).

Reactions in the art world were strongly positive. Citing writings by Ehrenzweig, Sir Herbert Read (1951), Jacques Maritain (1953), and Adrian Stokes (1955), whom Melanie Klein had analyzed (Read, 2002), Milner remarked on an emerging consensus on the role of the mystical in art. The oceanic feeling, which repeats the infantile experience of maternal embrace, was seen as "an essential part of the creative process." At the same time, there were differences between the two. Creativity "is the oceanic state in a cyclic oscillation with the activity of what Ehrenzweig calls the surface mind, with that activity in which 'things' and the self, as Maritain puts it, are grasped separately not together" (Milner, 1987b, pp. 196-97)

Milner added an appendix to the second edition of *On Not Being Able to Paint*, in which she summarized her point of view. She also proposed that different patients are inhibited in their creativity because it represents masturbation (p. 154), or a loss of control of their sphincters, or a perceptual letting go that would lead to extreme undifferentiation between their bodily openings and their products (p. 150). She reported the disappearance of her sense of self while she was united with her art during the creative process.

> The process always seemed to be accompanied by a feeling that the ordinary sense of self had temporarily disappeared, there had been a kind of blanking out of ordinary consciousness; even the awareness of the blanking out had gone, so that it was only afterwards, when I returned to ordinary self-consciousness, that I

> remembered that there had been this phase of complete lack of self-consciousness. (Field, 1957, p.154)

Milner consistently theorized about fusion experiences when inner and outer were at one; but what she reported as her conscious experience of creativity was instead a loss of differentiation that was consistent with Ehrenzweig's theory. There was no moment of identification when Milner thought that she was her artwork; there was instead an oblivion to her self and her environment, in which her artwork alone existed. Milner was possibly aware of the discrepancy. She raised the question, implicit in Ehrenzweig's theory, that something more than a return to the breast was taking place, because the blankness of "no-differentiation" may be "a necessary prelude to a new integration" (Field, 1957, pp. 155-56). She suggested that "the great innovator in art...is...creating what is, because he is creating the power to perceive it" (p. 161).

Beginning with Ehrenzweig and Milner, psychoanalytic writers on undifferentiation have often associated its neonatal experience with Freud's discussion of the oceanic feeling. In my view, this equation is an error. Undifferentiation is a type of simplification that involves reduction to a precursor of whatever may be the present differentiation. Undifferentiation should not be confused with the construction of a highly abstract unity within a unitive mode. The oceanic feeling involves an imposition of the idea of a unified self onto the experience of the perceptible world. The experience is not lacking in self-consciousness but, to the contrary, is self-consciousness extended universally. In the oceanic feeling, the unity of an already integrated or unified self-representation is imparted to the world, unifying the disconnected multiplicity of external phenomena into a holistic concept, a concept of the world being a whole. Feelings for the self are extended to the world in the process (Merkur, 1998, 1999). The oceanic feeling is an instance of highly abstract unity within multiplicity. It is not an experience of comparative undifferentiation. Undifferentiation may be a prelude for experiences of mystical unity, as it is for creative experiences; but it is not to be confused with the integrative component of the overall process. Buddhists, for example, practice mindfulness in order to achieve dedifferentiation, but they employ entirely different, "concentrative" meditations in order to attain the unitive experiences that they term *samadhi*.

Whether comparative undifferentiation is to be counted precisely as mystical, its integral role in the creative process warrants its inclusion in psychoanalytic discussions of the mystical. Fromm did not use the term "undifferentiation," but he recommended its achievement when he advocated Zen Buddhist meditation and the "bare attending" procedure of

Theravadin Buddhist mindfulness meditation. Importantly, Buddhist claims notwithstanding, undifferentiation is never complete. Bare attending is always attending to something, for example, to one's own breathing. The psyche never undifferentiates to the point of zero mentation without becoming unconscious. At a certain point in Theravadin Buddhist practices of "bare attending," the mind begins to generate ideas about undifferentiation, for which reason the meditation that is known as *satipatthana,* "mindfulness," is also known in its advanced stages as *vipassana*, "insight."

WINNICOTT ON THE ILLUSION OF CULTURE

When Winnicott (1967a, 1971) expanded his theory of creative illusion to become a general theory of culture, his theory secured an enduring but unacknowledged place for the mystical within psychoanalysis. The illusion of objectivity is a paradox not only as a verbal formulation, but also as a physical quiddity. It is the true nature of things, a "paradoxical logic" (Fromm, 1960) at the heart of reality.

> A good object is not good to the infant unless created by the infant. Shall I say, created out of need? Yet the object must be found in order to be created. This has to be accepted as a paradox, and not solved by a restatement that, by its cleverness, seems to eliminate the paradox (Winnicott, 1963a, p. 181).

Because Winnicott expressed himself in terms of illusion and paradox and did not claim to be a mystic, the mystical character of his theory has generally gone unrecognized. But the evidence is emphatic. Consider the following summary of his theory, which Winnicott addressed to a popular audience in 1970:

> The fact is that what we create is already there, but the creativeness lies in the way we get at perception through conception and apperception. So when I look at the clock, as I must do now, I create a clock, but I am careful not to see clocks except just where I already know there is one. Please do not turn down this piece of absurd unlogic--but look at it and use it. (Winnicott, 1986, p. 52)

None of the classical Western mystics--nor any other psychoanalytic mystic --dwelled more happily in paradox, thinking and speaking in exquisitely impossible formulations.

Because Winnicott (1967a) regarded culture in its entirety as a creative illusion, his treatment of paradox and illusion as intrinsic to the whole of human culture arrived him at a *coincidentia oppositorum*, "coincidence of opposites," as is typical of mystical systems of thought. Winnicott's formulation has the advantage, however, of being completely rational. More than any other psychoanalytic writer, Winnicott unpacked the logical implications of Freud's ontology and epistemology, that the world of sense perception exists objectively but can only be known subjectively through ideas whose original complement originate in body-based imaginations. By placing the paradox of subjectivity about objective reality at the center of human culture, Winnicott drew attention to the philosophic stance to which Freud had committed psychoanalysis. If the teddy bear is the paradigmatic instance of a transitional object, it is simultaneously the paradigmatic instance of human knowledge. Everything that we know is known in the same fashion that a transitional object is known. "An element of illusion enters into the realistic libidinal cathexis of external reality" (Rycroft, 1955, p. 36). As Modell (1991, p. 229) phrased it, "Although Winnicott did not use the term *construction of reality*, this is essentially what he described under the heading of creativity." Hood (1992) concurred: "Even perception could not be objectively contained....Object themselves are solidified intentionalities revealed in a transitional space spread out to encompass and, indeed, to define culture, a reality to which one is necessarily educated" (p. 154). A subjective appreciation, consisting of sense perception, emotion, wishing, and thinking, is applied to an objectively existing reality, converting the noumenal thing-as-such into a phenomenon of human experience. Every phenomenon is an illusion, and yet it is also such knowledge as we may possess of reality. J. Jones (1992) concluded:

> All knowledge is transitional and interactional in Winnicott's sense. *Discursive reason and imaginative creation interpenetrate.* Pragmatic realities constrain imaginative reconstructions while creative reinterpretations reframe empirical experience. *No hard and fast line can be drawn between objective and subjective spheres or between the products of reason and of imagination"* (pp. 235-36; Jones's italics).

Fromm had expressed an equivalent perception of reality by adopting a perspective that viewed Aristotelian and paradoxical logic in dialectic with each other. He implied but did not find words to express his experience of holding both aspects of the dialectic in tension simultaneously.

Winnicott instead found easily accessible, common sense language with which to express his mystical insight.

In drawing attention to the paradox of subjectivity about objective reality, Winnicott pointed to the intrinsic mysticality of philosophical realism. Winnicott did not call his position mystical because it was not necessary to do so. Realism, understood as a subjective appreciation of a reality that exists objectively, is inherently and inalienably a philosophy of the *coincidentia oppositorum*. Moreover, transitional phenomena--and, indeed, a healthy appreciation of realism--have the additional feature of emotionally intense experience. "This intermediate area of experience, unchallenged in respect of its belonging to inner or external (shared) reality, constitutes the greater part of the infant's experience and throughout life is retained in the intense experiencing that belongs to the arts and to religion and to imaginative living, and to creative scientific work" (Winnicott, 1953, p. 242).

Because creative illusion, the *coincidentia oppositorum* of human subjectivity and objective reality, is present in all creativity, the whole of the creative process might arguably fall under the scope of the mystical. In an article entitled "The Integrative Function in Creativity," Hart (1950) raised the relevant question: "Is the creative process itself essentially an integrative one, resulting from synthetic processes in the unconscious?" (p. 2). His observation that "the creative, original mind reaches out for a more comprehensive integration and reality mastery" (p. 9) suggests that creativity may in its entirety be a practical or pragmatic externalization of the mystical. Rank, Milner, and Ehrenzweig recognized that artists experience union with or nondifferentiation from their work during intense moments of its creation; but they thought it appropriate to distinguish the mystical from the creative by treating creative experience as a developmentally advanced application of the oceanic feeling. The collapse of the theory of primary narcissism falsifies the developmental component of their thinking and invites the construction of other formulations. A contrary use of semantics, that seeks to equate rather than differentiate aesthetics and mysticism, has been advanced by Meg Harris Williams (1997, 2000), who built on studies of aesthetic experience that she co-authored with Donald Meltzer (Meltzer & Williams, 1988).

EHRENZWEIG ON UNCONSCIOUS ORDER

Working concurrently with Winnicott on culture, but from his own perspective as a teacher of art, Ehrenzweig (1957, 1964, 1967) treated Milner's concept of a "creative surrender" as a new point of departure. He now suggested that gestalt psychologists who divided the field of perception were incorrect to assume that attention is necessarily focused on the figure to the exclusion of the ground. Painters must continue to perceive the entire canvas while they attend to each brush stroke (Ehrenzweig, 1964, p. 383). He suggested that they rely on a process of unconscious perception.

> It is a common experience to see a painter stop in his work: a mien of doubt creeps into his face; he steps back from his canvas and views it with a vacant stare that focuses on nothing in particular. Through this stare he can divert his attention from the prominent, obtrusive "figure" pattern and is able to take in the entire field of vision. All details, figure and background alike, are scanned with equal acuity, just as in horizontal listening all polyphonic voices are given the same significance. Now and again some inconspicuous detail will momentarily come forward and sink back into the surrounding blankness. At last some obscure detail is found that had upset the balance of the painting; the search is over. (p. 385)

Ehrenzweig noted that Paul Klee had discussed the allocation of attention to both the "inside" and "outside" of the figure as "multidimensional." Klee had also noted a second example of the attentional phenomenon.

> He...compares the interpenetration of inside and outside space with the interaction of polyphonic voices in music....Hearing polyphonic voices in music has received a technical name--horizontal listening--as opposed to the normal vertical hearing of a single melody underscored by a harmonic background of merely accompanying voices. The narrow focus of normal perception can attend only to a single "figure," the melody, and must necessarily suppress the rest into an indistinct "ground." Listening to one melody will automatically prevent us from attending to the other accompanying voices which recede into the harmonic background. But the control of the polyphonic structure requires from the composer and performer that they keep an equally firm grip on the entire fabric of music, not merely on a single melody. (Ehrenzweig, 1964, pp. 383-84)

Ehrenzweig suggested that psychoanalysts' practice of "evenly hovering attention" is a third instance of the same attentional process. "Freud found that inconspicuous, seemingly disconnected details, lacking properties of good gestalt, are more likely to contain the key to the meaning of unconscious fantasies. Hence it is necessary to counteract the conscious attraction of conspicuous features and treat the entire material with equal diligence" (p. 385). Ehrenzweig's idealization of analytic behavior described the attitude of analysts who listen "with the third ear" in order to perceive phenomena that have never as yet been formulated. Many analysts believe, however, that theories make perceptions possible; they implicitly listen for data that confirm their theories.

Ehrenzweig argued that the creative use of attention is accomplished by devoting conscious attention to the figure, while unconscious perception scans the ground. Conscious experience of the ground remained comparatively undefined or vague, as during normal attention; but the attention consciously allocated to the ground made it possible for unconscious perceptions to manifest consciously, supplying the perceptions that consciousness could not make on its own.

> The narrowly focused beam of normal attention can select only one of many possible constellations. The unfocused dispersed type of attention is free from the compulsion to make such a choice. It can grasp in a single act of comprehension several mutually incompatible constellations. (p. 386)

Ehrenzweig claimed that unconscious perception "is totally blank as far as conscious memory is concerned" (p. 384). He suggested that unconscious perception cannot be experienced consciously because it conforms with the principles of the primary process. "Unconscious phantasy does not distinguish between opposites, fails to articulate space and time as we know it, and allows all firm boundaries to melt in a free chaotic mingling of forms" (Ehrenzweig, 1967, p. 3). To account for the "rigorous organization" that unconscious perception nevertheless imparts to art, Ehrenzweig suggested that unconscious perception has a developmental history that commences with the oceanic feeling and passes through oral, anal, and Oedipal phases of psychosexual development. This history imparts structure to the unconscious. "Seen in this way, the oceanic experience of fusion, of a 'return to the womb', represents the minimum content of all art" (p. 121). "It would be misleading to call this near-mystic experience of modern art in any way pathological" (p. 121).

Ehrenzweig's theory was one of several formulations in the 1960s (Gill, 1963; Schur, 1966; Noy, 1969) that overthrew Hartmann's reduction of the id to drive energies (Hartmann, Kris, & Loewenstein, 1951, p. 94) and reinstated the Freud-Abraham model of psychosexual development as structured contents of the repressed. Dreamwork might be atemporal and fluid, but the repressed is sequential and structured. Ehrenzweig's assumption that the developmental structure of repressed fantasies is simultaneously a structure of unconscious *perceptions* was a corollary of Milner's theory that images, symbols, or fantasies inform creative perceptions of external reality. Age-appropriate fantasies at the primary-narcissistic, oral, anal, and Oedipal stages shaped the ego's conscious perceptions during childhood and continued to inform the unconscious perceptions of adults.

Because "perception too, like any other ego function, develops by a slow process of differentiation," Ehrenzweig (1967, p. 263) understood dedifferentiation to be occurring when a person undertakes what Milner had called a "creative surrender."

> "Relaxation" is not the right word for this shift in ego functioning; it is rather a substitution of a more intense concentration for our normal one. These shifts between dedifferentiation and redifferentiation constitute an ego rhythm which must go on undetected for most of the time; in creative ego function the rhythm is deepened until it touches on levels of dedifferentiation that are beyond all rational understanding. (Ehrenzweig, 1964, p. 387)

We may acknowledge that there is unconsciousness of whatever creative processing is going on during this shift in ego functioning without subscribing to Ehrenzweig's overstatement that consciousness experiences the ground of attention as a "full blankness." The concept of "blankness" should not be reified. It has validity only as a metaphor for not knowing. The ground of attention remains within consciousness, as a kind of inattentively perceived background. Simultaneously, there is more or less patient but expectant hope for an as yet unknown creative idea or motion to emerge, and there may also be reflective awareness of not yet knowing its content.

Ehrenzweig argued that consciousness oscillates between dedifferentiation and redifferentiation under normal conditions, resulting in continuous creativity of a low-grade order. "It makes little sense to call this periodic decomposition of the surface ego a 'regression'. It is part and parcel of the ego rhythm which makes perception work" (Ehrenzweig, 1967, p. 263). The extent of the dedifferentiation depends on the level of unconscious perception that comes into play. The more archaic, the less differentiated, and the farther from the operations of consciousness. Mystical experience involves an interruption of normal oscillation. "Temporary dedifferentiation if it is extreme, as in oceanic states, implies a paralysis of surface functions and so can act very disruptively" (p. 177). Importantly, Ehrenzweig's theories of dedifferentiation were not based on data, but were instead suggested by the interior logic of his theoretic model.

Ehrenzweig was criticized for referring to *unconscious* perception. His critics suggested that the process that he described must technically be *preconscious* "inasmuch as it assists conscious rational thought" (Ehrenzweig, 1964, p. 384). Ehrenzweig insisted, however, that the creative process was inconsistent with preconscious activity. His argument was persuasive.

> Preconscious processes, unlike unconscious scanning, are readily accessible to conscious introspection; they are outside the focus of conscious attention solely because another thought happens to occupy attention. The process of unconscious scanning, by contrast, is disturbed by any attempt at introspection; it depends on conscious "blankness" and to that extent disrupts conscious thought. (Ehrenzweig, 1964, p. 384)

Ehrenzweig's attribution of unconscious perception to the primary process is nevertheless unfeasible. Ehrenzweig credited the creative process with considerably higher function than Freud attributed to the primary process. He suggested that artistic imagination performs conceptual operations.

> What has not been sufficiently realized is that unconscious *per*cepts on the level of the primary process build disjunctive serial structures of so wide a sweep that they can easily accommodate these contradictory (disjunctive) *con*cepts of primary process phantasy. Far from being chaotic, the primary process precisely matches undifferentiated id content with serial structures of exactly the same degree of undifferentiation. (Ehrenzweig, 1967, p. 262)

Whether the creative process performs perception, we do not know. We can say, however, that it definitely has access to the results of the ego's perceptions of external reality. It is not a pre-ego function, it is a post-ego function. It is not a primary process, but a tertiary one (see also Arieti, 1964; 1971; Merkur, 2001). Ehrenzweig did not appreciate--or did not allow himself to appreciate--that his theories could not be reconciled with a conventional model of the psyche.

Not only does creative imagination work conceptually--a conclusion whose self-evidence in the contexts of science and technology is beyond dispute--but creations of the imagination are endowed with an integrity.

> In any kind of creative work a point is reached where our power of free choice comes to an end. The work assumes a life of its own, which offers its creator only the alternative of accepting or rejecting it. A mysterious 'presence' reveals itself, which gives the work a living personality of its own....[There is a] conversation-like intercourse between the creator and his own work and the need of the artist to treat his work like an independent being with a life of its own. (Ehrenzweig, 1967, p. 84)

We may treat Ehrenzweig's personification of creative works as an exaggeration, while recognizing that creative works resemble ideals in being inanimate loved objects whose autonomy and integrity are respected (see Pruyser, 1974, p. 254).

CONCLUDING REFLECTIONS

Psychoanalysts were able to acknowledge the presence of the mystical in art without endorsing mysticism as a valid appreciation of reality (Bychowski, 1951; Greenacre, 1958; Rose, 1964, 1971, 1972, 1980). The psychoanalytic mainstream was similarly untroubled by Milner's theory that the creative process projects unconscious fantasy as an aesthetic illusion in art.

Winnicott's concept of transitional objects was widely embraced, but its paradox was generally tolerated on a "let's pretend" basis and not taken to heart as a mystical truth. The poverty of Winnicott's prose contributed heavily to the misunderstanding. Winnicott once candidly advised students who were about to hear him lecture, "What you get out of me, you will have to pick out of chaos" (Milner, 1987b, p. 246). His essays typically present brilliant but isolated theoretical insights, without connection to each other and without a logical progression to the essay.

When Ehrenzweig (1953, 1967) applied the theory of creative illusion not only to the arts but also to reality-testing and the sciences, he was understood to have openly asserted the validity of mysticism. But he was an art teacher writing about art and not a clinical psychoanalyst writing about psychoanalytic treatment. His cachet carried little weight with most analysts, and his work has remained largely unknown to the psychoanalytic mainstream.

The theory of creative illusion that Milner, Winnicott, and Ehrenzweig developed among them was nevertheless a major contribution to the psychoanalysis of the mystical. If scientific knowledge, no differently than art, is a creative illusion that is projected onto sense data, we are all of us psychologically mystics, whether we are conscious of the fact or not. Conversely, we cannot know whether mysticism is philosophically true or valid. Like all knowledge, it is an illusion. What we can say, however, is that it is psychologically healthy and may possibly be true.

Six

D. W. Winnicott's Analysis of the Self

Winnicott contributed originally to the psychoanalysis of the mystical not only with his concept of creative illusion, but also with his theories of early ego development. Here again he showed himself a member of the Middle School of British psychoanalysis by attempting to reconcile Freud's ideas of primary and secondary narcissism with Melanie Klein's paranoid-schizoid and depressive positions.

THE CAPACITY FOR CONCERN

Freud had invented psychoanalysis in the late 1890s to relieve hysterical symptoms through a course of treatment that lasted perhaps five or six weeks. When, following the First World War, the psychoanalysis of aggression was added to the analysis of psychosexuality, and treatments began to stretch on into years' duration, psychoanalysts tended increasingly to replace symptom analyses with character analyses. One discovery, initially by Sandor Rado (1928) in the treatment of depression, but subsequently generalized by Melanie Klein (1935), was the unanticipated finding that a thorough analysis of aggression can precipitate guilt, remorse, and a wish to make reparation. When the patient becomes aware of the extent and manner of aggression's counter-productivity, aggression loses its attraction; and more loving sentiments--empathy, forgiveness, tolerance, affection, bonding and so forth--are able to gain the upper hand. Some patients, preferring aggression over love, flee analysis at this juncture. Those who carry on renounce aggression and undergo moral transformations of lesser or greater extents.

At the time, Winnicott was a pediatrician. He was initially analyzed by James Strachey, beginning in 1924. When Klein declined to reanalyze him because she wanted him to analyze her son Erich, he received a Kleinian analysis from her colleague Joan Riviere. Winnicott qualified as a psychoanalyst in 1934, but he always maintained a critical distance from Klein's object relations theories. Klein referred to the morally transformative phase of clinical treatment as the patient's arrival at "the depressive position." Winnicott (1962c) regarded the discovery of the depressive position as "Klein's most important contribution, in my opinion, and I think it ranks with Freud's concept of the Oedipus complex" (p. 176). At the same time, Winnicott disliked the term "depressive position." He acknowledged that patients become depressed, but he drew attention to their motivation.

> The stage of concern brings with it the capacity to feel guilty. Henceforth some of the aggression appears clinically as grief or a feeling of guilt or some physical equivalent, such as vomiting. The guilt refers to the damage which is felt to be done to the loved person in the excited relationship. (Winnicott, 1950-55, p. 206)

The achievement of a capacity for concern was a major goal of Winnicott's clinical work. "The attainment of a capacity for making reparation in respect of personal guilt is one of the most important steps in the development of the healthy human being, and we now wonder how we did analytic work before we consciously made use of this simple truth" (Winnicott, 1948b, p. 91).

> In analysis one could say: 'couldn't care less' gives way to guilt-feeling. There is a gradual building up towards this point. No more fascinating experience awaits the analyst than the observation of the gradual build-up of the individual's capacity to tolerate the aggressive elements in the primitive love impulse. (Winnicott, 1958b, p. 24)

Winnicott agreed with Klein that the clinical phenomenon of the depressive position constituted the belated achievement of a developmental milestone that in health would have been attained by an infant of perhaps six months of age. "The Depressive Position is a normal stage in the development of healthy infants" (Winnicott, 1955a, p. 262). Its natural occurrence in health establishes the fact that children and, indeed, human beings are innately good. "Those who hold the view that morality needs to be inculcated teach small children accordingly, and they forgo the pleasure of watching morality develop naturally in their children, who are thriving in a good setting that is provided in a personal and individual way" (Winnicott, 1958b, p. 15).

> Religions have made much of original sin, but have not all come round to the idea of original goodness....

> Religion (or is it theology?) has stolen the good from the developing child, and has then set up an artificial scheme for injecting this that has been stolen back into the child, and has called it 'moral education'. Actually moral education does not work unless the infant or child has developed in himself or herself by natural developmental process the stuff that, when it is placed up in the sky, is given the name God. (Winnicott, 1963d, p. 94)

Extending his critique of conventional moral theories to the psychoanalytic work of Freud and Klein, Winnicott (1971) asserted that "the concept of the death instinct could be described as a reassertion of the principle of original sin" (p. 82). By the death instinct Winnicott referred, of course, not to entropy but to aggression and guilt.

Winnicott's comfort with moral discourse set him apart from both the ego psychologists and the Kleinians. Edward Glover (1945) had objected to Klein's object relations theories because, he claimed, they imported moral categories within psychoanalysis.

> In [Kleinian theory]...we can trace the outlines of a new religious biology. The ultimately moral values "good" and "bad" can be followed back to early fantasies of "good" and "bad" introjected breasts, and via the function of taking in the good and expelling the bad, to a "conflict" between the life and the death instincts which exists before any psychic organization is developed. Whatever else this may mean, it certainly represents a projection into biological science of moral values (p. 107).

Glover's accusation was unreasonable, however, because Klein followed Freud carefully in offering exclusively amoral, biological formulations. At a Scientific Discussion on January 27, 1943, Ella Freeman Sharpe, who belonged to the Freudian school, more judiciously acknowledged that Klein's views were no more moralistic than those of Freud, because morality had its basis in primary narcissism.

> Freud, Mrs Klein, all of us, agree that the infant's breast hallucination is the initial wish psychosis. The wish is represented as fulfilled and commands entire belief. Dreams and unconscious phantasies regress to this level of perception....
>
> From this core of belief in the actual good object within proceeds the belief in God immanent, the dweller in the inner-

> most, the ultimate certainty and reality. It is the secret of the contemplative life, the heart of mysticism. She is in me and I in her. It is immaterial if one says God instead of Mother. 'One altogether, not by confusion of substance but by unity of Person.' It is an ultimate psychotic belief in a non-bodily separation from the first object and this is wish-psychosis (King & Steiner, 1991, p. 338)

Unlike both Freudians and Kleinians, Winnicott welcomed the implication that psychoanalytic theory cannot remain within an amoral biological framework, because moral categories are inevitable parts of human psychology. "From my personal point of view, the work of Klein has enabled psycho-analytic theory to begin to include the idea of an individual's *value*, whereas in early psycho-analysis the statement was in terms of *health* and neurotic *ill-health*. Value is intimately bound up with the capacity for guilt-feeling" (Winnicott, 1958b, p. 25).

UNIT STATUS

Winnicott made limited and selective use of Klein's theories, but he accepted her association of the depressive position with the infant's awareness of whole objects. "To reach the depressive position a baby must have become established as a whole person, and to be related to whole persons as a whole person" (Winnicott, 1955a, p. 264).

> We can say that at this stage a baby becomes able in his play to show that he can understand he has an inside, and that things come from outside. He shows he knows that he is enriched by what he incorporates (physically and psychically)....
>
> The corollary of this is that now the infant assumes that his mother also has an inside, one which may be rich or poor, good or bad, ordered or muddled. He is therefore starting to be concerned with the mother and her sanity and her moods. (Winnicott, 1945, p. 148)

Winnicott described the infant who had arrived at a capacity for concern in terms that applied equally well to Freud's concept of secondary narcissism, which involved the awareness of the bodily limitation of the self and the external location of all other physical realities.

The successful achievement of the developmental milestone is taken for granted whenever psychoanalysts discuss "illness and health in terms of neurosis" and "interpersonal relations." "Whole children are related to whole people. This cannot be said in a description of the earlier stages where infants are related to part-objects, or are themselves far from being established as units" (Winnicott, 1956c, p. 318).

In addition to "personalization" and "the appreciation of time and space and other properties of reality" (Winnicott, 1945, p. 148), Winnicott (1953) suggested that "every individual who has reached to the stage of being a unit" has also "an *inner reality*...an inner world which can be rich or poor and can be at peace or in a state of war" (p. 230). One aspect of the inner world provides a capacity to be alone.

> Although many types of experience go to the establishment of the capacity to be alone, there is one that is basic, and without a sufficiency of it the capacity to be alone does not come about; *this experience is that of being alone, as an infant and small child, in the presence of mother*. Thus the basis of the capacity to be alone is a paradox; it is the experience of being alone while someone else is present. (Winnicott, 1958a, p. 30)

Unit status makes communication possible (Winnicott, 1963a, p. 182) both intrapsychically and interpersonally. Referring to a case example, Winnicott (1971) remarked that in his presence, the child played for him to mirror. If the child had been alone, there would have continued to be a communication; but it would have proceeded "with some part of the self, the observing ego" (pp. 50-51).

Influenced possibly by the existential terminology of R. D. Laing, whose psychoanalytic training he supervised (Burston, 1996b, pp. 50-51), Winnicott (1971) associated unit status with the attainment of the concept of being (p. 152). A further consequence of unit status was its application in what Winnicott called the use of an object. Only when an object is known to be an object and individuation from it has taken place, can the object be used as an object. "The object, if it is to be used, must necessarily be real in the sense of being part of shared reality, not a bundle of projections. It is this, I think, that makes for the world of difference that there is between relating and usage" (Winnicott, 1969b, p. 103). Because it is conventional to speak of "using" people as a euphemism for their exploitation, it is crucial to appreciate that Winnicott intended the term "usage" in a literal sense. Object usage, as Winnicott described it, is the attitude which, when reciprocated, makes possible the dialogical relationship that Martin Buber called an encounter of I and Thou.

INFANTILE SOLIPSISM AS AN OBJECT RELATION

In thinking through the implications of Freud's and Klein's developmental theories, Winnicott avoided their technical terms and instead attempted to work the concepts out in more straightforward language. When he turned to imagine the stage prior to unit status, he famously attained his breakthrough insight during a scientific meeting in the early 1940s. He later reminisced:

> I have had a long struggle with this problem. It started when I found myself saying in this Society (about ten years ago) and I said it rather excitedly and with heat: '*There is no such thing as a baby.*' I was alarmed to hear myself utter these words and tried to justify myself by pointing out that if you show me a baby you certainly show me also someone caring for the baby, or at least a pram with someone's eyes and ears glued to it. One sees a 'nursing couple'.
>
> In a quieter way today I would say that before object relationships the state of affairs is this: that the unit is not the individual, the unit is an environment-individual set-up. The centre of gravity of the being does not start off in the individual. It is the total set-up. (Winnicott, 1952, p. 99)

Winnicott's remarks on the "environment-individual set-up" described reality, as seen by an external observer, during the infant's experience of neonatal solipsism. "The object, or the environment, is as much part of the self as the instinct is which conjures it up" (Winnicott, 1945, p. 155). Freud's approach to infantile solipsism had conceptualized primary narcissism as a vicissitude of libido, but Winnicott was instead interested in its implications for the analysis of the ego.

> We can build theories of *instinct* development and agree to leave out the environment, but there is no possibility of doing this in regard to formulation of *early ego development*. We must always remember, I suggest, that the end result of our thinking about ego development is primary narcissism. In primary narcissism the environment is holding the individual, and *at the same time* the individual knows of no environment and is at one with it. (Winnicott, 1955b, p. 283)

In his later years, Winnicott (1971) avoided the term "narcissism" "because I am not sure that it is what I mean" (p. 17). He referred to the earliest developmental phase as a "holding" phase when "the infant and the maternal care together form a unit" (Winnicott, 1960d, p. 39), and he credited an infant in the holding phase with the mental activities of primary process, primary identification, auto-erotism, and primary narcissism (p. 44). Dovetailing with Ehrenzweig's theories of the developmental differentiation of perception, Winnicott (1988, p. 116 n) endorsed Glover's (1930, 1968) theory that the newborn ego--better, the sense of self--begins in a state of unintegration and only gradually synthesizes the ego out of ego nuclei that are each formed in response to one or more early experiences. "It may be assumed that at the theoretical start the personality is unintegrated, and that in regressive disintegration there is a primary state to which regression leads. We postulate a primary unintegration" (Winnicott, 1945, p. 149). Glover had thought in terms of a gradual synthesis of memories of ego experiences. Spitz's (1955) theory that the infant's sense of self is initially limited to a "mouth ego" could be understood as one of the items that aggregates and coalesces into the body ego. Winnicott seems, however, to have taken for granted something akin to Federn's concept of a mental ego that antedates the body ego.

> With a good-enough technique the centre of gravity of being in the environment-individual set-up can afford to lodge in the centre, in the kernel rather than in the shell. The human being now developing an entity from the centre can become localized in the baby's body and so can begin to create an external world at the same time as acquiring a limiting membrane and an inside. (Winnicott, 1952, p. 99)

The concept of primary unintegration enabled Winnicott to develop psychoanalytic theories that accounted for a variety of psychological phenomena that existentialists had explored in terms of the individual. For example, Winnicott explained existential anxiety as anxiety about the regression of the self prior to its achievement of unit status. When "the ego changes over from an unintegrated state to a structured integration...the infant becomes able to experience anxiety associated with disintegration" (Winnicott, 1960d, p. 44). At the same time, existential anxiety was the manifest content of an unconscious object relation.

> The infant...is at this first and earliest stage in a state of mergence, not yet having separated out mother and 'not-me' objects from

> the 'me', so that what is adaptive or 'good' in the environment is building up in the infant's storehouse of experience as a self quality, indistinguishable at first (by the infant) from the infant's own healthy functioning.
>
> At this early stage the infant does not register what is good or adaptive, but reacts to, and therefore knows about and registers each failure of reliability. Reacting to unreliability in the infant-care process constitutes a trauma, each reaction being an interruption of the infant's 'going-on-being' and a rupture of the infant's self. (Winnicott, 1963d, p. 97)

THE TRANSITIONAL STAGE

Winnicott's concept of primary identification allowed him to locate Klein's paranoid-schizoid position within his own theory of early ego development. Winnicott postulated an intermediate or transitional stage that occurred after the initial developmental stage of unintegration but prior to the achievement of unit status. Here primary identification functioned as a foundation for the processes of projective and introjective identification (Winnicott, 1971, p. 94) that characterized Klein's paranoid-schizoid position. Objects are recognized in a paradoxically subjective way.

Winnicott (1953) initially proposed the term "transitional object" to designate the type of object that belonged to the transitional stage. He referred to the paradox of creative illusion when he remarked that the baby is permitted "to be mad in one particular way that is conceded to babies" (p. 83). In other contexts, he replaced the stage-specific term with the more general concept of a "subjective object" or "subjectively perceived object" (Winnicott, 1962b). "The term subjective object has been used in describing the first object, the object *not yet repudiated as a not-me phenomenon*" (Winnicott, 1971, p. 93). The term captured the paradox of the infant's situation. "I have used this term subjective object to allow a discrepancy between what is observed and what is being experienced by the baby" (p. 152).

To name the type of interaction that proceeds with subjectively perceived objects, Winnicott proposed the term "object-relating."

> In object-relating the subject allows certain alterations in the self to take place, of a kind that has caused us to invent the term cathexis. The object has become meaningful. Projection mechanisms and identifications have been operating, and the subject is depleted to the extent that something of the subject is found in

> the object, though enriched by feeling. Accompanying these changes is some degree of physical involvement (however slight) towards excitement, in the direction of the functional climax of an orgasm. (Winnicott, 1969b, p. 103)

"Object-relating" was Winnicott's designation of the mentality that manifests, in Buber's terms, in an I-It relation to another person.

Winnicott's concept of the transitional stage differed from Klein's idea of the paranoid-schizoid position in addressing the *quality* of relating while being indifferent to the content. For Klein, it was a question of part objects. For Winnicott, it was immaterial whether relating was done to the breast or to the whole body of the mother. In both cases, the object is subjectively perceived and treated as a thing and not as a person. One characteristic of behavior toward subjective objects is a ruthlessness that is oblivious to concern.

> If one assumes that the individual is becoming integrated and personalized and has made a good start in his realization, there is still a long way for him to go before he is related as a whole person to a whole mother, and concerned about the effect of his own thoughts and actions on her.
>
> We have to postulate an early ruthless object relationship. This may again be a theoretical phase only, and certainly no one can be ruthless after the concern stage except in a dissociated state. But ruthless dissociation states are common in early childhood, and emerge in certain types of delinquency, and madness, and must be available in health. (Winnicott, 1945, p. 154; see also Winnicott, 1950-55, p. 206).

Winnicott remarked that the concept of ruthlessness presupposed a vantage point in later development. "The infant does not feel ruthless, but looking back (and this does occur in regressions) the individual can say: I was ruthless then! The stage is one that is pre-ruth" (Winnicott, 1955, p. 262).

Reasoning that conscious communication presupposes unit status, Winnicott imagined that the transitional stage involves no communication that is consciously recognized as such.

> In so far as the object is subjective, *so far is it unnecessary for communication with it to be explicit.* In so far as the object is objectively perceived, communication is either explicit or else dumb.

> Here then appear two *new* things, the individual's use and enjoyment of modes of communication, and the individual's non-communication self, or the personal core of the self that is a true isolate. (Winnicott, 1963a, p. 182)

Winnicott speculated that the transitional stage might be brief and might possibly involve intermittent moments of unit status. "The baby can meet the reality principle here and there, now and then, but not everywhere all at once; that is, the baby retains areas of subjective objects along with other areas in which there is some relating to objectively perceived objects, or 'not-me' ('non-I') objects" (Winnicott, 1962b, p. 57).

THE FALSE SELF

Winnicott's theory of early ego development had important clinical consequences. He suggested that the infant's sense of self originates through primary identification with the mother's responses to the infant. Wholesome and defective senses of the self have their basis in the vicissitudes of relations with the mother of primary identification.

> What does the baby see when he or she looks at the mother's face? I am suggesting that, ordinarily, what the baby sees is himself or herself. In other words the mother is looking at the baby and *what she looks like is related to what she sees there*. All this is too easily taken for granted. I can make my point by going straight over to the case of the baby whose mother reflects her own mood or, worse still, the rigidity of her own defences. In such a case what does the baby see? (Winnicott, 1967b, p. 131)

Winnicott adopted the concept of a false self from patients who experienced themselves as inauthentic (Winnicott, 1960c, p. 140). For example, one patient "had the feeling all her life that she had not started to exist, and that she had always been looking for a means of getting to her True Self" (p. 142). Winnicott saw the false self in a variety of pathological intensities, but also as a component of health.

> Normally, this is no more than saying that...one is not always saying what one thinks, and that it pays to put forward a self for social acceptance that is not what one really is at heart.
>
> Many people do not find this easy. They find it dishonest to be acceptable socially....

> More ill people find all this a major problem. They live a life that is perhaps successful and socialized, even partly well socialized. But they gradually feel more and more dishonest, or less and less real. Eventually, (not really knowing what they are doing at all), they switch over to living from the true self...and this means an abandonment of all that has been built up on a basis of the false self. (letter to Nicholas Latimer, January 2, 1964; as cited in Burston, 1996b, p. 64)

"The false self is built up on a basis of compliance" (Winnicott, 1965, p. 133), initially with the mother, but later also with many other people.

> Through this false self the infant builds up a false set of relationships, and by means of introjections even attains a show of being real, so that the child may grow to be just like mother, nurse, aunt, brother, or whoever at the time dominates the scene....
>
> In the extreme examples of False Self development, the True Self is so well hidden that spontaneity is not a feature in the infant's living experiences. Compliance is then the main feature, with imitation as a speciality. (Winnicott, 1960b, pp. 146-47)

The false self has a place within Winnicott's system of thought that approximates inauthenticity in existentialism. Where Fromm had treated alienation as a symptom, Winnicott (1965) discussed the false self in ego psychological terms as a defense. "The compliant false self...is...a defence organization that is based on the various functions of the ego apparatus and on self-caretaking techniques. This relates to the concept of the observing ego" (p. 9). Winnicott adopted the term "observing ego" from Sterba (1934) but his implicit reference to de-personalization or de-realization arrived him at a concept that compares instead with Fairbairn's (1943, 1963) "internal saboteur" or "antilibidinal ego."

> With the true self protected there develops a false self built on a defence-compliance basis, the acceptance of reaction to impingement. The development of a false self is one of *the most successful defence organizations* designed for the protection of the true self's core, and its existence results in the sense of futility. I would like to repeat myself and to say that while the individual's operational centre is in the false self there is a sense of futility, and in practice we find the change to the feeling that life is worthwhile coming

> at the moment of shift of the operational centre from the false to the true self, even before full surrender of the self's core to the total ego. (Winnicott, 1955b, pp. 291-92)

In all of its intensities, "the existence of a False Self results in feeling unreal or a sense of futility" (Winnicott, 1960c, p. 148). In adopting his concept of the false self from patients' self-descriptions, Winnicott followed Klein's practice of reifying the manifest content of patients' fantasies. Postulating the existence of a psychic structure on the basis of patients' self-reports is an instance of the methodological error that Whitehead (1925) termed "the fallacy of misplaced concreteness." Winnicott's discussion of a pair of self-representations, a false self and a true self, might be better treated as an account of the vicissitudes of a single psychic structure, the sense of self or reflective self-representation. It is unearned and superfluous to assume from the existence of a sense that the self is false, that a true self exists simultaneously, either secretly in consciousness or unconsciously. The sense that the self is false is a self-reproach, a feeling of inadequacy, a self-evaluation as having failed to achieve a higher and desired-for standard of aspiration. The fantasy that the self is false, rather than deficient or inadequate, harbors hope for a second self that is uncontaminated or true, even as it displaces self-knowledge that the self-representation is defective.

THE TRUE SELF

In agreement with Rank, Milner, and Ehrenzweig, Winnicott attributed creativity to the unconscious sources of the self. In a book review of W. R. D. Fairbairn's *Psychoanalytic Studies of the Personality* (1952), Winnicott took the occasion to remark that neither Fairbairn nor Klein regarded "primary psychic creativity" as "a human property." In their view, "an infinite series of introjections and projections form the infant's psychic experience" (Winnicott & Khan, 1953, p. 420). For Winnicott, primary psychic creativity manifested in the neonate's creation of the breast. "From the child's point of view the mother was created by the child. The mother met the child's primary creativity, and so became the object that the child was ready to find" (Winnicott, 1956a, p. 311). Winnicott (1971) followed Ehrenzweig in linking creativity with the psyche's undifferentiation. "It is only...in this unintegrated state of personality, that that which we describe as creative can appear" (p. 64). Winnicott (1960c) suggested that primary creativity was integral to the formation of the true self. "The True Self does not become a living reality except as a result of the mother's repeated success in meeting the infant's spontaneous gesture or sensory hallucination" (p. 145).

In another formulation, Winnicott (1960c) used the term "true self" in an inconsistent manner that referred to both the inborn source of primary creativity and the ego organization that primary creativity builds up. "Periodically the infant's gesture gives expression to a spontaneous impulse; the source of the gesture is the True Self, and the gesture indicates the existence of a potential True Self" (p. 145). Slippage back and forth from the unconscious source of creativity to a healthy ego organization occurs also in Winnicott's discussion of the relation of the true self to the sense of reality.

> At the earliest stage the True Self is the theoretical position from which come the spontaneous gesture and the personal idea. The spontaneous gesture is the True Self in action. Only the True Self can be creative and only the True Self can feel real. Whereas a True Self feels real, the existence of a False Self results in a feeling unreal or a sense of futility. (Winnicott, 1960c, p. 148)

The true self that feels real conforms with the reality principle of the ego. It is implicitly a healthy ego organization that is alternative to the false self defense.

In yet another formulation within the same article, Winnicott (1960c) used the term in yet a third way, when he tried again to clarify what he was having difficulty expressing. "At the earliest stage the True Self is the theoretical position from which come the spontaneous gesture and the personal idea" (p. 148). The spontaneous gesture manifests primary creativity; the "personal idea" is the idea of individuated personhood on whose attainment unit status and object usage both depend.

Winnicott was referring to the unconscious source of primary creativity when he claimed a precedent for his concept of true and false selves in the early views of Freud.

> It would appear to me that the idea of a False Self, which is an idea which our patients gives us, can be discerned in the early formulations of Freud. In particular I link what I divide into a True and a False Self with Freud's division of the self into a part that is central and powered by the instincts (or by what Freud called sexuality, pregenital and genital), and a part that is turned outwards and is related to the world. (Winnicott, 1960c, p. 140)

The validity of Winnicott's reading of Freud depends on the sense in which the true self is to be linked to sexuality and the false self to external perception. As ego organizations, both the true and the false self are conscious phenomena. At the same time, a "true self" ego organization integrates the instincts within its creativity, where a "false self" defends against both sexuality and creativity while complying with the external world. Or, to put the theory another way, Winnicott's true self refers to a healthy integration of id and ego, by which instinct is enabled to manifest in creativity.

The true self, I suggest, is not an ego *structure* but a *process* that involves a self-representation that integrates both id and ego in a co-ordinating way. It is the ego organization that is active in creativity. The true self is experienced as true because it is genuinely pleasurable; and "it is creative apperception more than anything else that makes the individual feel that life is worth living" (Winnicott, 1971, p. 76). "Individuals live creatively and feel that life is worth living or else...they cannot live creatively and are doubtful about the value of living" (p. 83). "The artist has an ability and the courage to be in touch with primitive processes which the psycho-neurotic cannot bear to reach, and which healthy people may miss to their own impoverishment" (Winnicott, 1965, p. 132).

Winnicott's association of creativity with the true self meant that inhibitions of creativity coincided with the falseness of the self. A true and creative self might persist in hiding as a secret life that a false personality conceals; but in extremely severe cases of demands for conformity, for example, in concentration camps and totalitarian political circumstances, creativity may entirely disappear (Winnicott, 1971, pp. 79-80).

Like Rank and Fromm, Winnicott recognized that the goal of psychoanalytic treatment, to provide relief from repression, cannot be achieved on its own. Any thorough-going treatment of repression will restore the capacity for creativity, including but not limited to sexuality.

WINNICOTT AND EXISTENTIALISM

Winnicott made occasional use of existentialist terminology. He had been concerned with early ego development and its clinical consequences from the 1930s onward; but he began to express some of his ideas in the technical language of existentialism in the late 1950s, when he was supervising the psychoanalytic training of R. D. Laing, who was an existential psychiatrist both before and after his Tavistock years (Burston, 1996b, pp. 50-51). Winnicott implicitly recognized that he was formulating an object relations approach to topics that interested existentialists. He identified the sense of being with infantile solipsism (Winnicott, 1971, p. 94).

Unlike Rank and Fromm, Winnicott was not content with the solitary perspective that existentialist terminology implied. His was an object relations theory. He theorized that the manifest content of seemingly solitary existential phenomena are properly analyzed in terms of the mother-infant dyad. Winnicott (1960d) asserted, for example, that the true self that receives "good enough" mothering experiences "a continuity of being."

> [The] central or true self....could be said to be the inherited potential which is experiencing a continuity of being, and acquiring in its own way and at its own speed a personal psychic reality and a personal body-scheme. It seems necessary to allow for the concept of the isolation of this central self as a characteristic of health. (p. 46)

The novelty of Winnicott's formulation rested on his insight that there is no such thing as a baby. Because the sense of being, or going-on-being, rests on a solipsistic appreciation of the facilitating environment as a subjective object, the core of the true self, which is experienced phenomenologically as isolated, is the manifest content of an unconscious process of object-relating (Winnicott, 1971, p. 94). The object-relating proceeds with an experience of the human and non-human environment that is perceived subjectively as portions of the self.

Winnicott (1963c) suggested that the infant's experience of a continuity of being constituted "a kind of blue-print for existentialism."

> All the processes of a live infant constitute a *going-on-being*, a kind of blue-print for existentialism. The mother who is able to give herself over, for a limited spell, to this her natural task, is able to protect her infant's going-on-being. Any impingement, or failure of adaptation, causes a reaction in the infant, and the reaction breaks up the going-on-being. (p. 86)

It is because being, or going-on-being, involves an object relationship that the true self is able to entertain a concept of self toward which it can be true. Authenticity is a kind of object-relating that proceeds within the true self. "Feeling real is more than existing; it is finding a way to exist as oneself, and to relate to objects as oneself, and to have a self into which to retreat for relaxation" (Winnicott, 1967b, p. 137).

WINNICOTT AS AN EXTROVERTIVE MYSTIC

Winnicott also made use of the language of mysticism. He nowhere called himself a mystic and would have disavowed the term had he been called one. According to his wife Clare, Winnicott was raised in a "profoundly religious" Wesleyan family (Goldman, 1993, pp. 116, 117), and his occasional uses of the term "mysticism" reflect the traditional Wesleyan Methodist association of mysticism with Quietism, a form of extreme inwardism that Methodists rejected. Consider the following statement: "In thinking of the psychology of mysticism, it is usual to concentrate on the understanding of the mystic's withdrawal into a personal inner world of sophisticated introjects" (Winnicott, 1963a, p. 185). Although Winnicott disapproved of the experiential inwardness that he designated as "mysticism," he was sensitive to its variations and complexity. "Every mood is there and the unconscious fantasy of the mood ranges from idealization on the one hand to the awfulness of the destruction of all that is good on the other--bringing the extremes of elation or despair, well being in the body or a sense of being diseased and an urge to suicide" (Winnicott, 1971, p. 123).

For the purposes of this study, the mystical has been defined in terms of condensation and unitive thinking or, metaphorically, Eros, the drive to unity, and its many manifestations and vicissitudes throughout life. Winnicott's concern with infantile solipsism, primary creativity, the true self, its persistence throughout life, its pathology, and its psychoanalytic treatment, all fall under the scope of the mystical. This definition of the mystical corresponds, not entirely precisely, with usage in the academic study of comparative mysticism, for which Quietism is an example of a subcategory of mysticism that may be classified both as "introvertive" (Stace, 1960) because it looks exclusively inward, and as "impersonal" (Lindblom, 1962) with regard its conception of the divine as an impersonal quiddity. Haartman (2004) persuasively demonstrated that although Methodists avoided the term "mysticism," they valued several varieties of unitive experiences, for example, of the omnipresent power of God that informs and unites the whole of creation. Methodist experiences of justification and sanctification are not mystical, as Methodists define the term, but they are mystical as defined by students of comparative mysticism. At the same time, they differ from the experiences of Quietists. Methodist experiences are both "extrovertive" (Stace, 1960) in that they pertain to the external world of sense perception, and "personal" (Lindblom, 1962) in that they conceive of the divine as a personality.

From the perspective of comparative mysticism, Winnicott's thinking about psychoanalysis may be recognized as decidedly mystical, even though it was an extrovertive type of mysticism that neither Milner nor Winnicott knew to call mystical. Consider, for example, Winnicott's explicit assertion that his own point of view balanced mystical inwardness with an engagement with external reality.

> Without straining the language of everyday use I may talk of my behaviour in the world of external (or shared) reality, or I may be having an inner or mystical experience, while squatting on the ground contemplating my navel....
>
> There are those who place emphasis on the 'inner' life, who think that the effects of economics and even of starvation itself have but little importance as compared with mystical experience. Infinity for those in the latter category is at the centre of the self, whereas for the behavourists who think in terms of external reality infinity is reaching out beyond the moon to the stars and to the beginning and the end of time, time that has neither an end nor a beginning.
>
> I am trying to get in between these two extremes. If we look at our lives we shall probably find that we spend most of our time neither in behaviour nor in contemplation, but somewhere else. I ask: where? And I try to suggest an answer. (Winnicott, 1971, pp. 122, 123)

Because Winnicott restricted the term "mysticism" to introvertive, impersonal mysticism, he saw himself as pursuing a middle course between mysticism and action in the world. In the 1920s, historians of religion might have called his stance "prophetic" and contrasted it with "mystical" (Heiler, 1932); Fromm, certainly, has been called "prophetic" in this sense of the term (Burston, 1996a). Contemporary students of comparative mysticism would not hesitate, however, to assess Winnicott's position as an instance of extrovertive mysticism. His was a different kind of mysticism than the introvertive mysticism that he mistakenly assumed to be the whole of mysticism.

Winnicott expressed much the same, one-sided view of mysticism in an obituary for James Strachey.

> Intellectual honesty in living leads to the stake and did nearly lead Strachey as a conscientious objector to prison. In terms of mysticism and psychedelics, intellectual honesty takes one only to a personal view of the bird of paradise. It is perhaps only in the cultural sphere that intellectual integrity becomes actual, and can be a permanent feature. This was James Strachey as I saw him. (Winnicott, 1969a, p. 509)

Once again, if we allow a perspective in the comparative study of mysticism, we may understand Winnicott to have advocated an extrovertive mysticism that applied introverted mystical ideas to the world of sense perception. The *coincidentia oppositorum* of the creative illusion is perhaps the outstanding example of Winnicott's extrovertive mysticism. Extrovertive mysticism can also be seen in his notion that infantile solipsism is similarly paradoxical in its inclusion of the maternal environment within the self. Equally paradoxical is Winnicott's formulation of unit status, which involves an internalized object relationship with a capacity for object usage.

MYSTICAL EXPERIENCE

Winnicott expressed an early version of his fundamental insights about mysticism in the course of a discussion of theism.

> One may meet with an astoundingly deep recognition of certain aspects of internal reality in people who nevertheless do not acknowledge that the people who inhabit them are a part of themselves. An artist feels as if a picture was painted by someone acting from inside him, or a preacher as if God speaks through him. Many who live normal and valuable lives do not feel they are responsible for the best that is in them. They are proud and happy to be the agent of a loved and admired person, or of God, but they deny their parenthood of the internalized object. I think more has been written about bad internalized objects similarly disowned than about the denial of good internal forces and objects.
>
> There is a practical point here, for in the analysis of the most satisfactory type of religious patient it is helpful to work with the patient as if on an agreed basis of recognition of internal reality, and to let the recognition of the person origin of the patient's God come automatically as a result of lessening of anxiety due to the analysis of the depressive position. It is necessarily dangerous for the analyst to have it in his mind that the patient's God is a 'fantasy object'. The use of that word would make the patient feel as if the analyst were undervaluing the good object, which he is not really doing. I think something similar would apply to the analysis of an artist in regard to the source of his inspiration, and also the analysis of the inner people and imaginary companions to whom our patients are able to introduce us. (Winnicott, 1935, p. 133)

This formulation from 1935 anticipated Fromm's (1955b) concept of idolatry. It also pointed to the paradox of unit status, which recognizes the unit status of other people and can imagine the unit status of God. Winnicott's designation of God as "the good object" foreshadowed his appreciation, seven or so years later, that there is no such thing as a baby. The goodness that is attributed to God may be an endowment of an illusion with goodness derivative of the true self; but because the true self is an undifferentiated appreciation of the infant-mother dyad, the attribution of goodness to God may not impoverish primary creativity. It may simply be a transferring onto God of the goodness of the "environmental mother" of the holding stage.

Winnicott's reflections on infantile solipsism within the dyad culminated in a classic paper, entitled "The Capacity to be Alone" (1958a), where Winnicott advanced the insight that solitude involves an object relation. "The capacity to be alone depends on the existence of a good object in the psychic reality of the individual" (pp. 31-32). Winnicott attributed the capacity to be alone to an infant's healthy development through infantile solipsism. "Maturity and the capacity to be alone implies that the individual has had the change through good-enough mothering to build up a belief in a benign environment. This belief is built up through a repetition of satisfactory instinctual gratifications" (p. 32).

Winnicott followed Freud in maintaining that no developmental stage is ever completely outgrown and dissolved. "The *early stages are never truly abandoned*, so that in a study of the individual of whatever age all the primitive as well as the later types of environmental requirements will be found" (Winnicott, 1988, p. 158). Because the capacity to be alone depends on the ego's relation to the facilitating environment not only in infancy, but throughout life, Winnicott (1958a) advanced an original theory of solipsistic mystical experiences.

> I would now like to go a little further in speculating in regard to the ego-relatedness and the possibilities of experience within this relationship, and to consider the concept of an *ego orgasm*....At the moment I wish to leave out consideration of the pathological...and to ask only whether there can be a value in thinking of *ecstasy* as an ego orgasm. In the normal person a highly satisfactory experience such as may be obtained at a concert or at the theatre or in a friendship may deserve a term such as ego orgasm, which draws attention to the climax and the importance of the climax. It may be thought unwise that the word orgasm should

> be used in this context; I think that even so there is room for a discussion of the climax that may occur in satisfactory ego-relatedness. One may ask: when a child is playing, is the whole of the game a sublimation of id-impulse? Could there not be some value in thinking that there is a difference of *quality* as well as of *quantity of id* when one compares the game that is satisfactory with the instinct that crudely underlies the game? The concept of sublimation is fully accepted and has great value, but it is a pity to omit reference to the vast difference that exists between the happy playing of children and the play of children who get compulsively excited and who can be seen to be very near to an instinctual experience....we leave out something vital if we do not remember that the play of a child is not happy when complicated by bodily excitements with their physical climaxes.
>
> The so-called normal child is able to play, to get excited while playing, and to feel satisfied with the game, without feeling threatened by a physical orgasm of local excitement.....In my opinion, if we compare the happy play of a child or the experience of an adult at a concert with a sexual experience, the difference is so great that we should do no harm in allowing a different term for the description of the two experiences. Whatever the unconscious symbolism, the quantity of actual physical excitement is minimal in the one type of experience and maximal in the other. We may pay tribute to the importance of ego-relatedness *per se* without giving up the ideas that underlie the concept of sublimation. (pp. 34-35)

Federn (1952, p. 353) had previously conceptualized ecstasy as a solipsistic mental orgasm. What was new in Winnicott's formulation was his assertion that the ecstasy is not solitary but instead involves an internalized object relationship. Experience of a good-enough facilitating environment is an integral component of both infantile solipsism and mystical ecstasy; and a similar conjunction of sexual experience and ego-relatedness is to be seen in happy play, friendship, a concert, and the theater.

Revisiting the concept five years later, Winnicott (1963a) further developed its implications for mystical experience. "Perhaps not enough attention has been paid to the mystic's retreat to a position in which he can communicate secretly with subjective objects and phenomena, the loss of contact with the world of shared reality being counterbalanced by a gain in terms of feeling real" (pp. 185-86). The mystic who is alone is simultaneously in communion with objects and phenomena that are perceived solipsistically as subjective components of himself. At the same time, these objects and phenomena contribute to the feeling that self is real. Winnicott's formulation collapsed Freud's distinction between the oceanic feeling of earliest infancy and theistic mystical experiences, such as Deutsch (1989) had addressed. There is no such thing as a baby; solipsism is always unconsciously interpersonal. Mysticism does not have to be connected secondarily with religious theism; the template for theism is already present in the environmental mother of earliest infancy.

THE INCOMMUNICADO ELEMENT

Because the capacity for communication required unit status, Winnicott concluded that the core of the personality that is a lifelong residue of infantile solipsism permanently preserves a non-communicating isolation from external reality.

> I suggest that in health there is a core to the personality that corresponds to the true self of the split personality; I suggest that this core never communicates with the world of perceived objects, and that the individual person knows that it must never be communicated with or be influenced by external reality....Although healthy persons communicate and enjoy communicating, the other fact is equally true, that *each individuate is an isolate, permanently non-communicating permanently unknown, in fact unfound.*
>
> In life and living this hard fact is softened by the sharing that belongs to the whole range of cultural experience. At the centre of each person is an incommunicado element, and this is sacred and most worthy of preservation....the traumatic experiences that lead to the organization of primitive defences belong to the threat to the isolated core, the threat of its being found, altered, communicated with. The defence consists in a further hiding of the secret self, even in the extreme to its projection and to its endless dissemination. Rape, and being eaten by cannibals, these are mere bagatelles as compared with the violation of the self's core, the alteration of the self's central elements by communication seeping through the defences. For me this would be the sin against the self. (Winnicott, 1963a, p. 187)

Winnicott's concept of the incommunicado core of the true self arrived him at a formulation of "quietude...linked with stillness" that is tantamount to the introspective mysticism that he otherwise rejected. "I am putting forward and stressing the importance of the idea of the *permanent isolation of the individual* and claiming that at the core of the individual there is no communication with the not-me world either way. Here quietude is linked with stillness" (Winnicott, 1963a, pp. 189-90). In a later phrasing, however, Winnicott (1965) located the isolation of the true self within an active life in the world, arriving at the extrovertive mystical stance that was his own.

> A principle governing human life could be formulated in the following words: only the true self can feel real, but the true self must never be affected by external reality, must never comply. When the false self becomes exploited and treated as real there is a growing sense in the individual of futility and despair. Naturally in individual life there are all degrees of this state of affairs so that commonly the true self is protected but has some life and the false self is the social attitude. At the extreme of abnormality the false self can easily get itself mistaken for real, so that the real self is under threat of annihilation; suicide can then be a reassertion of the true self. (p. 133)

In this formulation, the isolation of the self is less an experiential state of being than a desideratum, an ego ideal, toward which the true self aspires.

BELIEF-IN

In correspondence with the Jungian analytical psychologist, Michael Fordham, Winnicott (1987) wrote that whenever critics accused him of being irreligious, it "always turned out that what they were annoyed about was that I was not myself religious in their own particular way" (p. 75). The distinction in Winnicott's mind between being religious and being religious in a particular way also informs his application of his ideas about the capacity to be alone to the circumstance of religion. Rather than to conceptualize religion in terms of the divine object of its belief, Winnicott discussed the very capacity for belief or, as he preferred to say, belief-in. Fromm had similarly written of faith as an attitude, but Winnicott added that belief-in has its foundation in the infant's relation to the facilitating environment. Once the capacity for belief-in has been established developmentally in relation to the environmental mother, it can be applied at later developmental stages to the objects of religion (Winnicott, 1963d, p. 93).

Winnicott's concept of "belief-in" was consistent with his maintenance of methodological agnosticism in psychoanalysis. In the course of a discussion of the transitional object, Winnicott (1989) noted the religious parallel.

> In theology the same thing appears in the interminable discussion around the question: is there a God? if God is a projection, even so is there a God who created me in such a way that I have the material in me for such a projection? Aetiologically, if I may use a word here that usually refers to disease, the paradox must be accepted, not resolved. The important thing for me must be, have I got it in me to have the idea of God?--if not, then the idea of God is of no value to me (except superstitiously). (p. 205)

The capacity for belief-in God is a psychoanalytic concern, and a capacity for belief-in must exist before it is possible to reach the further question of the existence of God, without foreclosing the issue through neurotic inhibition. Winnicott left open the possibility, addressed explicitly by Pruyser (1974), that if a capacity for belief-in does exist, the question of belief in God as distinct from belief in something else may not be a psychoanalytic concern, because it might be considered analogous to a preference for jazz over against classical music. Psychoanalytic concern pertains to the clinical question of mental conflict, whether a particular belief-in causes or is symptomatic of mental suffering that can be relieved through psychoanalysis.

Winnicott (1963d) connected his understanding of "belief-in" with Freud's concept of the superego, which he viewed as a benign agency: "The good alternative has to do with the provision of those conditions for the infant and child that enable such things as trust and 'belief in', and ideas of right and wrong, to develop out of the working of the individual child's inner processes. This could be called the evolution of a personal superego" (p. 94). For Winnicott, the superego has pre-Oedipal foundations in the facilitating environment of earliest infancy. The internalization of the mother is at work in the pre-moral capacities for object relating, belief-in, and ego orgasm, and also in the intrinsically moral capacities for concern and object usage, and the capacity to be alone. In keeping with his appreciation of the superego's positive features, Winnicott (1960a, p. 470) noted, "It is in health only that the classical superego...can be observed."

Because healthy infantile development involves the achievement of the capacity for belief-in, religiosity develops spontaneously and naturally in health.

> In regard to religion, and the idea of a god, there are clearly the extremes of those who do not know that the child has a capacity to create a god so that they implant the idea as soon as possible, and there are those who wait and see the results of their efforts to meet the needs of their developing infant. These latter, as I have already said, will introduce the family gods to the child when the child has reached to the stage for their acceptance. In the latter case, there is the minimum of set pattern; in the first case the set pattern is what is wanted, and the child can only accept or reject this essentially foreign thing, the implanted god concept. (Winnicott, 1963d, pp. 100-1)

In tracing both the capacity to be alone and the capacity for "belief-in" to the infant's relation to the facilitating environment, Winnicott was implicitly accounting for the theistic unitive experiences that would have been known to him from his Methodist upbringing. He was presumably familiar with Methodist accounts of justification experiences; but even if he was not, the Methodist hymns that he enjoyed singing throughout his life, for example, while walking up and down the stairs in his home (Kahr, 1996, p. 105), were filled with mystical ideas of the omnipresence of God, his spirit, and power.

WINNICOTT'S CLINICAL TECHNIQUE

Winnicott's theories led him to conceptualize psychoanalytic treatment as a process that facilitates primary creativity and, with it, the patient's access to the true self. Because Rank and Fromm had similar therapeutic ambitions, they redesigned their clinical techniques in order to further their goals. Winnicott's clinical procedures conformed with the technical innovations that Sandor Ferenczi and Michael Balint had devised, beginning in the early 1930s. Like Balint, Winnicott believed that the psychoanalytic process was not an artifact of psychoanalytic technique. Psychoanalytic technique was nothing more than an adjunct to a spontaneously occurring therapeutic process. "What we become able to do enables us to co-operate with the patient in following the *process*, that which in each patient has its own pace and which follows it own course; all the important features of this process derive from the patient and not from ourselves as analysts" (Winnicott, 1955b, p. 278).

Winnicott conceptualized the therapeutic process in terms of the true self's actualization. "At the extreme of illness I see the true self as a potentiality, hidden and preserved by the compliant false self" (Winnicott,

1965, p. 9). Winnicott conceptualized the therapeutic process in terms of early ego development; but his theories of early ego development were reconstructions that were based on clinical work with older children and adults. Because he retrojected into infancy the sequence of events during psychoanalysis, his reasoning was circular. Rank and Fromm dispensed with the trope of infancy, while working directly with the here-and-now of the psychoanalytic situation. Winnicott unwittingly achieved much the same practical end by watching for allegedly developmental milestones in the psychoanalytic situation.

> For a full understanding, however, it must be remembered that the *early stages are never truly abandoned*, so that in a study of the individual of whatever age all the primitive as well as the later types of environmental requirements will be found; and in child care as well as in psycho-therapy it is necessary all the time to be watching for the emotional age *at the moment* in order that the appropriate emotional environment can be provided. (Winnicott, 1988, p. 158)

Winnicott found it more effective to work with the patient's subjective experiences than to engage the patient in an intellectualized theoretical understanding of the patient's defense mechanisms. "In the False Self area of our analytic practice we find we make more headway by recognition of the patient's non-existence than by a long-continued working with the patient on the basis of ego-defence mechanisms" (Winnicott, 1960c, p. 152). The false self *was* a defense mechanism, but the therapeutic process was not facilitated by its discussion. What helped was talking about the patient's experience of unreality. Knowledge about was unhelpful; direct experience, knowledge of, was where therapy could be accomplished.

To facilitate the patient's transition from the object-relating of the transitional stage to the unit status and object use of the stage of concern, Winnicott followed Freud in recommending that the patient be kept in a state of deprivation. "The change of the object from 'subjective' to 'objectively perceived' is jogged along less effectually by satisfactions than by dissatisfactions" (Winnicott, 1963a, p. 181). The frustration of the patient was to include a benign but uncompromising withstanding of the patient's aggression.

> [The analyst] will find that after 'subject relates to object' comes 'subject destroys object' (as it becomes external); and then may come '*object survives* destruction by the subject'. But there may

> or may not be survival. A new feature thus arrives in the theory of object-relating. The subject says to the object: 'I destroyed you', and the object is there to receive the communication. From now on the subject says: 'Hullo object!' 'I destroyed you.' 'I love you.' 'You have value for me because of your survival of my destruction of you.' (Winnicott, 1969b, pp. 105-6)

Thinking in Kleinian terms of the expulsion or evacuation of the unwanted portions of the self, Winnicott (1969b) suggested that "the destruction plays its part in making the reality, placing the object outside the self" (p. 106). Rank had addressed equivalent clinical phenomena as attainments of negative will.

Apart from these specific recommendations regarding particular phases of the therapeutic process, Winnicott advised analysts to follow Ferenczi (1932) and Balint (1937) in offering humanity, kindness or at least benign tolerance that avoided re-traumatizing patients.

> Good enough adaptation *by the analyst* produces a result which is exactly that which is sought, namely, a shift in the patient of the main site of operation from a false to a true self. There is now for the first time in the patient's life an opportunity for the development of an ego, for its integration from ego nuclei, for its establishment as a body ego, and also for its repudiation of an external environment with the initiation of a relatedness to objects. (Winnicott, 1956b, p. 298)

Winnicott's remarks concerning the analyst's management of countertransference similarly implied the compassion, kindness, and caring that Ferenczi had recommended. "In particular I have had to learn to examine my own technique whenever difficulties arose, and it has always turned out in the dozen or so resistance phases that the cause was in a countertransference phenomenon which necessitated further self-analysis in the analyst" (Winnicott, 1955b, p. 280). Winnicott (1960b) objected to the expanded uses of the term countertransference that were becoming fashionable among Kleinian analysts.

> Would it not be better at this point to *let the term countertransference revert to its meaning* of that which we hope to eliminate by selection and analysis and the training of analysts? This would leave us free to discuss the many interesting things that analysts can do with psychotic patients who are temporarily re-

> gressed and dependent for which we could use Margaret Little's term: the analyst's total response to the patient's needs. (p. 164)

Winnicott recognized that the provision of a good-enough environment cultivated the patient's dependency. "The patient must become highly dependent, even absolutely dependent, and these words are true even when there is a healthy part of the personality that acts all along as an ally of the analyst and in fact tells the analyst how to behave" (Winnicott, 1960b, p. 163). The patient's security in the environment that the analyst provided made possible the patient's engagement in "a regression in search of the true self" (Winnicott, 1955b, p. 280). Building on the work of Balint, Winnicott (1955b) suggested that there are "two kinds of regression in respect of instinct development, the one being a going back to an early failure situation and the other to an early success situation" (p. 282). Regression to the early success situation is integral to the therapeutic process. "The patient needs to reach back through the transference trauma to the state of affairs that obtained before the original trauma" (Winnicott, 1963e, p. 209)

> One has to include in one's theory of the development of a human being the idea that it is normal and healthy for the individual to be able to defend the self against specific environmental failure by a *freezing of the failure situation*. Along with this goes an unconscious assumption (which can become a conscious hope) that opportunity will occur at a later date for a renewed experience in which the failure situation will be able to be unfrozen and re-experienced, with the individual in a regressed state, in an environment that is making adequate adaptation. The theory is here being put forward of regression as part of a healing process, in fact, a normal phenomenon that can properly be studied in the healthy person. (Winnicott, 1955b, p. 281)

Importantly, Fromm's effort to engage his patients in an interpersonal relationship along the lines of Buber's dialogical encounter of an I with a Thou cultivated an emotional state in the patient that was very similar to the therapeutic regression of Winnicott's patients to the early success situation of the true self. Fromm offered himself as an object for the patient's empathic encounter in order to arrive the patient swiftly at the sense of well-being that Winnicott required his patients to come to on their own. Although the styles of the two techniques appealed to different client populations, they provided patients with closely similar corrective emotional experiences. The experiences differed, however, in their relations to reality.

Perhaps because Winnicott did not share Fromm's social agenda, he was unconcerned about the dream-like quality of regressed experience. Winnicott's goal was the patient's belated completion of early ego development; and in Winnicott's (1963b) view, "that which has been dreamed and remembered and presented is within the capacity of the ego-strength and structure" (p. 254).

Winnicott's use of play techniques in the psychoanalytic treatment of children led him to claim that "in playing, and perhaps only in playing, the child or adult is free to be creative" (Winnicott, 1971, p. 62). Winnicott saw free association as play on the part of adult patients (p. 59). When an analyst's interpretations are offered with a light touch as possibilities, speculations, and guesses, they constitute play on the part of the analyst. The psychoanalytic situation ideally involves analyst and patient playing together. "If the therapist cannot play, then he is not suitable for the work. If the patient cannot play, then something needs to be done to enable the patient to become able to play, after which psychotherapy may begin" (Winnicott, 1971, p. 63).

The analyst's attempt to engage the patient in play ran the risk of being experienced by the patient as a demand for compliance (Winnicott, 1971, pp. 59-60). Rank had interpreted the patient's resistance as negative will, a developmental precursor of creative will. Winnicott instead regarded resistance as evidence that the analyst's attempt to play had failed and was counterproductive. Winnicott agreed with Balint (1969) that the process of regression, initially to the transference trauma and eventually to the early success situation, resolves the resistance spontaneously. Implicitly agreeing with Rank, Winnicott (1971) attributed curative value to the patient's playful experience of creativity (p. 59).

Winnicott portrayed himself in writing as an extreme example of the silent analyst; but Modell (1985) noted that his case presentations indicate "a fairly active stance." Khan (1974, p. 205) explained that Winnicott's practice of "not-interpreting" occurred during a late phase of an analysis, after "intensive analytic work" had successfully mitigated the patient's resistances, and the analyst needed only to hold the patient while the patient discovered her authentic being.

Effective interpretation had to avoid the patient's compliance. Otherwise the analyst would be a subjectively perceived object and a false self would be inculcated in the patient. "This interpreting by the analyst, if it is to have effect, must be related to the patient's ability *to place the analyst outside the area of subjective phenomena*" (Winnicott, 1969b, p. 102). Even when the analyst permitted the patient to maintain unit status, the analyst had to avoid upstaging the patient. "The patient's creativity can be only too easily stolen by a therapist" (Winnicott, 1971, p. 67).

> It is only in recent years that I have become able to wait and wait for the natural evolution of the transference arising out of the patient's growing trust in the psychoanalytic technique and setting, and to avoid breaking up this natural process by making interpretations. It will be noticed that I am talking about the making of interpretations and not about interpretations as such. It appalls me to think how much deep change I have prevented or delayed in patients *in a certain classification category* by my personal need to interpret. If only we can wait, the patient arrives at understanding creatively and with immense joy, and I now enjoy this joy more than I used to enjoy the sense of having been clever. I think I interpret mainly to let the patient know the limits of my understanding. The principle is that it is the patient and only the patient who has the answers. (Winnicott, 1969b, pp. 101-2)

Winnicott drew the traditional distinction between the analyst's interpretation and the patient's insight or understanding. He recognized that the latter alone was therapeutic. Writing of the treatment of children, he stated: "The significant moment is that at which *the child surprises himself or herself*" (Winnicott, 1971, p. 59). Stifling the patient's creativity by interpreting too much ran the risk of being traumatic for the patient.

> The student analyst sometimes does better analysis than he will do in a few years' time when he knows more. When he has had several patients he begins to find it irksome to go as slowly as the patient is going, and he begins to make interpretations based not on material supplied on that particular day by the patient but on his own accumulated knowledge or his adherence for the time being to a particular group of ideas. This is of no use to the patient. The analyst may appear to be very clever, and the patient may express admiration, but in the end the correct interpretation is a trauma, which the patient has to reject, because it is not his. He complains that the analyst attempts to hypnotize him, that is to say, that the analyst is inviting a severe regression to dependence, pulling the patient back to a merging in with the analyst. (Winnicott, 1960d, p. 51)

Winnicott's notion of an effective interpretation was consistent with his understanding of the contribution of the maternal environment to the formation of the true self during the holding stage. The challenge is to allow the patient to see the patient reflected in the analyst's interventions.

> Psychotherapy is not making clever and apt interpretations; by and large it is a long-term giving the patient back what the patient brings. It is a complex derivative of the face that reflects what is there to be seen. I like to think of my work this way, and to think that if I do this well enough the patient will find his or her own self, and will be able to exist and to feel real. Feeling real is more than existing; it is finding a way to exist as oneself, and to relate to objects as oneself, and to have a self into which to retreat for relaxation. (Winnicott, 1967b, pp. 137-38)

Like Rank and Fromm, Winnicott was in favor of non-analytic interventions whenever they were warranted and effective. Anti-social tendencies in children warranted child care, not analysis (Winnicott, 1956a, p. 315). Psychotic disorders benefited from analyses of early ego development rather than interpretations of the Oedipus complex. "If our aim continues to be to verbalize the nascent conscious in terms of the transference, then we are practising analysis; if not, then we are analysts practising something else that we deem to be appropriate to the occasion. And why not?" (Winnicott, 1962a, pp. 169-70).

CONCLUDING REFLECTIONS

Winnicott provided an object relations approach to early ego development that traced the infant-mother dyad from infantile solipsism through a transitional (paranoid-schizoid) stage to the stage of concern involving unit status and objective objects. This theory allowed him to understand pathologies of the self as consequences of environmental failures that the infant understands solipsistically. The retreat from the environment, which the infant experienced as an inhibition of the self and its creativity, leaves a false self in its wake. The false self is symptomatic of the repression of primary creativity. Therapy is accomplished through regression, first to the transferential intensity of the false self, but eventually to the true self at its core. Because the theory reconstructed early development by retrojecting the stages of therapeutic change into infancy, its clinical utility is unaffected by revisions in our knowledge of infantile development.

In Winnicott's model of the psyche, the relation of infant and mother in early ego development is invariably paradoxical. In the solipsistic holding stage, the facilitating environment is included within the self; in the transitional stage, transitional phenomena are subjective objects that both are and are not parts of the self. And in the stage of concern, when objects are objective, they are paradoxically also internal, providing emotional support and danger in imagination, despite their physical externality and absence. In all of the developmental phases, the confluence of subjective fantasy and objective reality makes everything illusory.

Because Winnicott equated "mysticism" with the interiorism of Quietism, he did not call himself a mystic; and the psychoanalytic mainstream has embraced large portions of his thought in ignorance that his views were mystical. From the perspective of the comparative study of mysticism, Winnicott's theories and clinical technique may be counted as a distinctive formulation of extrovertive mysticism. Winnicott saw mystical experience as an ecstatic consciousness, an ego orgasm, of the incommunicado element at the solipsistic core of the self; and he regarded religious ideas of God as heirs to early infantile appreciations of the mother, variously as a facilitating environment, subjective object, and objective object. In the absence of a "good enough" experience of the mother during infancy, religious ideas of God have no appeal; and atheism joins the false self as a symptom of self pathology.

Although Winnicott did not use the terms as I do, theism, as he understood it, is a manifestation of the mystical, as I define the term; and a person with a false self organization is, among other things, a failed mystic who has substituted a compliant false self for the mysticism of his true self. Whether a person with a false self organization is an unconscious mystic whose true self is repressed, or is only a secret mystic whose true self is conscious but kept private, depends on the severity of the illness.

Seven

The Cosmic Narcissism of Heinz Kohut

Heinz Kohut, the founder of self psychology, regarded his work as an outgrowth of Heinz Hartmann's formulations of ego psychology, and Hartmann agreed. Long after his break with ego psychology, Kohut (1990b) reminisced: "I am very happy that he [Hartmann] still read the manuscript of my *Analysis of the Self* (1971) and gave it his approval" (p. 285). Like Hartmann's ego psychology, Kohut's self psychology limited the contents of the unconscious to psychic energies and allocated all ideation and mental structure to consciousness. Kohut's concept of the cohesion of the self recast Thomas M. French's characterization of ego strength in terms of the ego's integration and its resilience. The consensus among psychoanalytic mystics that integration pertains to the total personality was shared by neither Hartmann nor Kohut, for whom integration was limited to the ego or self, respectively.

Kohut did not claim to be a mystic. He gave one interview where he expressed belief in God, but he was otherwise extremely reticent about personal matters. He kept secret, for example, that he was of Jewish descent. He was named Wolf Hersh in Yiddish at his circumcision in 1913 and was bar mitzvahed at the Mullnergasse synagogue in 1926. He fled Austria after the Nazi Anschluss in 1938. Many close friends at the University of Vienna during the 1930s were nevertheless unaware that he was Jewish, as were his colleagues at the Chicago Psychoanalytic Institute. Kohut told no Jewish jokes, never spoke Yiddish, and appeared baffled when Jewish cultural traditions were mentioned. In Chicago, he attended the Unitarian Church in Hyde Park on a regular basis, befriended its minister, and sometimes spoke to the congregation (Strozier, 2003, pp. 245, 252-53). The mystical character of self psychology must speak for itself.

Self psychology as a whole is explicitly concerned with narcissism, which it conceptualizes as a discrete developmental line that commences with primary narcissism and ends with the mature narcissism of adulthood. Self psychology may consequently be seen in its entirety as a psychology of the mystical. Kohut referred to mystical experiences only rarely. The principal discussion occurs in his 1966 article, "Forms and Transformations of Narcissism." Near the beginning of the essay, Kohut noted the versatility of narcissistic states: "In certain psychological states the self may expand far beyond the borders of the individual, or it may shrink and become identical with a single one of his actions or aims" (p. 429). Expansions of the self to become co-extensive with all being, or the perceptible cosmos, and its shrinkage to become nothingness, are classical varieties of mystical experience. The article's major consideration of mysticism, which speaks of the self's "participation in a supraindividual and timeless existence," may be quoted in full.

> More difficult still, however, than the acknowledgment of the impermanence of object cathexes is the unqualified intellectual and emotional acceptance of the fact that we ourselves are impermanent, that the self which is cathected with narcissistic libido is finite in time. I believe that this rare feat rests, not simply on a victory of autonomous reason and supreme objectivity over the claims of narcissism, but on the creation of a higher form of narcissism. The great who have achieved the outlook on life to which the Romans referred as living *sub specie aeternitatis* do not display resignation and hopelessness but a quiet pride which is often coupled with mild disdain of the rabble which, without being able to delight in the variety of experiences life has to offer, is yet afraid of death and trembles at its approach....
>
> Only through an acceptance of death, Goethe says here, can man reap all that is in life....I have little doubt that those who are able to achieve this ultimate attitude toward life do so on the strength of a new, expanded, transformed narcissism: a cosmic narcissism which has transcended the bounds of the individual.
>
> Just as the child's *primary empathy* with the mother is the precursor of the adult's ability to be empathic, so his *primary identity* with her must be considered the precursor of an expansion of the self, late in life, when the finiteness of individual existence is acknowledged. The original psychological universe, i.e., the primordial experience of the mother, is "remembered" by many people in the form of the occasionally occurring vague reverberations known by the term "oceanic feeling" (Freud, 1930, pp. 64-73). The achievement--as the certainty of eventual death is fully realized--of a shift of the narcissistic cathexes from the self to a concept of participation in a supraindividual and timeless existence must also be regarded as genetically predetermined by the child's primary identity with the mother. In contrast to the oceanic feeling, however, which is experienced passively (and usually

> fleetingly), the genuine shift of the cathexes toward a cosmic narcissism is the enduring, creative result of the steadfast activities of an autonomous ego, and only very few are able to attain it. (Kohut, 1966, pp. 454-56)

Kohut validated a mystical perspective when he wrote that adult experiences of the oceanic feeling are fleeting experiential counterparts of a cosmic narcissism that is a rarely achieved, characterological development. J. Jones (2002, p. 29) noted that Kohut referred, a few pages later in the same essay, "to some kind of psycho-spiritual practice," when he asserted that "a genuine decathexis of the self can only be achieved slowly by an intact, well-functioning ego; and it is accomplished by sadness as the cathexis is transferred from the cherished self to the supraindividual ideals and to the world with which one identifies" (Kohut, 1966, p. 458). Kohut was more allusive but no less coherent in an earlier paper, where he asserted that "Freud's hypotheses of primary narcissism and primary masochism...lie within the theoretical framework of introspective psychology" (p. 227). In claiming that primary narcissism (Freud, 1914a) is a theory that is premised on evidence that is available through introspection, Kohut referred unmistakably to the oceanic feeling.

Kohut insisted on the scientific rigor of his thinking. He claimed that he spoke "scientifically, i.e., psychologically, about an area to which certain philosophers and theologians refer as existential malaise or existential anxiety" (Kohut, 1978c, p. 751). Like Winnicott, Kohut sometimes explicitly distanced himself from what he described as "mysticism."

> The assertion that the presence of empathy is beneficial per se is a scientific hypothesis and not an outgrowth of vague sentimentality or mysticism. It is the former because it suggests an explanation for certain observable contents and/or sequences of events in man's psychic life; it is not the latter because it is not the expression of hopes or wishes and/or of an openly espoused or more or less hidden morality. The fact is that this hypothesis can be used for the purposes of those who have a moral stake in this area or whose mystical and sentimental bent will lead them to overplaying and overextending its significance--in particular, for example, by seeing it as the *only* psychotherapeutic agent that needs to be paid attention to. (Kohut, 1991, p. 544)

Because Kohut discussed mysticism in popular terms as an unscientific intuitionism, he found his insistence on the scientific character of his thinking to be sufficient grounds to reject allegations of the mystical character of self psychology. His was a psychoanalysis of the mystical but not, in his view, a mystical psychoanalysis. The mysticism that he disavowed was, however, a popular rather than a scholarly understanding of the cross-cultural phenomena. When mysticism is instead defined on the criteria of the academic study of religion, it can be meaningful to speak of "rational mysticism" (Bakan, 1966), along with natural theology (Paley, 1819; C. Webb, 1915), as an approach to religion that is premised, like science, on the evidence of nature and reason. Jones (2002, p. 29) noted a rare passage where Kohut called for precisely such a mysticism. Kohut (1985) wrote:

> The survival of Western man, and perhaps of mankind altogether, will in all likelihood be neither safeguarded by "the voice of the intellect" alone, that great utopian hope of the Enlightenment and Rationalism of the 18th and 19th centuries; nor will it be secured through the influence of the teachings of the orthodox religions. Will a new religion arise which is capable of fortifying man's love for its old and new ideals...the transformation of narcissism into the spirit of religiosity...could it be that a new, rational religion might arise, an as yet uncreated system of mystical rationality...? (p. 70)

In the same essay, Kohut (1985, p. 71) called for psychoanalysis's "amalgamation with mystical modes of thinking." I would like to suggest that Kohut was calling for public acceptance of what was already the case: that self psychology is a thoroughly mystical approach to psychotherapy. Kohut asserted that a developmental progression from the primary narcissism of the newborn to the cosmic narcissism of adult maturity is natural, valid, and primary. "If I were asked what I consider to be the most important point to be stressed about narcissism I would answer: Its independent line of development, from primitive to the most mature, adaptive, and culturally valuable" (Kohut, 1972, p. 615). Interpersonal ("object") relations are implicitly derivative and secondary.

Kohut acknowledged that his privileging of primary narcissism was a matter of personal inclination.

> [I] postulate two separate and largely independent developmental lines: one which leads from autoerotism via narcissism to object love; another which leads from autoerotism via narcissism to higher forms and transformations of narcissism....I am inclined to believe that the imputing to the very small child of the capacity

> for even rudimentary forms of object love (not to be confused, of course, with object relations) rests on retrospective falsifications and on adultomorphic errors in empathy. (Kohut, 1971, p. 220)

Presumably inspired by Glover's and Winnicott's ideas of early ego development, which he applied instead to the self, Kohut (1971, p. 29) postulated that a "*stage of the fragmented self* corresponds to the developmental phase to which Freud (1914a) referred as the *stage of autoerotism.*" This correlation of self with id made Kohut's thinking incommensurate with Winnicott's discussions exclusively of the ego. Kohut (1971, p. 31) coordinated the subsequent stage of narcissism (Freud, 1914a), which involved the ego, with what he called the "stage of the cohesive self." In Kohut's view, the clinical treatment of patients who suffer analyzable narcissistic issues induces a transference that reactivates, or regresses to, the cohesive self. Treatment is contraindicated when the transference risks reactivating the underlying fragmentation.

> The pathogenic nucleus of the analysand's personality becomes activated in the treatment situation and itself enters a specific transference with the analyst before it is gradually dissolved in the working-through process which enables the patient's ego to obtain dominance in this specific area. Such a process must, however, not be set in motion if the transference regression would lead to a severe fragmentation of the self, i.e., to a chronic prenarcissistic stage in which even the narcissistic bonds with the therapist (which are characteristically established in the analysis of narcissistic personality disorders) are destroyed. (Kohut, 1971, pp. 13-14)

Kohut (1977) expressed the same concept in a different manner when he wrote: "The deepest analysis of either one of these two clinical manifestations ["the grandiose self...and...the idealized object"] does not, however, lead to a bedrock of drives, but to narcissistic injury and depression" (p. 173). A fragmented self, to which narcissistic injury and depression revert at their deepest level, underlies the cohesive self. The regression to undifferentiation that Milner, Ehrenzweig, and Winnicott welcomed for the access it provided to the wellsprings of creativity, Kohut instead feared. Narcissism, as he understood it, could not tolerate a creative surrender. What Kohut diagnosed as healthy narcissism accordingly remained a false self by Winnicott's standards.

Freud (1914a) had suggested that primary narcissism is outgrown sometime during early infancy only to be replaced, on the one hand, by a secondary narcissism that is devoted to the body-ego and, on the other, by object-relations. Kohut asserted that the replacement of primary narcissism by concepts of self and others traced only a single developmental line. He suggested that primary narcissism also subdivides into two further forms of narcissism: the grandiose self, and the idealized parent imago.

> The equilibrium of primary narcissism is disturbed by the unavoidable shortcomings of maternal care, but the child replaces the previous perfection (a) by establishing a grandiose and exhibitionistic image of the self: *the grandiose self*; and (b) by giving over the previous perfection to an admired, omnipotent (transitional) self-object: *the idealized parent imago*. (Kohut, 1971, p. 25)

Kohut's parenthetical description of "self-object" as "transitional" acknowledged the derivation of his concept from Winnicott's idea of transitional or subjectively perceived objects.

In his early formulations, Kohut invoked the term "narcissistic cathexis" in order to justify his developmental assumption; but he used the term to mean not libido directed at the self, but self-love that may be directed at either the self or an object. "Narcissism, within my general outlook, is defined not by the target of the instinctual investment (i.e., whether it is the subject himself or other people) but by the nature or quality of the instinctual charge" (p. 26). Kohut's re-definition of narcissistic cathexis makes no sense in the context of Freud's theories, but can be seen as logically necessary if one postulates a developmental line that extends from infantile narcissism to the cosmic narcissism of mystical experience. A developmental line presupposes the continuity of some quiddity that undergoes development. When Kohut abandoned the concept of psychic energy, he referred to the continuous factor as the self. "The postulate of a single, central self leads toward an elegant and simple theory of the mind--but also toward an abrogation of the importance of the unconscious" (Kohut, 1978a, p. 659). If a mystical vision of the self is to be found at both the deepest unconscious and highest conscious levels of the mind, its relation to consciousness is reduced to the status of a secondary variable.

Kohut's ideas of both childhood development and clinical progress proceeded from the premise that the naive solipsism of archaic narcissism, which is reactivated in the oceanic feeling, is optimally reconciled with the objective nature of reality. This project may be described in mystical terms as a gradual transformation of the one to provide a place for the many within itself. Infantile narcissism imagines its infinity; mature narcissism recognizes the finite self as a component that participates within a greater infinity. Kohut conceptualized the transformative maturation as a neutralization of archaic narcissism that makes possible the development of its "higher forms." His theory of narcissistic pathology followed in logical corollary. Neither primary narcissism nor its adult reactivation as the oceanic feeling could reasonably be considered pathological. Pathology had instead to be attributed to the psyche's handling of its narcissism. Pathology arose when an individual failed to acquire the developmental structures with which to organize her inalienable narcissism within the world of her experience.

Pathology was due not to psychic conflict but to arrested development. It was a question not of psychic structures in conflict with archaic narcissism, but of a deficit of structures that were able to modulate archaic narcissism. "The therapist is...not helping the patient increase his mastery over endopsychic processes by making the unconscious conscious (as is the case in the structural disorders), but is attempting to prevent the disintegration of the self by stimulating and supporting the cohesion-producing activity of the patient's reasoning function" (Kohut, 1977, p. 107). Narcissistic rage was symptomatic of the arrested development (Kohut, 1972, p. 644).

In the absence of developmentally acquired structures, a therapist could behave in a manner that avoided exacerbating the deficit. Kohut (1977) recommended a "two-step sequence--step one: empathic merger with the self-object's mature psychic organization and participation in the self-object's experience of an affect signal instead of affect spread; step two: need-satisfying actions performed by the self-object" (p. 87). The analyst's function as the patient's selfobject provides the patient with sufficient safety to reactivate archaic narcissism at whichever stage of development it had been arrested in early childhood. The developmental acquisition of neutralizing structures could then be resumed (Kohut, 1971, pp. 123-24).

What Kohut regarded as curative was not the analyst's conformance with his two-step procedure, but the patient's recovery from the analyst's failures to do so. "The analyst aims at psychic reintegration of the need by reconstructing the period when, as he knows, the need was phase-appropriate and growth promoting. Nongratification of the intensified and distorted need while yet acknowledging appropriateness of its precursor in childhood constitutes *optimal frustration* for the analysand" (Kohut, 1978b, p. 558). Optimal frustration was to be achieved, however, by attempting not to frustrate. "However correct an analyst's theories are, and however open-minded he is in applying them, he cannot avoid erring many times in his understanding of the analysand and in the explanations he offers to him"

(Kohut, 1984, p. 69). The analyst's errors require the patient to develop compensatory structures. "Each small-scale, temporary empathic failure leads to the acquisition of self-esteem-regulating psychological structure in the analysand--assuming, once more, that the analyst's failures have been nontraumatic ones" (Kohut, 1984, p. 67). The result is a gradual increase in self-esteem that provides the strength to resist the reactivation of archaic narcissism.

> Each optimal failure will be followed by an increase in the patient's resilience vis-à-vis empathy failures both inside and outside the analytic situation; that is, after each, optimal new self structures will be acquired and existing ones will be firmed. These developments, in turn, lead to a rise in the patient's basic level of self-esteem, however minimal and by itself imperceptible to analysand and analyst each such accretion of structure may be. (Kohut, 1984, p. 69)

The theory of therapeutic action that was implicit in Hartmann's ego psychology was explicit in Kohut's self psychology. Where ego psychologists aim at increasing ego strength, Kohut aimed at increasing the coherence of the self. In both cases, the analyst aspired to therapeutic changes that were limited to increased resilience, partly through de-sensitization and partly by modifying symptoms (or "defenses") to become more socially adaptive than they had been. Neither school shared Freud's ambition to reduce repression. Hartmann saw no way to reduce the intensity of the id's instinctual energies, and Kohut (1966, p. 458) echoed Hartmann when he wrote that "a genuine decathexis of the self can only be achieved slowly by an intact, well-functioning ego."

Kohut's analyst August Aichhorn had pioneered the psychoanalytic treatment of juvenile delinquents; and Kohut credited Aichhorn's (1936) clinical technique with the inspiration of his own understanding of the analyst's function for the patient. Kohut wrote:

> Anna Freud (1951) described Aichhorn's technique as follows: "Owing to the peculiar narcissistic structure of his personality, the impostor is unable to form object-relationships; nevertheless he can become attached to the therapist through an overflow of narcissistic libido. But his narcissistic transference will set in only where the therapist is able to present to the impostor...a glorified replica of his own delinquent ego and ego ideal" (p. 55).

> In suggesting that the analyst offer himself actively to the patient as an ego ideal, Aichhorn neither differentiated between the ego ideal and its precursor, the idealized parent imago, nor did he assign a separate and special position to the grandiose self. (Kohut, 1971, p. 161)

Building on Freud's (1921) theory that a hypnotist is introjected by the hypnotic subject as the latter's ego ideal, Sachs (1925), Alexander (1925), Glover (1927), Nunberg (1928), and Strachey (1934) had explained that the analysand treats the analyst as her ego ideal or superego. Sterba (1934) departed from the consensus by asserting that the analysand identifies with the observing function of the analyst's ego. Ego psychology followed Sterba even though Bibring (1937) and finally Freud (1940, p. 175) insisted that patients introject their analysts within their superegos. The distinctive component within Aichhorn's (1925) formulation and clinical technique flowed from his realization that juvenile delinquents' narcissism limits both their superegos and their experiences of their analysts. They have ready access to their ego ideals but only limited tolerance for conscious experiences of conscience. They will similarly either derogate and ignore their analysts, or idealize them. In order to establish any therapeutic rapport whatsoever, Aichhorn encouraged the option of idealization. As Kohut appreciated, analysts are idealized when and because they are viewed as selfobjects.

The process of empathic rupture and repair alerts the patient both to the separateness of his analyst and to the renewals of the analyst's esteem. With sufficient acquisition of self-esteem, the patient develops sufficient resilience to be able to seek out real life circumstances that permit the maintenance of self-esteem. "The essence of the psychoanalytic cure resides in a patient's newly acquired ability to identify and seek out appropriate selfobjects--both mirroring and idealizable--as they present themselves in his realistic surroundings and to be sustained by them" (Kohut, 1984, p. 77).

Because Kohut's self psychological formulations can in part be phrased in structural terminology (Josephs, 1989), we may understand Kohut to have asserted that a narcissistic patient who depends for his self-esteem on his analyst's function as a selfobject, experiences the analyst's esteem as self-esteem, and gradually introjects a capacity for self-esteem within his superego. These therapeutic principles correspond precisely to Silberer's (1914) favorable view of mysticism as a modification of the psyche through the articulation and integration of unconscious conscience. Freud's (1914b) definition of his therapeutic aims in terms of transference and resistance differentiated psychoanalysis from Silberer's account of mysticism, and the same considerations apply to Kohut's self psychology. Improving ego-superego relations is not the same as undoing repression.

The better to make himself available to his patients as a self-object, Kohut famously introduced a modification in ego psychology's practice of the psychoanalytic situation. Kohut (1959) argued that introspection and empathy form the distinctive data base of psychoanalysis, and he recommended that analysts maintain a consistently empathic attitude toward their patients. "There are indeed moments in an analysis when even the most cogent and correct interpretation...is...unacceptable to the patient who seeks a comprehensive response to a recent important event in his life, such as a new achievement or the like" (Kohut, 1971, p. 121).

Kohut (1984) appreciated that in recommending empathy, he was conceptualizing a two-body psychology: "Whereas the traditional analyst is on the lookout for discrete 'mechanisms' tied to the functioning of a mental 'apparatus,' the psychoanalytic self psychologist acknowledges his own impact on the field he observes and, through such acknowledgment, broadens his perception of the patient through empathic contact with the data of the patient's inner experiences" (pp. 111-12). Because empathy disturbed neither an idealizing nor a mirror transference, it permitted the patient to experience a relationship with the analyst, as was necessary for the patient to be able to make use of analytic interpretations. "First the analysand must realize that he has been understood; only then, as a second step, will the analyst demonstrate to the analysand the specific dynamic and genetic factors that explain the psychological content he had first empathically grasped" (Kohut, 1977, p. 88). Kohut (1984, p. 82) defined empathy as "the capacity to think and feel oneself into the inner life of another person. It is our lifelong ability to experience what another person experiences, though usually, and appropriately, to an attenuated degree." He naively regarded empathy as a kind of perception, when it is better regarded as a speculative, imaginative conjecture about other people's inner experiences.

Kohut (1971, p. 300; 1977, pp. 304) emphasized that empathy was not to be confused with sympathy. He was not urging an analytic posture of friendliness. "An unusually friendly behavior from the side of the analyst, at times justified by the need to create a therapeutic alliance, is no more advisable in the analysis of narcissistic personality disturbances than it is in the analysis of transference neuroses" (Kohut, 1971, pp. 88-89). "All the evidence now available indicates that being nice, friendly, understanding, warmhearted, and in possession of the human touch cures neither the classical neuroses nor the analyzable disturbances of the self" (Kohut, 1977, p. 95). "The analyst's behavior vis-à-vis his patient should be the expected average one--i.e., the behavior of a psychologically perceptive person vis-à-vis someone who is suffering and has entrusted himself to him for help" (Kohut, 1977, p. 253). At the same time, Kohut (1977) maintained that "the analyst must behave humanly, warmly, and with appropriate empathic responsiveness" (pp. 253-54). The average expectable attitude included a measure of support. "The [patient's] maintenance of self-esteem--and indeed of the self--depends on the unconditional availability of the approving-mirroring selfobject or of the merger-permitting idealized one" (Kohut, 1972, p. 645). The approval that a patient experienced during the mirror transference was less therapeutic, however, than the internalization of psychic structures during the introjection of idealizing transference. "In analysis, the patient's decisive rise in self-esteem was associated more with the availability of an idealizable selfobject than with experiences of direct mirroring" (Kohut, 1984, p. 147).

In 1977, when Kohut parted company with ego psychology, he presented his system of self psychology as separate but equal.

> Self psychology and classical (mental-apparatus) psychology do not need to be integrated; in accordance with a psychological principle of complementarity, they accommodate, side by side, both major aspects of man's total psychology: the psychology of Guilty Man (conflict psychology) and the psychology of Tragic Man (self-psychology). Although it is not necessary to integrate these two depth-psychological approaches, it can be done if one wishes to do so, albeit to the detriment of the scope of the explanatory power of sometimes the one and sometimes the other. Kohut, 1977, p. 206)

In the context of cosmic narcissism, Kohut was claiming that the mystical perception of the one in the many is not to be confused with the sensible perception of self among others. The narcissistic and object-relational lines of development remain distinct. The world might fairly be viewed from both mystical and non-mystical perspectives. It was appropriate to live with their complementarity without attempting their integration, because integration could only be achieved at the expense of one perspective or the other.

Kohut's posthumous publications were less charitable to ego psychology. He complained: "We are steeped in a morality-tinged theory about the therapeutic centrality of truth-facing that is interwoven with a comparably morality-tinged scientific model about the need to make the unconscious conscious" (Kohut, 1984, p. 141). Kohut's criticism of ego psychology's moralism proceeded from his own assumption of a phenomenological orientation (p. 142). Like Rank's will therapy, Kohut's self psychology ultimately valued authenticity above consensual morality. If one's personal values and integrity were narcissistic, the values and integrity that arise from loving others fell by the boards.

> The more deeply an analysis penetrates, the more clearly the analysand recognizes the essence of those deepest of his ambitions and ideals which make up his nuclear self, the narcissistic center of his personality, the more vivid and real becomes the analysand's experience of being able to choose and to decide, the more certain he feels of possessing access to the capacity of exercising his "free will"--whether he chooses to live in accordance with the reality-pleasure principle and, regretfully, curbs the expression of a part of his true self (as most of us do), or whether he chooses to transcend the reality-pleasure principle (i.e., to live "beyond the pleasure principle") and disregarding even his cherished body self, i.e., his need for biological survival, strives toward that fulfillment of his nuclear self which, in the symbolism of religion, is celebrated as saintliness and as eternal life....Once the nuclear self has been laid down, however, it strives--in analogy to the totality of the nonpsychological universe--to fulfill its life-curve. It moves, from the time of its consolidation (its birth) toward the realization of its ambitions and ideals, i.e., toward the realization of the aims of the structures which are the ultimate descendants of the child's grandiosity and exhibitionism and of the child's striving to merge with an idealized self object. And if an individual succeeds in realizing the aims of his nuclear self, he can die without regret: he has achieved the fulfillment of the tragic hero--not the painful death of Guilty Man who strives for pleasure but a death which is "beyond the pleasure principle." (Kohut, 1990a, pp. 212-13)

In closing this passage with an allusion to his 1966 discussion of the equanimity with which the cosmic narcissist greets the prospect of death, Kohut associated the authenticity of the self with its engagement in the mystical.

A further posthumous publication provided a concrete historical example of narcissistic spirituality that embraced God as a selfobject.

> Let me add to these examples of scientific and artistic creativeness the heroes of another sphere: those survivors of the concentration camps who did not lose their humanness during their dehumanizing ordeal because they felt themselves connected with per-

> sonified political or religious idealized figures....During the years in the camps they remained human beings--sharing their rations, for example---and when they eventually returned to freedom they were relatively free of the permanent psychological damage sustained by almost all other survivors. And then there were those touching isolated resisters to Nazi tyranny, standing up alone or in small groups (such as Jägerstätter in Austria and the Scholls in Munich), who, again, were supported by a feeling of merger with personified ideals. They gave over their total selves to these ideals during the time when they performed some of the most awe-inspiring acts of courage of our age. They had prophetic dreams in which God spoke to them--they were undoubtedly not "realistic," "mature," or "independent" in the conventional sense of these terms--and the support that sustained them came not from loving "objects" but from their deep involvement in the narcissistic dynamics of self-selfobject relationships. (Kohut, 1990b, pp. 324-25)

In all, Kohut proposed a theory and clinical technique for the treatment of pathological narcissism; but because his theory of human nature included a place for cosmic narcissism, his approach to psychoanalysis implied an uninterrupted developmental continuity from the psychotherapy of pathology to the spirituality--and potentially the spiritual direction--of cosmic narcissism. Kohut viewed the therapeutic process of self psychology from the perspective of narcissism when he summarized: "The modification of the archaic idealizing cathexes (their taming, neutralization, and differentiation) is achieved by their *passage through the idealized self-objects*" (Kohut, 1971, p. 43). As this formulation would pertain to the cultivation of cosmic narcissism, it would imply that a human spiritual director would optimally be experienced as a manifestation of the one.

CONCLUDING REFLECTIONS

Kohut's concept of narcissistic cathexes or, in his later terminology, a central self permitted him to treat pathological narcissism together with mysticism, creativity, and a good deal else as forms and transformations of narcissism. Kohut (1978a) emphasized the plurality and inconsistency of selves. "We recognize the simultaneous existence of contradictory selves, of different selves of various degrees of stability and of various degrees of important. There are conscious, preconscious, and unconscious selves; there are selves in the ego, the id, and the superego; and we may discover in some of our patients contradictory selves, side by side, in the same psychic agency" (p. 660). In other formulations, Kohut (1984) referred implicitly to the id, ego, and superego as components within the self: "An uninterrupted tension arc from basic ambitions, via basic talents and skills, toward basic ideals....is the dynamic essence of the complete, nondefective self" (pp. 3-4).

Kohut's emphasis on empathy and introspection, his invention of effective approaches in the treatment of narcissistic pathologies, and his recognition of a developmental sequence among narcissistic states, remain enduring contributions to psychoanalysis. Kohut was not the first advocate of empathy; Reik's (1936) criticism of empathy as an inadequate substitute for "listening with the third ear" remains cogent. Reik reserved stronger and more extended criticism, however, for the same kind of mechanical, intellectual analytic listening--listening for data to confirm theory, rather than listening to the patient--that Kohut opposed; and Kohut succeeded where Reik did not, at persuading ego psychologists of better ways to work. After decades of controversy as to whether self psychology was psychoanalytic or not, self psychologists have largely gone their own way, forming their own societies and training programs.

In my view, self psychology advanced our understanding of ego-superego integration but at the expense of abandoning the id-ego integration that Freud thought all important. Self psychology's therapeutic program accords with ego psychology's ambition to ameliorate defenses by making them more socially acceptable. Where ego psychology preserved Freud's clinical techniques well enough to continue to relieve id-ego conflict even though ego psychological theory disbelieves in the possibility of doing so, Kohut changed technique in order to implement Hartmann's perspective more fully, and so had neither the ambition nor the effect of reducing repression. Whether psychoanalysis is defined in a manner that includes or excludes self psychology is a political question. Gifted clinicians of all therapeutic schools--psychoanalytic and otherwise--routinely succeed clinically in ways that their theories cannot explain, and sometimes claim to be impossible. For present purposes, it suffices to remark that self psychology neither aspires to nor accomplishes the type of therapy--structural change in the unconscious that reduces the ego's recourse to repression--that Freud designed his techniques to accomplish. When Rank wrote of going "beyond psychoanalysis" and Fromm conceptualized the "transtherapeutic," they were seeking to build on Freud's foundation while additionally addressing ego-superego integrations. Rank approached the integrations through art, Fromm through existentialism, Zen Buddhism, and Marxism. Kohut came at the same topic of ego-superego integrations--he called them self-idealized selfobject cohesions--through the vicissitudes of narcissism. Neither Rank,

Fromm, Kohut, nor anyone else has had more than a partial view of the topic, which remains unfinished business for future research.

Eight

Hans W. Loewald and Psychic Integration

Marjorie Brierley (1947, 1951) associated the concept of psychic integration with mysticism when she suggested that the Christian mystical life aims at an integration of the ego and the superego, whereas psychoanalysis promotes the integration of the id together with the ego and the superego. The concept of psychic integration implied by Wälder's concept of multiple function was subsequently elaborated further by Hans W. Loewald, an American ego psychologist who frequently departed from Hartmann by reverting to Freud. Loewald is best known for an article entitled, "On the Therapeutic Action of Psycho-Analysis" (1960), that marked the beginning of ego psychologists' disaffection with the program that Anna Freud and Heinz Hartmann had established. Bergmann (2000) summarized:

> For Loewald the aim of psychoanalysis is the resumption of growth rather than the resolution of conflict. Regression during analysis leads to integration on a higher level. Psychoanalysis does not end with the resolution of the transference, but rather by the permanent internalization of the analyst as a new and more mature object. The image of the analyst as a mirror, so important to Freud, gave way to an emphasis on a two-person psychology in which the process of interaction between analyst and analysand is crucial. (p. 61)

Loewald's emphasis on integration also challenged ego psychology's dualistic opposition of the ego and the id. His interest in the concept of psychic integration was informed by close readings of Freud's writings, as well as by his mysticism.

MYSTICAL EXPERIENCES

Although Loewald emphasized integration from his first paper onward, it was only in the 1970s, as the psychedelic era subsided and Eastern meditation practices began to flourish, that Loewald discussed mystical experiences in detail. His formulations privileged the quality of timelessness as a hallmark of mystical experience.

> At one extreme is the experience of eternity where the flux of time is stayed or suspended....Scholastic philosophers speak of the *nunc stans*, the abiding instant, where there is no division of past, present, and future, no remembering, no wish, no anticipation, merely the complete absorption in being, or in that which is....Time as something that, in its modes of past, present, and future, articulates experience and conveys such concepts as succession, simultaneity, and duration is suspended in such a state. Inasmuch as this experience, however, can be remembered, it tends to be described retrospectively in temporal terms which seem to approximate or be similar to such a state.
>
> States of this kind have been described by mystics and are in some respects akin to ecstatic states occurring under the influence of certain drugs or during emotional states of exceptional intensity. In conditions of extreme joy or sadness, sometimes during sexual intercourse and related orgastic experiences, at the height of manic and the depth of depressive conditions, in the depth of bliss or despair, the temporal attributes of experience fall away and only the now, as something outside of time, remains. (Loewald, 1972, pp. 141-42; compare 1978, p. 64)

This passage continued by connecting the experience of timelessness with Freud's remarks on the oceanic feeling.

Loewald discussed experiences of timelessness as rare events. "We know of exceptional and pathological states where the sense of time is "suspended"....in the height of bliss or the depth of despair, the temporal attributes of experience fall away; only a "now," outside time, remains" (Loewald, 1978, p. 64). Similar experiences of lesser intensity are commonplace, however: "All of us know...poignant moments that have this timeless quality: unique and matchless, complete in themselves and somehow containing all there is in experience" (p. 65). The universality of timeless experiences indicates that mystics differ from non-mystics in degree, but not in kind. Everyone is a little bit of a mystic, some few of us more so.

Loewald (1978) discussed experiences of timelessness as products of condensation (p. 65). This suggestion, offered briefly, represents a significant alternative to theories that mystical experience consists of a regression of the ego to early infantile levels of organization. In recognizing that condensation can represent all times as one, Loewald traced mystical experiences to the dreamwork. His views on ecstasy as a fusion of the drives similarly emphasized the id's role in mystical experience. "If you say that I am talking here...of an urge toward the bliss and pain of consuming oneself in the intensity of being lived by the id, you may be right. Ecstatic states, whether induced by drugs or religious and erotic ecstasies, may have this lure where love and self-destruction, Eros and Thanatos are merged into one" (Loewald, 1971a, p. 68).

Loewald (1973) explained ecstatic states as instances, in Kris's (1952) phrase, of "regression in the service of the ego."

> There are other situations and phenomena in adult life in which the subject-object distinction tends to become blurred or temporarily to vanish, as for instance in a passionate love relationship and other "ecstatic" states, which, while rare and exceptional, cannot be called pathological.
>
> We are dealing here with the fact that early levels of psychic development are not simply outgrown and left behind but continue to be active, at least intermittently, during later life including adulthood. They coexist, although overshadowed by later developmental stages, with later stages and continue to have their impact on them. Ernst Kris has discussed these and related problems under the title "regression in the service of the ego," and Freud referred to them as the "general problem of preservation in the sphere of the mind" or of the survival of earlier ego states. (Loewald, 1973, pp. 81-82)

Loewald did not cite Ehrenzweig, but his thought and, indeed, his neologisms were in approximate agreement. It would have been politically awkward--and unpublishable--for an American ego psychologist to have cited a Kleinian until very late in Loewald's life. Ehrenzweig (1948-49) had written of the dedifferentiation and redifferentiation of perception; Loewald (1973) expressed closely similar ideas in reference to the sense of reality: "The distinction between inside and outside--the basis for what we call object relations and objective reality--may become blurred or vanish for certain aspects and during more or less brief periods of reality organization; a dedifferentiation may take place by which the two become re-merged and subsequently re-differentiate from one another in novel ways--psychic events that are most important for the understanding of creative processes" (p. 82).

Loewald agreed with Freud's theory that mystical experiences have their prototype in neonatal experiences.

> We know states of identification where the boundaries between self and object world, between oneself and another person, are blurred or tend to vanish. In the early stages of human life, it seems, such boundaries are not yet established. We are not born with such discriminations, they develop gradually, becoming more or less firmly fixed in the course of childhood. The older, nondiscriminating forms of experience persist behind the more advanced ones. They may come to the fore under certain exceptional conditions: in psychosis, in situations of deep intimacy between people, in some drug-related and in ecstatic states. The intimacy of the infant-mother unity or bond is the prototype. (Loewald, 1978, pp. 35-36)

Loewald used the term "primary narcissism" in many of his writings (1951, 1962a, 1971b, 1978, 1979b), but at the end of his life he opted for a different concept. He had long worked with Freud's (1940) idea of the structural undifferentiation of the neonatal psyche, when he referred to "the ideal undifferentiated phase where neither id nor ego nor environment are differentiated from one another" (Loewald, 1962b, p. 47). Later, and possibly in reaction against Kohut's self psychology, he took the concept a step further. Because the infant's awareness of self originates at the same time as the infant's awareness of others, Loewald (1988b) suggested that "the term *primary narcissism* is imprecise and confusing when used to designate the absence of subject-object differentiation" (p. 17 n. 2). Already in 1962, in advance of Kohut, Loewald had argued: "The narcissistic cathexis, replacing object cathexis in internalization, is secondary and is founded on an older, 'primary' narcissism of which it is a new version" (pp. 264-65). A later formulation deleted the assumption that the original non-differentiation was narcissistic: "The differentiation, within the original matrix, of individual and environment involves the differentiation of narcissistic and object cathexis" (Loewald, 1976, p. 153).

DEVELOPMENT AS INTEGRATION

Loewald's discussions of mystical experience began in the 1970s, but he was concerned with the mystical from his first psychoanalytic publication onward. In an article entitled "Ego and Reality" (1951), Loewald argued that the ego and the sense of reality coincide in primary narcissism.

> We know from considering the development of the ego as a development away from primary narcissism, that to start with, real-

> ity is not outside, but is contained in the pre-ego of primary narcissism, and becomes, as Freud says, detached from the ego. So that reality, understood genetically, is not primarily outside and hostile, alien to the ego, but intimately connected with and originally not even distinguished from it. (Loewald, 1951, p. 8)

Where Winnicott explored the concept, important for object relations theory, that primary narcissism includes perceptions of the mother as a holding or facilitating environment, Loewald formulated a complementary concept that was relevant to existing concerns among ego psychologists. Because primary narcissism includes sense perceptions of external reality, the sense of self and the sense of reality are integrally related throughout life. Loewald's formulation may explain, as Winnicott's cannot, Winnicott's observation that the true self feels real, and the false self does not. Only a self that remains in contact with the sense of reality can feel real.

Freud (1919) had written of the ego's synthetic function, and Nunberg (1931) followed Freud in arguing that the action of Eros on the ego produces the synthetic function, one of whose earliest manifestation is primary narcissism. Loewald inverted the relation between the synthetic function and primary narcissism by interpreting the ego's synthetic function as a tendency to reassert primary narcissism throughout life.

> The ego mediates, unifies, integrates because it is of its essence to maintain, on more and more complex levels of differentiation and objectivation of reality, the original unity. To maintain or constantly re-establish this unity, in the face of a growing separation from what becomes the outside world for the growing human being, by integrating and synthesizing what seems to move further and further away from it and fall into more and more unconnected parts--this is part of the activity of the ego which constitutes it as an organization, in the sense of an agency that organizes. (Loewald, 1951, pp. 11-12)

Loewald (1951) saw the unconscious persistence of primary narcissism both as a motive for the ego's synthetic function and paradoxically as "the source of the deepest dread" (p. 17).

> The unstructured nothingness of identity of "ego" and "reality" represents a threat as deep and frightening as the paternal castration threat. It is the threat of the all-engulfing womb. Dread of the womb and castration fear, both....threaten loss of real-

> ity....Loss of reality, in the sense here intended,....means that the ego-reality integration sinks back, regresses to an earlier level of organization....Ego and reality, in a compulsion neurosis, regress to a magical level of integration, as they regress further in a schizophrenic reaction. (Loewald, 1951, pp. 16-17)

The dread of regression was responsible, in Loewald's view, for the ego's pursuit of ever more differentiated levels of organization. At the same time, the pull of regression--the attraction to the womb--leads to the compromise that is the synthetic function. Synthesis aspires toward unity, but it does so through an integration that is progressive. It does not dedifferentiate as regression does. It accepts higher orders of differentiation but then proceeds to integrate them.

Loewald (1951) also remarked that regression and progression proceed continuously. "If we look closely at people we can see that it is not merely a question of survival of former stages of ego-reality integration, but that people shift considerably, from day to day, at different periods in their lives, in different moods and situations, from one such level to other levels. In fact, it would seem that the more alive people are (though not necessarily more stable), the broader their range of ego-reality levels is" (p. 20).

Loewald's concept that the unconscious persistence of primary narcissism produces the ego's synthetic function, the psyche's tendency toward integration, a dread of regression, and continuous fluctuations in regression and progression, formed a paradigm of ego development into which Loewald fitted further observations over the years. Breaking with Hartmann's ego psychology, Loewald appealed to the precedent and authority of Freud in implicating the id in the integrative activity of the psyche.

> In *An Outline of Psychoanalysis*, [Freud wrote:] "the aim of the first of these basic instincts [Eros] is to establish ever greater unities and to preserve them thus--in short, to bind together"....the aim of the instinct Eros...is clearly seen in terms of integration. It is: "to bind together." (Loewald, 1960, p. 234; citing Freud, 1940, p. 148)

Ego psychology had so biologized Freud's concept of Eros, reducing it from a drive to unity in the cosmos to an instinct of sexuality in animal life, that Loewald's citation of Freud was radically innovative for its time. Loewald reverted to the structural hypothesis as it stood when Nunberg and Sterba wrote around 1930, before the rise of Anna Freud's and Hartmann's ego psychology, with its intrinsic, irreducible antagonism of the ego and the id.

Loewald (1960) differed from Freud and Nunberg, however, in crediting the id with thinking. "The undifferentiating unconscious is a genuine mode of mentation which underlies and unfolds into a secondary process mentation (and remains extant together with it, although concealed by it)" (pp. 64-65).

Again breaking with Hartmann's formulations, Loewald conceptualized the superego along lines consistent with Freud's (1923a) original intention that it account for "the higher, moral, supra-personal side of human nature" (p. 35). In Loewald's view, the superego, no less than the ego and the id, promotes the process of integration. "The superego...would represent the past as seen from a future, the id as it is *to be organized*, whereas the ego proper represents the id as organized at present" (Loewald, 1962b, p. 49). Superego materials are themselves gradually integrated within the ego. "During periods of psychic growth--in childhood as well as in adult life--the change of superego elements into ego elements is a continuing process, it seems. The superego itself, in its turn, receives new elements through interaction with the object world" (Loewald, 1962a, p. 272).

With the whole of the psyche implicated in the process of integration, Loewald (1978) conceptualized both regression and progression as integrative movements.

> We are dealing rather with a circularity or interplay between different levels of mentation....it looks as if there is a need for a conscient appropriation of unconscious experience as well as a need for reappropriating conscient modes (and the corresponding mental contents) into unconscious mental activity--and back again toward consciousness. What counts is this live communication, a mutual shaping, a reciprocal conforming, of levels of mentation. (p. 31)

Loewald's discussion of superego formation in terms of parental identifications that integrate object and subject, led him to challenge orthodox analysts' preoccupation with the Oedipus complex. He formulated the process of identification in a way that applied also to pre-Oedipal identifications.

> We can distinguish two types or stages of identification: those that precede, and are the basis for, object cathexes and those that are the outcome of object cathexes formed in the oedipal phase. The latter constitute the precipitate in the ego which Freud calls the superego; the former constitute the forerunners, the origins of the superego but are, considered in themselves, constituent

> elements of the ego proper. I think it correct to say that the early ("ego") identifications take place during stages of development when inside and outside--ego and objects--are not clearly differentiated, which is to say that the stage where "objects" can be "cathected" is not yet reached or that a temporary regression from this stage has taken place. The later type of identifications, the superego identifications, on the other hand, are identifications with differentiated objects of libidinal and aggressive cathexis....The later identifications thus can be based on the relinquishment of these objects. (Loewald, 1962a, p. 258)

In this formulation, the process of identification was a constant, but the level of the ego's development was a variable that determined whether the identifications contributed to the formation of the ego or the superego.

Loewald's (1952) *pro forma* conformance with psychoanalytic orthodoxy led him to define defense in terms of mechanisms that reflect the ego's shift, in connection with the oedipal stage, from a pleasure ego to a reality ego. "Defense, in the sense in which we speak of it in neurosis, and therefore to a certain degree in normal development, is based on that stage in the development of individual-environment configuration, of ego-reality integration, in which an organized ego and organized reality have been differentiated from each other" (p. 25). At the same time, Loewald's perspective on the pre-Oedipal development of the ego enabled him to endorse some of Melanie Klein's ideas about preoedipal defenses. In presenting Kleinian ideas to ego psychologists, Loewald both left Klein unnamed and avoided use of the term "defenses." He referred instead to processes that serve integration.

> On pre-oedipal levels the integrative processes are those introjective, projective, and identificatory interactions of a narcissistic and magical nature....In the analysis of psychotic states, and of many character disorders, it is these early, predefensive processes of integration, of relatedness to the environment, that represent the main subject and the main problem of our therapeutic endeavor. (Loewald, 1952, pp. 25-26)

Understanding introjection and projection, no differently than the defenses of the oedipal stage, as contributors to ego development, Loewald conceptualized defense in an original manner. Departing from ego psychology's view that defense divides the psyche into defense and defended-against, Loewald looked to the outcome of healthy defense in childhood when defense proves to be a prelude to higher order integration. "Instead of viewing psychic organization as being in the service of defense, we may view defense as being in the service of psychic organization" (Loewald, 1980a, p. 176).

Loewald (1988b) also addressed the topic of sublimation as a component within his model of psychic integration. Freud (1905) had defined sublimation as a means by which drives are "diverted from their sexual use and directed to other ends" (p. 178) "*without* involving repression" (Freud, 1914a, pp. 94-95). E. Jones (1915, p. 82), followed by Glover (1927, p. 491) and Anna Freud (1966, pp. 44, 52, 175), instead asserted that sublimation was a type of displacement, although Anna Freud also acknowledged her father's view that sublimation "pertains rather to the study of the normal than to that of neurosis" (p. 44). The incoherence of postulating a healthy displacement--a wholesome flight from reality--was concealed but not eliminated when Hartmann limited the discussion of sublimation to psychic energy. Hartmann imagined that psychic energies comes in two varieties, sexual and aggressive, that these varieties can be mixed and "neutralized" as though they were an acid and a base, and that sublimation is accomplished through neutralization. Hartmann (1950; 1955) acknowledged that sublimation involves more than neutralization alone, but he never developed a useful formulation. Hartmann (1955) maintained that "sublimation...allows a certain amount of discharge of the original tendencies, provided that their mode (and, often, their aims) have been modified" (p. 231). Kris (1956) argued precisely to the contrary, that what was essential to sublimation was not neutralization, but a change in energy's goal. "Sublimation...refers to the displacement of energy discharge from a socially inacceptable goal to an acceptable one....the more acceptable, i.e., 'higher,' activity can be executed with energy that has retained or regained its original instinctual quality" (pp. 26-27). Loewald (1988b) side-stepped the conundrum by conceptualizing sublimation in terms of the mystical. "Sublimation is a kind of reconciliation of the subject-object dichotomy--and atonement for that polarization (the word *atone* derives from *at one*) and a narrowing of the gulf between object libido and narcissistic libido, between object world and self" (p. 20).

> The "lowest" and "highest" are enveloped as one within an original unitary experience; one *is* the other, and later they can stand for one another, the body and its powers a symbol of the godhead, the deity a symbol of the living sexual body. It is the original unity that is in the process of being restored, or something of it is saved, in sublimation; there is a symbolic *linkage* which constitutes what we call meaning....In such a view, the transmutations of sublimation reveal an unfolding into differentiated ele-

> ments of a oneness of instinctual-spiritual experience: oneness stays alive as connection. (Loewald, 1988b, p. 13)

In Loewald's formulation, value-laden terms such as "higher" and "socially appropriate" are replaced by value-neutral concepts such as unitive and integrative.

Because Loewald saw integration and not the discharge of psychic energy as the psyche's over-riding imperative, he took exception to Freud's (1920a) "Nirvana principle," which held that "the dominating tendency of mental life, and perhaps of nervous life in general, is the effort to reduce, to keep constant or to remove internal tension due to stimuli" (pp. 55-56). Although Freud introduced the term "Nirvana principle" only in 1920, he had attributed pleasure to the reduction of energic tension from his hypnotherapy days onward (Strachey, in Freud, 1894, p. 65). David Rapaport (1960, p. 782; Rapaport & Gill, 1959, p. 802) had interpreted the Nirvana principle as a way of talking about entropy and equated it with the death drive. This formulation made sense of the long-standing puzzle of the death drive, but it left the pleasure principle out of account. Loewald (1960) solved the problem by making the pleasure principle contingent on Eros.

> Satisfaction now has to be understood, not in terms of abolition or reduction of stimulation leading back to a previous state of equilibrium, but in terms of absorbing and integrating stimuli, leading to higher levels of equilibrium....Satisfaction, in this context, is a unifying experience because of the creation of an identity of experience in two systems. (p. 239)

If satisfaction is produced through integration, no further explanation is needed for the ecstasy that attends a mystical experience.

PSYCHOANALYSIS AS INTEGRATION

Freud and Nunberg had credited repression with interrupting the synthetic function of the ego, and they regarded the analytic dissolution of repression as all that had to be accomplished clinically for the synthetic function to be able to resume its operations. These ideas were in abeyance under the hegemony of Hartmann's ego psychology until Loewald restated them.

> The ego's acceptance and inclusion of the repressed may, from the point of view of the constancy or Nirvana principle, be seen as nothing but a defensive operation of a higher order than re-

> pression. But from the point of view of the ego, defense has been replaced by acceptance, the ego has been enriched. For the ego it is a gain in its organization and functioning. (Loewald, 1973, p. 74)

Freud credited the synthetic function with the ego's organization of symptoms as habitual defenses. The restructuring of defenses as adaptations--the therapeutic goal of Hartmann's ego psychology--accomplished something more than was possible for the synthetic function, and Loewald discussed the accomplishment as an instance of integration. The observation implied a novel understanding of the relation of psychoanalysis and the mystical. Where Fromm had seen mysticism as transtherapeutic, and both Milner and Winnicott had seen psychoanalysis as removing inhibitions that blocked both creativity and the mystical, Loewald saw therapeutic change itself as an integrative process in the service of Eros. Psychoanalysis was not a complete program of mysticism, but it was intrinsically and inalienably mystical.

Loewald (1960) conceptualized psychoanalysis as a technique that promoted regression as a prelude to integration (p. 224). By regression, he alluded explicitly to Kris's (1952) phrase "regression in the service of the ego," but he also implied Ehrenzweig's concept of a comparative dedifferentiation of the unconscious. Loewald credited interpretation with promoting regression at the same time as it proceeds from a higher integrative level, belonging to the analyst, toward which the patient can aspire.

> The interpretation takes with the patient the step towards true regression, as against the neurotic compromise formation, thus clarifying for the patient his true regression level, which has been covered and made unrecognizable by defensive operations and structures. Secondly, by this very step it mediates to the patient the higher integrative level to be reached. (Loewald, 1960, p. 240)

Not only do interpretations free the psyche of its stagnation, but interpretations also commence the very task of integration.

> Interpretations establish or re-establish links between islands of unconscious mentation and between the unconscious and consciousness. They are translations that do not simply make the unconscious conscious or cause ego to be where id was; they link these different forms and contents of mental life, going back and forth between them. There are interpretations upward and interpretations downward. What is therapeutic, I believe, is the

> mutual linking itself by which each of the linked elements gains or regains meaning or becomes richer in meaning--meaning being our word for the resultant of that reciprocal activity. (Loewald, 1979a, p. 382)

Loewald did not use the terms, but he explicitly advanced the concept that interpretations are inevitably suggestive, didactic, or, in Austin's (1975) sense of the word, performative.

Modelling the termination of the psychoanalytic process on the resolution of the Oedipus complex, Loewald asserted that the outcome of a successful analysis involved the introjection of the analyst within the patient's superego.

> The analytic situation re-embodies this [Oedipal] interaction and the termination of analysis leads, if things go well, to a healthier resolution of the Oedipus complex than the patient had been able to achieve before, and to a more stable superego. Patients at the termination of treatment frequently express a feeling of mutual abandonment that, if analyzed, becomes the pathway to the relinquishment of the analyst as an external object and to the internalization of the relationship. This is similar to the experience of emancipation in adolescence, which repeats the oedipal struggle on a higher level. (Loewald, 1962a, pp. 267-68)

Loewald's formulation was consistent with the views of Sachs (1925), Alexander (1925), Glover (1927), Nunberg (1928), Strachey (1934), Bibring (1937) and Freud (1940), all of whom linked the analyst to the patient's ego ideal or superego. Freud (1940) acknowledged that a pedagogical relationship is inevitable. "If the patient puts the analyst in the place of his father (or mother), he is also giving him the power which his super-ego exercises over his ego, since his parents were, as we know, the origin of his super-ego. The new super-ego now has an opportunity for a sort of *after-education* of the neurotic; it can correct mistakes for which his parents were responsible in educating him" (p. 175).

TWO-PERSON PSYCHOLOGY

Winnicott adhered to the concepts of neutrality, abstinence, and mirroring when he imagined the analyst's function as a remedial mothering that provides "good enough" environmental mothering for the patient. His thinking was very much in line with a trend that conceptualizes the psychoanalytic situation by analogy to the mother-infant dyad. Loewald avoided the distorting prism of early childhood analogies and worked instead with Freud's (1940) view of after-education through superego introjection. Freud (1937, p. 146) had written: "In the same way [as its formation around age six], the super-ego in the course of an individual's development, receives contributions from later successors and substitutes of his parents, such as teachers and models in public life of admired social ideals." Loewald saw the psychoanalytic situation as a further instance of the same process. "The analyst, in the analytic situation, offers himself to the patient as a contemporary object" (Loewald, 1960, p. 249).

Loewald discussed an aspect of the parent-child relationship that was relevant to the parental task of promoting the integration of the child's psyche.

> The parent ideally is in an empathic relationship of understanding the child's particular stage in development, yet ahead in his vision of the child's future and mediating this vision to the child in his dealing with him. This vision, informed by the parent's own experience and knowledge of growth and future, is, ideally, a more articulate and more integrated version of the core of being that the child presents to the parent....The child, by internalizing aspects of the parent, also internalizes the parent's image of the child. (Loewald, 1960, p. 229)

"Parental recognizing care reflects more, as it were, to the child than what he presents; it mediates higher organization" (Loewald, 1978, p. 15).

Subscribing to the view that the patient's self-knowledge is the paramount goal of psychoanalysis, Loewald saw little value in the mainstream aspiration to mirror patients. Analysts are more useful to their patients when they provide empathic knowledge from a more advanced level of development.

> The patient, who comes to the analyst for help through increased self-understanding, is led to this self-understanding by the understanding he finds in the analyst....the analyst structures and articulates, or works toward structuring and articulating, the material and the productions offered by the patient....A higher stage of organization...is thus reached, by way of the organizing understanding which the analyst provides. The analyst functions as a representative of a higher stage of organization and mediates this to the patient. (Loewald, 1960, pp. 238-39)

Analysts' fears of their own narcissism were responsible for their traditional disavowal of their influence on their patients. "It seems to be the fear of moulding the patient in one's own image that has prevented analysts from coming to grips with the dimension of the future in analytic theory and practice, a strange omission considering the fact that growth and development are at the center of all psychoanalytic concerns" (Loewald, 1960, p. 230).

Revisiting the topic near the end of his life, Loewald (1988a) was unapologetic for recommending that therapists should respond fully to patients' treatment of them as admired role models.

> Psychotherapists, if they are worth their salt, have certain characteristics in common with professions of a different cast, with priests, rabbis, ministers, the old-fashioned doctor, who at their best function also as significant models of steady convictions, whatever their content, and of compassionate concern and dedication....The patient's placing the therapist in some such position is not simply a matter of "transference" to be "resolved" but of deeply felt needs and hopes for loving guidance, which in a good treatment situation may be met by means and in ways the patient had not known or anticipated. (pp. 55-56)

Loewald (1988a) asserted that analysts deal with the very phenomena that were traditionally the domain of professional religious: "Psychotherapists attend to the unseen world of the patient's psyche and of his unconscious, the abode of what in other contexts were, and are, called gods, demons, and ancestral spirits, or of those secret forces in nature that, thanks to Freud, are somewhat less secret and more amenable to mastery" (p. 56).

THE MORAL CHARACTER OF PSYCHOANALYSIS

Loewald stopped short of using Freud's word "after-education." He did propose a limited curriculum, however, when he described psychoanalysis as an intrinsically moral process. Because people are moral, psychoanalysis is obliged to address the topic of their morality (Loewald, 1978, p. 7). Psychoanalysis has an original and expanded understanding of morality, because it includes unconscious as well conscious responsibility (Loewald, 1978, p. 8). Moreover, psychoanalysis is itself a moral enterprise. The moral concerns of psychoanalysis are not limited to "the psychological roots of morality" but extend to "the moral implications of our therapeutic goals and practices" (Loewald, 1971c, p. 96). In making the unconscious conscious, psychoanalysis calls every patient to account for his or her unconscious.

> To acknowledge, recognize, understand one's unconscious as one's own means to move from a position of passivity in relation to it to a position where active care of it becomes possible, where it becomes a task worthy of pursuit to make one's business and concern those needs and wishes, fantasies, conflicts and traumatic events and defenses that have been passively experienced and reproduced....
>
> Such appeal, to begin with, comes from the outside and becomes internalized as an aspect of the superego. Psychoanalysis as a method of treatment, it seems to me, has this tension toward assuming responsibility for oneself, that is to learn by being instructed in self-knowledge, in repeating oneself knowingly, to take over this function of active repetition: to become a self....I think it is an unwarranted limitation, at this stage of our science, to maintain that self-knowledge, making the unconscious conscious, transforming id into ego, is a purely "objective" matter of self-observation and self-understanding and not a moral phenomenon and activity in and of itself. In this respect our theory is far behind the best in our practice and technique. (Loewald, 1971c, pp. 95-97; see also 1978, p. 11)

Loewald's understanding of moral responsibility led him to appreciate guilt as a integrative force in the psyche, whose experience motivates atonement and reconciliation.

> If without the guilty deed of patricide there is no individual self worthy of that name, no advanced internal organization of psychic life, then guilt and atonement are crucial motivational elements of the self. Guilt then is not a troublesome affect that we might hope to eliminate in some fashion, but one of the driving forces in the organization of the self. The self, in its autonomy, is an atonement structure, a structure of reconciliation, and as such a supreme achievement. (Loewald, 1979b, p. 394)

Loewald was here tacitly discussing the significance for his own perspective on psychic integration, of Klein's concept of the depressive position and Winnicott's view of the capacity for concern.

NORMALCY AND MYSTICISM

Loewald's theory that the ego and the sense of reality are bound up together provided him with a basis to critique the secular sense of reality that is normative in Western culture.

> The estrangement of man from his culture (from moral and religious norms that nevertheless continue to determine his conduct and thus are experienced as hostile impositions) and the fear and suppression of controlled but nondefensive regression is the emotional and intellectual climate in which Freud conceived his ideas of the psychological structure of the individual and the individual's relationship to reality. (Loewald, 1952, p. 29)

Like Fromm, Loewald challenged mainstream psychoanalysis for participating in the pathology of Western culture.

> Psychoanalysis has taken for granted the neurotically distorted experience of reality. It has taken for granted the concept of a reality as it is experienced in a predominantly defensive integration of it. Stimulus, external world, and culture, all three, on different levels of scientific approach, representative of what is called reality, have been understood unquestioningly as they are thought, felt, experienced within the framework of a hostile-defensive (that is regressive-reactive) ego-reality integration. (Loewald, 1952, p. 30)

Loewald (1978) suggested that "religious experience, primary narcissism, and the unconscious were tied together" (p. 72). A religious way of life is a necessary foundation to a scientific one. "I believe it to be necessary and timely to question the assumption, handed to us from the nineteenth century, that the scientific approach to the world and the self represents a higher and more mature evolutionary stage of man than the religious way of life" (Loewald, 1960, p. 228). Loewald maintained that the pure rationality espoused by science is disconnected from the living sources of the psyche and needs to be grounded in the unconscious and mystical. "We would lose ourselves...if we were to lose our moorings in the unconscious and its forms of experiencing which bespeak unity and identity rather than multiplicity and difference. We know madness that is the madness of unbridled rationality" (Loewald, 1978, pp. 56-57).

Arguing in a fashion parallel to his observation that self-knowledge places a demand on consciousness for moral responsibility, Loewald maintained that integration of the earliest levels of the psyche necessitates an embrace of undifferentiation, "the impersonal or nonpersonal beginnings and levels of psychic life" (Loewald, 1978, p. 47). Loewald suggested that repression of the psyche's mystical core was responsible for mainstream psychoanalysts' failure to validate religion (p. 74). Loewald raised the possibility that psychoanalysis might contribute positively to religion, implicitly by making conscious and integrating the psyche's mystical core.

> Instinctual life and religious life both betoken forms of experience that underlie and go beyond conscious and personalized forms of mentation....we may be at a point where psychoanalysis can begin to contribute in its own way to the understanding of religious experience, instead of ignoring or rejecting its genuine validity or treating it as a mark of human immaturity. (Loewald, 1978, p. 73)

PSYCHOANALYSIS AND EXISTENTIALISM

Prior to his immigration to the United States, Loewald had studied philosophy with Martin Heidegger, "and I am deeply grateful for what I learned from him, despite his most hurtful betrayal in the Nazi era, which alienated me from him permanently" (Loewald, 1980b, pp. viii-ix). Conversant with existentialism prior to his analytic training, Loewald routinely discussed psychoanalysis in terms that facilitated interdisciplinary comparisons.

> Man is understood in psychoanalysis as tending toward higher organization, further development of his unconscious life forces. He tends to become a person. The development of a more conscious life involves a continuous appropriation of the unconscious levels of functioning, an owning up to them as potentially *me*, ego. This appropriation, this owning up, integrating the id into one's life context as an individual self, is then a developmental task or, in a different framework, an existential task. I believe that Heidegger's concepts of *Geworfenheit*--man is thrown into the world, unplanned and unintended by himself--and *Entwerfen*--the taking over and actively developing the potentialities of this fact--have grown in the same soil. (Loewald, 1978, pp. 18-19)

Loewald's clinical technique was conventional and conservative. His conformance with mainstream technique reflected his belief that Freud had designed psychoanalysis to address much the same developmental concerns that later occupied Heidegger. "Psychoanalysis, I believe, shares with modern existentialism the tenet that superpersonal and transcendental aspects of human existence and of unconscious and instinctual life...can be experienced and integrated convincingly--without escapist embellishments, otherworldly consolations and going off into the clouds--only in the concreteness of one's own personal life, including the ugliness, trivialities, and sham that go with it" (Loewald, 1977, p. 416).

Loewald's perspective on existentialism differed from the approaches of other psychoanalytic mystics. Rank redesigned depth psychology from top to bottom in order to compete with existentialism. Fromm accepted existential formulations verbatim but limited their significance by fitting them into a larger dialectic. Having reformulated early ego development, Winnicott noted points of affinity with existentialism; but Loewald, who presumably knew existentialism best, simply carried on as a psychoanalyst. Loewald possibly considered it impolitic to discuss existentialism more extensively; but possibly he believed that psychoanalysis--better, psychoanalytic mysticism--had nothing to learn from Heidegger's formulations.

PSYCHOSIS

Loewald's view of the integrative process provided him with a distinctive approach to the treatment of psychosis. He suggested that Klein was correct in conceptualizing early infantile development in psychotic terms; but to her concern with object relations and Margaret S. Mahler's theories of separation-individuation (Mahler & Furer, 1968; Mahler, Pine, & Bergman, 1975; Mahler, 1979a, 1979b), Loewald added his own view of an opposing tendency toward union.

> Problems of self-object differentiation, with its inherent issues of the polarity between individuation and merging union, probably are not less but more universal and deep-seated than psychosexual conflicts of the oedipal nucleus of neurosis. They are what some have called the psychotic core of our mental life, an expression that should be understood in the same sense in which we speak of the Oedipus complex as the nucleus of neurosis. Such expressions refer to pathogenicity, not to pathology itself. All of us are heirs to this psychotic core. That is the important truth in Melanie Klein's work, as much as many of us disagree with her

emphasis, her metapsychological elaborations and speculations and her technical procedures. (Loewald, 1979a, pp. 377-78)

Presumably taking a cue from phenomenological and existential psychiatry, Loewald suggested that psychotic patients cannot be understood, nor effective interventions offered, unless an analyst is able to resonate empathically with the patient's level of subject-object dedifferentiation.

> Unless the analyst grasps that he is, on the now pertinent level of the patient's mental functioning, drawn into this undifferentiated force field, he will not be able to interpret adequately the transference meanings of the patient's communications. To do so, he has to be in touch with that mental level in himself, a level of which for him, too, the distance and separateness between himself and the patient are reduced or suspended. Ego boundaries, the whole complex individuating organization of self-object differentiation tend to dissolve. The difference between the patient and the analyst is that the former is at the mercy of that primitive level (inundated by it or disavowing it), whereas the analyst is aware of but not given over to it. (Loewald, 1979a, p. 379)

Loewald suggested that if a psychoanalyst is to empathize with a psychotic patient, he or she must have access to personal experience of subject-object dedifferentiation. Loewald implied that an analyst with no experience of mystical states was at a comparative disadvantage. Here was a practical argument on behalf of the psychoanalyst's practice of mysticism, to set beside Loewald's theoretical claims about integrating the psyche's neonatal nondifferentiation.

THE SUBJECTIVITY OF NATURE

In his final publication, *Sublimation* (1988b), Loewald touched on some cosmological implications of his mystical psychoanalysis. For Loewald, the subjectivity that an infant experiences during the neonatal stage of nondifferentiation, when it conceptualizes neither self nor objects, was an objectively existing subjectivity on the part of nature.

> Individual human mentation...would be but one instance or manifestation of *natura naturans*, of nature's "subjectivity." This subjectivity is vaster, "all embracing," in comparison to human individual mentation. The dynamic unconscious (Freud's "true

> psychic reality") is closer to subjectivity understood as nature's activity (Rolland's and Freud's "oceanic feeling") and is the enabling factor, in continuity with nature's subjectivity, for individual mentation and for consciousness. Ultimately it is in individual consciousness that a world of objects and an objective world are presented to a subject; one has no standing without the other. The mechanistic view of nature in scientific materialism carries objectivism to an absurd extreme whereby subjectivity in the just outlined sense is entirely eliminated from the world. Psychoanalytic theory still struggles with this heritage but is in the forefront of efforts to break the hegemony of the modern scientific *natura naturata* interpretation of reality ["which is nature considered as the world of distinct substances or objects"]. (p. 79)

Loewald argued that the existence of human subjectivity is only possible if subjectivity is an activity on the part of nature, that is, if subjectivity has ontological reality in and for nature. People can find things meaningful to them if and only if meaning exists as such.

Loewald rightly recognized that Freud's (1920a) theory of Eros and Thanatos similarly attributed objectively existing, ontological reality to meaning.

> It is noteworthy that Freud's last instinct theory--that which describes life (or love) instincts and death (or destructive) instincts--is in keeping with an interpretation of nature as *natura naturans*. He extends the concept of *Trieb* in such a way that it stands for the spontaneous activity of the universe, of which man's psychosomatic life, and particularly his unconscious, is but one manifestation. He concluded [Freud, 1937, p. 246] that the two fundamental principles governing "events in the life of the universe and in the life of the mind" as postulated by the pre-Socratic philosopher Empedocles--namely *love* and *strife*--"are, both in name and function, the same as our two primal instincts, Eros and destructiveness." (Loewald, 1988b, pp. 79-80)

In appealing to Freud's precedent, Loewald affirmed the particular part of Freud's theory of drives to which even his closest adherents had objected: that the unconscious psychological motives of sexuality and aggression are to be traced to metaphysical principles of Eros and Thanatos that exist in nature and not in biological organisms alone.

Loewald was correct, however, in perceiving the logical necessity that psychoanalytic interest in human subjectivity has ontological implications for the existence of meaning in the world. Psychoanalysis is philosophically inconsistent with scientific materialism and cannot be otherwise.

CONCLUDING REFLECTIONS

Psychoanalytic mysticism came of age with Loewald. Rank located mysticism "beyond psychology," Fromm called it "transtherapeutic." Milner, Ehrenzweig, Winnicott, and Kohut connected mysticism with earliest childhood and occasional repercussions in later life. Loewald instead argued that both psychic development and psychoanalysis were integrative from bottom to top. The therapeutic process was not to be contrasted with integration. The psyche's natural healing process was itself integrative. It was the particular type of integration to which the psyche resorts when dealing with repression.

Using exclusively secular language, Loewald made the case that psychoanalysis has intrinsically religious concerns that are neither otherworldly, supernatural, nor mythological. Nature itself possesses a subjectivity. If most psychoanalysts failed to recognize the validity of religion, it was because they conformed with the pathology of contemporary Western culture. Religion is as repressed in our time as sexuality was in Freud's era.

Nine

Wilfred R. Bion's Transformations of O

Wilfred R. Bion (1897-1979), the most important of the second generation of Kleinian object relations theorists, was a Neoplatonist. Although he discussed the Kabbalah in private conversations (Bléandonu, 1994, p. 228; Grotstein, 1997a, p. 78; 2007, p. 117), his literary references to mystics were limited to the pagan and Christian Neoplatonists (Bléandonu, 1994, p. 212). He referred by name to Plato, Aristotle, the Pythagoreans, Euclid, Proclus, St. Augustine, Meister Eckhart, John Ruysbroeck, St. John of the Cross, Pascal, Berkeley, Kant, and Teilhard de Chardin (Bion, 1961, p. 173; 1965, pp. 55-56, 139, 147, 159, 162, 171; 1989, pp. 38-39; 1994, p. 313). His knowledge of Neoplatonism was not casual. He constructed equivalents within psychoanalysis even for minor details of late Neoplatonism. Rather than tailoring his mysticism to suit psychoanalysis, Bion tailored psychoanalysis to suit his Neoplatonism.

Plato's theory of forms was foundational to Bion's approach to psychoanalysis. Bion attributed thinking to the impact of ideas on the human mind: "This differs from any theory of thought as a product of thinking, in that thinking is a development forced on the psyche by the pressure of thoughts and not the other way round" (Bion, 1962b, p. 111). "If there is such a thing as a mind, or character, or personality, it cannot be assumed to correspond to the physical formation. All of us need...to wonder why we think there is a personality where the body lies" (Bion, 1990, pp. 13-14). True thoughts are discovered, not invented. "Nobody need think the true thought: it awaits the advent of the thinker who achieves significance through the true thought" (Bion, 1970, p. 103). Bion (1965) explicitly acknowledged his theory's debt to Plato: "I shall borrow freely any material that is likely to simplify my task, starting with Plato's theory of Forms....The object, of which the phenomenon serves as a reminder, is a Form" (p. 138). Bion also signalled his debt to Plato by posing for a photograph that is printed as the frontispiece of *Cogitations*, a posthumous collection of his occasional writings. The photo shows Bion reading the works of Plato (Bion, 1994).

Bion's mysticism is often treated as an idiosyncrasy that can be ignored by analysts who value his contributions to their secular practices of psychoanalysis. Others who admire his early work think that he ceased to be worth reading at the point in this career when he began openly to discuss mysticism. Bion's mysticism was not, however, an adventitious or detachable superstructure to otherwise secular theories. His theoretic contributions flowed from his Neoplatonism. Loewald had understood therapeutic change as intrinsically integrative. Bion conceptualized the very procedures of clinical psychoanalysis as a mystical practice. The analyst serves implicitly as the analysand's spiritual director. Both analyst and analysand meditate. When therapy is successful, both achieve "transformations of O," which was Bion's term for mystical reversions from the perceptible many to the intelligible forms of the unknowable godhead.

BETA-ELEMENTS

Because Freud had developed psychoanalysis on the clinical evidence of neurosis, Bion's clinical work with psychotics created both opportunity and need to develop original formulations. In Bion's view, psychotics have thoughts that they are apparently unable to think.

> The inability of the psychotic to 'digest' his experience mentally...contributes to the situation with which most observers are familiar, namely the easy accessibility to the *observer* of what should be the psychotic's unconscious. These elements remain detectable because the patient cannot make them unconscious. They are...also...not available to him. (Bion, 1994, p. 71)

An external observer may know that a psychotic's delusions, hallucinations, motor compulsions, and so forth are coherent and meaningful as symbols of latent thoughts; but psychotics have no such awareness. Winnicott (1971) expressed the conventional view of psychosis when he extrapolated from Freud's (1900) view of dream hallucinations to the waking hallucinations of psychotics: "Hallucinations are dream phenomena that have come forward into the waking life and...hallucinating is no more of an illness in itself than the corresponding fact that the day's events and the memories of real happenings are drawn across the barrier into sleep and into dream-formation" (p. 78). Bion appreciated, however, that the conventional view is inadequate. Freud's theory of the dream-work cannot be made to explain the latent coherence of psychotic symbolism because Freud attributed the latent dream content to preconscious wishful thinking during the day previous to the dream. All that the unconscious dreamwork accomplishes, in Freud's model, is the recasting of preconscious thinking into the mental imagery of the dream. The clinical evidence of psychosis requires a more complex formulation. Psychotics' preconscious egos are affected by their psychoses and incapable of formulating the latent thoughts that psychotic productions symbolize. The latent coherence of psychotic thoughts requires either a modification in Freud's theory of the dream or a new theory to be placed alongside it. Because Freud (1923a, 1923b) attributed unconscious rationality to the superego, which undergoes symbolization in dreams "from above," I have elsewhere proposed that the unconscious superego, rather than the preconscious ego, should be credited with the latent content of dream hallucinations (Merkur, 2001). Bion's proposal, by contrast, was much more radical. Rather than to explain mental phenomena in terms of intrapsychic processes, Bion opted for Plato's forms. Psychotics can have thoughts that they cannot think whenever Platonic forms manifest through them without their knowledge.

To describe the thoughts that psychotics have but cannot think, Bion postulated the existence of what he called "beta-elements." Beta-elements are thoughts that cannot be used in thinking because they "lack a capacity for linkage with each other" (Bion, 1962a, p. 22). They include "sense impression" and "emotions," but "they are not so much memories as undigested facts" (pp. 6-7). In other words, beta-elements are mental representations of Platonic forms that a psychotic possesses but does not comprehend. Whether representation of the forms is acquired through sense perceptions of the forms embodied in the perceptible world, or through internal perception of the forms embodied in the sensory stimuli and instincts of the human body, the forms are represented mentally as beta-elements through a kind of parrotry or mimicry that replicates without understanding what is being conceptualized.

Bion's theory of beta-elements offered a solution to an unsolved difficulty of classical and Kleinian theory. In order to account for the hereditary ideas of the Oedipus complex, Freud invoked J. B. Lamarck's widely rejected theory of the inheritance of acquired characteristics (Paul, 1976; Freud, 1987, pp. 94-95). Melanie Klein (1952) avoided naming Lamarck when she wrote: "The fact that at the beginning of post-natal life an unconscious knowledge of the breast exists and that feelings towards the breast are experienced can only be conceived of as a phylogenetic inheritance" (p. 117). Working with a Neoplatonic metaphysics, Bion was able to account for inborn ideas without further to-do. Bion (1965) stated: "I claim Plato as a supporter for the pre-conception, the Kleinian internal object, the inborn anticipation" (p. 138). Bion avoided Klein's use of the term "knowledge," however, because he maintained that newborns do not initially know the Platonic forms that are embodied within them. He suggested that an infant begins without a "conception" of the breast but has an innate "pre-conception" that meets its "realization" through the actual encounter with the breast. "Conception...results when a pre-conception mates with the appropriate sense impression" (Bion, 1962a, p. 91) "The conception is initiated by the conjunction of a pre-conception with a realization....the theory that the infant has an inborn disposition corresponding to an expectation of a breast may be used to supply a model" (Bion, 1962b, p. 111). "I shall suppose that an infant has an inborn pre-conception that a breast that satisfies its own incomplete nature exists. The realization of the breast provides an emotional experience" (Bion, 1962a, p. 69). The inborn preconception consists of the mental representation of an instinctual urge to seek that on which to suck. The infant does not have an inborn mental image of the breast. The mental representation of the sucking instinct is initially a wish for an object that is not as yet known to be the breast. In a similar fashion, "the mating of this...Oedipal pre-conception with the realization of the actual parents gives rise to the conception of parents" (Bion, 1963, p. 93).

Despite the elegance of Bion's formulation, Klein was not persuaded of the validity of Neoplatonism. Bion (1965) stated that "Melanie Klein objected in conversation with me to the idea that the infant had an inborn pre-conception of the breast, but though it may be difficult to produce evidence for the existence of a realization that approximates to this theory, the theory itself seems to me to be useful as a contribution to a vertex I want to establish" (p. 138). Bion's candid remark that his theory was "useful" to establish a vertex that he happened to want constituted an admission that his theory subserved his philosophy and was not a necessary conclusion from the evidence of psychoanalysis.

BION'S SYSTEM OF EMANATION

Making bold to speak on behalf of psychoanalysis, Bion asserted that "the psychoanalytic vertex is O" (Bion, 1970, p. 27). By O, Bion referred to the divine without invoking more traditional theological baggage than he expressly chose to affirm.

> I shall use the sign O to denote that which is the ultimate reality represented by terms such as ultimate reality, absolute truth, the godhead, the infinite, the thing-in-itself. O does not fall in the domain of knowledge or learning save incidentally; it can be 'become', but it cannot be 'known'. It is darkness and formlessness

> but it enters the domain K[nowledge] when it has evolved to a point where it can be... formulated in terms derived from sensuous experience. (Bion, 1970, p. 26)

Bion (1970, p. 88) invoked both the Neoplatonic doctrine of the "emanation" of the divine from higher to lower hypostases and the Christian myth of "incarnation" in which God became man (Bion, 1970, p. 88). Both postulated an unknowable Godhead that was ulterior to the immanence, presence, or manifestation of God. In a tidy wordplay, Bion (1990, pp. 28-29) remarked that the Godhead was the noumenon, the unknowable reality behind phenomena, whereas the immanent God was numinous, which is to say, is experienced as holy or sacred. Mystical union with the incarnation of O was possible. "The religious mystic claims direct access to the deity with whom he aspires to be at one" (Bion, 1970, p. 87). "It is possible through 'incarnation' to be united with a part, the incarnate part, of the Godhead" (Bion, 1965, p. 148).

Bion used the term O in a consistent and complex manner. He chose the letter O to abbreviate the word "origin" (Bion, 1965, p. 15), "representing the unknowable ultimate reality" (p. 140). O "is a 'thing-in-itself', which can never be known" (Bion, 1970, p. 87) because "the godhead is formless and infinite" (p. 88). At the same time, Bion drew on the language of medieval Christian mystics and asserted that O is knowable in relation to human beings under a different aspect than its infinite formlessness. He followed Meister Eckhart and Jan Ruysbroeck in contrasting the Godhead and God (Bion, 1965, p. 139). God in his essence is the unknowable godhead; God in his immanence is instead intimately knowable. "The relationship with God is possible, but not with the Godhead" (p. 155).

Agreeing precisely with the designation of Christ as the *logos*, "Word," in the Gospel According to St. John, Bion equated the incarnation of O with Platonic forms. "The emphasis is altered by Christian Platonism....this may be seen most clearly expressed in the doctrine of the Incarnation" (Bion, 1965, p. 139). "The [same] domain [is] investigated, whether it be called Platonic memories, or religious incarnations" (p. 155). "The significance of O derives from and inheres in the Platonic Form" (p. 138). Platonic forms are present in the mind not as ideas about forms, but as instances of the forms themselves. This identity of forms with thoughts of the forms constitutes incarnation, as Bion interpreted the term; it also constitutes mystical union. "The phenomenon of Good or Beauty would not then be that which "reminds" the personality of a Form (pre-conception) but is an incarnation of a part of an independent Person [i.e. God]....The phenomenon does not 'remind' the individual of the Form but enables the person to achieve union with an incarnation of the Godhead" (Bion, 1965, p. 139).

Bion sometimes expressed his doctrine of form by reference to the unity and trinity of God. "Eckhart considers Godhead to contain all distinctions as yet undeveloped....It cannot be the object of Knowledge until there flows out from it Trinity and the Trinity *can* be known" (Bion, 1965, p. 162). Like the Trinity, Unity was a form appropriate to God and inapplicable to the godhead. "The object represented by the Platonic Form may also be represented in mystical terms such as 'One is one and all alone and every more shall be so'" (p. 138).

Bion's thought on the unity and trinity of God nodded in the direction of the mathematical metaphysics of Neopythagorism, which had been a traditional component of Neoplatonism in late antiquity. "An intrinsic feature of the transition from the 'unknowability' of infinite Godhead to the 'knowable' Trinity is the introduction of the number 'three'. The Godhead has become, or been, mathematized" (Bion, 1965, p. 170).

The equivalence of the Incarnation with Platonic forms meant that O was incarnate in and as all things. "It is possible through phenomena to be reminded of the 'form'" (Bion, 1965, p. 148). The distinction between the unknowable godhead and the knowable God applied also to the manifestations of O in and as phenomena. "My theory would seem to imply a gap between phenomena and the thing-in-itself and all that I have said is not incompatible with Plato, Kant, Berkeley, Freud and Klein, to name a few, who show the extent to which they believe that a curtain of illusion separates us from reality" (p. 147). "What the absolute facts are cannot ever be known, and these I denote by the sign O" (p. 17). The sign O "stands for the absolute truth in and of any object....it can be known about, its presence can be recognized and felt, but it cannot be known. It is possible to be at one with it" (Bion, 1970, p. 30).

> To qualify O...I list the following negatives: Its existence as indwelling has no significance whether it is suppose to dwell in an individual person or in God or Devil; it is not good or evil; it cannot be known, loved or hated. It can be represented by terms such as ultimate reality or truth. The most, and the least that the individual person can do is to be it. (Bion, 1965, pp. 139-40)

For Bion, O was both the unknowable godhead ulterior to all phenomena and the one and triune God with whom mystical union is possible. The incarnation of God was a stage in the transformation of O that was simultaneously the forms of Plato, the absolute truth, and the thing-in-itself of all phenomena. Just as the incarnation of God, viewed from a human perspective, was evident as the forms, so the transformations of O in the many could be seen either in their order of cosmogenesis or in the sequence of mystical reversion to O. The absolute truth or things-in-themselves of all phenomena were no other than beta-elements, the mental representations of forms that are experienced as things-in-themselves. As beta-elements, the incarnate God has psychological relevance for human beings.

BION'S MENTALIST COSMOLOGY

Integral to Bion's Neoplatonic mysticism was a mentalist cosmology. Mind was not necessary limited to organic beings. Its existence within the cosmos outside organic phenomena was to be entertained as a tenable consideration. Bion (1994) wrote: "The classic psycho-analytic view supposed the mind or personality to be identical with the physical identity of a person. The object of my proposal is to do away with such a limitation and to regard the relationship between body and mind (or personality, or psyche) as one that is subject to investigation" (p. 314). In suggesting that mind was not necessarily limited to the "physical identity of the person," Bion allowed for the possibility of Platonic forms.

Plato's theory of forms is implicit in the sense in which Bion described phenomena as beta-elements. In an explicit statement of his cosmology, Bion (1994) wrote:

> I shall suppose a mental multi-dimensional space of unthought and unthinkable extent and characteristics. Within this I shall suppose there to be a domain of thoughts that have no thinker. Separated from each other in time, space and style, in a manner that I can formulate only by using analogies taken from astronomy, is the domain of thoughts that have a thinker. This domain is characterized by constellations of alpha-elements. These constellations compose universes of discourse that are characterized by containing and being contained by terms such as, 'void', 'formless infinite', 'god', 'infinity'. This sphere I shall name by borrowing the term, 'noösphere' from Teilhard de Chardin. (p. 313)

The "mental...space of [the] unthought and unthinkable" referred to the godhead of O. The "domain of thoughts that have no thinker," in the second sentence of the quotation is the realm of Platonic forms and their phenomenal appearance as beta-elements. The "domain of thoughts that have a thinker," mentioned in the third sentence, consists of mental elements that thinking creatures can use in thinking. The three domains--the unknowable O, the forms that are phenomena, and thoughts about phenomena--comprise the whole of reality. They together form what the modern Jesuit mystic, Teilhard de Chardin, termed the "noösphere," the domain of the noetic that is God.

Although Bion referred to Plato, a closer parallel to his metaphysical system may be found in the Christian Neoplatonism of the Cappadochian fathers, St Basil of Caesarea and St Gregory of Nyssa, who had regarded sense phenomena as thoughts produced in the mind of God. Where Plotinus, the pagan founder of Neoplatonism, had followed Plato in treating the Indefinite Dyad as a formless material substance out of which the further forms are formed, Basil and Gregory maintained "that material beings are produced by a meeting of purely spiritual and intelligible qualities and that there is no material substratum apart from these qualities" (Armstrong, 1955, p. 55). Bion implied a similar regard for physical reality as a mental construction within God. Beta-elements are mental phenomena that seem not to be. They are instead experienced as external realities. "Beta-elements are not felt to be phenomena, but things in themselves" (Bion, 1962a, p. 6). Whether external realities exist that underlie beta-elements is nevertheless unknowable. "The breast, the thing in itself, is indistinguishable from an idea in the mind. The idea of a breast in the mind is, reciprocally, indistinguishable from the thing itself in the mouth....The realization and the representation of it in the mind have not been differentiated" (Bion, 1962a, pp. 57-58). A beta-element "partakes of the quality of inanimate object and psychic object without any form of distinction between the two" (Bion, 1963, p. 22). "The concept of beta-elements includes only sense-impressions, the sense impression as if it were a part of the personality experiencing the sense impression, and the sense-impression as if it were the thing-in-itself to which the sense-impression corresponds" (Bion, 1962a, p. 26). We experience Platonic forms incarnated as beta-elements; but all that we know about the beta-elements are thoughts that conceptualize them as ideas of external realities. We have no access to external realities by which to confirm their externality. Insofar as they exist externally--if they do so--they are unknowable. And so too is God. "In any object, material or immaterial, resides the unknowable ultimate reality, the 'thing-in-itself'" (Bion, 1970, p. 87). "According to Kant the thing-in-itself cannot be known" (Bion, 1962a, p. 67).

Hamilton (1982, p. 251) remarked that "Bion blurs Kant's distinction between *a priori* and sensible knowledge when he proposes equivalences between the 'things-in-themselves' and the 'beta-elements'--that is, the raw, pure, discrete sense-impressions. Because both are ultimately unknowable....Bion subsumes the noumenon under a corporeal conception." Bion (1990) had, however, both considered and disputed such a reading of Kant: "Some philosophers would disagree...but I think, nevertheless, that there is a great deal to be said for the idea that he did regard noumena and things which are noumenous as related to the thing-in-itself" (p. 84).

Bion's reference to "things which are noumenous," which equates all material and immaterial objects with the thing-in-itself, was consistent with the view that all things are in and of God.

> When the noumena, the things themselves, push forward so far that they meet an object which we can call a human mind, there then comes into being the domain of phenomena. We can guess, therefore, that corresponding to these phenomena, which are something that we know about because they are us, is the thing itself, the noumenon. The religious man would say, 'There is, in reality, God'. (Bion, 1990, p. 28)

Bion's mentalist cosmology was consistent with his disinterest in the views of other psychoanalytic mystics. He must surely have been aware of the views of other psychoanalytic mystics, particularly those in London whom he knew personally; yet he nowhere engaged their thought in his writings. The concept of creative illusion that Milner, Winnicott, and Ehrenzweig shared, took for granted that physical matter has objective existence and sought to explain how it is that we organize the raw data of our senses into coherent and recognizable perceptions. The theory can easily be given a Platonic spin, but it cannot be reconciled with Bion's claim that mind is the only empirical existent. There was no point of contact between Bion's subjective idealism and other analysts' philosophical realism. In a mentalist cosmos, coherent and recognizable perceptions are immediately given. They are not produced laboriously outside awareness by neurophysiological processes of sensation, because physical matter does not exist.

Bion's disengagement from collegial discussion concealed a fundamental flaw in his theory system. Ehrenzweig's distinction between the comparative undifferentiation of a newborn's perception and the dedifferentiation of previously differentiated perception gives the lie to Bion's cosmology. If beta-elements cannot be used in thought, it is because they are *de*differentiated. What is merely comparatively *un*differentiated can be used in thought, and indeed is being so used in a comparatively undifferentiated way. Bion's claim that sense impressions are indistinguishable from psychotic productions is not valid. Both phenomenologically and theoretically, they are distinct. Had Bion attempted to respond to the consensus among

Ehrenzweig, Winnicott, and Loewald regarding undifferentiation, the over-simplicity of his Neoplatonism would have been transparent. Undifferentiation and dedifferentiation require different clinical strategies; and Bion's treatment of psychosis as though it were infantile undevelopment is at least one reason that his theories did not dramatically improve psychoanalysts' success in the treatment of psychotics.

PROJECTIVE IDENTIFICATION

Although Bion's posthumously published notes indicate that he initially viewed beta-elements as sense impressions, by the time that he began to publish his ideas he regularly maintained that beta-elements add emotional content to sense impressions. The emotional content makes it possible for psychotics to express desire, hatred, and other motives by means of beta-elements whose conceptual content they remain unable to comprehend. Beta-elements are not "thought." "Beta-elements are suitable for evacuation only--perhaps through the agency of projective identification" (Bion, 1962a, p. 13). By invoking the process that Klein (1946) termed "projective identification" (see also Segal, 1979, pp. 116-19; Grotstein, 1981a; Ogden, 1982), Bion avoided the notion that the transmission of a beta-element involves agency or activity on the parts of either the patient or the analyst. When, for example, a patient consciously adopts a posture as a victim, there is inevitably a corresponding idea of being in relation to a victimizer. We speak of "projection" and "transference" when the patient consciously thinks of the analyst as the victimizer. We speak of "projective identification" in other cases, when the patient is unaware both of feeling a victim and of feeling the analyst to be a victimizer. Klein discussed projective identification as a fantasy. Bion (1961) recognized its interpersonal effect on others: "The analyst feels that he is being manipulated so as to be playing a part, no matter how difficult to recognize, in somebody else's phantasy" (p. 149). When projective identification occurs, the patient unconsciously behaves in a way that manipulates the analyst into behaving as the unconsciously fantasized victimizer--for example, by getting angry, or indifferent, or another order of adversarial. Because projective identification is an unconscious communication from the patient to the analyst's unconscious, it occurs without the analyst's knowledge, consent, or agency. The analyst is acted upon by the patient.

Analysts respond to projective identification in various ways. Freud's contemporaries and later ego psychologists regarded projective identification as a type of countertransference, or emotional response by the analyst to the patient, that was to be kept from interfering with the analyst's task of analyzing the patient. Beginning in the early 1950s, Heinrich Racker, a Kleinian analyst, championed the use of the countertransference as a diagnostic tool that allows an analyst to learn the content of an unconscious phantasy that a patient can communicate unconsciously without being able to formulate verbally (Racker, 1968). Racker expected analysts to self-observe and self-analyze their countertransferences, before using them to deduce their patients' unconscious phantasies, and to formulate verbal interventions regarding the phantasies they inferred. Relational psychoanalysts have more recently come to appreciate that at least part of the time analysts will act on their countertransference emotions before they become conscious of them, for example, fulfilling the assigned role of victimizer; and it is only in retrospect of an "enactment" that the analyst will become conscious that a projective identification has occurred, will think about the process, and will respond verbally in an effectively therapeutic manner (Maroda, 2004).

Of the various types of countertransferences, Bion limited his discussion to projective identification alone. Bion (1990, p. 122) insisted on a strict definition of countertransference as "one's *unconscious* feelings about the patient." He consequently restricted the term to Freud's original usage. All else that his contemporaries were calling "countertransference" he regarded as conscious feelings. Projective identifications of which an analyst has become aware and can interpret to the patient belonged to the category of conscious feelings. Neither empathy nor idiosyncratic neurotic responses to patients drew Bion's attention as a theorist, presumably because projective identification alone was useful for his Neoplatonic purposes. Projective identification is the only variety of countertransference that is completely unconscious in both the patient and the analyst. Bion accordingly saw "projective identification as the single most important form of interaction between patient and therapist" (Ogden, 1982, pp. 25-26). In Klein's theory, the patient is unconscious of the phantasy that is transmitted to the analyst; and the analyst is unconscious of having received the phantasy until his or her emotional response to it becomes subject to self-observation. Bion's theory of projective identification replaced Klein's concept of phantasy with his own concept of beta-elements. For Bion, projective identification described the unique circumstance by which beta-elements in the patient are transmitted to the analyst, who receives them equally unthinkingly as beta-elements. "Beta-elements lend themselves to projective identification when that mechanism is employed to evacuate a part of the personality, but are useless, or at best unsuited, for use in thinking" (Bion, 1965, p. 44). Because beta-elements are used in projective identification, they superficially resemble "a confused state," but are actually "coherent and purposive" even though they are not understood by the patient (Bion, 1962a, pp. 22, 24). Bion also suggested that beta-elements "are influential in producing acting out" (p. 7).

For Bion, projective identification alone among the varieties of countertransference was a vehicle by which Platonic forms may *emanate* from person to person without being thought. Through projective identification, Platonic forms may be transmitted from a person who cannot think to a person who can. In this manner, the many, which begin as beta-elements, commence their process of reversion to unity.

BION'S THEORY OF THINKING

Bion began his theorizing about thinking by treating psychotics' inability to think as a product of motivation. "The psychotic with his hatred of reality evades the installation of the reality principle. His intolerance of frustration makes for intolerance of reality and contributes to his hatred of reality. This leads to reinforcement of projective identification as a method of evacuation" (Bion, 1994, p. 53).

Bion (1994) proposed that the psychotic hatred of reality motivates an inhibition of what he called the "alpha-function," which "is concerned with, and is identical with, unconscious waking thinking designed, as a part of the reality principle, to aid in the task of real, as opposed to pathological, modification of frustration." Alpha-function underlies "attention, storage of memory, thinking, the positions, consciousness attached to sense organs, notation, passing of judgement, motor discharge" (p. 54). Bion (1962b) initially suggested that alpha function "convert[s] sense data into alpha-elements and thus provide[s] the psyche with the material for dream thoughts and hence the capacity to wake up or go to sleep, to be conscious or unconscious" (p. 115). "Alpha-function transforms sense impressions into alpha-elements which resemble, and may in fact be identical with, the visual images with which we are familiar in dreams, namely, the elements that Freud regards as yielding their latent content when the analyst has interpreted them" (Bion, 1962a, p. 7). In later formulations, Bion revised his assertion. "Alpha-elements are a later stage of beta-elements...dream-work-alpha operates on beta-elements and not directly on sense data" (Bion, 1994, p. 183). The terms "alpha" and "beta" do *not* represent a causal sequence between the respective elements. Bion named "alpha-function" and "beta-elements" in the alphabetical order of their formulation. He happened to arrive at his theory of alpha-function first, and interpolated beta-elements into his theory only later.

The term "dream-work-alpha," which Bion later replaced with "alpha function," indicates the debt of Bion's model to Klein's concept of phantasy. Klein had extended Freud's concept of the dreamwork (Hayman, 1989), and Bion developed the concept further. Alpha-function begins by converting mental elements that are not thoughts into elements that can be used in thinking. It transforms beta-elements into alpha-elements by thinking about them and thereby converting them into thoughts (Bion, 1994, p. 182). Through alpha-function, the human mind comes to know the Platonic forms that its beta-elements contain. In knowing, the mind is engaged in thinking and reasoning in a realistic manner.

Bion's concept of the reality principle preserved the term but not the concept of Freud. For Freud, reality consisted of the physical world of sense perception, and conformance with the reality principle required a person physically to love and to work. For Bion, reality consisted of things-in-themselves that forced thinking on the mind. Conformance with the reality principle in Bion's mentalist cosmology was accomplished by thinking. The mystic, experiencing perceptible phenomena give way to a union of all being, was conforming with Bion's reality principle.

Bion regarded alpha-function as a more elegant theory than Freud's (1911) account of the primary and secondary processes. Where Freud postulated two mental processes, Bion claimed that unconsciousness was not a process but a condition of beta-elements. In Bion's theory, there was only a single process, the alpha-function, and it was responsible for both the dreamwork and thinking (Bion, 1962a, p. 54). Bion did not clarify how alpha-function accomplishes all of the many activities that he attributed to it; but it might be helpful to think of the core of alpha-function as the process of thinking about conscious mental experiences. The sense data and emotions that comprise beta-elements do not involve thinking. In thinking about beta-elements, the alpha-function transforms them into alpha-elements that can be thought both with and about. Alpha-elements include both the perceptual hallucinations of dreams and the abstract concepts of waking thought

An important corollary of Bion's concept of alpha-function is its modification of the concept of unconsciousness.

> Without alpha-elements it is not possible to know anything. Without beta-elements it is impossible to be ignorant of anything: they are essential to the functioning of projective identification; any unwanted idea is converted into a beta-element, ejected from the personality, and then becomes a fact of which the individual is unaware, though he may be aware of feelings of persecution stimulated by it. (Bion, 1994, p. 182)

Bion implied that a psychotic who is conscious, in the ordinary sense of the term, of hallucinations, delusions, compulsive urges, and so forth, is nevertheless unconscious or unaware in the sense of unthinking and uncomprehending. Beta-elements can be present within the sensorium; but because they cannot be linked through associations, they remain isolated and unconscious. Conversely, the activity of alpha-function in generating dreams during sleep and unconscious waking phantasies is, in Bion's sense of the term, a kind of consciousness because awareness or comprehension is involved.

When alpha-function is attacked, psychotics lose the ability to discern that there is anything other than beta-elements--anything other than psychic reality.

> Since its [alpha's] destruction makes it impossible to store experience, retaining only undigested 'facts', the patient feels he contains not visual images of things but things themselves. Reciprocally, things themselves are regarded by him in the same way as non-psychotics and the non-psychotic part of his personality regard 'thoughts' and 'ideas'; they are expected by him to behave as if they were visual images in his mind. (p. 97)

Freud (1939) had written that when there is "a domination by an internal psychical reality over the reality of the external world...the path to a psychosis lies open" (p. 76). Bion agreed, but omitted other important aspects of Freud's concept of psychical reality. Freud (1911) had written: "The strangest characteristic of the unconscious (repressed) processes, to which no investigator can become accustomed without the exercise of great self-discipline, is due to their entire disregard of reality-testing; they equate reality of thought with external actuality, and wishes with their fulfilment--with the event--just as happens automatically under the dominance of the ancient pleasure principle" (p. 225). Where Freud wrote of a "disregard of reality-testing," Bion wrote exclusively of an active attack on the reality principle. In much the same way that Bion addressed projective identification to the exclusion of other types of countertransference, he used Freud's concept of psychical reality only in reference to psychosis. For Freud, involvement with psychical reality might be so pleasurable that reality is disregarded. Children's play, aesthetic experience, and so forth, all involve an indulgence of psychical reality. For Bion, however, a reversion to psychical reality was always intensely negatively motivated and pathological. An emotionally motivated attack on alpha function causes the psychotic loss of contact with reality. "Attacks on alpha-function, stimulated by hate or envy, destroy the possibility of the patient's conscious contact either with himself or another as live objects" (Bion, 1962a, p.9). For Bion, Freud's concept of "psychical reality" covered too much. "An attack on alpha-function made through the agency of projective identification" (Bion, 1994, p. 217) arrived the mind at its default position: beta-elements that are mental, but are not thoughts. The disintegration of thought into the dissociated beta-elements that compose the many was a psychotic condition and was not to be equated with dream-work-alpha products such as play and aesthetic experience.

THE GRID

Bion asserted his stance as an object relations theorist when he wrote, "An emotional experience cannot be conceived of in isolation from a relationship" (Bion, 1962a, p. 42). He was referring simultaneously to relations among people and to the relation of people to the incarnation of O. In the same way, Bion's definition of the links between human beings was implicitly also an analysis of O. Bion posited Love (L), Hate (H), and Knowledge (K)--effectively supplementing Suttie's (1935) restatement of Freud's (1920a) duality of sex and aggression with a consideration of the noetic. The links among L, H, and K, and the absence of links that Bion expressed as -L, -H, and -K, were interpersonal relations. They were transformations of O that could be observed clinically in patients' associations and precipitated by analysts' interventions. In similar ways, the development of pre-conceptions through sense perception into conceptions, and of conceptions through abstraction into concepts, were transformations of O that could be observed and influenced clinically.

Bion (1963, 1989) created a diagram, which he termed the grid, that plotted the various categories on a graph. It assigned a row each to beta-elements, alpha-elements, dream thoughts (including dreams and myths), pre-conception, conception, concept, scientific deductive system, and algebraic calculus. Bion assigned vertical columns to the analyst's activities: definitatory hypotheses, the Greek letter psi (signifying a countertransferential misunderstanding), notation, attention, inquiry, and action. The function of the grid was to provide graph categories that were descriptive of the psychoanalytic process. Meltzer (1998) termed it "the periodic table of psycho-analytical elements" (p. 324), but it was also considerably more. Bion (1963) remarked: "The grid as the representation of an instrument used by the analyst in scrutinizing the patient is equally a representation of the material produced by the patient as an instrument for scrutinizing the analyst" (p. 81). The grid may also be understood as a typology or categorizing of mentation that Bion regarded as discrete transformations of O. "The Grid is an attempt to describe the progressive development of thought from concrete to highly abstract levels" (Symington & Symington, 1996, p. 33). As a classification of divine hypostases, the grid imparts a late Neoplatonic dimension to Bion's system. Emanations were both vertical and horizontal in the fourth and fifth century systems of Proclus and pseudo-Dionysius the Areopagite. Bion's grid is arranged sequentially, from top to bottom, in the order of the reversion from the many (beta-elements) to pure forms (algebraic calculus). Its columns, which concern the analyst's thinking, are sequential from left to right.

Using projective identification as the prototypical clinical instance of emanation, Bion integrated his Neoplatonism with Freud's concern with sexual dualism under the terms "container" and contained."

> Container and contained are susceptible of conjunction and permeation of emotion. Thus conjoined or permeated or both they change in a manner usually described as growth. When disjoined or denuded of emotion they diminish in vitality, that is, approximate to inanimate objects. Both container and contained are models of abstract representations of psycho-analytic realizations. (Bion, 1962a, p. 90)

These two orientations toward relationship were each operable everywhere in Bion's system. There were containing and being contained at L, H, and K, in pre-conception, conception, and concept, beta-element and alpha-elements, and so on.

PSYCHOANALYSIS AS A PRACTICE OF MYSTICISM

With the patient's projective identification of beta-elements into the analyst for the analyst to convert by means of alpha-function into alpha-elements, the reversion from phenomena to the unknowable godhead was begun. The analyst's task, in Bion's model, was to receive projective identifications, to perform alpha-function on them, and to return the alpha-elements to the patient in order to facilitate the patient's achievement of alpha-function. In this way, both analyst and patient would pursue transformations in O. The analyst's role had its precedent in the activity of an infant's mother.

> In the situation where the beta-element, say the fear that it is dying, is projected by the infant and received by the container in such a way that it is "detoxicated", that is, modified by the container so that the infant may take it back into its own personality

> in a tolerable form. The operation is analogous to that performed by alpha-function. The infant depends on the Mother to act as its alpha-function.
>
> Stating this in other terms, the fear is modified and the beta-element thereby made into an alpha-element. Restating this less abstractly still, the beta-element has had removed from it the excess of emotion that has impelled the growth of the restrictive and expulsive component; therefore a transformation has been effected....The change that is brought about by the mother who accepts the infant's fears, is one that is brought about later in personalities whose development is relatively successful, by alpha-function. (Bion, 1963, p. 27)

Bion did not cite Loewald's (1960) concept of the parents' and analyst's mediation of higher psychic organization; but he referred to the same developmental and clinical phenomena. He was not content to speak of differing complexities of thinking, but instead referred categorically to thinking as distinct from not thinking.

Bion suggested that a nursing mother performs alpha-function while in a state of reverie. Milner had proposed that analysts employ the term "reverie" for creative and mystical states because the term "phantasy" was overworked (Field, 1957, p. 163). The term "reverie" had also been popularized by the phenomenological philosopher Gaston Bachelard (1987); but Bion defined reverie in a very limited way, much as he had limited countertransference to projective identification and Freud's concept of psychical reality to the circumstance of psychosis. Bion (1962a) wrote:

> The term reverie may be applied to almost any content. I wish to reserve it only for such content as is suffused with love or hate. Using it in this restricted sense reverie is that state of mind which is open to the reception of any "objects" from the loved object and is therefore capable of reception of the infant's projective identifications whether they are felt by the infant to be good or bad. In short, reverie is a factor of the mother's alpha-function. (p. 36)

Bion's restriction of "reverie" to instances "suffused with love or hate" confined discussion to sex and aggression. By transforming emotions into alpha-elements, reverie was a means to revert beta-elements to O.

The analyst's task was to provide alpha-function for patients who had not acquired sufficient alpha-function in the course of their childhood.

"The next step is for the analyst to bring his attention to bear....A state of reverie conducive to alpha-function, obtrusion of the selected fact, and model-making together with an armoury limited to a few essential theories ensure that...interpretations can occur to the analyst with the minimum disturbance of observation" (Bion, 1962a, pp. 86-87).

Bion (1978, p. 7; 1990, pp. 67, 88, 127) claimed Freud's "free floating attention" as a precedent for his own views on analytic listening. His phrasing "free floating," where "evenly suspended" and "evenly hovering" are the common translations, indicates an unacknowledged debt to Theodor Reik's (1948, p. 157) idiosyncratic translation of Freud's *gleichschwebend*. Like Winnicott and Kohut, Bion frequently neglected to acknowledge his intellectual sources and is easily but wrongly assumed to have been far more innovative than he was. Bion's approach to analytic listening was also indebted to Martin Buber's philosophy of I and Thou: "As soon as I can understand what it means when I can see a body lying on a couch, the *live* relationship between me and you, and you and me (either direction) has become a dead relationship between I and it, and it and me, and you and it, and it and you" (Bion, 1990, p. 14; see also 1989, pp. 37-39). Like Fromm, Bion combined the influences of Reik and Buber in his own approach to analytic listening.

> In the course of analysis it is wrong for the analyst to allow himself either memories or desires, the one being the future tense of the other, because memories and desires are opaque. They hide what is going on. This, I believe, is equally true of understanding. While you are *trying* to understand what the patient says he goes on talking and you do not hear what he says. (Bion, 1990, p. 88)

Bion described the analyst's reverie as an alternate state of consciousness. "The total process depends on relaxed attention; this is the matrix for abstraction and identification of the selected fact" (Bion, 1962a, p. 87). The analyst's reverie required an avoidance of distractions. Where Milner had discussed faith in the creative process of the unconscious, Bion discussed faith in unconscious processing as a faith in O. "The discipline that I propose for the analyst, namely avoidance of memory and desire...increases his ability to exercise 'acts of faith'" (Bion, 1970, p. 34). "The exercises in discarding memory and desire must be seen as preparatory to a state of mind in which O can evolve" (p. 33). While avoiding distraction by memory and desire, an analyst was to engage in meditation.

> Psychoanalytic 'observation' is concerned neither with what has happened nor with what is going to happen but with what *is* happening. Furthermore it is not concerned with sense impressions or objects of sense. Any psychoanalyst knows depression, anxiety, fear, and other aspects of psychic reality whether those aspects have been or can be successfully named or not. These are the psychoanalyst's real world. Of its reality he has no doubt. Yet anxiety, to take one example, has no shape, no smell, no taste; awareness of the sensuous accompaniments of emotional experience are a hindrance to the psychoanalyst's intuition of the reality with which he must be at one. (Bion, 1967, p. 17)

> The only point of importance in any session is the unknown. Nothing must be allowed to distract from intuiting that. (Bion, 1967, pp. 17-18)

The goal of the analyst's meditation was the psychoanalytic process; it was simultaneously a mystical union. "No one who denudes himself of memory and desire, and of all those elements of sense impression ordinarily present, can have any doubt of the psycho-analytical experience which remains ineffable" (Bion, 1970, p. 35). "The analyst has to *become infinite* by the suspension of memory, desire, understanding" (p. 46). "The psychoanalytic vertex is O. With this the analyst cannot be identified: he must *be* it" (p. 27). Bion (1967) went so far as to recommend his meditative practice as a way of life. "These rules must be obeyed *all* the time and not simply during the sessions. In time the psychoanalyst will become more aware of the pressure of memories and desires and more skilled at eschewing them" (p. 18).

Bion's failure to cite Ehrenzweig's discussion of the analyst's evenly hovering attention was consistent with his Neoplatonism. Both Kleinian thinkers regarded the analyst's listening state as a cultivation of dedifferentiation that had a mystical potential. Where Ehrenzweig thought of mystical union as a regression to infantile solipsism, Bion rejected the theory of infantile solipsism and instead imagined that the infant's psyche consisted of a complete unintegration of beta-elements that had not as yet been linked through alpha-function. For Bion, mystical experience was a regression, but not in the psychoanalytic sense of the term. Implicitly for Bion, as explicitly for the Neoplatonists of late antiquity, mystical experience was an *epistrophe*, a "reversion" of the decline of the one into the many through an ascension of the many to the one (see Lloyd, 1990, p. 126).

In Bion's view, being O was the ordinary condition of reality. It was only being attentive to it that was rare. "I consider it rather to be a state always present, but overlaid by other phenomena, which screen it....its full depth and richness are accessible only to 'acts of faith.' (Bion, 1970, p. 36). The purpose of the analyst's union with O was the production of psychoanalytic interpretations on its basis. When an analyst achieves union with O, his interpretations proceed not from knowing about O, but from participating in O and its transformations in both himself and his patient. An interpretation was optimally to arise out of the analyst's union with O, as a self-analytic insight into beta-elements that the patient had projectively identified into the analyst; and the analyst's verbal presentation of the insight to the patient as an interpretation would serve, in its turn, to catalyze the patient's transformation in O. "The interpretation is an actual event in an evolution of O that is common to analyst and analysand" (Bion, 1970, p. 27). Interpretations are always at risk of promoting intellectual knowledge (Bion, 1970, p. 30); but their "value therapeutically is greater if they are conducive to transformations in O; less if conducive to transformations in K" (Bion, 1970, p. 26). "The interpretation should be such that the transition from *knowing about* reality to *becoming real* is furthered" (Bion, 1965, p. 153).

The analyst's achievement of a transformation in O--alpha-functioning on his own behalf by self-observing and self-analyzing the patient's projective identifications--required the analyst to attain alpha-elements that were pertinent to the beta-elements of the patient. Intervening with these alpha-elements facilitated a similar transformation in O on the part of the patient (Bion, 1965, p. 148). Bion conceived of clinical psychoanalysis as a pursuit of mystical experience on the part of both analyst and patient. By means of reverie and alpha-function, the analyst achieves transformation in O for himself, and facilitates a parallel transformation in the patient.

Although Bion's language for discussing psychoanalysis was radical, his clinical practice involved a fairly conventional psychoanalytic frame. Bion kept to regular set hours, the patient lying on a couch and attempting to associate freely, the analyst out of view, aspiring to anonymity, saying very little, and limiting comments so far as possible to observations regarding the patient's associations. What Bion said to patients consisted generally of fairly conventional Kleinian interpretations (Grotstein, 2007, p. 30). Bion nevertheless conceptualized the psychoanalytic process as a practice of mysticism that pursued and facilitated transformations in and of O.

THE MYSTIC

Bion (1970) discussed the mystic as a person who manifested a pre-conception that he termed the "messianic idea."

> The idea that is messianic may be confused with the person; he may believe he is the messiah. The person I call 'the mystic'....The terms 'mystic' and 'genius' are interchangeable. Mystics appear in any religion, science, time, or place. Such persons 'contain' the 'messianic idea'. (Bion, 1970, p. 110)

Bion (1970, p. 84) universalized the messianic myth by treating the Christ story as a cultural variation that expressed a more advanced version of the same myth that underlies the Oedipus narrative. Both stories expressed the necessary tragedy of the messiah, mystic, or genius. Bion defined myth as "a primitive form of pre-conception and a stage in...communication of the individual's private knowledge to his group" (p. 92). In keep with this definition, Bion maintained that "components of the Oedipal myth...operated as a pre-conception" (p. 67). The messianic idea was similarly a Platonic form that was inborn as a pre-conception.

Both dreams and myths are vehicles for the expression of pre-conceptions. "The dream has fresh significance if it is regarded as a private myth" (Bion, 1963, p. 92). "The private myth, corresponding to the Oedipus myth, enables the patient to understand his relationship with the parents" (p. 66). "Some myths are public rather than private, for example, the Oedipus myth" (p. 64). "The Oedipal myth in addition to the place it already occupies in analytic theory" should be "recognized as an essential part of learning in primitive stages of development" (p. 66). Because all thought has its ultimate basis in the inborn categories constituted by pre-conceptions, "the genetic stage of thought is that of dream or myth" (Bion, 1965, p. 29).

Like Klein's internalized objects, the myths of interest to Bion functioned as mental images. "The components of these myths that I wish to use are those which pictorialize, in the sense of internal pictures or symbols that we make for ourselves, features that might turn out to be the psycho-analytical elements that I seek" (Bion, 1963, p. 65). Unlike Klein's internalized objects--and Jung's archetypes--Bion's myths concerned processes, activities or scenarios and were not limited to entities or objects. "Myths...*represent* the evolution of O" (Bion, 1970, p. 85).

Bion maintained that psychopathology arises when a person's pre-conceptions are unable to render family relationships comprehensible.

"This private myth, in its investigatory role, if impaired or maldeveloped or subjected to too great a stress, disintegrates; its components are dispersed and the patient is left without an apparatus which would enable him to comprehend the parental relationship and so adjust to it" (Bion, 1963, pp. 66-67).

In Bion's view, the myths that express pre-conceptions concern morality, knowledge, and conflict about knowing. With this formulation, Bion implicitly accepted Glover's (1945) charge that Klein's system was mythological because it was ethical; but Bion countered that mythico-ethical thinking is intrinsic to humanity. Bion initially identified three inborn myths.

> 1. There is a god or fate, omniscient and omnipotent though modelled anthropomorphically. This god belongs to a moral system and appears to be hostile to mankind in his search for knowledge, even moral knowledge.
>
> 2. In all, penetration into, or ingestion into, or expulsion from a blissful place or state is prominent. Sexual knowledge and pleasure is a prominent feature of the knowledge sought and forbidden.
>
> 3. In Eden and Oedipus myth there is a stimulation of forbidden desires--the serpent incites desire for the fruit: Oedipus instigates the search for the criminal; in the Babel myth there is a significant variation--the people come together and are dispersed, the language is one and replaced by a number of languages. The Sphinx incites to curiosity by its riddle. (Bion, 1963, p. 65)

Klein's inner world of breasts, genitalia, and parents can be described as a mythology only metaphorically; they were intended by Klein as a continuation of Freud's program of universal de-mythologization. Bion's additions to Klein's theory of internalized objects were instead explicitly religious and mythological. Whatever one may think of Bion's choice of myths, his concern was well taken. Most people in all cultures and eras have been both ethical and religious. People generally entertain moral standards whether they live up to them or not. People also generally believe in providence, fate, miracles, magic, luck, or another manner of metaphysical intervention in human affairs, whether or not they personally claim such an experience. The distribution of these two mythical ideas--ethics and miracles--is so very nearly universal that a psychoanalytic explanation is warranted.

The "messianic idea" was a fourth myth that Bion introduced in a later publication. It concerns the individual who is engaged in manifesting

O, whether through creativity, mysticism, or otherwise (Bion, 1970, p. 117). The myth included the impact of the mystic on his social group. "Any formulation felt to approximate to illumination of O is certain to produce an institutionalizing reaction. The institution may flourish at the expense of the mystic or idea, or it may be so feeble that it fails to contain the mystical revelation" (p. 81).

In Bion's (1970, p. 92) view, the messianic idea complemented and continued the Oedipus myth whose importance Freud had recognized. In both cases, the unknowability of O is represented in myth as a prohibition of knowledge, and the individual who seeks to know O--the messiah, mystic, or creative genius--must defy O, as represented in myth by fate or God or the gods, in order to aspire to O. With this assertion of the Oedipus complex, Bion was claiming that mysticism was inborn, normative, and the optimal goal of human development.

THE CLINICAL BION

The views that Bion expressed in his psychoanalytic writings were not fully consistent with the views that he expressed informally in lectures and seminars that he gave toward the end of his life. Bion's writings present theories, but in his clinical work Bion professed to have almost no use for theories.

> Analysts talk and argue about Kleinian theory, Freudian theory, Abrahamian theory and so on, as if they had forgotten that behind all these theories there are people who are actually suffering....as analysts we are not concerned with *theories*; we are concerned with, 'What shall I say to this man?'....With a new patient it is of course useful to fall back on a certain amount of psychoanalytic theory when there is very little else to go on; it is useful for about three sessions. Giving interpretations after that without the necessary information encourages the patient to think that the analyst doesn't need evidence. (Bion, 1987, pp. 201-2, 170, 210)

Another significant discrepancy that emerges from Bion's oral presentations was his attitude toward mysticism. Bion (1990) denied that he was a mystic. He asserted: "My knowledge of mysticism is through hearsay" (p. 68). In his view, "A mystic may be able to say that he has direct relationship with God, without the intervention of any other agency" (p. 24). An analyst, by comparison, "has to be a kind of poet, or artist, or scientist, or theologian" (p. 17). Bion is perhaps better viewed as a mystical theologian than as a mystic.

Bion also stated that he had "never found out anything which has not already been discovered" (p. 101). The statement may be accepted at face value. Bion's major contribution was hermeneutic. He conceptualized psychoanalysis from a perspective that was informed by Christian Neoplatonism and resulted in a unique phrasing of psychoanalysis. Bion disclosed his literary purpose, I suggest, if we interpret the following analogy as a tacit self-description.

> I have no objection to saying, 'Let's get up tomorrow at sunrise'. I do not believe the earth stays stationary while the sun rises in a certain position, goes round and sets in another. But I would not want to reform the ordinary way of talking. I still think it is useful for people like us. But on the other hand, I would not advocate the abolition of heliocentric astronomy on the grounds that it is in conflict with geocentric language of getting up in the morning. (Bion, 1990, p. 155)

Where Federn, Milner, Winnicott, Loewald and other psychoanalytic mystics had expressed themselves primarily in secular terms, while quietly intimating their mysticism at appropriate junctures for the benefit of attentive readers, Bion opened psychoanalytic discourse to an explicit and open exploration of the mystical, apparently by offering what he regarded as a "geocentric language." Grotstein (2004b) suggested that Bion's "use of religion was an attempt to use it metaphorically as a psychoanalytic 'vertex' or point of view, namely, as a psychoanalytic instrument" (p. 1084); but Bion nowhere indicated that his use of Christian Neoplatonism was intended merely as metaphor.

CONCLUDING REFLECTIONS

Bion openly paraded his mystical theology, making O, his concept of God, central to his presentation of psychoanalysis. He discussed a largely conventional practice of psychoanalysis from a mystical point of view, seeing in it an intrinsically mystical activity. If he opened the topic of mysticism for explicit, professional discussion, he did so at a considerable price. Bion's concept of O has proved popular among psychoanalytic mystics, metaphysicians, and theologians, but each takes the term in a different direction. Bion's metaphysics were Platonic or Idealist and did not require the postulation that physical matter exists. Bion's theory proceeds on the basis that all we know of matter are mental elements that portray physical matter. The objective reality of matter does not enter experience or Bion's discussion. Almost everyone who has worked with Bion's concept of O instead affirms that both mind and matter exist, and each attempts to make sense of Bion in a way that--for the most part unwittingly--contrives to reconcile Bion's Idealism with a common sense view of the material universe. The solutions are various and mutually inconsistent. They reflect divergent metaphysical and religious speculations, and they do not forward our understanding of psychoanalysis, mysticism, or God.

Consider, for example, some obvious limitations that Bion took over from Neoplatonism. His theories nowhere departed from the rigidly automatic, intellectual determinism for which pagan Neoplatonism was notorious in the Christian and Jewish worlds. There is no freedom of will in Bion's mystical theology. There are the infallible and unvarying mechanics of transformations in O. Bion generally contented himself with asserting that the unknowable godhead O is entirely beyond discussion, but the discussion of a particular case led him to discuss the implication that O is so devoid of content as to be an uncaring, impersonal existent.

> There is an urge to exist; it is felt to be something which doesn't care whether you are a dog, a bitch, or a beautiful woman--it is completely indifferent. The mother may die, the offspring may be eaten up, but all in the service of this force. If the human race blew itself out of existence with the neutron bomb, the force to exist wouldn't mind in the least--it would be just one more discarded experiment. So the patient can be afraid of being used simply as a means of perpetuating existence.
>
> I don't think it would be the slightest good saying that to the patient, but it is something that would be useful to me if I were analysing this patient because I would expect everything to fit into that basic theory. I would expect it to crop up all the time--the patient waging war against this force, wanting to remain a person, a beautiful person, and not liking being a slave to that force, that power, that energy....I am using the word 'existence', but I am trying to describe something which has no human characteristics....The individual piece of life--whether it is a dog, or a plant, or a human being--is simply one little particle in this total existence. The force doesn't mind what happens to it any more than we mind what happens to single cells of our skin which we shed and don't even know we have worn them out. (Bion, 1987, pp. 164-65)

Bion's three volume novel, *A Memoir of the Future* (1991), expressed the same theology in a passage of dialogue: "But don't you think it pathetic that when Science and its brood of astronomers leads unmistakably to the discovery of our insignificance in contrast with those gigantic forces--novae, super novae, black holes and the rest--someone is sure to apply a mental first-aid dressing and hurl us back into the downy comfort of ignorance. Doesn't that depress you?" (p. 573). Grotstein (2007, p. 3) remarked that for Bion, "The evolved human being--the mystic--is capable of 'negative capability', the tolerance of doubt, frustration, and uncertainty, but is also able to tolerate the cosmic meaninglessness of being (existence)." Bion's neglect of Klein's concept of gratitude and reparation (Bléandonu, 1994, p. 40, 211-12) reflects the indifference that he attributed to O.

Discussions of O, so it seems to me, are unhelpful departures from methodological agnosticism in psychoanalytic work. They do not advance psychoanalytic theorizing but instead by their arbitrariness foreclose research options by prejudicing thinking now in one speculative manner, and now in another. Bion's concept of O assumes that God is impersonal and is not a person with whom one might have a dialogical relationship. Grotstein unpacks Bion's thinking--in my view accurately--when he formulates that human beings are responsible for transforming the impersonalism of O and the meaninglessness of the universe into human appreciation of the personal values and meaningfulness of human life. Most psychoanalysts would agree that people project meanings onto the meaninglessness of physical matter; but methodological agnosticism--the standard that Freud maintained--avoids entering into the question whether meaning is real or an illusion. Bion's concept of O, that people project meanings onto an O that is absolute reality but utterly unthinkable and meaningless, affirms a metaphysics of ultimate meaninglessness. There is, in such a theology, no room for the personal and intensely meaningful God of the Bible, the Qur'an, or Hindu *bhakti*. O is assuredly consistent with Neoplatonism and Neo-Vedantin Hinduism; but from a biblical standpoint, it is an idolatry. If a metaphysical concept such as Bion's O is to be part of psychoanalysis, it needs to be addressed in a responsible, professional manner. Utter unknowability and meaninglessness may not be stipulated arbitrarily. The theological propositions have to be argued persuasively against alternative metaphysical possibilities.

I am myself persuaded that any such effort must fail, because faith would not be faith if it were capable of being proven. A category mistake is made whenever faith is misrepresented as knowledge. I also see no reason to confound issues by misrepresenting metaphysics and theology as psychology. If clinicians wish to extend the scope of psychoanalysis beyond psychotherapy to include spiritual discernment--and why not?--I would strongly urge that the metaphysical and theological aspects of their work be identified as such, and that appropriate methodological standards be required. The comparative study of religion and philosophical theology are specialized disciplines of academic research, each with professional research standards. Both disciplines will require adaptation to meet clinical needs. Ongoing efforts to coordinate theology with the natural sciences are a further existing body of learning that may bear on our concern, but they are presently nowhere near to reaching the critical mass that would give us an intellectually responsible natural theology, religion, or spirituality. Although a satisfactory paradigm has yet to emerge, the old paradigm has clearly failed us. The days of dogmatism, ethnocentricity, and apologetics are long since past. Taking a bit of Neoplatonism, Zen or Kabbalah and adding it to psychoanalysis is indefensible. Why take one bit and not another?

Leavy (1995) argued for the continuing importance of separating psychological work from mystical faith-claims.

> I think it is important to pursue this examination in a literally agnostic way, neither presuming nor excluding the divine origins of the mystics' experiences. If the religious believer cannot allow this bracketing of faith, i.e. a suspension of judgement on its "reality," then he would do well to avoid any psychoanalytic consideration at all. And if the skeptical psychoanalyst cannot allow that the faith of the mystics be taken seriously enough to bracket it, he might also better abandon the quest. (p. 354)

Where methodological agnosticism permits psychoanalysts of all persuasions to aspire to a consensus, the accommodation of faith-claims within psychoanalysis leads rapidly to the divisiveness of religious dogmatism. The result can only be a fragmenting of psychoanalysis along denominational lines. Analysts who speak deeply out of their own religious tradition largely speak only to it, as for example Moshe Halevi Spero (1992) and Randall Lehmann Sorensen (2004). If psychoanalytic mysticism is to thrive, the temptation to preach to the choir must be resisted.

At several crucial points in his model, Bion revealed himself as a dogmatic "top-down" thinker who made selective uses of clinical phenomena (for example, countertransference, psychical reality, and reverie states) that agreed with his conceptual model, while he ignored other aspects of the phenomena (for example, undifferentiated perceptions) for whose explanation his Neoplatonic model was inadequate. He conceptualized psychoanalysis as a Neoplatonist, and he ignored what he was unable to employ within his system of Neoplatonic mysticism. In this manner, he offered, in my view, a *truncated* theory of psychoanalysis. At the same time, his own clinical work was inconsistent with his theory precisely at such junctures. He theorized, as we have seen, that projective identification, uniquely among an analyst's possible experiences of the patient, merits interpretation; but his clinical statements placed no such limitations on the analyst's intuitions. As precedent, Bion (1987, p. 241) cited Freud's remark, "I learned...to follow the forgotten advice of my master Charcot, to look at the same things again and again until they themselves began to speak." In Bion's (1980) view, "While I am trying to understand what the analysand is telling me, I have to guess, I have to conjecture until the patient can give me some more convincing evidence; then I may be able to feel reasonably sure of my interpretation" (p. 102). An analyst should allow "exercise of his speculative imagination" (Bion, 1997, p. 46). And again:

> Every psychoanalyst has to have the temerity, and the fortitude which goes with it, to insist on the right to be himself and to have his own opinion about this strange experience which he has when he is aware that there is another person in the room. Pressure against this is considerable....Forget...both what you knew and what you want, to leave space for a new idea. A thought, an idea unclaimed, may be floating around the room searching for a home. Amongst these may be one of your own which seems to turn up from your insides, or one from outside yourself, namely, from the patient. (Bion, 1980, p. 11)

In a less formal phrasing, Bion (1978) described his internal process as free association: "During this time I, as usual, had plenty of free associations of my own (which I keep to myself because I am supposed to be the analyst)" (p. 238).

Neville Symington (2004a), who attended Bion's workshops at the Tavistock Clinic and the Institute of Psychoanalysis, remarked that "Bion, I believe, saw freedom as being elemental to psychoanalysis and any erosion of freedom within psychoanalysis being a betrayal of its true nature" (p. 175); but Bion (1978) claimed that he objected "to guiding the person, because I cannot believe that I know how to conduct my own life." Bion was concerned with the patient's autonomy because it alone was therapeutic.

> The object...is to introduce the patient to the most important person he is ever likely to have dealings with, namely, himself. It

> sounds simple; in fact it is extremely difficult. One is always liable to affect the patient with one's own views, both those consciously held and others one is not consciously aware of--the counter-transference. The main object is to help the patient to be less frightened of his own horrible self--however horrible he thinks he is. (Bion, 1978, p. 5)

These avowals of the traditional practice of neutrality notwithstanding, Bion did not approach analysis as a one-person psychology. Where Loewald had described the analyst--and the parent--as speaking from a more mature developmental level, Bion referred to the analyst's--and the mother's--provision of alpha-function, a higher stage in the evolution of O. The intrinsically educative or pedagogical role of the analyst was not the focus, however, of Bion's clinical ambition. Perhaps more candidly than any analyst before him, Bion recognized that analysts' interventions are performative; they make things happen. "Every interpretation means that a change takes place--if it is a correct interpretation. The puzzling situation which has been made clear by the interpretation at once disappears; it is once again an entirely new situation in which there are new problems" (Bion, 1987, p. 13). Bion expressly urged analysts to anticipate their patients' growth and to speak to it.

> In any session, evolution takes place. Out of the darkness and formlessness something evolves. That evolution can bear a superficial resemblance to memory, but once it has been experienced it can never be confounded with memory. It shares with dreams the quality of being wholly present or unaccountably and suddenly absent. This evolution is what the psychoanalyst must be ready to interpret. (Bion, 1967, p. 18)

Bion's concept of the evolution of O expressed in mechanical, deterministic terms the same clinical phenomenon that Winnicott described as the patient's creativity. Some ideas and feelings, some insights, that did not exist, consciously or unconsciously, come into being in response to a successful intervention--and the intervention may even be the analyst's choice to be respectfully silent at a particular moment.

Bion's theoretic formulations were not equal to his clinical sensitivity. The need to account for the production of psychotic hallucinations confronted him with the realization that the dreamwork is a kind of thinking, so that conventional ways of differentiating the primary and secondary processes do not hold. To solve the theoretical problem, Bion reverted to

Freud's "Formulations on the Two Principles of Mental Functioning" (1911), where Freud had written: "It is probable that thinking was originally unconscious, in so far as it went beyond mere ideational presentations and was directed to the relations between impressions of objects, and that it did not acquire further qualities, perceptible to consciousness, until it became connected with verbal residues" (p. 221). Here was a clear statement that a type of thinking, that is, of reasoning abstractly, operates unconsciously with sensations; but unconscious thinking does without further qualitative aspects of the sensations that can only be apprehended by means of consciousness (p. 220). In this way, Bion derived from Freud his postulate that the dreamwork and unconscious thinking are a unified mental function. The corollary that it is possible "to cultivate a capacity for dreaming while awake" (Bion, 1994, p. 215) followed directly. Bion's concept of alpha-function is not an adequate solution to the theoretical puzzle of the intelligibility of the latent content of psychotic hallucinations, but it brought a long neglected piece of Freud's theory to renewed attention.

To complete his account of the latent intelligibility of psychotic productions, Bion took recourse to Plato's theory of forms. If the intelligibility is instead to be traced to the mind, as most psychoanalysts believe, Bion's concept of alpha-function may be placed alongside Fromm's ideas of conscience and the unconscious production of universal symbolism, Milner's and Ehrenzweig's revision of the theory of primary process, and Winnicott's ideas about the internalization of both the environmental mother and the unit status mother at the foundation of superego's capacity for concern. Psychoanalytic mystics have repeatedly detected evidence of the existence of a higher mental function, or group of functions, that have escaped conventional ways of thinking about the unconscious. The topic awaits further research.

Ten

James Grotstein and the Transcendent Position

Los Angeles psychoanalyst James S. Grotstein refers to himself as a Kleinian. He was initially trained in the classical tradition of American ego psychology; but when Wilfred Bion taught at the Los Angeles Psychoanalytic Institute, Grotstein sought supervision with him. Because Bion believed that only the person who was in the room with a patient could possibly know how best to respond, he treated Grotstein as a colleague rather than as a supervisee. Finding Bion's supervision disappointing, Grotstein chose instead to learn from Bion by being re-analyzed by him (Grotstein, 2002). Grotstein is a versatile, prolific, and highly original contributor to many different aspects of psychoanalysis. My present concern with his mysticism addresses only a portion of his oeuvre.

THE INTELLIGENT CREATIVITY OF THE DREAM

Grotstein's approach to the mystical had its basis in the following dream. Grotstein (1981b) reported:

> When I was a second year medical student I had a dream the night before the final examination in pharmacology which I remember across the years as follows: the setting was a bleak piece of moorland in the Scottish Highlands engulfed by a dense fog. A small portion of the fog slowly cleared and an angel appeared surrealistically asking, "Where is James Grotstein?" The voice was solemn and litanical. The fog slowly re-enveloped her form as if she had never existed or spoken. Then, as if part of a prearranged pageant, the fog cleared again but now some distance away, at a higher promontory where a rocky crag appeared from the cloud bank revealing another angel who, in response to the first angel's question, answered as follows: "He is aloft, contemplating the dosage of sorrow upon the Earth." (p. 359)

Grotstein reacted to his dream as do many people who have religious or mystical experiences or who know the "aha!" experience of creative inspiration. He knew that he could not have produced the experience by himself. The dream exhibited features that were beyond the powers that he attributed to his sense of self. Grotstein (1981b) wrote: "I was deeply impressed, mystified, and bewildered. I knew that I had experienced the dream, but I did not know who wrote it. I wanted desperately to be introduced to the writer who could write those lines" (p. 359). Grotstein's reaction to his dream was a rational response to the creativity of its manifest narrative. In the article discussing his dream, he also cited some dreams that exhibit "creative *thinking* and *planning*," such as the famous dream of the chemist August Kekule von Stradonitz, whose image of snakes biting each other's tails solved the puzzle of the benzene ring (p. 409). Grotstein also cited a well-known clinical phenomenon as further evidence of the creativity of dreams. Dreams are sometimes able to disclose unconscious materials that cannot be accessed through free associations (p. 409).

Grotstein (1981b) concluded that "this creative, exploratory aspect of the dream bears testimony to the 'thinker' behind the dream" (p. 409). "The dream represents the product of an intelligence or coherence that has access to memory and hidden emotions and can construct for the dreamer and analyst a narrative that is capable of meaningful decipherment" (Grotstein, 2000b, p. 19). "In this respect it is a revelatory function" (Grotstein, 1981b, p. 410). Grotstein recognized that Freud never adequately accounted for dreams' intelligent creativity. Freud (1900) had famously assigned the unconscious dream-making function to an irrational process, consisting of condensation, displacement, and considerations of representability, that translated the latent content of the dream into symbolism. He acknowledged that the latent content of the dream may contain intelligent, rational materials, but he suggested that these materials originate as preconscious thinking during waking hours prior to the dream. Freud (1923a, 1923b) later revised his model, dividing the rational input between the preconscious ego and the superego, to which he now attributed the dream censorship. Rational intelligence in the latent content of a dream, such as Kekule's ideas about the benzine ring, might be argued *ex hypothesi* as preconscious materials that first became conscious only following a detour into the unconscious dreamwork (Kris, 1950). However, the dream's access to the preconscious cannot explain its access to autobiographical materials to which free association, the preconscious process *par excellence*, has no access. Moreover, Grotstein recognized that latent content formation aside, the unconscious symbol-forming function is itself capable of highly intelligent, rational thinking, inventing a fantasy scenario, organizing its imagery, and so forth. The dream not only has a latent story line, but also a manifest script, casting, stage direction, set decoration, and a great deal else. To account for "the awesome, god-like, arcane, mysterious nature of dreams" (p. 372), Grotstein (1981b) opted for Bion's concept of the alpha-function, which attributes both the dreamwork and abstract, conceptual thinking to a single mental process (pp. 361, 410).

Grotstein tried to work with Bion's theory in a variety of ways. He began by accepting Bion's model that a dream or, during wakefulness, an unconscious phantasy is produced whenever the alpha-function transforms beta-elements into alpha-elements. To account for the infant's capacity to communicate with the mother, Grotstein (2000b) rejected Bion's theory that infants acquire their alpha-functions from their mothers, and instead postulated that a rudimentary alpha-function is inborn (p. 26, n. 7; p. 299; 2007, p. 46). Grotstein (1981b) suggested that "the dream is something like an evacuation of nighttime accretions of mental stimuli...relayed communicatively to an audience who experiences *dramatic communication* in such a way as to undergo the phenomenon of *relief*" (p. 362; Grotstein's italics). "I actually see an almost infinite number of sorties back and forth between the two of highly coded messages which, in their dynamic reciprocal feedback, finally forge an acceptable dream narrative" (p. 364). Personifying the two functions within dreams as the Dreamer Who Dreams the Dream and the Dreamer Who Understands the Dream (p. 361), Grotstein compared them with "the crying infant" and "the containing mother" (p. 364). In this formulation, the Dreamer Who Dreams the Dream personified beta-elements, and the Dreamer Who Understands the Dream personified the alpha-function that makes the beta-elements tolerable. In keeping with Bion's equation of both beta-elements and O as the "thing-in-itself," Grotstein treated the Dreamer Who Dreams the Dream as "a Divine Self" by contrast with the individual self of the Dreamer Who Understands the Dream (p. 365).

Twenty years later, when Grotstein (2000b) incorporated his article within a book, he presented a significantly changed model. He referred to the Dreamer Who Dreams the Dream as the "Ineffable Subject" and the Dreamer Who Understands the Dream as the "Phenomenal Subject"; and he identified them as the id and the ego, respectively (p. xvii). This formulation departed from Bion's system in crucial ways. Bion had allowed only a single mental process, the alpha-function. What had not been processed was unthought and, as such, unconscious; and whatever had been processed was subject to consciousness because it had become thought. Bion's idiosyncratic uses of the terms unconscious and conscious were inconsistent with common psychoanalytic usage. Grotstein's effort to reconcile Bion's theory with ego psychology's structural model radically shifted several of Bion's concepts. Where Bion had made thinking and unconsciousness mutually exclusive, Grotstein concluded that if dreamwork was a kind of thinking, thinking must be allocated to the id. To correlate alpha-function with the id, Grotstein proposed a considerable revision to both concepts:

> I am seeking ways to rescue the id specifically and the unconscious generally from what I believe has been a prejudice--that it is primitive and impersonal, rather than subjective and ultra sophisticated...it bubbles with infinite creative possibilities and bristles with our indifference to it. (Grotstein, 2000b, p. xvi; see also Grotstein, 1990c, p. 280).

Rycroft (1956), Khan (1974, p. 87; 1983, pp. 49-50), and Noy (1969, 1979, 1982, 1985) had earlier argued for the creativity and sophistication of the id. Grotstein innovated by adding Bion's concept of alpha-function to their model. Citing the work of Daniel Stern and Robert Langs, Grotstein (1990b) proposed that the id had to be credited with less fantasy and greater realism than was generally recognized:

> Perception of reality, rather than fantasy or drives, is the deepest and most forceful component of the unconscious. This conclusion suggests, first of all, that Freud was more correct than we had thought regarding his first theory of psychoanalysis, that of the censorship of traumatic memory. Second, it suggests that there needs to be a shift in our conception of the relative importance of *reality* and *imagination* as etiological factors in mental illness. Thus, traumatic reality experience may be primary, and our capacity for imagination (primary process) may have been instituted in order to regulate it through the production of fantasies. (p. 150)

Grotstein (2007) further suggested that, contrary to Bion, alpha-function and alpha-elements occur prior to beta-elements. "The *alpha-element* may have an earlier beginning in the Ideal Forms...and exist on a gradient of transformational sophistication as it proceeds. The term '*beta-element*' should...be reserved for pre-processed sensory stimuli" (p. 46).

> When O intersects our emotional frontier and makes an impression there of its presence, the initial response is the formation or appearance of an *alpha-element* (personal). It may either continue in its transformational course into dream elements, contact-barrier, and memory, or come to be rejected by the mind and de-

> graded *after the fact* into '*beta*-elements' and thereby remain 'impersonal.' (pp. 61-62).

This revision of Bion's system undercuts one of its basic premises. If the beta-elements are decay products or reifications of alpha-elements, psychotic hallucinations cannot be cited as evidence for the existence of "thoughts without a thinker."

Grotstein nevertheless followed Bion in taking flight from psychology to metaphysics in order to account for unconscious rationality. At the same time, Grotstein rejected Bion's mentalist cosmology. Acknowledging that there are such things as physical matter, human bodies, bodily impulses, and the unconscious mental representation of impulses as drives, Grotstein opted for vitalism (Grotstein, 2000b, pp. xiv, 76, 101; 2001; 2004a, p. 101), the doctrine that matter is alive and thinks (see Skrbina, 2005).

Grotstein's attribution of alpha-function to the id had several corollaries. In updating his theory of the two Dreamers, Grotstein (2000b) reversed the relationship of mother and baby. It was now the internal mother (id) who made the dream for the baby (ego), and not the baby who made it for the mother. Because dream images were a kind of thinking, dreams had to be "messengers of information" and "Freud's discharge theory" had to be "replaced by an information theory" (Grotstein, 1980, p. 492). "The instinctual drives comprise semiotic signs that are *signifiers*, not the *signified*. As such they designate, but do not ultimately constitute, internal mental states....They are messengers, not the message itself" (Grotstein, 1990a, p. 35). Grotstein (1986) also built on Bion's suggestion that psychosis is characterized by a failure of alpha-function. "Defective or absent alpha function... constitutes not only an ego defect, as has commonly been thought, but also an id defect; that is, the psychotic does not have sufficient functioning of primary process to transform the data of personal experience into dreams, phantasies, or personal myths--only into hallucinations or delusions, which are the failures of phantasies and dreams" (p. 100). "All pathology can be considered to be id pathology, that is, pathology that results from an inadequate transformation of 'O'....mental health is a direct function of successful dreaming/phantasying and, conversely,...all psychopathology is a function of insufficient or defective dreaming/phantasying" (Grotstein, 2004a, pp. 99-100).

PSYCHOANALYSIS AS MYSTICISM

Like Bion, Grotstein (2000b, p. xxvi) asserted that "psychoanalysis constitutes a transcendental enterprise." "The analyst, without realizing it, is a practicing mystic" (p. xxx); and the patient's task is to attain a mystical union. "The task of psychoanalysis is not the attainment of insight but, rather, the use of insight to attain transcendence over oneself, over one's masks and disguises, to rebecome one's supraordinate subject. This task involves a transcendent reunion with one's ineffable subject" (p. xxvii).

Grotstein recognized the circularity of the mystical transformations of Bion's O, but he nowhere remarked that Bion was indebted to Neoplatonism for the concepts of the declension of the one into the many and the mystic's returning ascension to the one. Grotstein (1996) wrote:

> *"O" is inchoate and occurs before P-S--and awaits our transcendence of the depressive position so that we may be rejoined--for a moment--with it....*
>
> There seems to be an inherent circularity in the concept of "O," i.e., it is within us, around us, and beyond us...yet we also temporarily proceed from it, through it, and toward it...."O," as our mystically directed trajectory fulfills Plato's conception, "That which is always becoming"--but is never really attained. (pp. 118-19; Grotstein's italics)

Because Grotstein adheres to a philosophical realism that posits both mental experience and an objectively existing material universe, his presentations of Bion's views consistently interpolate innovations that aim to reconcile Bion's mentalist cosmology with a common sense understanding of physical matter. For example, the passage immediately above continued: "This circularity hints at a cosmic continuum--and even at-one-ment--between the personal Unconscious 'O' (immanent or incarnate, in the Heideggerian sense) and cosmically transcendent 'O'" (Grotstein, 1996, p. 119). It is only because Grotstein postulates an objectively existing cosmos that is external to the psyche that he postulates an O that transcends the cosmos, in addition to the O that acts within the psyche. Bion's formulations pertained only to the latter, because his theories bracketed or were non-committal regarding the existence of physical matter.

Grotstein also phrased the circularity of the declension-ascension process with reference to an intrapsychic personification of O that he called the Background Presence of Primary Identification. He suggested that the Background Presence undergoes development from primary narcissism to the numinous presence that it is later felt to be (Grotstein, 2000b, p. 18). Grotstein identified the Background Presence with O and credited it with engaging the self in a relationship (p. 21). The Background Presence encourages the self to return to unity with itself (p. 26).

Explicitly locating conventional Kleinian emphases on unconscious phantasy within the mystical circle, Grotstein (2000b) explained that the "diaspora" (p. 26) of the Background Presence that transforms beta-elements into knowledge involves a detour through phantasy. The dream issues from O and returns to it (p. 11). He credited the dreamwork with endowing experiences with emotional content. "We must first 'dream' (while awake as well as asleep)--that is, imaginatively create and phantasize--our emotional experiences through *primary process*--before we can discover, accept, and own them" (p. 41). When the dreams of night and both the unconscious phantasies and free associations of waking hours fail to complete the return through K to O, neurosis occurs and therapeutic interventions may be needed to restore motion along the mystical circle (p. 21).

THE TRUTH DRIVE

Grotstein's (2004b) effort to reconcile Bion's theories with ego psychology's versions of the id and the ego led him to postulate the existence of a truth drive. In Bion's mentalist cosmology, truth existed, but reality had no existence apart from truth. O was both Absolute Reality and the Truth. Truth might go unrecognized as beta-elements or be known as truth through alpha-function; but Freud's concept of a reality principle sufficed to account for the motivation to know and be transformed in O. Grotstein's philosophical realism disclosed Bion's formulation as simplistic. The ego sense perceived external reality, and the reality principle described its efforts to discern what was real and what was not. Truth is not limited, however, to objects of sense perception. It is instead concerned with relations among thoughts. Truth may pertain to a correspondence between thoughts and objects of sense perception; it may pertain to a wholly internal coherence among thoughts. Because the concept of O is completely abstract, its knowledge and transformations all concern truth; and the reality principle, as traditionally formulated, does not suffice to account for the quest for O.

To solve the problem, Grotstein (2004b) postulated a "truth drive" that conforms to "a truth principle." "It purportedly seeks and transmits as well as includes....'O'" (p. 1081). At the same time, Grotstein took the indifference and meaninglessness of O into account. Through the analytic process, O undergoes transformation from the absolute truth, the impersonal and meaningless noumenon ulterior to all things, to become intensely meaningful, personal truth. "Unconscious consciousness (attention, intuition) and the truth drive....subserve...the quest for and perception of emotional truth that must first undergo a transformation from the Absolute Truth about Ultimate Reality (intolerable truth, indifferent reality) to tolerable truth through the mediation of alpha-function" (p. 1092). "Ultimately, Bion's O is about the emotional truth of the psychoanalytic session in both the analysand and analyst" (p. 1084). "The *beta*-element is *not* O; it is O's protoemotional descendant--that is, the *beta*-element is the emotional sense *impression* of O" (Grotstein, 2007, p. 59).

Grotstein (2007) simultaneously affirmed the illusion of the cosmos; but this was illusion in Winnicott's sense. "What we commonly call reality is itself an illusion that disguises the Real (O)" (p. 123). "What we believe we experience is a 'virtual reality'--a Reality that has become 'virtued' ('laundered') by the refractions of phantasy, imagination, illusion, and symbolization, leaving us with a 'cooked' 'Real' (O) suitable for our timid digestion" (p. 124).

NUMINOUS EXPERIENCES

Grotstein recognized that experiences of O might be either ecstatic or horrific, depending on the attitude and maturity of the individual. The variable consists of "whether the individual who is in contact with [O]...has or has not effectively *transcended the depressive position and the depressive anxieties associated with it and has also transcended mourning object (K) loss*" (Grotstein, 1996, p. 114; Grotstein's italics). Even an experience that was filled with dread of O constituted progress along the mystical circle. "Although most of us shudder and shrink away from the dread of the Real (O), the power to encompass and countenance it qualifies one as having undergone a transformation in O, which corresponds to a numinous, spiritual experience" (Grotstein, 2000b, p. 273).

Grotstein (2000b) used the term *numinous*, a neologism that Rudolf Otto (1950) invented as a technical term in the academic study of religion. For Otto, numinous experiences involved feelings of the uncanny, the sacred, the demonic, the awesome, and the miraculous. Numinous experiences may or may not include theistic ideas. Otto explicitly equated numinous experiences with religious experiences in general, and he treated mystical experiences as a subcategory. All mystical experiences are numinous, but not all numinous experiences are mystical. Paul Pruyser (1974) argued that numinous experiences invariably contain a cognitive component that consists of the recognition of a "limit situation," or limit to the process of thought. It is not possible, for example, to think of more than infinity, less than nothing, a real number prior to one, and so forth (see also Merkur, 1996). At these and all comparable points in one's thinking, an emotion arises in regard for the unthinkable, which is among the varieties of feeling that Otto categorized as numinous. I have elsewhere suggested that the devotion of emotion to the unthinkable constructs the unthinkable as the object of a relationship, unconsciously crediting it with a mind that possesses subjectivity, and so transforms the empty or null concept of the not-thinkable into a positive concept of the transcendent (Merkur, 2006). Reality-testing may depersonify the sense of numinosity, resulting in a wholesome capacity for wonderment, awe, fascination, humility, immediacy, and tranquility in the face of life's mysteries.

Grotstein's references to the numinous generally agreed closely with Otto. For example, Grotstein (2000b) defined the numinous in terms of "the sense of awe and wonder and inward journey (into the self) associated with the mystical and meditative contact with the ineffable" (p. 255). He also employed the term "preternatural," meaning "beyond natural," in acknowledgement of the "complexity of our being alive and human--in the presence of the mystery inherent within others" (p. xxiii). These "exceptional qualities and capacities that we once attributed to gods, messiahs, and mystics" (p. xxiii) belonged, in Grotstein's view, to the Background Presence and its many derivatives.

Following Bion, Grotstein (2000b, p. 276) derived the pairing of the terms "Godhead" and "God" from the medieval Christian mystic Meister Eckhart as means to distinguish the unknowable essence of O from the knowable presence of O in human experience. Grotstein's O is not completely unknowable, however. The activity of thinking can be credited to it. "Godhood is the 'thinker' of the 'thoughts without a thinker' and the prime generator of *alpha*-elements" (Grotstein, 2007, p. 107). In yet another formulation, Grotstein offered a theology that was still closer to the views of Moses Maimonides (Bakan, Merkur & Weiss, 2009). Here mystical experience of God was considered an imagination that makes symbolic use of an aspect of the soul that is suitable as a carrier of the idea of immanence. "Since God is ineffable and inscrutable (never an object of contemplation), then the only way He can be known is through the projective attribution of some essence within us that is proximate, that is, through the ineffability of our unconscious (or, more specifically, of the Ineffable Subject of the Unconscious)" (Grotstein, 2000b, p. 139).

THE INEFFABLE SUBJECT

Limiting his discussion to the aspect of the divine or of the psyche that is akin to the divine that can be experienced and is then found to be numinous and preternatural, Grotstein (2000b) remarked that the divine is experienced as a mysterious, Ineffable Subject, in contrast with the Phenomenal Subject that psychoanalysis conventionally associates with the ego, self, and sense of agency (p. 122). The Ineffable Subject is an unconscious psychological subjectivity, a component within the psyche that is experienced as numinous. It is both an internal object and an internal subject, the Background Object of Primary Identification (Grotstein, 1981b, p. 369) and the Background Subject of Primary Identification (p. 370). In Bion's terms, the background subject-object was O in K, an intrapsychic manifestation of the ineffable. "The background subject-object aspect of 'I' seems to be associated with (O), that aspect of Universal Truth which is unknowable but approachable through (K)" (Grotstein, 1981b, p. 372). In the course of development, "the human being undergoes a series or sequence of caesuras in which (s)he experiences a sense of separation" from the background subject-object (p. 369).

> It is the principle of continuity which, in religious terms, can be called God, and in natural science, the guiding principles of natural laws. In Taoism, it can be seen as the unifying, hovering spirit of Oneness which binds all existence....In the sense that the background object is an object, it constitutes the "Other," the object of our experience, whereas, as subject, it expresses our subjective experience to be connected with a larger subjective "I"-ness (Grotstein, 1981b, p. 370).

In mystical experience, the Phenomenal Subject experiences the Ineffable Subject as cosmic in extent, and its own subjectivity as derivative of the greater subjectively that is ineffable (Grotstein, 2000b, p. 11). Subjectivity is a spiritual reality without whose discussion psychoanalysis is incomplete (p. xxviii). "Subjectivity not only dares to risk being the authentic sense organ for experience (i.e. for *being*) but becomes active by subjectivizing experiences as its own personal repertoire and finally links up with its sense of *agency* (intentionality, will, desire, conation, entelechy) to seek and to react to experience" (p. 121).

The Ineffable Subject may also be conceptualized objectively as a dynamic psychological process. "There exists a *Coherent Presence*, an *Intelligence*, or *Wisdom* that is preternatural in nature, that can be understood to function as a putatively 'divine' creator and organizer of unconscious mental life, including our (?) spontaneous free associative 'thoughts-without-a-thinker'" (Grotstein, 1996, p. 130). Grotstein (2000b) summarized "that what I am calling the Ineffable Subject has at least two functions: (1) pure being and (2) ineffable or oracular communication and agency, as in dreams, free associations, parapraxes, jokes, and symptoms" (p. 125). Further features of the second function included "the unconscious capacity for prescience or premonition" (p. xxviii) that Bion had mentioned.

ON PSYCHIC PRESENCES

In describing the Ineffable Subject as a "Background Presence," Grotstein classified it with a large group of psychological quiddities that are known in psychoanalysis as "psychic presences." "My term *psychic presences* is meant to convey the experience of intrapsychic preternatural entities, which present as images or phantoms and which we, in turn, reify as real" (Grotstein, 2000b, p. xix). Grotstein listed Jung's archetypes, the characters in Klein's unconscious phantasies, and Bion's preconceptions as theories about presences. Grotstein followed Thomas H. Ogden when he asserted that psychic presences may appear to have subjectivity but do not actually do so. "Ogden (1983), in his discussion of the internal object as an amalgam of projected self and object, asserts that '*if internal objects are thoughts...then they themselves cannot think, perceive or feel, nor can they protect or attack the ego*' (p. 229; italics added)--to which I add that *only subjects do*" (Grotstein, 2000b, p. 159). In correspondence, Grotstein (2001, personal communication) clarified:

> Internal objects are a myth. There is no such thing as [an] internal object. We do not take in objects. We paint them with the artistry of our autochthonous imagination. Internal objects do not think. The agency of what are erroneously called internal objects is the projective subjectivity of the subject's own self. Introjection is a myth.

In Grotstein's view, the psychic presences that have wrongly been called internal objects are recurring characters in the manifest contents of dreams, symptoms, and other manifestations of unconscious phantasies. Psychic presences are not centers of activity within the psyche. They may be portrayed as having subjectivity, but they have none. They may be portrayed as thinking, but they do not think.

The Background Presence is an example of an unthinking psychic presence. Correctly understood, it is "phantasied and mythical" (p. 18). It is not a division of the psyche, even though it seems to be so. It can be identified with the presence of God or, in Gnostic theology, with the Demiurge (p. 19). It includes but is not limited to God-representation (Rizzuto, 1979). It may develop, but it may also undergo attenuation that changes its theological identity (Grotstein, 2000b, p. 18).

No differently than the Background Presence, the Phenomenal Subject constitutes a psychic presence. Rejecting Freud's (1923a) claim that "the ego is first and foremost a bodily ego" (p. 26), Grotstein followed Tausk (1933) in suggesting that "the infant is born as a psyche and claims its body as its own, first by 'creating' it by way of identification through projection and then by discovery" (Grotstein, 2000b, p. 48). "The infant is born as a yet-to-be-embodied psyche, which soon enough becomes confronted with the intrusive neediness and demandingness of its "psyche-soma" as well as with the intrusive vicissitudes of the object world" (p. 118). Like the body ego, the self too is a psychic presence. "Self is the object reflection of Freud's *das Ich* ('I') and can be viewed from the instinctual, moral, rational, and subjective viewpoints" (p. 97).

It is the subjectivity of the psyche as a whole that underlies the Background Presence of the Ineffable Subject, the Phenomenal Subject, the body ego, and the self. "The psychoanalytic concept of the subject is inclusive of the whole personality and of its putative component selves" (Grotstein, 2000b, p. 118). "Whereas the Ineffable Subject is numinous, the Phenomenal Subject is secular, manifest, incarnate, palpable. I consider these two subjectivities to be...part of an overall ultimately indivisible subjectivity--the Supraordinate Subject of Being and Agency--which is both holistic and divided" (p. 141).

THE DUAL TRACK

Grotstein assimilated the differences between the Ineffable and Phenomenal Subjects to the familiar Freudian distinction between the id and the ego, the primary and secondary processes.

> My view is that the so-called id is another ego ("alter ego"...) and normally operates in parallel with the traditional ego, albeit with a different set of laws governing its functions. Each "ego" is so constituted as to process or encode the data of internal and external experience complementarily (objectively and subjectively). Another way of stating this is that primary process and secondary process are psychical partners that may appose and oppose one another (like the thumb and forefinger, for instance) but are not necessarily in conflict with one another. They function as if they constituted a *dual track*....and work toward a common purpose. (Grotstein, 1990a, p. 34)

To account for the mystical character of the unconscious, Grotstein turned to the theories of Ignacio Matte-Blanco, a psychoanalyst and metaphysician who claimed that unconscious and conscious thinking can be described mathematically (Grotstein, 1996, p. 112). Matte-Blanco (1959) expressed the core of his thinking on the mathematical formulation of the unconscious as follows:

> *The system Ucs treats the converse of any relation as identical with the relation. In other words, it treats relations as if they were symmetrical.*
>
> To quote an example, If John is the brother of Peter, the converse is: Peter is the brother of John. The relation which exists between them is symmetrical, because the converse is identical with the direct relation. But if John is the father of Peter, the converse is: Peter is the son of John. In this case the relation and its converse are not identical. This type of relation which is always different from its converse is called asymmetrical. (p. 2; Matte-Blanco's italics)

Matte-Blanco here substituted the concepts of symmetry and asymmetry for Freud's concepts of condensation and reality-testing, respectively. In the process, he arrived at mathematical formulations that converged with Fromm's distinction between the paradoxical logic of mysticism and the Aristotelian logic of science.

What was significant about Matte-Blanco's work for Grotstein's purposes was its treatment of the unconscious as a logical system. Matte-Blanco (1959) wrote:

> If laws of the system Ucs exist, and if they do not conform to the principles of scientific logic, they must conform to some logical system that at least in some respect is different from scientific logic. The laws of the system Ucs could then be the consequence of principles of this logical system; in any case they would conform to it. (p. 2)

The theory of infantile solipsism played no part in Grotstein's thinking. How were mystical experiences to be explained? Although Matte-Blanco's circular reasoning in the above quotation deduced the existence of a logical system from the consequences of the unearned assumption that it exists, his model provided Grotstein with the idea that mystical experiences are products of a distinctive type of thinking that the unconscious performs.

Through Matte-Blanco, Grotstein came to attribute mysticism to a distinct type of thinking, rather than to the unconscious persistence of infantile naiveté.

Loewald had offered a more elegant theory to the same general effect when he traced the timelessness of mystical experience to condensation. Condensation instantiates Eros. Unconscious symbol-formation includes a process that can condense anything with anything, accomplishing the unification of all things in one.

Inspired by Matte-Blanco's formulation, Grotstein (1996, p. 113) attributed the paranoid-schizoid position to the unconscious, dream-making activity of the alpha-function. Grotstein similarly attributed the depressive position to the conceptual thinking of the alpha-function. "The depressive position is the mediator of transformations from mythic P-S alpha function to K" (p. 113). This division of the alpha-function into two portions, one unconscious and the other not, reinterpreted Bion's theory in terms of the id-ego model that Bion had rejected. Generalizing further, Grotstein proposed that the "dual track" functions were not only different mathematico-logical procedures or processes but addressed different concerns. Each was a means to a different end. The normal, transient, and partial dissociation of conceptual thinking made possible self-reflection, intersubjectivity, and the capacity to mentalize the minds of others (Grotstein, 2000b, p. 84). Grotstein's division of alpha-function into dreamwork and thinking agreed with Noy's formulations of the primary and secondary processes and simultaneously converged with Winnicott's distinction between subjectively perceived objects and objectively perceived objects. Kohut and Loewald had expressed similar observations with reference to narcissistic cathexis and object cathexis.

Grotstein's phrase "dual track" made explicit that unlike previous psychoanalytic mystics he was not postulating a developmental sequence. He was not postulating a developmental phase of infantile solipsism; neither was he postulating its maturation into secondary narcissism and external reality. Rather, he was proposing a dialectical relation where two mutually exclusive points of view were routinely applied simultaneously to single concerns. Individuals regularly employ both the paradoxical (symmetrical) logic of mysticism and the (asymmetrical) Aristotelian logic of science, either simultaneously or in very rapid alternation. Dual track theory was Grotstein's version of Bion's lifelong fluctuation between the paranoid-schizoid and depressive positions.

AUTOCHTHONY

Grotstein most frequently expressed his ideas of the dual track with reference to the concepts of *autochthony* and *alterity*.

> Autochthony (from the Greek "born from the earth" or "native to" but used here in the sense of "born from [native to] the self")--solipsistic, syncretistic--is a birth phantasy in which the self is defined by its self-creation, and external objects are understood to owe their origin to having been created by the self. Autochthony exists in a dialectical relationship with *alterity*, the awareness of the Otherness of the object and cocreation by it and with it (i.e., the phantasy--and ultimate the realization--of the cocreation and defining of the self *by* external objects, by subjects, or by both). Autochthony designates omnipotent, imaginative self-creationism and the creation of the world of one's objects. It is dialectically counterposed to intersubjectivity and *social constructivism*, the realization of one's dependence on the other and of the absence of omnipotence--a realization that applies not only to one's birth but also to the cocreation with the other of one's personal reality. (Grotstein, 2000b, p. 38)

Grotstein's concept of autochthony was "inspired in part by Winnicott's (1971) conception of creativity which I seek to extend" (Grotstein, 1997b, p. 404; see also 2000b, p. 41). "We must first 'dream,' i.e., imaginatively create and fantasize our emotional experiences through primary process, before we can discover, accept, and own them accountably through secondary process" (Grotstein, 1997b, p. 420).

In agreement with Loewald, Grotstein regarded creation in phantasy as a progressive and integrative process. It was in no sense of the term a regression.

> When we use the term *regression*, we really mean *progression* of primitive awarenesses to the surface rather than the other way around....Structures do not regress. Perceptual content may, under certain circumstances, find access to the surface of awareness and therefore rise to meet the sense organ receptors of the perceptual apparatus--and of intuition. This "progression" takes place in terms of the return of the repressed in mental illness but also occurs normally on an ongoing basis. Creativity is but one normal facet of it. (Grotstein, 1981b, pp. 405-6)

At the same time, Grotstein (2000b, p. 39) intended his concept of autochthony to account for the narcissistic developmental line that Kohut had discussed. Grotstein distinguished between primary autochthony, which was equivalent to Winnicott's creative illusion, and secondary autochthony, "in which the infant defends against a differentiated traumatic external experience by claiming retrospective responsibility as agent where autochthonous phantasies are devised retrospectively" (Grotstein, 1997b, p. 407). Secondary autochthony was involved, for example, in the guilt that people feel over having been traumatized--the victim's phantasy of having been responsible for victimization.

Grotstein may have been thinking of extrovertive mystical experiences, a category that which includes but is not limited to the oceanic feeling, when he discussed a further example of autochthony, where alterity is perceived but autochthony is conceived and emoted.

> The infant may *perceive* itself to be separate from the object but simultaneously may emotionally *conceive* that the object is an extension of it. This form of thinking has been termed egocentric..., prereflective..., or cyclopean and is characteristic of Klein's (1946) paranoid-schizoid position. (Grotstein, 2000b, p. 156)

Grotstein neatly summarized the autochthonous implications of Winnicott's theory when he asserted that "what we commonly call reality itself is an illusion that disguises the Real (O)" (Grotstein, 2001, p. 130). Extending the same line of autochthonous reasoning, Grotstein (2001) went so far as to claim "that the concept of O transforms all existing psychoanalytic theories (e.g. the pleasure principle, the death instinct, and the paranoid-schizoid and depressive positions) into veritable psychoanalytic manic defenses against the unknown, unknowable, ineffable, inscrutable, ontological experience of ultimate being, what Bion terms 'Absolute Truth, Ultimate Reality'" (pp. 129-30)

ALTERITY

Grotstein has made brief references, at different junctures in his writings, to innovative ideas that will need further work before they become substantive theories. For example, his contributions on alterity consisted, for the most part, of images of alterity in dreams, phantasies, and myths. This concern for alterity-within-autochthony may be contrasted with alterity proper, on which Grotstein had little to say beyond invoking Klein's concept of the depressive position. To this generalization there is a notable exception.

> I believe that Kohut's (1971) formulations...following as they did in the footsteps of A. Reich's (1960) concept of self-esteem regulation in narcissism, offer formulations that allow for a broader extension of the concept of self-regulation beyond the newer concept of self-disorders. Insofar as Kohut's formulations hypothesize an independent development of the self vis-à-vis its relationship to objects, we now have a whole new way of conceiving of human motivation and psychopathology along lines first adumbrated by Freud....More specifically, Freud speculated that the libidinal instincts were counterposed to the ego instincts, the latter being directed toward the preservation of the self and the former toward the preservation of the race. Freud (1914a) later abandoned this distinction when he reformulated that the ego itself is the id's first object....
>
> I should like to rescue Freud's original hypothesis from the shadows into which he long ago retired it and amalgamate it with Kohut's (1971) theory of the duality of developmental agendas of the self....and offer a theory which speculates that each human organism, like its other primate analogues, is motivated toward *self-preservation* and toward *group preservation* via *innate altruism*--provided that there is a sufficiently intact bonding or attachment to a group unit. (Grotstein, 1986, p. 107)

In Grotstein's formulation, theories of infantile solipsism pertain to autochthony and provide an incomplete account of early development. When a dual track model is interpolated, a theory of altruism arises as an extension of Kohut's approach to narcissism.

THE TRANSCENDENT POSITION

Grotstein employed the term "transcendent" in a sense that was inspired by, but not limited to, its use by Kierkegaard and the existentialists. "Transcendent means having the ability to transcend our defensiveness, our pettiness, our guilt, our shame, our narcissism, our need for certainty, our strictures in order to achieve or to become 'one with O,' which I interpret as becoming one with our *aliveness*...or with our very *being-ness* (our *Dasein*...)" (Grotstein, 2000b, p. 300). A person attained the "transcendent position" during a moment of union with O. Grotstein (2000b) described the experience of the transcendent position as a "state of serenity that accompanies one who...is able to become reconciled to the experience of pure, unadulterated Being and Happening" (pp. 281-82). The "'transcendent position'...both supervenes and transcends the functioning of the paranoid-schizoid and depressive positions but also mediates the infinities and chaos of the Real" (Grotstein, 1996, p. 109).

Some of Grotstein's formulations of the transcendent position reflected the solipsism of Bion's Neoplatonism. "In the transcendent position the individual must forsake the presence of the object in order to look inward into his/her own subjectivity...the transcendent position is the quintessence of a subjectivity that transcends (for the moment) object relations" (Grotstein, 1996, p. 114; see also p. 124). Where Grotstein's reports of Bion's formulations implied introvertive mystical experiences, Grotstein's more independent formulations referred explicitly to extrovertive experiences of other people and the external world. Grotstein explicitly denied, for example, that the transcendent position was the sort of mystical experience that Neoplatonism privileged.

> The concept of a transcendent position does not constitute a whimsical journey into lofty, ethereal abandon, nor does it necessarily validate religion, spirituality, or the belief in God, except as a need by humans whereby they attempt to close the maw of the ineffable with an all-encompassing name. It is not in the oeuvre of W. Somerset Maugham's Larry Darrell, the protagonist in *The Razor's Edge* who sought "enlightenment" atop the Himalayas. In other words, it is not a blissful, "autistic enclave." O is one's reality without pretense or distortion. This reality can be a symptom, the pain of viewing beautiful autumn leaves, gazing on the mystique of Mona Lisa de la Giocanda, contemplating the horror of Ypres (for Bion), trying to remember Hiroshima, Nagasaki, Auschwitz, or Viet Nam, or resting comfortably beside one's mate trying to contemplate the exquisiteness and ineffability of the moment. (Grotstein, 2000b, pp. 300-301)

In this passage, Grotstein's examples of the transcendent position were consistently extrovertive.

The unity of the transcendent position was not an original, utter simplicity, but an all-inclusive integration. "In its comprehensive capacity for 'at-one-ment' the transcendent position reconciles virtually all the 'vertices' or cosmic perspectives which inform Bion's higher epistemological endeavors, i.e., the scientific, mathematical, spiritual, mystical, noumenal, and aesthetic, to which I now add the transcendent" (Grotstein, 1996, p. 128). The external orientation of the transcendent position could go so far as to involve an encounter with God as a numinous Other. In the transcendent position, "one can be in communion with a sense of an Absolute Truth that one can tolerate never really knowing" (p. 129).

Other formulations of the transcendent position were more in keeping with Grotstein's own ideas of simultaneously transcending and synthesizing the dual track of autochthony and alterity.

> The "transcendent position" represents the achievement of the state of meditative-like grace in which one experiences a serenity that transcends conflict....One has achieved the capacity for mourning, reparation, empathy, tolerance of ambivalence, and true love and caring. One must then continue his/her ontological pilgrimage to the next state, one of enlightenment and serenity where one is at peace with oneself and with the world, both internal and external. (Grotstein, 1996, pp. 127-28).

Achievement of the transcendent position was optimally to be experienced in clinical contexts by both the analyst and the patient simultaneously. "Perhaps the quintessence of my theme about the transcendent position is the concept of the presence of a '*Transcendent Subject of Being*,' which the analyst and his patient become or approximate becoming when a transformative evolution in 'O' occurs, i.e., a resonance with one's own respective 'O' as well as the 'O' that is communal between them" (Grotstein, 1996, p. 130).

Grotstein's formulation of the transcendent position can be taken in two senses. To engage in analytic listening "with the third ear" and to be receptive to intuition, in the manner of Reik and Fromm, was conceptualized by Bion as union with O that facilitated transformation in and of O. When the patient reciprocates, by associating freely in a self-analytic and insightful manner, both analyst and patient may be credited with being in the transcendent position. A distinction must be made, however, between the achievement of a transcendent moment and the acquisition of a habitual capacity for transcendent experiencing. Just as an analyst's calm may calm an anxious patient, an analyst may use the unobjectionable positive transference-countertransference to carry a patient, as it were, into a mutual achievement of the transcendent position; but any such clinical event can only be useful therapeutically for providing the patient with a glimpse of a characterological potential that has yet to be actualized. It is an insightful emotional experience that remains to be worked through. For the patient's attainment of the transcendent position to become more than a transference cure, the patient must internalize or introject the analyst's transcendent position, partly as new ego ideal content and partly as new self-representation content, until the patient comes to achieve what might, however metaphorically, be called transcendent object constancy. The completion of this achievement is, to my thought, implicit as a second sense in which Grotstein has sometimes discussed the transcendent position.

At the same time, I suspect that Grotstein may work clinically with a broader concept of the transcendent position than his literary formulations might suggest. Perhaps it is the spiritual, and not only mystical union with O, that we should include in the transcendent position. For example, an analyst may easily bring a patient through the interpretation of dreams to a numinous experience of wonderment at the unconscious process that Grotstein calls the Dreamer Who Dreams the Dream. The inculcation of wonder at the wisdom of the dream can readily serve as a point of departure for further experiences of the numinous, such as wonder at the latent content of free associations and parapraxes in session, and wonder also at self-analytic inspirations and insights.

Another aspect of Grotstein's formulation that warrants comment is the implication that clinical psychoanalysts should routinely inculcate the achievement of mystical experiences. Fromm asserted that analysts and their patients should seek Zen-like states in order to meet in moments of Buberian encounter. Grotstein urges that analysts and their patients should both attain union with O in states of reverie. In keeping with the differences in their clinical styles, Fromm and Grotstein found different mystical experiences to be useful therapeutically. Fromm sought undifferentiation and empathy; Grotstein's phrasing instead accommodates unitive modes. Because Fromm called his procedure transtherapeutic, it is Grotstein's formulation alone that raises the question, "But is it psychoanalytic?" In one of his kinder discussions of Jung's analytic psychology, Freud (1933) wrote: "We for our part...say: 'This may be a school of wisdom; but it is no longer analysis'" (p. 143). Should one say the same for Grotstein's project?

Whether an analyst qua analyst should be engaged in promoting mystical experiences is, in my view, part of the larger question of the place of "after-education" in psychoanalysis. Loewald argued that pedagogy is inevitable because neutral mirroring is and always has been a fiction. Bion argued that interventions are transformative. Grotstein has drawn the logical conclusion and added the transcendent position to the curriculum. Due to the tradition of contrasting analysis with suggestion, most psychoanalysts today remain uncomfortable admitting to their pedagogical functions. The need for pedagogy has long been recognized in analytic work with adolescents, children, and personality disorders of pre-Oedipal origin; most analysts nevertheless continue to subscribe to the fantasy that "classically analyzable patients" can be treated without pedagogy. The whole of psychoanalysis is nevertheless pedagogical. According to Freud, the neuroses are consequences of trauma, which is to say, of catastrophic learning experiences in childhood that inculcated distressing and counterproductive habits. Undoing repression, which is the very essence of clinical psychoanalysis (Freud, 1914b, p. 16; Fenichel, 1945, p. 573), is nothing but a remedial learning process. The historical happenstance that neurosis was assumed to be neurological until Freud established its psychological character has given longevity to medical tropes that have never been valid. Neither is a hermeneutic model the appropriate alternative to a medical one. Psychoanalysis is and always has been nothing but an after-education. The relevant question is not whether we should teach, but how we decide whether any individual topic belongs on an analyst's lesson plan.

Regarding the transcendent position, I would suggest that its internalization involves, among other features, the automatization of what Milner and Ehrenzweig called "creative surrender," which is indeed a distinctive achievement in therapy. If the onset of the capacity for concern or, as I have elsewhere called it, the capacity for relationality (Merkur, 2007) occurs as the neurotically inhibited ego ceases to repress positive superego functions such as empathy and conscience, the transcendent position involves a further shift in ego-superego relations. With increased trust, the ego delegates selected aspects of its "executive function" (Rangell, 1986) to the positive superego, merging real and ideal in maximal integration. Freud (1921) discussed the merger of real and ideal in connection with falling in love. A creative person's love affair with creativity is precisely parallel. It is the same rapturous process as being in love, but devoted to a different topic. The transcendent position pertains to the general application: it concerns the extrovertive mystic's love affair with the world.

I would further suggest that the mystical is irreplaceable for its power to overcome stranger anxiety (Spitz, with Cobliner, 1965) and its lifelong sequel, irrational prejudices and bigotries against entire categories of others, by rekindling love and trust for all humanity. If psychoanalysis is to be defined with Freud (1914b), as "any line of investigation" (p. 16) that addresses resistance and transference, then the undoing of stranger anxiety, however it is accomplished, must be counted within the scope of psychoanalysis.

INNOCENCE AS A DEVELOPMENTAL LINE

Grotstein generally discussed the transcendent position as both a position and a brief, transient attainment. At one point, however, he wrote of innocence as a spiritual line of development that was similarly in dialectical relation with both the paranoid-schizoid and the depressive positions (Grotstein, 2000b, p. 259). His thinking on the topic began with the observation that Freud and classical psychoanalysis had portrayed unconscious instincts as chaotic, untamed, and subjectively experienced as sinful and evil; whereas the British Middle School—Balint, Fairbairn, and Winnicott—had been followed by both Sullivan and Kohut in acknowledging "a primal innocence" that their therapeutic efforts sought to bring to consciousness (Grotstein, 1984, pp. 207-8). Innocence is not an autonomous state; it is an interactive one. "Innocence is the crucial element in a person's spiritual nature. It is greatly influenced by his or her inner nature and by the outer environment and cultural imperatives that confront this inner nature" (p. 213). Grotstein associated innocence with empathy (p. 203), implicitly because the sense of innocence is contingent on self-reflection in retrospect of empathy. Avoiding the terms "will" and "choice," Grotstein positioned the sense of self in between its moral self-evaluations: "Human nature's pristine component is a moral ambiguity between evil and innocence" (p. 208). The concept of a developmental line pertained to the repeated need to regain the sense of innocence once it has been lost. "The homeostasis or ecological concord that exists in every biological system, [is] that state of constancy whose moral term may be *innocence*. Curiosity and desire are perturbations to homeostasis and therefore to innocence" (p. 207). Because Freud had associated homeostasis with the Nirvana principle, a psychic motionlessness attained through a total expenditure of psychic energy, Grotstein's meaning would have been more clear had he referred not to homeostasis, but to the sense or balance that arises through the integration of the psyche's multiple functions. Innocence is a unitive, integrative achievement.

In his initial presentation, Grotstein (1984) suggested that "the ego ideal....represents primal innocence" (p. 221). In a later formulation, he suggested that Abraham's concept of the preambivalent stage and Fairbairn's concept of the preambivalent object both pertained to an early infantile condition of innocence. It is this innocence whose loss can be occasioned through acceptance of a sense of agency (Grotstein, 2000b, p. 260). Grotstein's formulation of innocence as both a position and as a developmental line may be seen as yet another psychoanalytic approach to topics of concern to existentialism. Grotstein's perspective had the novelty of a dual track model that by-passed and ignored the issue of individuation, while proceeding directly to the questions of innocence, anxiety, and innocence regained.

REMARKS ON CLINICAL TECHNIQUE

Grotstein announced a book on clinical technique several years ago, but it has yet to see publication. In the meantime, we have only passing comments. Grotstein followed Bion in conceptualizing psychoanalysis as a two-person mystical process.

> One can hypothesize that psychopathology represents an incompletion in the iterative transformational cycle of O-->K-->O and that one of our goals as psychoanalysts is to introduce our analysands to a self-reflection of, and repetitive contact with, their subject of being (rather than to enable them merely to understand themselves) so that with each recertification from this pilgrimage into a subjective solitude of being they emerge ever-more self-transcendent, that is, ever-more accepting of their being (*Dasein*), their subjectivity, their experiences, and their psychic responsibility for them. I believe this being "at one with the experience" is what Bion meant by "transformations in O." (Grotstein, 2000b, pp. 128-29)

This formulation presupposes a conventional psychoanalytic situation in the tradition of Klein and Bion, where the analyst perceives the patient's conscious and unconscious productions and, through reverie, alpha-function, and intuition, transforms it into knowledge (K). This knowledge is provided to the patient in the form of an intervention that the patient's Ineffable Subject is able to employ in order to continue the patient's progress toward O. What is novel in the procedure is the mystical discourse in which the analyst engages the patient.

Grotstein stated explicitly what Bion had only implied, that the injunctions for the analyst to proceed without memory, desire or understanding were intended to produce mystical experiences. "The analyst must be in...the 'transcendent position' (a state of reverie in O)" (Grotstein, 2000b, p. 264). "To be in a state of what Bion (1970) termed reverie, which connotes a 'transformation' or 'evolution in O,' one must be without memory, desire (intentionality), understanding, knowledge, or preconception. At that serene moment, the subject (which may also be God) just *is*--as a cosmic and ineffable being" (p. 258). "The ultimate rationale that the analyst should abandon (really, suspend) memory, desire, understanding, and preconception is to allow the analyst to keep the inner container empty of sense-derived prejudice so that s/he can all the more be able to 'look inward,' that is, intuit his/her own subjective responses to the analysand's projective (trans)-identifications" (Grotstein, 2000a, p. 692).

Grotstein discussed the rapport between the analyst and the patient in similar terms. "When the ineffable subject of the unconscious finds an external other who happens to be a psychoanalyst, then the two together constitute what the Greeks called the *psychopomp*, the conductor to the realm of lost souls" (Grotstein, 2000b, p. xv).

Grotstein (1994) understood the analyst's practice of abstinence as a necessity if he is to meditate while listening to patients.

> I think that in the discrepancy between the two proposed fates for abstinence lies the question of what really constitutes the analytic relationship. Is it an "I-Thou" (Buber, 1958), interpersonal, intersubjective relationship, where it would be understandable that one might believe that abstinence should be abandoned; or is it an unusual, even *unique* relationship that has to be specially constructed and maintained with disciplined care so that the unconscious may have its long-thwarted epiphany and a sacred cryptography can transpire?
>
> Some may argue, and I am one, that perhaps the most important provision that the analyst can proffer his/her patient is his/her discipline, forbearance, and his/her capacity to suspend his/her "memory and desires"...and thereby provide an identification with a "visual-cliff"...model for the patient's ability to suspend his or her needs and desires so that transformation and metamorphosis can occur. The mutuality and reciprocity of this bilaterally disciplined forbearance, suspension, and abstinence constitute the analytic covenant and are the analyst's most precious gift. (p. 598)

Reik (1948) had offered a similar concept of abstinence in Freud's name, when he recommended analytic "listening with the third ear." Buber had claimed, however, that the asymmetry of a patient-therapist relationship precluded the possibility of a true meeting. Buber (1958) wrote:

> The normative limitation of mutuality is presented to us in the relation between a genuine psychotherapist and his patient. If he is satisfied to "analyse" him, i.e. to bring to light unknown factors from his microcosm, and to set to some conscious work in

> life the energies which have been transformed by such an emergence, then he may be successful in some repair work. At best he may help a soul which is diffused and poor in structure to collect and order itself to some extent. But the real matter, the regeneration of an atrophied personal centre, will not be achieved. This can only be done by one who grasps the buried latent unity of the suffering soul with the great glance of the doctor: and this can only be attained in the person-to-person attitude of a partner, not by the consideration and examination of an object. In order that he may coherently further the liberation and actualisation of that unity in a new accord of the person with the world, the psychotherapist, like the educator, must stand again and again not merely at his own pole in the bipolar relation, but also with the strength of present realisation at the other pole, and experience the effect of his own action. But again, the specific "healing" relation would come to an end the moment the patient thought of, and succeeded in, practising "inclusion" and experiencing the event from the doctor's pole as well. Healing, like educating, is only possible to the one who lives over against the other, and yet is detached. (Buber, 1958, pp. 132-33)

Buber notwithstanding, Fromm and Bion had adapted Buber's concept of I-Thou encounter to their practices of analytic listening. Grotstein favored Buber's own understanding.

Grotstein (1995) recommended use of the couch precisely for its capacity to preclude a meeting between analyst and patient.

> Lying down facilitates a shift from the real to the imaginative, phantasmal, and illusory worlds....the analyst, strictly conceived, listens not to the speaking patient but to the text of associations from the patient's unconscious, for which the patient's conscious speech (free associations) is merely the "channel." Likewise, when the analyst interprets, he or she speaks to the unconscious through the conscious ego, not to the patient per se. The use of the couch facilitates this unique dialogue. (pp. 397-98)

Grotstein (1996) followed Bion in valuing "sensory deprivation in psychoanalytic technique" for its capacity to promote the ancient mystical "technique of *intuition*, taken in its literal sense: 'looking inward' by forswearing the glimpse of the external object" (p. 119).

The privileging of serenity over empathy while awaiting intuition of the patient's unconscious had its limitations for Grotstein, as for Bion. From Bion, Grotstein learned to impersonalize or de-personalize the patient in a fashion that was consistent with Bion's mentalist cosmos and was completely opposed, for example, to the Buberian encounter that Fromm advocated. "The concept of preternatural presences came to me as I was beginning to use a clinical technique that I had picked up from my own analyst, Wilfred Bion....I found myself listening not to an analysand per se (i.e., the person of the analysand who spoke) but to the seemingly depersonified text itself, which, from one point of view, was other than human or personal" (Grotstein, 2000b, p. xxiii). The patient was here not a Thou but an It.

CONCLUDING REFLECTIONS

Grotstein's model presupposes that the psyche consists, at bottom, of only a single process: the alpha-function. Loewald's concept of the psyche's fundamental nondifferentiation, and its acquisition of differentiation exclusively through mental structures, similarly imagined an intrinsically unified psyche. Grotstein has provided a contemporary Kleinian alternative to Loewald's ego psychological formulations. Secular equivalents of this model were advanced by George S. Klein (1976) and Morris N. Eagle (1984), who argued that the psyche consists exclusively of an ego, and by Charles Brenner (1994), who similarly proposed that the tripartite structural model be abandoned, in his version, because the psyche consists exclusively of compromise formations.

Freud (1923a) had proposed a unified psyche when he advanced the structural hypothesis, but he abandoned it in 1937 when he asserted that "we have no reason to dispute the existence and importance of original, innate distinguishing characteristics of the ego" (p. 240). Hartmann's (1958) concept of the primary autonomy of inborn ego apparatuses built on Freud's renunciation of the unity of the unstructured psyche. In the topographic hypothesis (Freud, 1900) and again in the structural hypothesis after its revision in 1937, Freud postulated inherent differences in the neurophysiology of the primary and secondary processes. The primary process acted at the frontier of the body and the mind; it was responsible for unconscious proprioception, including the unconscious proprioception of the physiological precursors of drives. The secondary process was neurophysiologically connected to external sensation, and it was responsible for unifying the senses through the simultaneity of their perception, which is the nature of consciousness. It was because the one process was hard-wired to sense inward and the other hard-wired to perceive outward that they conformed with a pleasure principle and a reality principle, respectively. The two mental processes ordinarily pooled the results of their thinking into a common reservoir, so that each could work with the other's products (Rycroft, 1956). The ego had recourse, however, to repression when it was at risk of being overwhelmed and paralyzed by the id's products. Therapy restored the common pool by reducing the danger of the repressed.

We can retain Grotstein's invaluable concepts about psychic presences, I suggest, without having to insist that the unconscious process that generates psychic presences is necessarily the only psychic process. Freud, for example, attributed the function of an internal object to the superego. "The ego...enters into the relation of an object to the ego ideal...and...all the interplay between an external object and the ego as a whole....may possibly be repeated upon this new scene of action (Freud, 1921, p. 130; see also: 1923a, p. 29). Grotstein's own considerations of the superego are consistent with a view of psychic presences as roles or personas that the superego constructs, much as the ego temporarily identifies with a variety of roles when engaged in play, in theatrical performance, and in all manner of walks of life. Grotstein (2000b) stated: "I think that the superego itself and the ego ideal are generally normal, no matter how seemingly distorted or malicious they may appear to be, and that what we see in pathological situations are the 'barnacles' of the patient's projective identifications, which obtund the appearance and expression of the normal superego and ego ideal" (p. 131).

Eleven

The Personal Monism of Neville Symington

Neville Symington, currently resident in Sydney, Australia, trained at the Institute for Psychoanalysis in London and for many years taught at the Tavistock Clinic in London. Symington and his wife, Joan Symington, attended several of Bion's workshops at the Tavistock and the Institute of Psychoanalysis and later co-authored *The Clinical Thinking of Wilfred Bion* (1996). Like almost everyone, the Symingtons re-interpreted Bion in a fashion that minimizes or eliminates Bion's philosophical idealism. The Symingtons' book argues for Bion's compatibility with the findings of empirical science. At the same time, Symington was inspired by Bion to undertake a thorough-going reconceptualization of clinical psychoanalysis from a mystical point of view. Where Bion was both carefully Kleinian and carefully Neoplatonic, Symington pursued a separate path. Because Symington (2002) used "a combination of ordinary language and what might widely be called religious language" (p. 6), his intellectual debts and technical concepts are not always transparent. Symington left the Roman Catholic priesthood before training as an analyst (Symington, 2007, p. xviii), is deeply read in philosophical literature, and favors the metaphysics of the Hindu Upanishads. His clinical style was influenced by the innovations of his analyst, John Klauber (Symington, 2007, pp. 3). Although Symington was trained and taught in the British Independent group, he was also attracted to Kleinian theories, which left him somewhat marginalized. He began to flourish as an original theoretician only after leaving London for Australia in 1985. Symington's psychoanalytic theories belong generally in the British tradition of object relations, but with greater debts to Fairbairn than to Klein and Bion (Symington, 1993b, p. 39). On the issue whether internal objects are inborn or acquired, Symington (1994, p. 121) opted for Fairbairn's concept that real people are internalized in the ego, and he opposed Klein's concept of internal objects that are inborn, instinctual, and projected onto people. He also followed Fairbairn in using conventional religious terms to discuss psychic processes, thereby creating "a religious mythology" as a technical terminology for psychoanalysis (Symington, 2002, p. 206; 2004a, p. 10); the practice originated with Suttie (1935). Symington (1994, pp. 39, 102, 115) also acknowledges the influences of Winnicott and Fromm.

In lectures that Symington gave at the Tavistock almost a decade prior to his major theoretical innovations, he characterized psychoanalysis in unitive terms that echoed the views of Fromm and Loewald. Symington (1986) placed symbiotic union and the integration of the personality in dialectic as alternative approaches to unity.

> There are two ways in which man can feel a unity. Either he clings to a unified system outside himself or he tries to unite something inside himself. In the first case the disunity within remains, but he protects himself from nameless dread by hanging on to a religion, a political ideology, a cultural value system, or national, tribal or familial traditions. This method can work well in a traditional society or one with a single value system, but given the pluralistic value system of the modern large conurbation it does not work as well, or is more likely to fail.
>
> The other way is for man to go into himself and forge his many different complexes into a cohesive whole. A person may achieve this without professional help, as Freud and Jung did, and as a certain number of people do, but he may need to approach a psychoanalyst. In the giving of meaning to the patient's utterances the psychic bits come together, slowly and hesitatingly, and form a cohesive unity. (pp. 46-47)

Symington (1986) suggested that psychoanalysis fosters the patient's unity in three ways. Patients have "an inner thrust to form a unity," but they need "the help of an analyst to get it unblocked" (p. 47). In addition to the analysis and dissolution of resistance, psychoanalysis promotes unity "through the analyst's capacity to bear the patient's anxiety" (p. 47). When an analyst maintains his own unity despite the patient's anxiety, the patient is calmed and enabled to discover unity in herself. Lastly, a good interpretation has a unifying effect. "The analyst makes interpretations to relieve anxiety, and to link the patient's contradictory thoughts and feelings" (p. 48).

Freud and Nunberg had originally drawn attention to the relation of the synthetic function of the ego to the therapeutic process, but their conceptualization of psychoanalysis as part of the larger project of Eros was neglected by ego psychology until Loewald revived it, with reference to psychic integration rather than to the synthetic function alone. Symington (2006, p. 93) suggested the concepts of "aggregate" and "unified" modes of the psyche. Because the term "aggregate" encompasses both the unintegration of the never previously integrated and the splitting or disintegration of existing unities, Symington's contrast of aggregate and unified modes of the psyche neatly rephrased Klein's concepts of the paranoid-schizoid and depressive positions in language appropriate to the unitive and mystical.

THE LIFEGIVER AND NARCISSISM

Symington accepted as valid Fairbairn's theory that the psyche thinks primarily in personal terms. "Erotogenic zones" were to be seen "not as independent determinants of libidinal aims, but as parts of the body which lend themselves in carrying degrees to the expression of *personal* aims" (Fairbairn, 1994, p. 32). For example, "in the early oral phase the natural object is the breast of the mother; but in the late oral phase the natural object becomes the mother with the breast. The transition from one phase to the other is thus marked by the substitution of a whole object (or person) for a part-object" (Fairbairn, 1941, p. 48). Fairbairn (1941) famously concluded that "the ultimate goal of libido is the object" (p. 31). "In accordance with this point of view, the pleasure principle will cease to be regarded as the primary principle of behaviour and will come to be regarded as a subsidiary principle of behaviour involving an impoverishment of object-relationships and coming into operation in proportion as the reality principle fails to operate, whether this be on account of the immaturity of the ego structure or on account of a failure of development on its part" (Fairbairn, 1944, p. 89). Fairbairn (1994) challenged Freud's theories of erotogenic zones on the grounds that "the data upon which the theory of erotogenic zones is based themselves represent something in the nature of conversion-phenomena" (p. 35). Hysterical symptom-formation accomplishes "the substitution of a bodily state for a personal problem" that "enables the personal problem as such to be ignored" (Fairbairn, 1994, p. 29; see Symington, 2004a, pp. 50-51). In this way, Fairbairn (1994) reversed "the classical theory of erotogenic zones...that the original libidinal orientation of the child is inherently autoerotic, and that an alloerotic or object-seeking orientation is only acquired at a later stage in the process of development" (p. 40). Fairbairn's theory of personal relations included an original way of conceptualizing the repressed. Fairbairn (1943) claimed that "what are primarily repressed are neither intolerably guilty impulses nor intolerably unpleasant memories, but intolerably bad internalized objects" (p. 62).

Addressing the topic of pathological narcissism from a Fairbairnian perspective, Symington concluded that self-love is neither the original infantile condition of the psyche, nor its abiding core in later life, but is instead a sequel to an inhibition of object relations. To choose self as one's love object is to fail to choose someone else; and this act of turning away from the object is central to narcissism (Symington, 1994, p. 122). Narcissism involves a turning away not from one or another specific person, such as the mother, or the father, but from all people without exception. Symington concluded that the bad object that is repressed in narcissism is a mental construct, a generalization, that signifies all objects simultaneously. He called it a "mental object" that has "psychic reality."

> We...need to be able to conceive of psychic realities that cannot be smelled, touched, seen, or heard. Examples of such realities are friendship, an hallucination, a dream, a thought, a feeling, an intuition, an intention, a judgement, truth, goodness, courage, confidence, inhibition, omnipotence, humbleness, cruelty, revenge, self-loathing, hatred, love, guilt, shame, deception. These are realities, in that we are capable of knowing them. They are psychic objects of knowledge. (Symington, 1993b, p. 12)

Symington's concept of a "psychic object" personified the traditional philosophical concept of the noetic or intelligible, an idea that can be thought but cannot be sense perceived or mentally imaged.

Symington (1994) conceptualized the mental object that is rejected in narcissism as an inner quality that he termed "the Lifegiver" (p. 122). Because the lifegiver is a mental object, "it comes into being within the self in the act of being chosen, of being desired" (Symington, 1993b, p. 47). In speaking of the lifegiver as a quality rather than, for example, a mental structure, Symington explained that qualities are both subjectively constructed and objective existing.

> This sounds paradoxical, but there are parallels in our social world; for example, friendship only comes into being in the act of being forged--so also the Lifegiver is a mental object which comes into existence in the act of being chosen. The act through which the Lifegiver is chosen brings about this mental reality as an inner possession. (Symington, 1994, pp. 122-23)

Like Milner and Winnicott's concept of creative illusion, the coincidence of subjective and objective in Symington's concepts of friendship and the lifegiver is, I suggest, intrinsically mystical.

Symington suggested that the lifegiver is both a quality and an internal object, indeed, is at the core of all internal objects.

> It is a mistake to say that the infant is seeking the breast or the mother. It is the breast, but it is also not the breast. It is the mother, but it is also not the mother. Instead, one has to posit the existence of an emotional object that is associated with the breast, associated with the mother, or in later life associated with the other person; it is *in* the other--an object that a person seeks as an alternative to seeking himself. If being emotionally alive means to be the source of creative emotional action, there has to be a turning to this object, and this object has to be taken in. I call this object the "*lifegiver*"....
>
> What is the nature of the *lifegiver*? It is a psychic object located in relation to a breast, a penis, a vagina, the self, the analyst, or the therapist. While it is not any of these primary objects of fertilization or nurture in itself, it has no existence apart from them. (Symington, 1993b, p. 35)

Symington's concept of the lifegiver involved a measure of paradox. The lifegiver is an object that is both transcendent and immanent. At the same time, it is the quality of being an object. It is that whose presence in the mother constructs the sense perception of the mother both as externally existing and as a person, rather than as a component part of the self. Loewald's concept of "object cathexis" that constructs an object as an object is an impersonal analog of Symington's lifegiver. If "object cathexis" constructs a percept as a quiddity external to the self, the lifegiver constructs it as both external and personal. The lifegiver endows percepts with personhood. Indeed, the lifegiver is the personhood within objects that constructs the objects as personal quiddities.

Working with the idea that "turning away from the lifegiver forms the core of narcissism," Symington (1993b, p. 39) extended the concept of pathological narcissism. He generalized that "this route, which is taken as a reaction to pain, is the source of all pathology" (p. 118). Symington (1994) suggested that almost all categories of psychopathology have their "origin in narcissism." Symington (2007) maintained that will reacts to trauma by freely choosing narcissism; pathology commences with the choice rather than the trauma. Symington did not accept Freud's (1926a) view that trauma is a condition of paralysis that precludes choice. Whichever view of the unconscious process is correct, Symington rightly drew attention to the presence of narcissism as a manifest symptom of all pathologies.

Agreeing with Fairbairn, Winnicott, and many others, Symington regarded the self as a construction of self-with-other. Because repression is directed at an internal object together with the part of the self that seeks it

(Fairbairn, 1944, p. 89), the self is diminished and damaged by the refusal of the lifegiver. "This turning away from the *lifegiver* is a turning against the self" (Symington, 1993b, p. 41). "By refusing the *lifegiver*, the individual has refused the inner principle of coherence, so he has the threefold problem of generating action, binding himself into a unity, and contending with the outside world" (p. 53). What remains is the false self (p. 103). Symington (2001) endorsed Winnicott's view that a sense of falseness, fraudulence, or imposture owes to a failure of creativity (p. 120). At the same time, because he rejected the theory of infantile solipsism, Symington did not accept Winnicott's idea of the true self (p. 24). Symington (1994) instead traced "the source of creative emotional action" to the lifegiver (p. 35), whose relationship to the self permits the latter to flourish in the manner that Winnicott characterized as the true self. "The autonomous creative source is the core of the self: the source of inner creative action" (Symington, 2004a, p. 92).

Like Fromm, Symington recognized creativity in the art of loving. "We often think of creativity in terms of art, music, and so on, but actually a much more basic creativity is the capacity to create a relationship" (Symington, 2001, p. 64). "Relation to a person requires a free creative act" (Symington, 2002, p. 116).

INTENTIONALITY

Freud (1923a) described the freeing of a patient's will as a goal of psychoanalysis. In making the unconscious conscious, psychoanalysis sets out "to give the patient's ego *freedom* to choose one way or the other" (p. 50). Explicit discussions of free will have otherwise been extremely rare in psychoanalysis. It has instead been conventional not to address the question. Rank and Fromm were exceptions in affirming the reality of will and free choice. So too was Symington (2002), who asserted that "freedom of choice is the defining element of human life." He also considered its existence a mystery. "We are autonomous free agents *and* determined by antecedent causes. The interpenetration of these two so that they are also a unity is a mystery" (p. 27). He suggested that freedom and determinism are different ways of appreciating reality that arise from the differences between the beta elements and alpha function of Bion's description. "One can think of beta elements as the deposit in us that determines the direction of our being and of alpha activity as our creative autonomous existence" (p. 27). Because Bion described alpha function as "that in the personality which was responsible for thinking" (Symington, 2002, p. 46), Symington implied that the human capacity for freedom of choice is to be related to the capacity for abstract thinking. However, he did not complete the theory, and the epistemological aspects of the paradox do not resolve the ontological puzzle. "The necessary and contingent nature of existence....are not two modes of existence but two perspectives on one reality....it remains mysterious how these two can coexist as one" (p. 28).

Symington (1994) expressed his concept of free will or, as he preferred to state, "intentionality," in commentary on his abandonment of the concept of psychic energy, or libido, and its replacement in terms of object relations as "a drive toward attachment" (p. 120). His formulation arrived at a concept very like Rank's location of will in the ego. "The ego takes its own self as love object. This means that a mental structure has been erected, and that the activity by which the ego has become its own love object is an intentional act....action from the ego implies choice, whereas action from the id does not" (Symington, 1994, pp. 121-22).

Because the ego was the locus of choice, the ego was empowered to choose its own authenticity. The concept of authenticity expressed in the language of one-person psychology what is better understood but more difficult to explain in relational terms as the ego's relation to conscience and to encounters with other people.

> It is a strange paradox that when you look at someone and you say, "Well, they're authentic", it's an authenticity that has arisen through having been chosen, and the choosing of it is what endows it with its authenticity. That, to my mind, is related directly to conscience, which comes as an inner invitation. I find it a bit more difficult to try to get across the thing about the person-to-person and the I-Thou. (Symington, 2001, p. 93)

Symington's (1994) claim that "the core of the self [is] the source of intentionality and action within the personality" (p. 53) had the corollary, explicit in Rank, that the unconscious ego function of repression is a willful choice. The lifegiver is "a mental object that the mind can opt for or refuse at a very deep level" (Symington, 1993b, p. 3). In narcissism, the lifegiver is "the object that is spurned" (p. 34). "There is a choice at this deep level, and the *lifegiver* is an inner and outer object....The bad inner objects have been fashioned through this basic refusal, not through the presence of a death instinct within" (p. 111). "Narcissism is chosen, in traumatic circumstances, at a deep level within the personality. As it is a choice, it is possible for that choice to be reversed. I take the view, however, that there can be traumata so severe that the human spirit collapses" (p. 81).

In agreement with Fromm, Symington associated psychopathology with a voluntary abdication of freedom. "The psychological distress that lands people in a mental hospital, that takes human beings to the psychiatric clinic or for psychoanalysis, is the suppression of their freedom. It is not just what brings a few individuals to seek treatment for their ills; it is THE cause of human distress" (Symington, 2002, p. 38). Symington also followed Fromm in recognizing willful evil as a cause of repression. "It is not possible for a human being to do something self-destructive and know it at the same time....in order to do something self-destructive, it is necessary to destroy awareness of the act" (Symington, 2002, pp. 110-11; see also 2004a, pp. 65, 67, 162). Like Bion, Symington (2004a, pp. 60-61) regarded the repressed as the whole of the unconscious. He had no place for Freud's theory of instinctual excitations that originate in the body and comprise an unrepressed portion of the unconscious (Symington, 1993b, p. 4).

Where Rank saw the counter-will as a positive step toward individuation, Symington viewed repression--and pathology--as a moral failing. Narcissism impacts negatively on both other people and the self. It is "the emotional state where the other does not exist; where reality is cancelled out; where a pseudo-self dominates the scenario" (Symington, 1994, p. 126). "Narcissism is an act of refusal of which taking oneself as love object is a compensatory mechanism and is secondary to the act of refusal" (Symington, personal communication, 2008). Because the narcissistic repression of the lifegiver was a willful choice, the refusal to acknowledge other people's personhood had moral implications. "The consequence of this refusal is guilt, which is not available to consciousness" (Symington, 1994, p. 123). The unconscious guilt might manifest through self-punishment (p. 123), a need for praise in compensation for failed self-confidence (pp. 123-24), destructiveness to self and others (p. 125), a savage super-ego (p. 156), and so on. Narcissism always incurs unconscious guilt (p. 156).

Willful choice was also the basis of therapeutic change. "What leads to psychic change is inner psychic action...[that] is made by the person alone, in their own freedom" (Symington, 1994, p. 92). It is always possible, at least in theory, to choose the lifegiver because narcissism is never complete. No matter how severely it may be repressed, the lifegiver persists unconsciously. Its conscious manifestation was the principal goal of psychoanalysis (p. 137).

THE INFINITE

Symington referred to the lifegiver as a mental object in publications of the mid-1990s. It was a subjective, psychological construction that could be interpreted in Winnicott's terms as a transitional object, a creative illusion. After 2000, he discussed it in an explicitly metaphysical manner. His claims were ontological. He called the lifegiver "the infinite in our being" and conceptualized it as "this basic element out of which we are all constituted" (Symington, 2001, p. 42). This shift from psychology into metaphysics reflected an open embrace of the teaching of the Hindu Upanishads.

> The true god is reached through a deep and sustained reflection on the nature of reality. In our Western tradition the philosopher who best represents this endeavour has been Spinoza....In the East the seers who are responsible for the school of thinking that produced the Upanishads showed the first and deepest understanding of what I refer to as the True God. God is not a term that is ever used by these seers--they use terms like the THAT, the Absolute, the Truth, or just Reality. Wilfred Bion called this same Reality O. (Symington, 2002, p. 103)

Symington followed Spinoza and the Upanishads in postulating a divine monism. All of reality is the one true god. God is the only existent.

> I think that what is referred to as the infinite, or Bion referred to as O or the absolute--it is not even right to say it's *in* the personality....Spinoza said, "There is just one substance, that is all there is, one reality"--but....it's beyond the mind to grasp how it can be manifested in different ways if it's one....But the real significance, the real emotional significance for us is that we are in it--so there is this dual constitution of the personality. (Symington, 2001, pp. 74-75)

To explain the emergence of mind in matter, Symington (2006) favors the "theory...called *panexperientialism*" which maintains "that mind and brain are just two ways of looking at one thing, and that mind-stuff exists in the most elemental particles of matter" (p. 32). The notion that everything in existence thinks is often called *panpsychism* (Skrbina, 2005) and its implication that everything possesses will and can be capricious famously provoked Einstein's objection, "God does not play dice."

Much as Symington admired the Upanishads for their monism, he valued the Western religions for their conceptualization of a personal God.

> The great contribution of Judaism, Christianity, and Islam was the realization that this absolute was personal. Therefore the

> whole drama in the history of God's covenant with the Israelites is a person-to-person situation.
>
> How the infinite is one but varied is a mystery; how the infinite is personal is also a mystery. (Symington, 2001, p. 12)

Symington's combination of the Hindu Upanishads' concept of the divinity of reality and the Western monotheisms' idea of a personal God brought him to approximate agreement with Loewald's concept of the subjectivity of nature.

The question of individuation from the infinite, which had occupied Rank, Fromm, Winnicott, and Loewald, did not arise in Symington's system because he did not subscribe to the theory of infantile solipsism. Symington instead followed Klein, Balint, Fairbairn, and many others in postulating an inborn distinction between self and others that makes object relations possible from birth onward. In Symington's formulation, the experience of intentionality defines the core of the self. The infinite confronts the self as the otherness of all else. An object relation between self and the infinite exists at the core of all further object relations from birth onward (Symington, 2001, p. 24)

Because the infinite is personal, denial of the personhood of another person through his or her narcissistic reduction to a subjectively perceived object, is a denial of the infinite within the person. It is a denial of the other person's being, in the existentialist sense of the term.

> It is common for us to hear someone complaining that he or she has been treated as a mere object by another....It is not perception or memory that is blotted out here, but the epistemological faculty. I apprehend another person not through the senses, but through knowledge....When I say I know a person....I am referring to the *being* of the other, and ontological reflection tells me that *being* is one and indivisible. (Symington, 2004a, pp. 75-76)

To express a person's individual being in relationship with the being of the infinite, Symington (2004a) introduced the phrase "participated being" (p. 77). "*Participated Being* is synonymous with *being*, but the former accents the fact that our *being* is a shared *being*" (p. 84, n. 1). Symington recognized the paradox inherent in his perspective.

> There are two aspects to *participated being*: it is both me and not me....I am it, and, at the same time, I am not it....In the religious

state of mind I act according to the principle that *participated being* has a claim upon me. (Symington, 2004a, p. 79)

Symington acknowledged the incoherence of his view that the many are one, but he insisted that reality is an incomprehensible mystery. "The contradiction is a mystery--the central mystery of existence. It is something that is clearly so; reality is a unity, yet our senses tell us it is diverse; a reconciliation of this contradiction is not possible" (Symington, 2002, p. 26; see also 2001, p. 160)

Like Bion and Grotstein, Symington did not limit himself to psychological remarks. He additionally advanced metaphysical faith-claims. He was also highly specific in his metaphysics. Symington (2004a, p. 104) rejected negative theology and the concept of creation *ex nihilo*, which are the traditional Western solution to the discrepancy between the many and the one. In keeping with his admiration of the Upanishads, he opted instead for the divinity of existence itself. In this way, he replaced an unknowable mystery with an explicit paradox. "Intrinsic to existence is that it is necessary, it is absolute, it cannot not-be. It just is. There can be no explanation for it....Existence is its own explanation" (Symington, 2004a, p. 104).

THE MYSTICAL CHARACTER OF CONSCIENCE

Where Fairbairn (1963) had distinguished the superego from the antilibidinal subject, Symington followed Fromm (1947) in referring to the two psychic processes as conscience and the savage super-ego, respectively. For Symington (1994, p. 157), conscience is part of health, while the superego is implicated in narcissism. The two psychic processes alternate. "The superego banishes conscience," but as the superego's intensity diminishes, conscience is able to manifest (p. 157). Because Symington conceptualized narcissism as a choice, he saw conscience and the superego as alternative consequences of choice. He further maintained that the neurotic guilt of the superego always masks valid guilt that has been incurred through the narcissistic refusal of relationality. "Where there is neurotic guilt or psychotic guilt, there is also real guilt that cannot be borne....conscience is stifled and replaced by a savage superego" (Symington, 2004a, p. 78).

Symington (1994) recognized that conscience is intrinsically relational. "When I choose to follow conscience it brings me into relation with an object" (p. 158). It is equally relational in its intrapsychic dealings with the self. Unlike the savage superego, conscience does not control, determine nor impel. "We feel conscience to be us, yet not us. We experience it as inviting us. To follow conscience is a free act, not an obligation" (Symington, 2001, p. 162).

Conscience manifests the infinite within the psyche. "Conscience....flows from that part of the personality that I refer to as the infinite....conscience is the subjective experience of the infinite within the personality" (Symington, 2001, p. 29).

> When I listen to my conscience I am attentive to a principle within me but which at the same time extends beyond me. It is *in* me but it is not *just* me; something has a claim on me which is at the same time greater than me....
>
> Conscience speaks for that reality whose praises were sung by the seers who wrote the Upanishads....it took the Buddha to realize that conscience was the manifestation of this reality. The Buddha stressed meditation just as did the seers of the Upanishads, but his realization that conscience was the organ of this reality gave his truth a practical application which had been lacking in a defined way within Hinduism....To act according to conscience is to pursue the good. (Symington, 1994, p. 155)

Where Freud and Loewald had privileged Eros as the imperative to unity that accounts for the psyche's synthetic and integrating processes, Symington (1994, p. 58) traced relationality to conscience, and so made loving relationships derivative of conscience. In this way, conscience was responsible, in Symington's (2001, p. 33) formulations, for the activities that Freud had credited to the synthetic function.

Symington credited conscience with an influence on ego strength. "Every time a person follows conscience, his or her ego is strengthened" (Symington, 2001, p. 163). He also saw knowledge as contingent on morality. "The virtuous act integrates the ego-parts. A product of integration of the ego-parts is knowledge; therefore the virtuous act is the pre-requisite for knowledge" (Symington, 1994, p. 168). The same line of reasoning led Symington to attribute creativity to conscience. "The moment that I have a truly creative thought I get a bit more self-knowledge...a truly creative thought is closely related to conscience" (Symington, 2001, p. 27). Human creativity was a type of thinking on the part of the infinite within the personality. "True thinking is creative--it comes from within--from the infinite" (Symington, 2001, p. 46).

For Symington, "obliteration of participated being" is the cause of psychopathology. Conversely, mental health requires "unimpeded access to participated being," which is to say, uninhibited intrapsychic relations between the ego and conscience (Symington, 2004a, pp. 77-78)

PSYCHOANALYSIS AS MORAL EDUCATION

Symington (2004a, p. 54) rejected Freud's ambition to construct psychoanalysis as an amoral natural science. He instead boasted that psychoanalysis provides the most sophisticated moral education that is presently available. The ambition to heal is a moral good (pp. 153-54), and the very concept of mental illness is a moral evaluation. "The diagnosis of what is mad as opposed to what is sane rests upon a value judgement for which there is no rationale. It arises out of a basic human conviction" (Symington, 2002, p. 20). Mental conflict is ubiquitous, and distress is sometimes appropriate (Symington, 1994, p. 122). Neither can psychosis be defined on amoral criteria. "When we say something is 'real', it is a value judgement and not a statement as to whether or not it exists. An hallucination exists, but we say it is not real. We distinguish it from a perception, which we say *is* real" (Symington, 2004a, p. 85).

Symington further suggested that emotions cannot be discussed amorally because they express moral value-judgments.

> Morality is defined according to actions towards the self or other on an axis of good and bad....It is not a question of whether people should judge in this way or not, but that they do. These emotional actions have moral tags attached to them....They are judged by the recipient; the feeling is the judgement. (Symington, 1994, p. 180)

People have an intrinsic knowledge of the categories of good and evil. Murder, stealing, and hating are wrong; generosity is good, and so forth (p. 111). To account for evil, Symington (2006) proposed "that the injurious element in the personality is so *because it is alienated*--in other words, it is not evil or, in our more familiar language, destructive inherently, but because it remains distanced from other parts of the personality....the prime task is not to banish them, but, rather, to embrace them" (p. 24).

Traditional religions address morality only in limited areas and generic terms. "The sphere of good and evil applies in many channels of human communication that have no law. The moral law, such as the Decalogue, only describes very general principles and they are all external, identifiable actions" (Symington, 1994, p. 111). Both conscience and psychoanalysis are capable of greater extent and precision. "Psychoanalysis has brought to the spiritual endeavour a knowledge of inner parts of the self and their manner of interacting. This was not scientifically known in the traditional religions" (p. 195). Symington illustrated with experiences that Howard Giffin reported in *Black Like Me.* Giffin, who was Caucasian, stained his skin black and went around America for a year in order to report on the African American experience.

> What he finds particularly upsetting is the 'hate stare', for example, travelling on a bus a white would stare at him with contempt and hatred. There is no law against this; no moral authority can legislate against it, and yet such behaviour is a source of great perturbation in the human community. (Symington, 1994, p. 111)

Symington concluded: "The contempt, hatred and cruelty that are enacted emotionally between man and woman, parents and children are *the* relevant spiritual locus in present-day structures of living" (p. 131).

Symington (2004a) rejected the conventional view that psychoanalysis provides a psychology of morality without itself being a moral endeavor. "Psychoanalysis aims to transform a pattern centred around hatred, blame, and revenge into one that centred around love and self-awareness" (p. x). Moral perspective was integral to psychoanalysis because psychopathology has its basis in narcissism. The manifestation of narcissism in the transference involves projective identification--a depositing of unacknowledged, unwanted parts of the self, and a surrender of their powers, into an external quiddity.

> What is transferred on to the analyst is a hated part of the patient's own self. This identification becomes known when the analyst can see that the patient is behaving in precisely the way that the parent is claimed to have behaved towards the patient. (Symington, 1994, p. 128)

Noting "that I meet the dark side of myself in the personal encounter with my analyst" (p. 131), Symington remarked: "That the greatest spiritual encounters occur in the emotional confrontation with the analyst is a momentous fact that has not been registered either by theologians or by psychoanalysis" (p. 130). It is here, after all, in the perception of the wrongdoing done to the analyst in the transference, that the patient learns remorse, atonement, and reparation. Similarly mystical significance attaches to interpersonal relations more generally. "The field for mystical union with the Ultimate is within the closest emotional bonds" (p. 136).

CONTEMPLATION AND ECSTASY

Symington regarded meditation and contemplation as processes of thinking about and experiencing abstract ideas.

> The seers of the Upanishads were contemplatives....they had an understanding of themselves and the universe as a single unity, and they then also realized the implications of what this meant for their own way of living. In the Christian tradition there have always been nuns and monks whose whole vocational dedication has been to attempt to achieve contemplation, and again it is contemplating the infinite, the absolute. (Symington, 2001, pp. 65-66)

Readers familiar with the fact that the Upanishads contain our earliest evidence of the ecstatic practices of yoga may be surprised by Symington's views on contemplation. Neither did Symington use the term "meditation" in the manner that has been popularized by the academic psychology of meditation since the 1970s, in reference to any of several practices of disciplined attention, of which yoga is an example. His terminology reflects his training as a Roman Catholic priest, but even then overlooks the ecstatic component of intellectualist mysticism, for example, in the writings of Meister Eckhart (Forman, 1990).

Symington associated contemplation with "what is called 'natural religion'--that is, religion the foundation of which resides naturally in mankind and the dictates of which are mediated through conscience" (Symington, 2004a, p. 80). A natural religion "accords with man's nature" and relies for its "authority upon reason" (Symington, 1993a, pp. 51-52). Contemplation was consistent with natural religion because it was philosophical in method (Symington, 2004a, p. 103). "The person who is in search of the motive that drives his actions in order to purify his intentions is engaged in spiritual activity. The mystic searches into himself, into the deepest layers of his being whence the power of action emanates" (Symington, 1994, p. 172). "Self-analysis...resembles very closely the inner search and ascesis of the mystics" (Symington, 2004a, p. 8).

In keeping with his philosophical approach to meditation and contemplation, Symington (2004a) asserted that "*the true mystic* feels himself to be the servant of a higher truth and distrusts visions and sensually satisfying experiences" (p. 11; emphasis added). Symington counted the Hebrew prophets among the true mystics. He credited them with the discovery of conscience (Symington, 2001, p. 28; 2004a, p. 99) and ignored the extensive discussion of "prophetic consciousness" in modern biblical studies (for example, see Merkur, 1985).

Because Symington limited "true" mysticism to philosophical theology, he took exception to the consensus view of ecstatic religious experience in the academic study of religion. Symington associated the experience of ecstasy with the *mysterium tremendum* of a God external to human beings. This God manifested to the senses and required submission in awe, as was characteristic of "primitive" or "revealed religion" (Symington, 1994, p. 95). "In revealed religion an almighty being suddenly overpowers an individual, who becomes enslaved to this extraneous force. This almighty being is referred to as God. This god is revealed in a moment of ecstasy" (Symington, 2004a, p. 101). The call of Mohammed was paradigmatic.

> In the midst of an ecstatic trance the teachings of Allah were revealed to Mohammed, who dictated them and had them transcribed onto tablets, which became the Koran. Mohammed himself was a slave in submission to the Voice of Allah. Thinking, which is an inner creative process, was crushed under the force of the ecstatic experience. (Symington, 2001, p. 156)

The ecstatic god of revealed religion represents the superego, which is "never purely internal but always embodied in outer figures or institutions and it is an agent within the personality" (Symington, 2004b, p. 64).

> This is a god that gets in the way of two people coming to know each other; a god who interferes with my thinking; a god who demands that I follow his instructions; a god who punishes me if I think for myself, who sanctions my sadism, encourages my masochism, hates my greed, my envy, and my jealousy, and so expels them into figures in the environment. It is a god who possesses me but despises me; a god who solves problems by obliterating them. (Symington, 2002, p. 100)

Agreeing with Bion, Symington (2002, p. 100) attributed the psychological erection of a revealed god as an instance of projective identification. "Projective identification is the activity generated by the narcissistic part of the personality and that *embodiment* in outer objects is integral to it" (p. 63). A revealed god is "a split-off part of the self taking possession of the whole personality....in the narcissistic part of the personality a wound has been incurred, and the god arises, having sustained an infinite insult, and takes over the personality" (pp. 157-58).

The problem with ecstasy, in Symington's view, was its engagement in projective identification with a revealed god--in Fromm's terminology, alienation and idolatry. "Being buried in an ecstatic object is....an action of the 'I'. Burial in the ecstatic object protects the ego from knowledge of its activity" (Symington, 1994, p. 167). "God commands, demands, and abhors freedom, whereas conscience *invites*" (Symington, 2002, p. 42). The process of projective identification could also be conceptualized as a deficit of individuation (Symington, 2001, p. 103). Symington saw individuation as necessary, but it was a therapeutic process that corrected pathology. It was not a developmental process that corrects immaturity.

Owing to the nature of superego gods, people sometimes choose atheism as a defense (Symington, 2001, p. 83). Symington regarded mystical contemplation as a healthy alternative. "The mystics set themselves to the task of getting a true god rather than this false one installed in consciousness" (p. 87). "A false god...strangles personal growth and creativity and a true god...promotes them" (p. 96).

Because Symington's remarks about mystical contemplation are mutually exclusive with his views on ecstasy, his analysis of an oceanic feeling that Milner reported provides an important illustration of his point of view. Milner wrote:

> I was one day driving over the mountain road to Granada in the Spring, the cone-shaped, red-earthed foothills all covered with interlacing almond blossom. Also it was the first sunny weather after days of rain, so that I was filled with exultation as we climbed higher and higher into the clear mountain air. I was full of that kind of exultation which make one above oneself. I felt powerful and important, as if it was somehow my doing that the country was so lovely, or at least that I was cleverer than other people in having got myself there to see it--I was certainly thankful that I was not as other men are. Then I noticed the character of the country was changing...but as soon as I tried to look back in my own mind, I found there was nothing there, only a rather absurd memory of my own exultation but no living vision of what had caused it. Then I remembered the Pharisee and the publican...at once the look of the country was different, I was aware only of it, not of myself at all, and always afterwards it was that bit of Spain that I seemed to possess in imagination. (Field, 1937, pp. 208-209)

Symington (2004a) commented: "When Marion Milner was *in* her exalted state, she saw neither the object nor herself....she was mad, but she became sane at the moment when she withdrew herself from the exaltation and observed the state she had been in....I am drawing a parallel between the ecstatic state...in revealed religion and the act of comprehension inherent in natural religion" (p. 109).

Symington's treatment of Milner's mystical experience as madness but her mystical theology as sane and commendable, betrayed a theologically motivated inability to differentiate psychosis and God-intoxication. Because conscience was divine, it had also to be both infallible and truthful, and departures from rationality could not be accorded spiritual validity. Divine conscience could mystically inspire great ethical wisdom; but if a religious experience was irrational, it was necessarily not a manifestation of conscience. Symington was not prepared to allow that "ecstasy" is, as I elsewhere claim, a sustained manifestation of creative inspiration and, in psychoanalytic terms, an experience of insight on mystical, religious, or spiritual topics (Merkur, 1999). Like all creative inspirations, ecstasies emerge from the unconscious during a temporary suspension of disbelief. They are felt to be valid or true for the duration of their occurrence, whether they happen to be manifestly rational or not. Indeed, it is the relaxation of ego functions, the creative surrender to the unconscious, that makes the manifestation of inspiration possible. As is well known, the inspiration phase of the creative process is succeeded by a return of critical thinking that is able to recognize the illusory character of the inspiration, to discount its excesses, and to value its original contribution (Wallas, 1926; Ghiselin, 1952; Merkur, 2001). In psychoanalysis, the evaluation phase of the creative process is termed "working through." Symington's praise for "vital realization" despite his antipathy for "ecstasy" is analogous to a fellow who likes a drink, places a firm limit at one beer, and speaks badly of anyone who enjoys anything stronger.

PSYCHOANALYSIS AS A NATURAL RELIGION

Because Symington advocated an ethico-mystical monotheism, his claim that psychoanalysis was a process of moral education was simultaneously a claim that psychoanalysis was a religion. "Psychoanalysis is a natural religion but not a revealed one" (Symington, 1993a, p. 53).

Symington (2004a) suggested that therapeutic change, as he understood it, is the same process that is called "conversion" in traditional religious contexts. He preferred to call it "awakening" in acknowledgement of its occurrence outside traditional religions.

> While most psychoanalysts have had patients who consciously affirm their commitment to truth, justice, and compassion but whose inner dispositions are utterly ruthless, they also frequently witness a transformation whereby what was initially a possession of the super-ego becomes a possession of the ego. In such an ego transformation the values that become part of the ego's structure are also the core values of mature religion: compassion, truth, and goodness. (Symington, 1994, p. 58)

Symington (2004a) also discussed the ego's integration of values to which it had previously only paid lip service as an achievement of "vital realization." "A combination of inner acts with the external catalyst brings about this transition from blindness to wakefulness or from *inert reality* to *vital realization*" (p. 5). Symington's terms "inert reality" and "vital realization" expressed the subjective aspects of Bion's beta elements and alpha function, respectively (p. 6). The mental act of realization was a prelude to the further realization of the act in the world (Symington, 1994, p. 131).

Vital realization cannot be achieved without addressing resistance. "The transformation from *inert to vital* mental reality is always a psychological crisis for the individual" (Symington, 2004a, p. 7). "The person has to face the wasted years and effort, and it is a challenge to take up new responsibilities" (p. 8). False gods are inevitably present in the transference and can be addressed in the analytic relationship (Symington, 2001, p. 124). Like Bion and Grotstein, Symington saw the patient's contact with the analyst as a means to contact the ultimate (p. 39).

Symington conceived of vital realization in a hermeneutic manner. It was not a question of bringing to consciousness materials that already existed unconsciously. Neither was it limited to Bion's concept of alpha function, which actualizes the potential in beta elements by thinking thoughts that previously had no thinker. Vital realization could additionally include the wholly original creation of thoughts that had no previous existence, either unconsciously or in potential (Symington, 2004a, p. 87). "I would define a creation as a reality the origin of which is generated in the mind" (p. 106).

CONSEQUENCES FOR CLINICAL TECHNIQUE

Like Fromm and Bion, Symington admired the I-Thou philosophy of Martin Buber (1958) and integrated it within his clinical technique in ways that Buber thought impossible. Symington was also influenced by Ferenczi's technique, which Balint brought to England and Winnicott adopted. Symington (1986, p. 3) cited Ferenczi's (1930) criticism of the classical psychoanalytic situation: "We found that the rigid and cool aloofness on the analyst's part was experienced by the patient as a continuation of his infantile struggle with the grown-ups' authority, and made him repeat the same reactions in character and symptoms as formed the basis of the real neurosis" (pp. 117-118). Balint applied Ferenczi's insight by abandoning abstinence while maintaining neutrality: "The analyst's role, for Balint, is to be *with* the patient as a sort of friendly equal. The patient needs to feel that the analyst is really *with* him or her and not 'up there'" (Symington, 1986, p. 304). For Symington, the clinical stance of the British Independent tradition formed a tidy fit with Buber's concept of meeting or encounter. "No friendship, no love relation, no analysis can last without the respect for the 'other' and the at-oneness that forms a bond between the two" (Symington, 1986, p. 253).

An analyst was not to adopt an artificial posture or attitude. He was not to presume authority. Interpretations were no more than educated guesses. "When I make one of these educated guesses I am conscious of my own uncertainty, and I watch the patient's response rather carefully to see whether it is confirmed, denied or qualified in some way" (Symington, 1986, p. 34). Interventions were not driven by standard theories but were instead to be tailored to each moment with each patient. An analyst was "encouraged to follow his own conscience," alert to the possibility that "a realization may come to...mind" while listening to the patient (Symington, 2001, p. 163). Realizations were also to be expected on the patient's part. "In an analysis creative moments of individual understanding are rather rare. When such moments do occur they cause a therapeutic shift, but a welter of preparatory work has to occur first. Also the analyst cannot just sit in silence session after session: he has to keep the conversation going but at the same time try not to say anything that will block the moment of insight from occurring" (Symington, 1986, pp. 33-34). Although an analyst was "to be unrelenting in stripping away the false consolations with which a narcissistic person is surrounded," it was important to be simultaneously "firm but empathic," "holding them,...as it were, with care and concern" (Symington, 1993b, p. 93; 2002, p. 140). The analyst's interpretations were less important than the emotional content of the analytic relationship (Symington, 2001, p. 117).

Like Fromm, Symington made Buber's concept of a "meeting" or "encounter" between an I and a Thou a central component of clinical work. Where Fromm made himself available authentically to patients, Symington additionally invited patients to reciprocate. Symington had been impressed when Bion, in a seminar at the Institute of Psychoanalysis in London, had suggested that "the analyst and patient were like a married couple, and interpretations needed to reflect the sort of equal interplay that typified such a partnership" (Symington, 2007, p. 260). In Symington's development of this idea, mutual personhood is the basis of the therapeutic process. "The naked fact of my personhood demands that she [the patient] be a person too" (Symington, 2001, p. 122). When the analyst is being seen by the patient as a person, the patient is obliged to own projections as internal fantasies (Symington, 2001, pp. 197, 143).

In a recent publication, Symington replaced his earlier references to "conscience" with the phrase "inner inviting presence." As well, the dynamic between analyst and patient is characterized in a way that harmonizes classical formulations about the patient's introjection of the analyst within her superego, and Bion's ideas about the analyst's mediation of alpha-function to the patient. Symington (2006) wrote:

> We are not persons full stop. We are constantly being called to be persons. I think I am a person, but then meet someone--perhaps a patient, perhaps my next-door neighbour, perhaps a work-mate--and I am blown hither and thither and I know I am in *aggregate* [disintegrated] mode, so my task is to start a work inside myself. It is the work of transforming this chaos into personhood. The *inner inviting presence* is to be master of the world and not this alien force pounding and invading the inner perimeter.
>
> The paradox, however, is this: the extent to which I am able to be a person gives the other inhabitant of my consulting-room the opportunity of being so also. This is, I believe, because I then embody my own *inner inviting presence*, and this has a generative effect upon the other. This faculty that I have been referring to passes beyond the sense of the outer words to the inner constituting mode of the other. If I am a person, it does not mean that I force the other into the way in which I am constituted....A person is fulfilled by the presence of another person, so there is an inherent need for the other to be different. If I, as psychoanalyst or psychotherapist, embody my own *inner inviting presence*, then it has a strengthening effect upon the *inner inviting presence* of the other. (p. 95)

When the patient fails to reciprocate the analyst's availability as a person, it is because resistance has intervened. "What is most powerfully resisted in all this is a meeting with the analyst as *person*, because if the analyst as *person* is met, then it forces the individual to create himself into a person. However, it also faces the individual with the terror of meeting a savage and crushing God within" (Symington, 2001, p. 85). Inviting a patient to meet on an I-Thou basis not only precipitates resistance, as Symington suggests, but in my own clinical experience consistently provokes a transference. Analysis of the transference, facilitating a reduction of the patient's resistance to immediate participation in an I-Thou encounter, may then become a focus of the therapeutic encounter.

Where analysts have traditionally been taught to listen for unconscious aspects of a patient's words, Symington (1993b) listened not for the unconscious in general, but specifically for "what has been refused" (p. 123). The presence of a savage superego indicates that conscience has been inhibited, and the clinician's task is to reverse the situation (Symington, 1994, p. 158). Symington's major technical innovation consisted of facilitating the manifestation of unconscious conscience. "Any interpretation that is really effective has to bring conscience into play....conscience then starts to invite the person to do something" (Symington, 2001, p. 31). Because projective identifications construct an analyst as a false god in the transference, analytic interpretations are misconstrued as accusations of guilt unless the analyst succeeds in catalyzing the process of realization in the patient (Symington, 2004a, p. 130).

Interventions are best phrased in a manner that carefully avoids the superego and instead addresses conscience (Symington, 2001, p. 119). In order to preserve the integrity of the patient's conscience and its production of realizations, Symington insisted on the analyst's adoption of classical neutrality, abstinence, and so forth. "It's terribly important to try to get hold of and allow conscience to function inside the person, not to rob him or her of a chance to make a judgement" (Symington, 2001, p. 33). Symington had no advice regarding when to speak and when to use silence to encourage the patient to speak. Both procedures might be appropriate, depending on which promoted realization in the patient at any particular moment (Symington, 2001, pp. 146-47).

Symington's concern to bring the patient's conscience into play led him to ignore the traditional analytic advice to speak only to productions by the patient that have fresh emotion attached to them at the time. Because Symington trusted conscience to produce fresh emotion during its realizations, he found clinical utility in raising pertinent issues from past sessions that did not happen to be part of the patient's current productions (Symington, 2001, pp. 125-26).

CONCLUDING REFLECTIONS

Symington's devotion to a personal monism led him to see moral transformation as a mystical process. His syncretism of the Western idea of a personal God with the Upanishadic idea of divine monism meant that all reality, including the psychoanalytic process, was simultaneously material and divine. A patient's achievement of Klein's depressive position, which Winnicott had called the capacity for concern, was for Symington a religious conversion, an "awakening" through "vital realization" to the lifegiver or infinite within the personality. Where analysts since Freud had conceptualized the patient's attainments of insight as secular events, Symington regarded the lifegiver's manifestation in a vital realization as a direct manifestation of the divine, a theophany in the consulting room.

Symington's way of conceptualizing the capacity for concern also dovetailed with Fromm's distinction between the superego and conscience. More clearly than Fromm, Symington saw conscience as the vehicle of the therapeutic. Pathology had its basis in narcissistic refusals of conscience at deep levels of the personality; and therapeutic change required conscious manifestations of conscience in vital realizations that the patient embraced and no longer refused. Symington agreed with Klein that the savage superego was part of the paranoid-schizoid position. He innovated the idea that conscience is integral to the depressive position. His theory had dramatic practical consequences for clinical technique. Rather than be limited, with Klein, to the critique of the patient's negativity--the analysis of paranoid-schizoid phantasies--Symington listened for the refused goodness within. Highly innovative interventions that facilitated the manifestation, growth, and original creativity of conscience flowed from his optimistic premise.

Symington's advice on clinical technique consistently exhibits the nuance, fine detail, and sensitivity of a master clinician. His theories, by contrast, tend to be categorical in their contrasts of health and morbidity. Although Symington was familiar with Bion's view that every human being goes back and forth on a continuous basis all day long between the paranoid-schizoid and the depressive positions, Symington opted instead for a radical contrast of narcissism and conscience, as though a conversion or "awakening" was a totalizing and permanent achievement. Symington's unearned assumption that narcissism, which manifestly has moral significance in its consequences for others, originates precisely through an intentional refusal of the lifegiver, made it impossible for him to follow Bion in regarding the narcissistic moments of everyone's daily life as inevitable and healthy. For Symington, good and evil were at issue. "There cannot be a healthy act of refusal of the infinite. It is like speaking of 'virtuous vice' (Symington, personal communication, 2008).

What is at stake in Symington's moralism is his monism. If conscience is no other than the infinite within the personality, the psyche can never be ignorant of the divine that is already present within it. The psyche must then be held accountable for its unconsciousness of the lifegiver and credited not with trauma-induced ignorance, but with a morally culpable act of refusing the divine. Had Symington worked with methodological agnosticism, rather than a commitment *a priori* to Upanishadic monism, other theoretic options would have been equally tenable.

Twelve

The Ecstasies of Michael Eigen

Michael Eigen practices psychoanalysis in New York City. He has been a mystic since childhood (Eigen, 1998a, p. 11) and read Fromm and Jung as a teenager (p. 182). As an adult, he encountered Freud and mainstream psychoanalysis after beginning work as a psychotherapist. Eigen earned a doctorate in psychology and trained analytically in classical ego psychology, with its emphases "on ego mechanisms, adaptation, ego's conflict with instinctual drives, social conditioning" (Eigen, 2004, p. 168). Henry Elkin was his major analyst (Eigen, 1993, p. 261). Eigen expanded his repertoire through his encounters with the work of Winnicott, Milner, and Ehrenzweig, who wrote "of spontaneous, affective ordering processes, in which order grows from the ground up rather than from a rationalistic order imposed top down" (p. 171). Eigen's further interests included "body therapies, phenomenological and existential philosophers, Gestalt psychology, Melanie Klein, D. W. Winnicott, and the British Independents, R. D. Laing and Harold Searles, and later, Kohut, Lacan, and Bion" (Eigen, 1993, p. 261). He reads Winnicott, Bion, and Lacan "on a weekly or monthly basis" and has given seminars on them for many years (Eigen, 2001a, pp. x, 164). He also knows the work of Rank and Matte-Blanco, and engages with the work of Grotstein (Eigen, 1986, p. 20 n. 31; 2004, p. 170).

Eigen's readings are personal appropriations. "I draw from texts and teachers and colleagues and friends--whatever hits me" (Eigen, 1998a, p. 163). "Deep down I think, 'I believe in lack of definition'" (Eigen, 2007a, p. 106). "I am not a scholar, a systematic reader, or follower of any school" (Eigen, 2001a, p. 166). "I love Lacan, but I twisted him out of shape" (Eigen, 1998a, p. 195). Similarly, he considers Winnicott's "Use of an Object" article to be "Winnicott's climactic paper and... all else in Winnicott must be reread in light of it" (Eigen, 1989, p. 244). Eigen's appropriation of Bion systematically reinterprets Bion's mentalist cosmology in terms of Eigen's belief in both ideas and matter (for example, Eigen, 2001a, p. 63; 2002, p. 166). Where Bion suggested that sense perception of physical reality is equivalent to and may be nothing but a hallucination, Eigen (2006a) asserts that hallucination contributes extensively to what we take to be reality

Eigen (1992, p. xx) identifies himself personally and professionally as a mystic. "If I do not draw from the Holy Spirit on a daily basis, I become a semi-collapsed version of myself" (Eigen, 1998a, p. 163). In some phrasings, Eigen asserts that mysticism and psychoanalysis each has its advantages: "I was able to reach places through prayer that I could not get to by analysis, although each made better use of the other possible" (Eigen, 1993, p. 260). In other statements, Eigen equally clearly asserts that psychoanalysis, no differently than anything else in existence, is mystical through and through. "From the first session I've ever had with anyone, I've always felt a sacred element in psychoanalytic psychotherapeutic work, and I've never quite understood the animosity so many analysts have had against the mystical" (Eigen, 1998a, p. 191).

Eigen is the sort of mystic who accesses mystical experiencing with the ease, for example, that many professional artists, writers, and musicians are able to access creative reveries. Although he enjoys and discusses mystical moments, he is more generally concerned with "mystical experiencing" and "mystical feelings," the apperception of the whole of experience in a mystical manner. Where Grotstein, for example, writes of the transcendent position as an occasional transient experience, Eigen knows the transcendent position for extensive parts of each and every day. Eigen brings his mystical sensibility to his work as an analyst, and he brings at least some of his patients to a capacity for mystical feeling that is akin to his own. "Mystical experiences provide models for aspects of therapeutic processes, and therapeutic processes tie mystical experiences to real living. I have seen individuals lost in mystical experiencing without a clue to what they were doing to themselves and others" (Eigen, 2001a, pp. 165-66). Using Lacan's term *jouissance* as a synonym for ecstasy, Eigen conceptualized psychoanalysis as a missionizing faith: "We are here to bring everyone to fulfillment. Our job is to bring *jouissance* into people's lives, to inspire people to a *jouissance* life" (Eigen, 1998a, p. 149). "There is no reason to place artificial limits on where or how far therapy should go. Throughout my career I have heard that therapy is not a religion, and must stop short of the religious dimension. Perhaps this is true for many practitioners but it has never been so for me" (pp. 41-42).

THE DIVERSITY OF MYSTICAL FEELINGS

Eigen criticized psychoanalytic discussions of mysticism for their preoccupation with solipsistic experiences. He accepted Freud's interpretation of the oceanic feeling "in terms of mother-baby fusion," but he insisted on the variety of mystical experiences (Eigen, 1986, pp. 8-9 n. 1; see also 1998a, pp.

13, 28). "There is an ecstasy of difference, as well as ecstasy of union, and all sorts of mixtures" (Eigen, 1998a, p. 36). Nightmarish ecstasies are perhaps the most important omission from psychoanalytic discussion. "Mystics themselves, while enjoying oceanic feelings, sometimes were...left terrified by the onset of a numinous awakening. They were overturned, and shaken to their core" (p. 190). Mystical experiences are extremely varied. "There are body ecstasies and transcendental ecstasies. Fear-rage ecstasies, erotic ecstasies, intellectual ecstasies, power ecstasies, hate ecstasies, love ecstasies. There is free-floating ecstasy almost any capacity can trigger and dip into. Hitler ecstasies. Saint Teresa ecstasies. Incessant amalgams of selfishness-surrender, twin ecstatic poles. Sensation, feeling, thinking, intuition, willing, imagining, believing, disbelieving, knowing, unknowing--all ecstasy vehicles." (Eigen, 2001b, p. 29). "There are mysticisms of emptiness and fullness, difference and union, transcendence and immanence....There are mystical moments of shattering and wholeness--many kinds of shattering, many kinds of wholeness. In moments of illumination, not only one's flaws stand out, one's virtues become a hindrance....Prophets attack our evil ways, but inspire us to new heights" (Eigen, 1998a, p. 13).

Eigen was referring specifically to Winnicott and Milner when he described the paradigm of psychoanalytic mysticism in general.

> In some basic sense the "oceanic" for these authors is no longer viewed pejoratively but as a dimension of subjectivity with hidden resources waiting for exploration and use. It is seen, essentially, as in traditional religions, as carrying a redemptive element, linked with the feeling of wholeness.
>
> This positive emphasis on regressive states is in contrast with much psychoanalysis of the past. (Eigen, 1980, p. 61)

Eigen credited Milner with an optimism that stood in marked contrast with the pessimism of Freud and most psychoanalytic writings. "She stands nearly alone in psychoanalysis in seeing plenitude rather than distress as the central source of personal growth" (Eigen, 1983, p. 157).

The diversity of mystical experiences requires a theory of the mystical that accounts for more than solipsism or, as Eigen's (1986, p. 151) phrases it, "objectless omnipotence." Freud's theory of primary narcissism was untenable because self and other acquire their meanings through differentiation from each other. "The sense of self can only exist in a relational or differentiated experiential field" (Eigen, 1980, p. 72). A state in which self alone exists is a contradiction in terms. Such a state cannot be a state of self, a primary narcissism, but could at most be a state of unintegration or undifferentiation (Eigen, 1981b, p. 143; 1983, pp. 171-2; 1986, pp. 147, 157). However, the concept of undifferentiation has difficulties as well. It is never absolute, but always and only relative or comparative.

> In reality, pure cases of fusion or self-sufficiency do not present themselves. One finds various amalgams with characteristic emphases. Pure union and distinction are abstract concepts that do not characterize living experience. Since in reality there are always varying degrees and qualities of separation and union, there is no reason to conceptualize the original self in terms of one pole without the other. It seems fairer to say that a basic ambiguity--a simultaneity of areas of distinction and union--represents an essential structure of human subjectivity, whatever developmental level. If one tries to push beyond these poles, the sense of self must disappear: to be undifferentiated and to exist is not possible. (Eigen & Robbins, 1980, p. 81)

The concept of comparative nondifferentiation might be allowed, but its equation with the oceanic feeling--an assumption that Milner, Ehrenzweig, Winnicott and others took for granted--is incorrect. Nondifferentiation may be related to the mystical, but mystical experiences are diverse.

> In unintegrated moments, one may experience a profound well-being one could have scarcely imagined possible. But all-consuming rages also rise and fall, as the emotional weather changes. Or one may be gripped by terror beyond words. In unintegration, one is not frozen into any one position. (Eigen, 1986, p. 335)

Eigen raised the question whether a concept with a negative prefix was necessarily the most useful way to formulate the experiential phenomenon. Rather than to speak of what was absent--differentiation--one might find greater value by identifying what is present in the experience.

> Those who write about this state are in touch with an experiential dimension of exquisite importance to themselves and others. But do such descriptive terms as nondifferentiation, fusion, oneness, and the like, really do justice to that which is being contacted? When Milner writes that what is crucial about such mo-

> ments is the creation of something new, doesn't she most basically mean a new sense of self and other? (Eigen, 1983, p. 164)

Eigen emphasized that he was not immediately concerned with the unconscious processes that manifest as creativity, nor with the achievement that is called creativity. Milner's formulations--and Winnicott's too--pertained to "a state of heightened consciousness: the sense of creativeness" (Eigen, 1983, pp. 168-69). Milner had asserted that "creativeness is not simply employed for defensive functions but is a condition of subjectivity as such. Milner postulated a primary creativeness, explained by nothing outside itself. If a heightened sense of subject-object union is an illusion, it is a crucial one" (Eigen, 1983, pp. 158-59).

For Eigen, Milner's discussion of the projection of gods and demons into the landscape, as a mystical analog of the artist's fusion with the artwork during the creative moment, was paradigmatic of mystical experiencing. A mystic experiences the numinous, sees light, feels ecstasy, senses the presence of God, receives inspirations, as creative illusions that impart meanings to, and transform the apperception of, the perceptible world. The experience of meaning in depth stems from the core of the psyche and speaks to the foundations of existence. Every attribution of meaning to mass-energy is an instance of "heightened sense of subject-object union."

A PERSONAL RELATIONSHIP WITH GOD

Most Christian, Jewish, and Muslim mystics have maintained that the soul remains distinct from God even at the climax of mystical experience. God may so occupy consciousness that the soul ceases to be aware of itself, but the experience is of being at one *with* God. Like Plotinus' Neoplatonic flight of the alone to the alone, the Vedantin Hindu aspiration to be *Atman*, the divine "Self," presupposes a God who is not a creator but is instead the substance of existence. A God who creates the substance is, by definition, always other than a soul that is created. Mystical experience of a God who transcends creation is, in scholarly terms, a communion rather than a union (Scholem, 1954), *unio sympathetica* rather than *unio mystica* (Heschel, 1962), or a personal mysticism rather than an impersonal mysticism (Lindblom, 1962). Eigen concurred with the scholarly consensus when he wrote: "My view (with Buber, Elkin) is that the soul's union with God is better described as communion (co-union), preserving the paradoxical distinction-union element" (Eigen, 1993, pp. 273-74).

> I do not think the sense of oneness can be what it is supposed to be, unless there is someone who is undergoing it and who can appreciate it. It is perhaps more appropriate to speak of a two-in-oneness or one-in-twoness. Pure merger and isolation are abstract terms which do not characterize living experience. Areas of union and distinction occur together, with one or the other more emphasized in a given situation. (Eigen, 1983, p. 171)

In other phrasings, Eigen referred to "dual unity" (Eigen & Robbins, 1980, p. 82), "dual union" (Eigen, 1983, p. 171), and "the I-yet-not-I" experience" (Eigen, in Milner, 1987b, p. 291).

Eigen speaks of an implicitly transcendent God who is known through acts of providence and grace. "There are people who do experience a sense of the living God, a wondrous, at times terrifying, uplifting sense of grace, the work of providence" (Eigen, 2002, p. 140). One of Eigen's (1998a) self-reports illustrate the necessity that union with a creator God be experienced as a dual unity.

> I mean a biblical God, the God of Abraham, Isaac and Jacob....But having said that I can step back and say: "Hey, well, what I mean by God could be anything, because I don't know...." In a sense God is a total unknown, and yet in others the very notion ties the so-called biblical, personal God closer to me than I am to myself....And then there are times one can just lift up one's hands and say, "Wow, all this out of nothingness!" (p. 193)

A creator God, radically transcendent and unknowable, remains distinct even in the most intimate mystical union.

The distinctness of God is similarly intrinsic to the enjoyment of a personal relationship with God. God may sometimes be encountered through God's actions on the soul during mystical experience.

> Buber...wrote, "All real living is meeting"....The self that enters an I-Thou relation is not the same as in an I-It relation. Oceanic fusion, absorption, or oneness would not do justice to the drama of self-other meeting and intersection that Buber points to. For one thing, the mystical moment may involve enormous upheaval, turbulence, overthrowing and reworking of self. A new meeting can change one's picture of what self and other can be. (Eigen, 1998a, p. 31)

In other cases, God may be encountered through interior dialogs between the soul and verbal inspirations that it receives. "I've been speaking with God since I was a little boy....I can't say that God hasn't answered. The Jewish God is quite a conversationalist" (Eigen, 1998a, p. 11).

Eigen conceptualized personal revelations from God with reference to a doctrinal distinction between the ineffability of God and the idea of God's intellect.

> In an ancient scheme, God is mediated through intellect....God is beyond thinking, beyond differentiation and limitation. Yet intellect and reasoning provide something of a ladder to the Beyond.
>
> God's intellect, then, is something of a misnomer. But it is associated with a divine plan, providence, self-sufficiency, self-completion. We get a taste of God through our higher function, a meeting of minds. Yet our higher function is mostly unconscious. We make little use of it. We are more given to lower functions. Little by little, we may be able to animate our reason and begin the ascent. Our intellect may make contact with God's intellect, taste the universal plan, or, more accurately, get a glimpse of the reason the intellect below God plants in us, the reason or intellect our nature allows us to see and use.
>
> The recovery and exercise of Reason jumpstarts the process but does not take us all the way. In the end, what can be known cannot be God, since God, being One, is beyond knowing, which involves duality. It is, finally, a certain ecstasy that brings us to God. We do not know how this happens. We feel our way into it and use suggestive words like "sinking" into God, "merging," being "filled" with God--filled with God, rather than saturated with forgetting. In such moments we forget world, life, lesser passions, ambitions. In such moments there is only God. We turn the unconscious inside out and reach the Fathomless. (Eigen, 2001b, pp. 8-9)

Eigen referred to the distinction between God and intellect as "an ancient scheme," accurately alluding to the Aristotelian and Neoplatonic traditions. At the same time, Eigen observed a contemporary psychoanalytic scheme, the distinction between O and K, Origin and Knowledge, in Bion's psychoanalytic theories.

Whether Eigen's metaphysics are correct or not, they have a coherent interior logic that belongs to the mainstream of the Western monotheistic tradition.

THE EXPERIENCED QUALITY OF OMNIPRESENCE

Eigen (1998a, p. 31) denies the possibility of defining mystical feeling. He instead employs a variety of tropes that commonly emphasize the experienced quality of omnipresence that attaches to the mystical. Eigen sometimes speaks in secular terms of the sense of aliveness at the core of being human. "There is...the thrill of being alive, of consciousness, of sensing" (Eigen, 2006b, p. x). "The ecstasy of being alive is the core of our existence" (Eigen, 2001b, p. 92). In other instances, Eigen (2001b, p. 35) writes of the mystical as light, which happens to be a frequent accompaniment of euphoria in his own mystical experiences.

Eigen also speaks of the sense of the numinous, with its awe, wonderment, urgency, majesty, mystery, and fascination. Eigen (1986) emphasized "the mystical, cosmic underpinning of affects....It is as mad to disregard the numinous in daily affairs as it is to run away from the pressing requirements of social-political-economic factors" (p. 211). Of the various components of the sense of the numinous, mystery is most explicitly concerned with cognition. Eigen emphasizes the element of mystery in connection with science and its relation to the mystical. "Mystery motivates and nourishes science....Discovery deepens mystery" (Eigen, 1998a, p. 18).

Eigen's references to aliveness, the numinous, and light discussed the mystical in straightforward terms. The mystical is omnipresent and available for experience. When Eigen discussed the omnipresence of the mystical with reference to the term "God," he drew attention to the paradoxical character of the experiences.

> I felt God more highly concentrated in Jerusalem than other places I visited. The golden illumination seemed to be part of the dry land, the old walls, the light. God was in the land, the air. Inner-outer luminous sensation, ineffable sensation. Perhaps sensation *is* ineffable. A lighting, heightening, awakening that the region's bitter pain fails to disconfirm. God is infinitely everywhere, but there are infinite fluctuations in infinity. This coheres with shifting numinous densities that characterize the influence of ancient gods on changing fortunes. (Eigen, 2007a, p. 18)

> There may be no end to God, but there are different God zones. I know this is not so, according to traditional logic: God must be the same everywhere, equi-perfect. But when one jumps into the God of experience, one finds variably pulsating areas of joy and horror. One swims around, area to area, sudden cold/warm spots in a sea, dumbfounding brews of bliss and terror. Once one enters this God, there is nowhere else to go. One cannot get to another person without God as a link. If one is suspended in a ghastly God zone, access to others is horrifying. (Eigen, 2001a, pp. 22-23)

Eigen recognizes that the paradoxes surrounding the presence of God arise from human psychology and not divine metaphysics. "To escape the difficulty of interacting with no-thing, we not only fill no-thing with things, but also relate to no-thing as a thing....One soothes or scares oneself into oblivion and tries to soothe-scare others as well" (Eigen, 1996, p. 46). The God of faith and understanding is transcendent, but the experiential sense of God's immediate presence is a psychological event within the mind. Confusion of the two categories leads to paradox. Like theological formulations, the experiential sense of God's presence is a kind of knowledge. Just as God differs from intellectual knowledge of God, God differs from experiences of God's presence.

In other formulations, Eigen happily arrives at paradoxical formulations by appropriating Lacan's term *jouissance*, "enjoyment," as a synonym for God. The primary paradox is dual unity, I-yet-not-I.

> For the moment, let us...call God *Jouissance*, and imagine originary, boundless *Jouissance*. Let us say, "In the beginning there is originary, boundless, *Jouissance*."
>
> If I, also, am God and ever beginning, then I, too, am originary, boundless *Jouissance*. But I am, also, not God, just plain me, a vessel of *jouissance*, a limit. You and I provide a playground for *jouissance* by placing limits on it....Our desires channel *jouissance*, filter it, make it this or that form....
>
> We hunger for originary *jouissance*, and originary *jouissance* hungers for us. But if originary *jouissance* is boundless, it is not merely lack of it that drives us. It is surplus, abundance, exuberance, the capacity for more and more life. (Eigen, 1998a, p. 136)

Working, as Eigen does, with an implicit doctrine of *creatio de nihilum*, "creation from nothing," as though nothingness were a divine substance from which creation was made, he also arrives at the further paradox that all is equivalent to nothing. "Pure *Jouissance*, absolute fullness, is also pure lack, the purity of Non-Being" (Eigen, 1998a, p. 139). "Not even zero is adequate to signify the purity of non-being. Lacan...envisions a lack so profound that zero fails to do it justice" (p. 139). As non-being, *jouissance* remains a fullness but has a ghastly, horrific quality.

> If *Jouissance* is the purity of Non-Being, then *Jouissance* must be....the background lack, a lack so purely lacking...that the universe can appear as ripples of lacks....*Jouissance* is not homogeneous. Its inhomogeneities are the sparks we live by. The purity of Non-Being has defects, gaps, ruptures, variations, dislocations. The purity of Non-Being is alive, therefore spontaneous....The purity of Non-Being surprises itself by fluctuations in the field of *jouissance*. (Eigen, 1998a, pp. 138-39)

> The dreads we know are hints of dreads we do not, perhaps cannot, know. The dread of dreads is a kind of negative counterpart to the Kabbalistic *Ein Sof*, God as unknown infinite, infinite of infinites. Only here it is God in utmost negative aspect, destroyer rather than bringer of life. (Eigen, 2001a, p. 62)

Fromm placed Aristotelian and paradoxical logic in dialectic and Grotstein conceptualized a dual track of alterity and autochthony. Eigen's distinction between materiality and the mystical arrived him at a similarly polarized worldview.

> We can experience the world "naturalistically" and "mystically," often together, an eye on each. We may be better off giving various sides of our nature their due than fighting truth wars. We have a lot to learn from the capacities that make us up, each making contributions to our sense of life. There is no sense in taking sides with one and throwing rocks at others, which is what we often seem inclined to do. Better to put our energy into learning how to use what is given to us, the ins and outs of our makeup. (Eigen, 2004, p. 11)

Paradox is wrongly thought exotic. It is commonplace. Where sense perception discloses the plurality of material things, abstract conceptual thinking discerns integrative processes--laws of nature, but also observations that we cannot or cannot as yet formulate in terms of demonstrable laws. The human capacity both to perceive and to think, and the discrepancies between the two, make every human being paradoxical and mystical in the manner that Fromm, Grotstein, and Eigen have remarked. It is only the fictions of impersonality and objectivity, the I-It perspective to which the physical sciences aspire, that has abolished open acknowledgement of paradox, mystery, and faith from our culture's public discourse.

ELKIN'S DEVELOPMENTAL THEORY OF THE SELF

The diversity of mystical experiences and, above all, their dual-unity refutes the theory that mystical experiences are regressions to infantile solipsism. At minimum, a relational theory of the self is required. In Eigen's (1992) view, "a sense of self and other go together. There is no such thing as self without other, or other without self" (p. xi). Eigen (1983) "believe[s] this basic experiential structure characterizes the self throughout all its developmental levels" (p. 171). He traces the dual-unity of the self to the capacity to identify.

> It is the capacity to identify that links the human race and links humankind with the cosmos. It may be shown that the phenomenological structure of the capacity to identify contains both distance and union elements, neither possible without the other. A certain structural "dual unity" characterizes human experience, both in the realms of self-other and mind-body relations. It characterizes our relation to creative symbols in general. (Eigen & Robbins, 1980, p. 82)

The capacity to identify may, I suggest, be considered an application of the more general function of condensation to the specific topic of the self.

To account for the origin of the self, Eigen works with a developmental theory that his analyst Henry Elkin proposed. Elkin (1958, p. 59) added Kleinian features to a primarily existential model. He commenced with several facts of early infant development. The smiling response, around three months of age, indicates at least some awareness of the otherness of the mother (Elkin, 1972, p. 392). The knowledge to smile indicates that the infant's "consciousness is *reflective*, implying self-awareness, and thus must have at least two objects, the self and a nonself" (p. 392). Next, the manipulation of objects by hand, around six months of age, indicates at least some body image and, presumably, a body ego (Elkin, 1958, p. 60).

Elkin regarded stranger anxiety, around eight months of age, as evidence of the infant's awareness of the difference between the otherness of the mother and the otherness of other people. Elkin (1972) consequently dated the capacity for concern, with its knowledge of whole objects, around eight months (p. 404). These three developmental milestones--the smiling response, physical manipulation, and stranger anxiety--provided anchorage for Elkin's speculations about infantile experience.

Elkin (1958) introduced the term "the primordial stage" to name the first six months of life when according to his theories the infant has yet to form a clear idea of physical reality (p. 61). He subdivided the primordial stage into two subphases, "preconsciousness" and "primordial consciousness" (Elkin, 1972, p. 392). His characterization of "preconsciousness" was a variant of the theory of nondifferentiation that avoided any suggestion of infantile solipsism.

> The child has no individually coherent psychic unity, or identity....its psychic identity is with the surroundings, especially the mother, and is inherently *collective.* For the unity of mother and child now extends from the biological into the psychic realm, so that the child absorbs (*ab-sorbere*: to suck in) not only her milk but her feelings, as conveyed by the quality of her touch, movements of limb and body, tones of voice, and perhaps even by the taste of her milk (p. 61).

Where Winnicott thought in terms of the environmental mother of primary narcissism, Elkin imagined an initial stage prior to the origin of the self. The "primordial erotic substratum of human life" involves a state of "collective identity" (p. 61) that is not yet differentiated into self and other.

Interpreting Elkin's theory, Eigen (1980) emphasized that "before the smiling response the infant can be said to be conscious (e.g., like an animal) but not self-conscious (i.e., in some way aware of its 'going on being')" (p. 71; see also Eigen, 1986, p. 155). Eigen (1986) argued that a single subjectivity animates both consciousness and self-consciousness. He argued that consciousness is self-reflective and generates transcendence in the process. The sense of a transcendent ego is a product of consciousness and is not consciousness's cause (p. 229).

Eigen (1980) integrated Elkin's idea of self-consciousness with Milner's and Winnicott's views on originary creativity when he accounted for the distinction of self and other that is implied by the smiling response. "In my belief it is the implicit awareness of the generative experience in the act of giving rise to the original sense of self and other--with areas of distinction and union--which most basically evokes the experience of wholeness" (p. 73).

> *The primary object of creative experiencing is not mother or father but the unknowable ground of creativeness as such.* Winnicott, for example, emphasizes that what is at stake in transitional experiencing is not mainly a self or object (mother) substitute, but the creation of a symbol, of symbolizing experiencing itself. The subject lives through and toward creative immersion (including phases of chaos, unintegration, waiting). What he symbolizes and seeks more and more of is the absorption of creative experiencing and the way this latter makes use of objects through successive waves of self-other awareness. Maternal or paternal object relations may subserve or thwart this experiencing but must not be simply identified with it. A similar argument could be made for the subject's immersion in the life of meaning as described by Lacan, or Bion's Faith in O. (Eigen, 1981a, p. 135)

Elkin's second developmental stage follows the smiling response and concludes with physical manipulation and the achievement *ex hypothesi* of a discrete body image. During this period, there are both consciousness and self-consciousness, but "the self can only be related to a unitary, all-encompassing *non-self* or other" (Elkin, 1958, p. 62). "A sense of time and space and of materially-distinct subject and objects" are not yet firmly established, and the infant's experience compares with "*mystical experience*, as manifest in dreams, fantasies, psychotic delusions, and states of religious ecstasy, aesthetic rapture, or erotic entrancement" (p. 62). Ordinarily, developmentally later aspects of self experience persist within mystical experiences. What appears from a later perspective as nothingness or void is, in infancy, the primordial other. "The integral self is the subject of consciousness only in the total form of mystical experience--that usually denoted as such--when it is confronted, in phenomenal terms, by nothingness or void, but in the mystical terms of the experience itself, by some immaterial, pre-phenomenal *other*" (p. 66). The primordial other may provoke a full range of positive and negative feelings.

> Total mystical relations, to an immaterial *non-self* or *other*, as we know from dream life, religion, and psychopathology--involve the total or absolute feelings, the consummate passions, that are symbolized by the mythological-religious conceptions of heaven and hell. Such feelings as ghastly dread, dire agony, tremendous

> awe and sublime bliss, import the unitary, undivided awareness of *numinous* power--absolute, infinite, "sacred" power, whether divine or demonic. (Elkin, 1958, pp. 66-67)

The infant's expression of its needs and their satisfaction by the mother take on mythic proportions because they are enacted between a primordial self and a primordial other.

> [The infant] soon finds that the *other* fails--if, in fact, only momentarily--to respond to his will. At this point there must take place in the child's mind, at repeated instances, a momentous primordial drama involving his images of the *Self* and the *Other*, such as is reflected in later total mystical experience. The child, in shocked awareness of his own frustrated will while beset by instinctive fears, doubtless falls into the state of *primordial anxiety*--a mystically ineffable, *awe-full* or *holy* terror....whatever the actual time span of the child's frustration, he passes through a subjective eternity of agonized *primordial doubt* about the existence of both himself and the *other*. Excruciatingly aware only of his unrequited need amidst nothingness, he may then, as in the conversion of psychotic excitement into stupor, pass into a state of numb insensibility and spiritual darkness, that of *primordial despair*. The child is finally saved from tormenting doubt and anxiety, or from despair, by the *other's* merciful intervention. This deliverance brings, in the literal sense, a *spiritual resurrection*--but to a new, regenerate state marked by the shift of numinosity from the self to the *Other*. For the child has realized that the self's very existence depends on the omnipotent and merciful love of the Other. (Elkin, 1958, p. 68)

The myths of death and rebirth, descent into hell and spiritual resurrection, have their infantile prototype in the primordial drama of despair and deliverance. "This deliverance from 'eternal darkness' is experienced as a mental-spiritual resurrection to a new, regenerate state in which the Self's initial, direct, and immediate identification with the Other is now *overlaid* by the infant's awareness of the Other as the eternal numinous Source of Being; that is, of light, or consciousness itself, along with the infinite, all-encompassing, protean cosmos which is manifest by the light" (Elkin, 1972, pp. 397-98).

In Elkin's theory, the period from approximately six to eight months of age, that is, from the beginning of manipulation until the onset of stranger anxiety, involves a body image of the mother who appears sometimes as a Divine Mother and sometimes as a Diabolic Mother (Elkin, 1972, p. 401). Coinciding with this splitting of the primordial Other into the divine and diabolic mothers is a distinction between the body ego, associated with the body image, and a "transcendental ego" that "remains detached from, or transcends, the body ego's affect-laden experience of physical immediacy" (pp. 405-6). The transcendental ego is heir to the primordial Other and, like it, is infinite (p. 406).

Eigen (1986, p. 155) emphasized that the phenomenological distinction between mental and bodily self experiences had been formulated in various ways by other analysts. Jacobson contrasted the mental and physical self. Kohut had referred to a mind-mind and a body-mind; and Greenson had distinguished the observing and experiencing ego. Once the distinction between mind and body is achieved, it proves extremely important.

> Our doubleness makes it possible for us to feel unreal to ourselves. We may ally ourselves with the ineffable or immaterial over/against the visible and material or vice versa....In physical illness, I-feeling can leave the body. In mental illness, I-feeling itself may vanish....Some capacities and dimensions seem more real in one area than another. (Eigen, 1992, p. 186)

Eigen (1992) suggested that "a split between a steellike mental ego and a diffuse, clinging, and explosive body ego....may be characteristic of the psychopathology of our age" (p. 187; see also: 1996, p. 103).

Elkin's theory of the origin of the self dispensed with the theory of infantile solipsism but nevertheless endorsed the theory that mystical experience is a regression to an early phase of cognitive development. The theory postulated a self-contradiction: primary love but also a "collective identity." Eigen's concept of the capacity to identify could be used to remove the inconsistency. *Ex hypothesi* children know self and other at birth; but the psyche's capacity to identify is able to construct syntheses of self and other, resulting in dual-unity experiences.

IDEALITY AS A DEVELOPMENTAL LINE

Elkin's reworking of Federn's pairing of bodily and mental ego-feelings as his own distinction between a body ego and a transcendental ego provided a location within his psychoanalytic model for the interpolation of existentialism's concerns with the transcendental. In taking over Elkin's interest in the transcendental, Eigen favored formulations that had a history within psychoanalytic theorizing. Unfortunately, his views do not cohere into a self-consistent theory.

Where Bion had invoked Plato's theory of forms, Eigen asserted the equivalence of ideas and ideals. "A physical object can be treated like a thing and destroyed. However, neither meaning nor meaninglessness can be destroyed. They are immaterial, invisible, unlocalizable and, in principle, infinite" (Eigen, 1996, p. 61). "Terms such as *ideal experience*, *ideal states*, and *ideal images* are usually related to some aspect of the felt sense of infinite perfection....all experience is ideal in a broad sense, invisible, intangible" (Eigen, 1980, p. 61 n. 1). "The mental self is....plugged into the ideal as well as real" (Eigen, 1996, p. 103).

Eigen's definition of the ideal in terms of "infinite perfection" emphasized his concern with idealization. Although ideals may be either wholesome or morbid, idealization is generally regarded as unrealistic. Ego psychologists tend to view idealization as a defense mechanism, while Kleinians see it as a by-product of splitting that always coincides with an equally extreme derogation of its opposite. In both approaches, "ideal experiencing usually involved something in disguise (e.g., mother, father, sex, hostility, etc.)" (Eigen, 1981a, p. 134), and the analytic task is to unmask the ideal by tracing it to its latent source. A minority tradition within psychoanalysis views idealization in a more complex fashion. Freud (1914a) initially described the ego ideal as heir to primary narcissism. Following Freud's (1923a) introduction of superego theory, which attributed its origin to the resolution of the Oedipus complex, Nunberg (1955) harmonized Freud's theories by discussing an ideal self as the neonatal foundation of the developmental line. In this way, idealization was made the fountainhead of both the structure called "the ego ideal" and individual ego ideals, or personally held values. Contributions that build on Nunberg's formulation typically proceed by pathologizing the ego ideal (for example, Reich, 1973; Chasseguet-Smirgel, 1985). Eigen's formulations proceeded to reverse effect by discussing idealization as a diagnostically neutral process whose individual uses may variously be wholesome or morbid. Eigen (1981a) treated "the problem of ideal experiencing in its own right, as a spontaneously unfolding human capacity related to existential concerns" (p. 134).

Eigen stressed the roles that ideality plays in Freud's thinking. Eigen drew attention to the implicit role of ideality in Freud's discussions of the devotion of love toward the "mental representation" or "imago" of the parents. "Ideal images play a central role throughout the Freudian corpus. They are virtually omnipresent--complexly interfacing with or against instincts and reality. Ideal qualities in one form or another appear as part of the object pole of instincts. In Freudian dramas *instincts seek an ideal imago*" (Eigen, 1979, p. 102).

In Eigen's view, precisely the same implicit role of ideality is to be recognized in the process that Freud termed "sublimation." Here ideality belonged to abstract concepts rather than mental images, but the devotion of instincts toward the ideal remained constant. "The systematic treatment of ideal experience as a derivative of instinctual drives is part of what Freud referred to as his Copernican revolution" (Eigen, 1986, p. 50; see also 1998a, p. 29).

Rephrasing Ehrenzweig's view of the mystical foundations of the developmental layering of the unconscious, Eigen (1981a) emphasized that ideal states are continuous with the ideal images and ideal qualities that preoccupied Freud. "In Freudian dramas the ideal imago variously saturates one's own body, ego, mother, father, and so on to a wide range of possibilities (e.g., feces, feet, science, nation, God)" (p. 134). Eigen offered a variety of arguments in opposition to the conventional view that ideality is a manifest content whose latent significance is otherwise. The ideal cannot be derived from the experience of the breast, as Kleinians maintain, or the environmental mother, as Winnicott suggested, because experience of the ideal precedes the sense perception. The mother is experienced as ideal because ideal states are primary (Eigen, 1986, p. 161) "If the mother as mother (or part of mother or maternal functioning) is gradually discriminated from early ideal images projected on or fused with her, the critical implication is that the creation of ideal images precedes the perception of mother *qua* mother or, at least cannot be derived from her" (Eigen, 1979, p. 102).

> Ideal feelings can inform many objects of experience and so cannot be accounted for by any one of them. The capacity for beatitude creates what mother can be and transforms sex into Eros. The propensity to experience ideal moments is irreducible and constitutive, not simply derivative. (Eigen, 1986, p. 50)

The presupposition of ideal experiencing in discussions of ideal states that involve the mother is not affected by the question whether newborns are solipsistic or instead enjoy interpersonal relationships. Whether the ego is its own ideal or the mother is, "a sense of the infinite" ideality is being presupposed (Eigen, 1986, p. 161).

The developmental history of the ideal begins prior to the differentiation of self and other, when it begins to generate ideal selves and others. Following the achievement of the body image, ideality is applied differently to the mind and the body. "Ideal feeling may take the form of omniscience in the mental self, omnipotence in the body self" (Eigen, 1996, p. 104). Freud (1913) had referred to "omnipotence of thought" in connection with belief in magic; but Winnicott (1963a) had placed a positive value on the illusion of omnipotence in the infant's construction of the mother: "At this early stage the facilitating environment is giving the infant the *experience of omnipotence*; by this I mean more than magical control, I mean the creative aspect of experience" (p. 180). For Eigen, omniscience and omnipotence might each be wholesome or morbid or a mix of the two. "Omnipotence tends to refer to the exercise of limitless power in physical terms, of mind over matter. Omniscience refers to more purely mental power, mind over mind" (Eigen, 1996, p. 96).

In keeping with the ego ideal's role in creativity, Eigen (1980) regarded the ego ideal as a discrete "structural" development of the more general process of ideal experience (p. 70). It is a development specifically of the ideal imago (Eigen, 1982, p. 78). The "ego ideal function" helps to "direct inspiration into culturally meaningful forms" (Eigen, 1980, p. 70). "The ego-ideal may come to act as a nodal point for the convergence and transformation of symbolic expressions of ideal and material experience. Insofar as the ego-ideal helps to stimulate and support creative activity it often also serves as a symbolic mirror of creativity itself" (Eigen, 1982, p. 78).

PATHOLOGIES OF IDEALITY

Eigen conceptualized morbid vicissitudes of ideality. "What we face in therapy is the result of transformations that failed to happen, aborted evolution, and the deformations that have taken their place" (Eigen, 1999, pp. 202-3). The most devastating pathology of ideality corrupts the sense of aliveness. "In the Bible, one's base is God, in Bion's terms (loosely speaking), O (at-onement). But what if one's O, one's very sense of aliveness, is off--poisoned, warped, traumatized, malformed?" (Eigen, 2002, p.120). "Making the unconscious conscious is no guarantee of either goodness or health, if madness and sin permeate all psychic structures" (Eigen, 2004, p. 78).

In other cases, the capacity for mystical experiencing is intact, but people are unable to integrate their mysticism within their lives in wholesome ways (Eigen, 1998a, p. 42). Omniscience, insufficiently restrained by awareness of material realities, becomes pathological through its very extremism. "Omniscience murders experience....One truncates experience to fit one's preconceptions" (Eigen, 1996, p. 97). "When we hate we think we are or ought to be God....we want our will to be done" (Eigen, 1986, p. 211).

> Omniscience is rooted in an invisible sense of boundlessness....The mind's immateriality seems to spread through physical existence....it seeks to master and triumph over it, to wrest its secret. Its transcendence, however, easily becomes perverse, losing respect for competing powers. Omniscience manipulates omnipotence....
>
> Our journey in the sense of the infinite is, ironically, limited not by realistic finitude (which is its raw material), but rather by our discovery of alternate infinities, infinite pretensions. (Eigen, 1986, pp. 330-31)

Citing Freud but using Fromm's term, Eigen (1986) listed idolatry as a pathology. Freud "pointed out how, even in love, perhaps especially in love, idolatry is always self-idolatry (megalomania) at bottom" (p. 9). Conceptions of heaven ran similar risks.

> Mystical visions of heaven on earth offer a challenge. I believe that this is so for many kinds of mysticism that espouse a love of human dignity (hate mysticisms are obviously exclusive). The ethical challenge to individuals in heaven is whether or not heaven is inclusive or exclusive. The contracted individual lives in contracted heavens. To what extent can therapy enrich the flow of heavenly-earthly life, mediate heaven-earth interweaving, while not denigrating heavens that are beyond reach? Perhaps it is the denigrating attitude--earth denigrating heaven, heaven denigrating earth--that keeps the brakes on, whether cynically sour or righteously idealistic. Denigration is a kind of self-irritant through which one keeps a hold on oneself.
>
> Earth does not exhaust heaven, nor heaven earth. Visions of concordance make room for otherness. Prophets and mystics tend to emphasize brotherly-sisterly love, helping one another, respect for sameness-otherness. In actuality, ambitious, aggressive, rivalrous, envious individuals/groups have made ambitious, aggressive, rivalrous, envious use of heaven. Heaven becomes a club, banishing rivals or undesirables. In keeping with a visionary-humanitarian tradition that values the least of us, Jesus turned things upside down, making heaven for the bottom, not only the top (the top have a tougher time getting into *his* heaven). It did not take long to reverse the reversal, insofar as heaven remains a pawn of domination-submission. That does not nullify

> heaven or make it less real: It is real all the more. (Eigen, 1999, pp. 203-4)

THE CLINICAL TREATMENT OF MORBID IDEALITY

When self-consciousness, ideality, a mental ego, omniscience, omnipotence, and the ego ideal are appreciated as a developmental line that occurs spontaneously in health but may also become pathological, conventional clinical approaches are patently mistaken.

> Ideal experience is a basic human capacity and emerges spontaneously in the course of human development. Since in some sense it is free floating and can merge with virtually any material object, it cannot be reduced to any single object or set of objects with which it comes to be identified. It is a generic capacity and its relation to particulars is riddled with problems. To explain the felt sense of infinite perfection or an intimation of immaterial boundlessness solely in terms of their material occasions (mother, breast, father, penis, etc.) seems at best careless; it assumes what it needs to understand. (Eigen, 1980, p. 73)

Any procedure that denies the integrity of ideality by treating it as a symptom that is symbolic of materiality is denying health and insisting on pathology. The analytic task is to distinguish the healthy and the morbid within ideality, not to pathologize ideality as such.

Equally misguided, despite proceeding in the opposite direction, were Kohut's efforts to develop a therapy of the ideal that failed to allow an equal place to materiality.

> Kohut's (1971, 1977) formulations provide a good illustration of the problem which arises when ideal and material realities are implicitly confused (not united). He is one of a growing group of analysts to place great importance on the constructive use of ideal feelings in the course of therapy. Oceanic states are no longer to be taken as second-class citizens but as a source of inspiration and sense of wholeness, a kind of "home base" of the human self. He describes an early sense of oneness in which ideal feelings come to fluctuate between self and other, a fluidly oscillating god sense ("I am God" and/or "You are God"). (Eigen, 1979, pp. 101-2)

Eigen presumably had similar objections to existential therapy, with its neglect of physiological impulses and the unconscious.

In Eigen's view, therapeutic change requires a differential analysis of the ideal and the material that facilitates their relationship.

> Ideal feelings can be profound sources of inspiration and healing. What is required is a growth in sophistication. The person must come to see that his ideal feelings are not one with his products (or medium), at the same time one values both dimensions. In creative work a tension must be tolerated between ideal feelings and the facts of life. It is, in part, this tension which art explores. The result of psychoanalysis should be a more vital and effective interplay between ideal feelings and the capacity for work. (Eigen, 1983, p. 161)

The interplay between the ideal and the real pertains omnisciently to mystical experiencing and omnipotently to creative activities.

The analytic task is to bring the patient to a capacity for wholesome mystical experiencing. The following clinical vignette will illustrate.

> "You wreck everything you touch. You leave damage in your wake."
>
> "That's what I'm afraid of."
>
> "You'll wreck your feeling for me, like you wrecked your girl-friend's feeling for you."
>
> "Or you'll do something wrong I can't let go, and I won't be able to stay because things went bad."
>
> "Like your girlfriend left you."
>
> "Yes. People don't recover from each other. Things don't go on. There is a rage inside or a void that makes life impossible."
>
> My mind goes back to the glass house and wonders if it forms as protection against rage and void, to bind them, keep them in or out. Or whether it come because support for interflow is lacking and rage arises to penetrate it, create flow. Dan describes both, no either-or. But rage and void seem linked.
>
> We're quiet. I feel myself start to smile. He beams. "It's totally glorious, isn't it," I say.
>
> He is beaming, tears streaming, sparkling. (Eigen, 2002, p. 105)

Eigen's interpretation reflected on the conjunction of the materiality of rage and damage and the ideality of glory, enabling his patient momentarily to attain and more longitudinally to introject Eigen's sense of the numinous.

Eigen criticized conventional treatment strategies that avoided mystical perspectives because they were predicated on the assumption that the mystical is a regression to infantile solipsism. His remarks specifically addressed Margaret Mahler's theories of separation-individuation but pertained equally aptly to the mainstream of ego psychology as a whole.

> According to Mahler's scheme, if the patient goes back far enough he is left with the choice of being isolated or merged, in either case nonexistent. In light of this scheme no wonder emphasis is so often placed on building good defenses rather than risk becoming lost in the imagined vacuum of the psychic depths. (Eigen, 1980, p. 73)

Eigen (1986) expressed parallel reservations about clinical strategies that worked with the concept of undifferentiation. They risked discouraging creativity by failing to maintain tensions and harmonies among differentiated phenomena (p. 353). Analytic emphasis on the de-construction of the highly differentiated must be balanced by support for the project of reconstruction. It is a question not only of intellectual insights into the constrictions of overly rigid higher differentiations, but also of the immediate clinical experiencing of ecstasy.

TREATING A MYSTIC

In *The Psychoanalytic Mystic* (1998a), Eigen presented a case study of a woman who was caught up in being a mystic. She sought and attained many mystical experiences, but she had never learned how to integrate them within her life.

> The very *experience* of changing states can be highly charged, numinous. The amazing diversity and extremes of experiencing can give rise to a sense of awe and mystery....Often the mystic of changing states is manic....Every movement opens new vistas, new thrills. The passing years leave no rings inside, no ripples outside. He is as blank at the end, as the beginning, although his life may be in ruins.
>
> The manic mystic short-circuits the states he spies. It is enough to see them, to taste them a bit before spitting them out

> as aesthetic, religious, or psychological products. The manic mystic is able to avoid being changed by the states that thrill him. This is different from the mellowing of the seasoned mystic, who is deeply affected by what he goes through, and undergoes corrective transformations (Eigen, 1998a, pp. 102-3)

Eigen's term "manic mystic" alluded to the Kleinian concept of the manic defense, which deploys euphoric states while avoiding the capacity for concern (Winnicott, 1935).

Eigen's patient approached mysticism like an artist who lived only for her art and had no life outside it. "Most of her life she did not mind a threadbare existence, since her life was filled with *self-feeling*. Cosmic suffering and joy commingled to maker her life full, rich, meaningful. The moment was enough" (Eigen, 1998a, p. 108; Eigen's italics).

The denial of self-concern that is integral to the syndrome of manic mysticism is masochistic (Eigen, 1986, p. 123). Whenever the manic defense cannot be maintained, self-concern emerges into consciousness, producing devastation. The suffering that manifests in between manic moments creates a dependency on mystical experiences, and mystical experiencing becomes an addiction.

> She lived from heightened moment to heightened moment. Life was cosmic drama with a cosmic glow. She moved from union to union, suffering agonizing disruptions of union. As often happens with individuals who possess a strong appetite for union, she tended to live alone. (Eigen, 1998a, p. 104)

Eigen (1998a) did not find his patient's mysticism problematic as such. "What is important is not mysticism versus other domains, but lack of growth within the mystical domain itself" (p. 112). "Her precocious mystical capacity helped and harmed her. The gratification she got from her mystical capacity held her together. At the same time, it decreased motivation to develop her intellectual and practical potential" (p. 104). Eigen summarized his clinical strategy:

> I never felt my job was to make Dolores into a different person, to make her more "realistic"....I was willing to accept that what most people called reality would be meaningless to her....What was most important was that she make the most of the home and world *she* lived in. (p. 112)

What was required was not a diagnosis of mysticism but a differential analysis. Dolores needed insight into the particular ways that she was both using and misusing mysticism.

> So much of her experience was organized around a nuclear sense of rightness and certainty. She stayed close to what felt right for her, and when she found what felt right, there was no room for doubt.
>
> That the mystical richness of life should have something in common with her mother's unconscious snobbery was unthinkable....
>
> It never dawned on Dolores to develop a critical stance towards the...area of life she felt certain her mother did not invade. (Eigen, 1998a, pp. 104, 110)

Eigen's work with Dolores brought her to think critically and become psychologically minded about her mysticism, without challenging mysticism as such (Eigen, 1998a, p. 113). The critical self-understanding that Dolores learned to achieve proceeded within mysticism, on criteria that she found acceptable as a mystic. "Dolores got a first hand glimpse of what in literature and religion has variously been described as *hubris, original sin, pride, vanity, narcissism, folly, madness, egocentricity, selfishness*" (p. 113).

TREATING A MEDITATOR

Another case study discussed the treatment of a man who wanted help with his anger, primarily in connection with his family, but also with regard its impact on his practice of meditation.

> Ken came for help with an abusive temper....He was committed to Buddhist meditation and found that while meditating his anger would fade and he would open. But....instead of meditative calm carrying over into family life, the latter exploded the former, and Ken would become helplessly furious. (Eigen, 1996, p. 188)

Ken's use of meditation as a means to soothe himself was not problematic. His inability to integrate the benefits of meditation with the remainder of his life epitomized his general difficulty in integrating his love for his family with his capacity to be abusive. Meditation was an instance of self-abuse that provided Eigen with the opportunity to offer interpretations that were simultaneously intrapsychic and interpersonal.

> Meditation centered him, yet masked a tyrannical demand that life not be life, his wife not be his wife, his child not be his child.
>
> We worked on building a capacity to move between states, a capacity for transitions....
>
> In time he realized that he tried to get from meditation the calm he never got from his parents....That it did not work in daily living does not mean it did not work at all. (Eigen, 1996, p. 189)

DEATH AND REBIRTH IN PSYCHOANALYSIS

As a young man, Eigen independently discovered the mystical process that he today regards as a precedent and model for psychotherapeutic change.

> If you follow the pain all the way, you pass through a barrier.
>
> I discovered this accidentally one day when I was a young man and just terribly unhappy. It happened once on a bus. I doubled over in agony and went deeper and deeper into it. At some point there was a semiblackout and everything reversed, passing through a vaginal opening into heavenly sky. Stars. Light. Radiance. (Eigen, 2001b, pp. 66-67)

Elkin, Winnicott, and Bion provide Eigen with psychoanalytic formulations for the discussion of the therapeutic movement from agony into joy.

> Elkin writes of a loss and recovery of primordial consciousness linked with death-rebirth dramas of the early self. Winnicott writes of breakdown and spontaneous recovery in sessions. Bion writes of coming alive, being murdered, then feeling all right. These are profiles of a basic rhythm or psychic pulse that can get damaged. When this rhythm stops, the psyche stops breathing, Parts of what we call character structure trace pathos of strangulation and paths where freedom flows, mixed arteries of psychic flow and blockage.
>
> The sense of rebirth functions as a kind of unconscious archetype or template that helps process the movement between trauma and recovery. Of course, trauma can overwhelm recovery, and, as Freud points out, there are all kinds of attempts at recovery. (Eigen, 2004, p. 75)

Eigen followed Elkin in conceptualizing infantile experience as the prototype or template of the death-and-rebirth process.

> Bad times come and break up this nice feeling. Say, hunger hits and pain, then agony disturbs, devours well-being....The infant is plunged into dread, perhaps screaming in rage to offset the terror. The boundless, immaterial Other may now be experienced as insensitive, inscrutably menacing, abandoning, persecuting--perhaps a primordial devil.
>
> If the agony mounts and becomes unbearable, the infant may grow numb, stuporous, pass into oblivion. At some point, the infant's mother brings relief. The caretaker tries to fathom what is wrong and mend things, and consciousness blooms again. The light of primordial self and other re-emerges from darkness, this time with more emphasis on the bountiful Other, whose merciful intervention enables restoration of aliveness. God restores my soul, my spirit returns from death.
>
> I think something of this pattern remains as a basic organizing sequence, a rebirth pattern informing emotional life. Some or all of these phases may be traversed at different times. (Eigen, 2004, p. 38)

Eigen (1986, p. 209) suggested that various cultural institutions have sought to organize the death-and-rebirth process. For example, the mystery ceremonies of classical antiquity attempted to provoke the experience in their initiates, while the pattern was expressed in the myths of dying gods. "Biblical rebirth images involved healing damage or cleansing corruption: the blind will see, the lame walk, the burden of sin will be lifted" (Eigen, 2004, p. 18). Psychoanalysis implicitly belongs in the same historical lineage.

In a formulation early in his career that drew on the terminology of ego psychology, Eigen discussed the psychoanalytic process in close detail.

> The pattern described in Carl's case was, in general, typical: (1) disillusionment with the outer world and the possibility of a truly meaningful life in it; (2) a drawing of libido inward toward a barely sensed ego experience; (3) intense panic-dread of disintegration; (4) intense sense of emptiness, in which it is discovered that the emptiness is alive and full; (5) sighting and uniting with an ego structure which is experienced as the underlying inde-

> structible sense of self--a compressed, dense, magnetic I-kernel, a seeming final contracting point of the I; (6) a perception of some intrinsic merit in the world, usually a beatific experience, however momentary, and the reversal of libido flow, so that a two-way current of outflow and inflow can occur. It is as though the discovery and exploitation of the safety zone of the I--an inviolable I within a hidden enclosure--makes possible the generosity which allows the other to become genuinely attractive. A deeper constancy of his own I has been disclosed to the patient, so that he is more able to grant this deeper sense of I to others. (Eigen, 1973, p. 5)

Eigen was indebted to Winnicott for the technical procedure of allowing the patient to endure agony until reflective awareness of the negative transference begins to occur spontaneously. Ferenczi (1988) had discovered the process of spontaneous recovery, which Balint (1932, 1969) had conceptualized as malignant regression developing spontaneously into a therapeutic regression in the service of the ego. In this way, the patient, regressed initially to the catastrophic trauma ("basic fault"), regressed still further to the happy time prior to the trauma. Eigen remarked on the vicissitudes of spontaneous recovery in psychosis and psychotherapy.

> Madness capitalizes on the relationship between self-attack and rebirth. In psychosis, the individual....may be frozen, in terror of dying, or weep with pity and joy in sight of Eternity. These states can fluctuate rapidly....They may be pitted against, merged with, or split off from each other. If left to themselves, they do not usually get anywhere....It is the rare individual who can go through such a tailspin by himself and then be made better by what he has passed through.....Even in good therapy, it seems something of a miracle when the phases of a death-rebirth sequence come together properly. (Eigen, 1986, pp. 209-10)

Eigen recommended that when a patient's self-observation discloses the negative transference as an inefficient or counterproductive defense, the patient has reached the point where a transference interpretation will be found acceptable.

> One does not try to discourage the negative transference by prematurely interpreting it....The patient makes important maturational gains by being allowed to have the new sense of energy and

> freedom his hate brings him vis à vis the therapist. Acceptable interpretations at this point concentrate on helping to deepen the patient's emerging sense of self, introduce the patient to the art of shifting perspectives, and provide an exhilarating taste of the dimension of meaning....More direct interpretations of the negative transference may be used when it is necessary to slow down the pace of treatment or to provide enough of an orientation so that the patient does not feel forced to terminate. If the therapist successfully protects the negative transference, the patient in time spontaneously reveals his vulnerability and longing and himself interprets the self-protective use of his ambivalence. At this point transference analysis is ego-syntonic and the patient can genuinely use his own and the analyst's observations concerning the shifting meanings of their relationship. (Eigen, 1977, p. 31)

The dissolution of the negative transference may manifest in euphoria, an explosion of *jouissance*. "There are psychoanalytic ecstasies. One follows agonies to the point of reversal, opening to *jouissance*, exquisite self-other perception, staying and staying with the feel of oneself and another" (Eigen, 2004, p. 168).

In a therapeutic context, the experience of rebirth is an insight that remains to be integrated within the psyche, by means of working through.

> In repeated contact with his expressive acts the person becomes more thoroughly identified with an underlying sense of generativity and renewal. He lives more and more in the rebirth experience. His time becomes the time of creativity, of absorption: a primordial or natural time with its own rhythms, turnings, juttings, caesuras, curves. (Eigen & Robbins, 1980, p. 85)

Where Elkin and Winnicott thought of a unidirectional movement from death to rebirth, Eigen was influenced by Bion's concept of continuous back-and-forth movements between the paranoid-schizoid and depressive positions. Eigen (2004, p. 75) speaks of death and rebirth as a continuous rhythm or pulse.

> In psychotherapy rebirth is modest, if far-reaching....No matter how great one's epiphany, sooner or later one's ordinary personality resurfaces....Over and over, we fall apart and come together....The agonies of the self are never left behind but....We learn to work better with what we are given, to be surprised by

> our gifts, and to be less afraid of ourselves. (Eigen, 1992, pp. 43, 100)

Eigen understands both the secondary gains of illness and repetition-compulsion as aspects of the death-and-rebirth process that have taken morbid turns.

> Once the psyche sets off in a wrong direction, it dreads the process of resetting itself....One has more or less adapted to oneself. One's adaptations themselves may cause pain, but they offer some illusion of control or safety....
>
> One does not merely go around the same old circles with no results. Repetition is not just a sign of being mired in self-destructive patterns but an opportunity, a challenge, a chance to do better.
>
> One appreciates more keenly that repetition is necessary and built into life.... Repetition gives us a chance to learn, to dig more deeply. It provides a frame of reference to transcend, a home base for exploration. (Eigen, 1992, pp. 218-219)

Eigen (1992) emphasizes that the death-and-rebirth pattern is a metaphor and not a theoretic explanation (p. 7). The pattern is also highly variable (p. 3). A patient's achievement of a sense of rebirth does not guarantee therapeutic success. Like any other insight, a rebirth must be worked through and made real (Eigen, 1996, p. 55)

THE WHIRLWIND

Eigen treats the biblical narrative of Job as an example of another major type of psychoanalytic process. In contrast with the death-rebirth pattern, Job suffered catastrophe, a devastation from which there could be no recovery, a disaster that could be survived but could not be repaired. Unable to put his catastrophe behind him, he envisioned God in a whirlwind and was freed to move on.

> Job contracts to the *pain point*, the place where there is nothing but pain. The pleasure he has in his body, his family, his flocks is taken away. The story dramatizes this movement in external, common-sense terms. The losses are real: real people, real animals, real body.

> One may also read the story of Job in psychological terms. The animals, family, and body are expressions of an alive-and-well self, the self in plenitude. When trauma is severe enough and wounding great enough, the alive-and-well self moves through pain and torment towards death. Job becomes pure pain, torment, living hell. One wonders how much he can bear.
>
> Job's paradox is that at the point of maximum intensity, a breakthrough occurs: he sees God. Pain is transformed to joy. A moment of expansion begins. All is lost, then heaven opens. New flocks, new family, and healed body express the expansive moment. Life is renewed. (Eigen, 1995, pp. 191-92)

Eigen understands catastrophe as a psychic wound so severe that the capacity to dream is damaged. The catastrophe is neither conceptualized in images nor experienced with affect. There is no possibility of undertaking the further tasks of ameliorating imagery and transforming affect in the direction of rebirth. Analytic treatment of catastrophe seeks to promote "actual growth in primary processing ability and a distinct evolution of dream work" (Eigen, 1995, p. 188).

Eigen recognizes catastrophe in a variety of phenomena. Impasse in the therapeutic situation can be a clinical manifestation of catastrophe.

> The thing that does not change, the permanence of a shifting impasse point or barrier in personality and psychotherapy, forces practitioner and patient to be still. One may object to sitting like Job while one's life is collapsing. But Job did more than ride out the storm. His complaints, recriminations, outrage, and agony shook inner and outer heavens....The intensity mounted and the reversal came: a vision of the Creator's mysterious power--the awesome shock of the malleability of everything in His hands. A life can be given, crushed, reshaped, and restored: "Yea though He slay me, yet will I trust Him" (Job 13:15). (Eigen, 1992, p. 29)

Eigen most frequently discussed catastrophe in terms taken from Bion for whom beta-elements were primary data that could not be analyzed further. In other formulations, Eigen resolved psychic catastrophe into components. For example, Eigen's clinical advice on how to avoid being a "Job's comforter" interprets the patient's condition as resistance to aliveness.

> People who have undergone grave, deadening processes in order to survive cannot take too much life in the analyst. The analyst

> learns to keep stimulating aspects of the session within semi-tolerable bounds....As the patient is able to tolerate more aliveness, the analyst may allow his own personality more play. (Eigen, 1996, p. 93)

Eigen (1992) elsewhere noted that "in the Bible, a whirlwind is often associated with the leveling of arrogance" (p. 178). Again, using Bion's term "murderous superego" for the object that cannot be dreamt, Eigen (2005) wrote:

> The murderous superego aims destructive energy at aliveness, turns the latter against itself, absorbs or channels its power, adding life to destructive force. On a relatively superficial level, an individual may say, "Why bother living if you're going to die." The capture of aliveness by destructive energy is more than this statement implies. Negative momentum reaches a point where life is part of destruction (rather than the reverse) and infusions of aliveness automatically empower destructive action. (p. 144)

Rather than a sense of renewal, patients who have undergone the whirlwind arrive at a sense of survival and consolation. There is no sense of a new start that makes good the previous loss. Catastrophic loss remains permanent and irremediable, but what remains possible can be accepted with optimism as a lesser good that is good-enough. "I have had patients who, after nearly destroying themselves, return from the Great Destruction with inner peace....Where there had been walls and impossibilities, they now see opportunities for living" (Eigen, 1998a, p. 168).

KABBALISTIC TIKKUN

Freud conceptualized the psychoanalytic process in terms of inhibition, the lifting of repression, and the manifestation of drives. Both the death-and-rebirth pattern and the Job pattern can be seen as ways of making the unconscious conscious. Due perhaps to his original training in ego psychology's practice of defense analysis, Eigen has also noticed a third basic pattern that is common to some therapeutic processes. Where ecstasy can be detected within the manifest structure of morbidity, there is no need for a therapeutic procedure that enables unconscious ecstasy to manifest consciously. Rather, the therapeutic task is to free manifest ecstasy from the morbid structure in which it is embedded, so that the patient can access ecstasy in a less conflicted manner.

The basic therapeutic strategy may be found in Winnicott's (1963d) discussion of the treatment of psychopathy in a child.

> Compulsive wickedness is about the last thing to be cured or even stopped by moral education. The child knows in his bones that it is *hope* that is locked up in the wicked behaviour, and that *despair* is linked with compliance and false socialization. For the antisocial or wicked person the moral educator is on the wrong side" (p. 104).

Eigen (1975) remarked on the pattern with regard to psychopathy. "It seems to me a serious therapeutic error, or at least an oversimplification, to hastily attribute the sense of power derived from various forms of psychopathic violence simply to frustration or a feeling of impotence" (p. 10). "A clinical point is that in attempting to remove illness, one may damage what is most alive and creative in the individual" (Eigen, 1999, p. 187).

> It seems essential that dissociated psychopathic as well as schizoid tendencies receive integration by central or communal ego structures in the course of authentic personal growth....It is desirable that they undergo transformation within the context of the therapy relationship itself so that destructive acting out is minimized....It is both crude and subtly oppressive to try to undercut the patient's pathology without helping to bring to light and assimilate the capacities and tendencies that the pathology embodies. (Eigen, 1975, pp. 11-12)

Eigen's technical procedure was once again to wait out the negative transference until spontaneous recovery began to take hold. Only after the patient began to experience his negativity as unwanted did Eigen commence with more active interventions.

> In each of the cases presented the patient's psychopathy was experienced as a natural, inevitable phase of a total process. It began gradually or explosively, built up to a sustained, fairly long-lasting peak, and with periodic bursts, subsided, its purpose apparently accomplished. A teleological sense was part of the experience. Once accomplished the powers, energies, or functions released took their place as a part of the total personality, some deep-seated dissociation overcome or diminished. Deep aggression was liberated and tested out in the form of outright hostility,

> trickery and deception, or defiant self-hatred. Since an important tendency previously left out of development now entered into communion with and eventually was balanced by other aspects of the self, it could begin to undergo transformation into the active virtue it pointed to: realistic effectiveness and practical self-assertion. The hold of guilt or idealized goodness was, in some instances, self-consciously defied, broken down by means of systematic or persistent immoral and criminal acts. As past identifications broke down, a more fully human sense of self, linked with the capacity for self-forgiveness, emerged. In certain important respects a morality beyond guilt, based on a sense of existential brotherhood, spontaneously appeared to develop. The main thrust of the patients' immoral and criminal actions seemed to reflect a determined concretizing of the right to be and the ability to do, the "I am" and "I can." (Eigen, 1975, p. 18)

Revisiting the topic of psychopathy twenty years later, Eigen (1996) reconceptualized the moral structure of psychopathy with appropriate attention to its ecstasy.

> A psychopath (sociopath)...has too much of the wrong kind of conscience: an *immoral conscience*....The psychopath....feels wronged and aims to set things right. The world owes him better, his just deserts. He recoils against life's injustice and takes life into his own hands to supply the necessary corrective....To whatever crimes or sins he commits, his superego whispers or, more likely, shrieks or cackles, "It is only just." Ego analysis is futile without addressing the...force that underwrites the persistent self-congratulatory, mocking superego. (Eigen, 1996, p. 64; see also p. 92)

Eigen's thinking here dovetailed with Symington's (1993) understanding that narcissism involves a denial of conscience together with a rationalization of wrong-doing as justified. Morality is not lacking. It is present but perverse.

Eigen generalized the pattern of liberating ecstasy from negativity and made the mystical character of the pattern explicit.

> A goal of analysis is to unmask the hidden god sense displaced or mixed up with some mundane reality. The question of who or what carries the god sense or how one's ultimate sense of power

> is distributed at a given time is critical for understanding the nature of the subject's distress and the direction of his movement. In work at the deepest levels of character it is necessary to search out and clarify the subject's relation to his power source with its ideal penumbra (or core) and chart how the subject maintains and gives away power in complex ways. (Eigen, 1979, p. 103)

Eigen's concept of the ghastly, horrible *jouissance* of non-being is perhaps the extreme instance of ecstasy embedded in negativity.

> One of life's cruel tantalization is that there are black hole ecstasies, mutilated ecstasies, damaged and damaging ecstasies, including evil imaginings, evil dreams. Ecstasy plays in damaged keys. One keeps aiming at the ecstasy in the warp, pressing buttons to heighten it. There is a sense one can undo the warp by feeding on ecstatic twists. (Eigen, 2001b, p. 17)

The personification of a black hole ecstasy in the form of a persecuting object improved the patient's prognosis. "A therapist might be quite happy if a patient who is a nonexistent 'person' should be lucky enough to fall into the hands of...a devil and risk a breakthrough into life" (Eigen, 1996, p. 106). A patient suffering a black hole ecstasy might nevertheless dream of positive ecstasy that was unavailable to waking life. The therapeutic task was then to facilitate the integration of the dream's optimism into the waking emptiness and horror (p. 95).

Eigen recognizes a historical precedent for his clinical strategy in the Kabbalistic practice of *tikkun*, "repair, healing." In the sixteenth century cosmogony of Rabbi Isaac Luria, God's initial effort to create the universe ended in a catastrophe, when the light and fire of divine holiness proved too strong for its material vessels to contain, and the vessels shattered, trapping holy sparks in their shards. A second work of creation brought the universe as we know it into being. The task of *tikkun*, "repair," requires a liberation of holy sparks from the *kelipot*, "shells," that imprison them, so that they may be returned to God (Scholem, 1954; Berke & Schneider, 2003; Fine, 2003).

> Aliveness, Kabbalah tells us, is shattered, sparks thrown in all directions. Wherever you find yourself, there are sparks waiting to be redeemed, waiting for your partnership, your work. (Eigen, 2005, p. 79)

The Kabbalah's debts to Neoplatonism--and possibly Bion's interest in the Kabbalah--account for the compatibility of the Lurianic program of *tikkun* with Bion's ideas of transforming beta-elements into alpha-elements that can be elevated through K and F to O (Eigen, 1998b, p. 188). In the Kabbalistic model, the general task of *tikkun* that will result in the arrival of the messianic era is practiced by individual Kabbalists as a personal program of moral and spiritual transformation. Since the seventeenth century, a personal *tikkun* has been conceptualized specifically as the soul's healing.

FURTHER ASPECTS OF EIGEN'S CLINICAL TECHNIQUE

Eigen's approach to the clinical situation blends elements of classical technique with thorough-going innovations. He stands with Freud in the Socratic tradition of seeking self-knowledge, but he understands self-knowledge as a quest that the analyst and patient share. "By its nature psychotherapy is extraordinary. Two individuals meet alone together to discover the truth about a life. The idea of truth orients the direction of discourse, although attempts to be truthful are flawed" (Eigen, 1992, p. 43). There is, at the same time, no possibility of discovering truth. Truth is God, and God is ineffable. What can be known is necessarily not God, but something short of God, short of the truth. "The very fact of symbolization is already a kind of castration at the heart of the real. No matter how joyous our joy, it is through a glass darkly" (Eigen, 1998a, pp. 14-15).

Eigen is not content with the mainstream attitude that the patient's autonomy is to be protected through the analyst's avoidance of teaching. Where Loewald recognized the patient's assumption of responsibility for her unconscious as a moral transformation, and Symington regarded psychoanalysis as a process of moral education, Eigen addresses deeper and earlier developmental issues. Eigen seeks to formulate the clinical phenomenon of the origin of emotion. Freud (1926a) maintained that a trauma, which by definition is paralyzingly painful to experience, is afterward repressed in order that paralysis not be perpetuated. Therapeutic progress begins with a sufficient processing of trauma that excruciating pain begins to be tolerable, and it carries on through the further processing of the emotional response to the trauma that reduces its pain and, if possible, replaces pain with solace and even joy. Eigen sees this process, which Freud originally formulated in terms of "abreaction" and "catharsis," as an emotional education. "Psychotherapy has grown up as an attempt to further emotional education. The complexity and subtlety of therapeutic processes teach us that simplistic notions of taming and training can be misleading" (Eigen, 1992, p. 180). Emotional education is intrinsically a transformation of mystical experiencing from the black hole ecstasy of non-being into the euphoria of ecstasy. Because Eigen sees himself as an emotional educator, he does not limit himself to analyses of what his patients have already achieved. "Many of my interventions are not directed to the details of transference to the 'real relationship' in therapy, but to emergence of new capacities and to the tone or spirit of communications" (p. xii).

Traditional aspects of the psychoanalytic situation take on original nuances in Eigen's practice. Rejecting Ferenczi's recommendation that analysts show kindness to their patients (Eigen, 1996, p. xix), Eigen endorsed Freud's call for the analyst's abstinence on the unprecedented argument that mystics have traditionally favored abstinence because it facilitates their attention to their work.

> Since the dawn of self-awareness some form of asceticism has been used, virtually universally, as a consciousness-raising technique. It appears to have functioned both to heighten awareness for its own sake and as one of the perennial revolutionary media to offset the toxic side-effects of civilization. It is thus not surprising to find radical psychoanalysis, a consciousness revolution of critical importance, an advocate of abstinence as a catalyst for the work of self-transformation. (Eigen, 1973, p. 1)

Eigen (1975) similarly endorses Freud's call for the analyst's neutrality, which he understands as "uncensoring awareness--the cognitive essence of compassion" (p. 17). He follows Bion's practice of avoiding memory, understanding, desire, and expectation, not continuously through each session, but at the beginning of each session (Eigen, 1998a, p. 175). Eigen is attentive, however, not only to projective identifications but to whatever his patients may produce. He is also flexible in his responses. "I do not have a party line, a dogma about just how I am supposed to be with every patient. I am willing to shift ground, try different styles, try to locate some way of being/experiencing that might work" (Eigen, 1996, p. 216).

Eigen conceptualizes the analyst-patient relationship through a series of partial formulations. He objects, for example, to ego psychologists' view of the analyst as an auxiliary ego, and he offers in its place a formulation that refers to the primary process. "The patient *experiences*, if initially through the analyst, the possibility of *someone* processing what could not be processed....The analyst is not only an *auxiliary* ego for the patient, but an...*auxiliary primary processor*" (Eigen, 1996, pp. 144-45).

Another formulation speaks instead in relational terms that are consistent with the import, although not the wording, of Fromm's appreciation of Buber.

> The therapist is often called upon to witness the massive mutilation and impoverishment of our most basic feelings and capacities and participate in the (re)constitution of an injured soul from the ground up....The therapist's own sense of distinction-union vis-à-vis the patient in his care will likely be...crucial....
>
> Patients are radically threatened, baffled, and confused by how near and far they feel to themselves and others. This distance-closeness is not something that is "curable." It is an elemental given, our raw material, a condition of our beings. Therapy provides a new distance-closeness field in which these terms begin to redefine and spontaneously reorder themselves. (Eigen, 1986, pp. 311-12)

In the analyst's meeting with the patient, the analyst makes contact and is available to be contacted, to whatever degree of emotional intimacy or distance the analyst determines. The patient, typically more damaged and incapable of equivalent intimacy, follows the analyst's lead, gradually abandoning fears and embracing a capacity for authentic intimacy that had never previously been known.

At the same time, an analyst must have the capacity to follow the patient's lead, so that the patient may feel known to and contacted by the analyst. "There are individuals who need a therapist who has gotten...adept at going through agony--nowhere sequences" (Eigen, 1998a, p. 173). Balancing an open display of aliveness with respect for the patient's pain requires continuous readjustment as the patient progresses. "The therapist attempts to time his use of frustration and gratification in such a way that the patient is able to bring together and begin to integrate polar experiences which were previously dissociated or overwhelming" (Eigen, 1977, p. 29).

Analytic interpretations of childhood object relations play an integral role in Eigen's cultivation of the therapeutic relationship.

> James's capacity to create ideal experience had become impaired owing to destructive aspects of his relations to his parents. The early ideals he had projected on his parents were returned to him in poisoned and debased forms. He learned to keep idealizing tendencies to himself, with the result that periodic bursts of chaotic inflation alternated with strong demoralizing tenden-

> cies....The modification of parental images through therapy allowed his desire for ideal communion to come into the open. This was especially expressed and carried forward in his relationship to the analyst....It was critical for him to learn that both his and my sense of intrinsic goodness persistently regenerated itself and, whatever our failings, remained essentially incorruptible. (Eigen, 1980, pp. 68-69)

Among the capacities that the patient introjects from the analyst is the capacity for faith. The analyst trusts to the psychoanalytic process of spontaneous recovery from morbid states through the acquisition of access to mystical experiencing. It is a faith in human nature and in God simultaneously. "There is a fidelity to this sacred something, the very mystery of who we are" (Eigen, 1998a, p. 25). It is the analyst's task to maintain faith even when the patient cannot (Eigen, 1992, p. 3). Both the analyst and the patient need to be honest about the limitations of their knowledge (Eigen, 1986, p. 334), in order to be clear about their reliance on faith. Eventually the analyst's faith in the process comes to be shared by the patient. "As the individual's sensitivity to moment to moment nuances and possibilities of his work quickens, he becomes more committed to a lifestyle aware of dangers inherent in premature closure operations. He learns not only to expect the unexpected but to rely on what the unforeseen must teach him" (Eigen & Robbins, 1980, p. 85).

Under optimal conditions, the analyst's faith creates a container that makes possible the patient's immersion in her agonies.

> Therapy provides a chance to dip into original madness in manageable doses. Winnicott (1989, pp. 128-29) envisions going through bits of madness and repeatedly making spontaneous recoveries. It is crucial that the therapist does not try to "push" the patient into "sanity" and disrupt what needs to happen. The therapist needs to help the individual find his own rhythm and way of going in and out of what bothers him. (Eigen, 1999, p. 167)

It is inevitable, however, that optimal conditions will not always be met. The analyst's strength falters, and his efforts to be with the patient in her agony lead him to join the patient in being overwhelmed by the agonies.

> Something was poisoning her, killing her, making her stuporous. I had urges to fight it and give in to it at the same time. In a way,

> I did both. For periods, I went under with her, knocked out by lethal forces. Years of going through horrific states taught me I would resurface and come back in time. How does one convey such learning to another? How does one help another develop resilience?
>
> From time to time, Lucy found someone with her where no one had been before. We were in blank, noxious deadness without any contact, having lost a sense of each other's existence. Now and then we jostled or bumped each other in our lightless world. Sometimes we came up to breathe, moments of reprieve, then back to malignant nowhere....
>
> The O we had reached was a sort of anti-O, a null-O, an O of poisonous blankness. It is important to stress that this poisonous blankness was very real, the only real reality while we were in it. When it gripped us, the idea of hope seemed like child's play. (Eigen, 1998a, pp. 175-76)

Conventional views of succumbing to a patient's distress as the technical error of a *folie à deux* fail to acknowledge that every analyst has finite strength. Every analyst eventually succumbs, and every analyst is eventually guilty of transference-countertransference enactments (Maroda, 2004)--perhaps not with every patient, but with every patient whom the analyst finds particularly difficult to help. Faith carries the analyst through. In the process, doing therapy becomes a growth opportunity for therapists.

> Therapy is as much for the therapist as for the patient.. A therapist uses therapy to evolve equipment to do therapy. One tries to let oneself think and feel as therapy is going on. A lot of therapy work goes on unconsciously between meetings. One comes to the next meeting with work needed the meeting before. (Eigen, 2001b, p. 76)

CONCLUDING REFLECTIONS

Although Eigen counts himself among the psychoanalytic mystics, his clinical work is often regarded as a pioneering contribution to the American school of relational psychoanalysis, which arose in the 1980s through a synthesis of British Independent and American interpersonal points of view. In Eigen's work, psychoanalytic mysticism has become a practice of spiritual direction. He helps mystics with their mysticism and meditators with their meditation. He conceptualizes the therapeutic process in mystical metaphors: death-and-rebirth, enduring the whirlwind, and the *tikkun* of ecstasy trapped in shards of negativity. The variety of secular and religious tropes that he employs, permit him to work with both secular and religious patients. Most of his views can be expressed in methodologically agnostic, psychological formulations. It is primarily the equation of plenitude and nothingness that leads him into metaphysics and paradox.

Intriguingly, Eigen does not discuss mystical awakening, the conversion of a secularist to become a mystic, as a psychoanalytic activity. With secularists he is apparently content to speak of aliveness, joy, and creativity, without adding that he regards the three idealities as numinous and divine. Another intriguing lack is Eigen's address of moral issues largely in passing as matters of course. Patients' achievements of the capacity for concern are not a topic that is prominent in his writings and may not be a major consideration in his clinical work. His metaphysics suggest that the omission may be dogmatic. Eigen interprets the experienced sense of divine presence not as a revelation by God to the soul, but as an actual presence of God, a theophany within the soul. This metaphysical doctrine, inherited from Bion, that all being is the divine non-being O, requires Eigen to treat both euphoric and horrific ecstasies, *jouissance* of both wonderment and non-being, as equally O and undifferentiatedly divine. The therapeutic process, involving spontaneous recovery from trauma, is a movement of God--the O of the patient--from horror to joy. Because meaningful moral discussion is precluded by the divinization of suffering, morality has very little place in Eigen's description of the therapeutic process.

Eigen's occasional remarks on morality nevertheless disclose a passionately moral individual whose convictions happen to remain considerably unintegrated with his theoretical model. Eigen (2007b) expressed a similar assessment of his limitations in a recent talk at the graduation exercises of the New York University Postdoctoral Program in Psychotherapy and Psychoanalysis. Looking to the future, he suggested that "the edge of the possible" might be developing a clinical "response capacity" to address our present "Age of Psychopathy, in which triumphal psychopathic manipulation of psychotic agonies hold masses of people in thrall."

Afterthoughts

This book project began with my realization that a contemporary definition of mysticism in the academic study of religion would evaluate a small but notable group of psychoanalysts as having been both extrovertive mystics and attentive to mystical concerns in their contributions to psychoanalytic theory and practice. My goal has been to provide a history of psychoanalytic ideas about the mystical, together with a compendium of clinical advice about working with the mystical in clinical psychoanalysis. If I have persuaded my readers that the analytic writers whom I have surveyed deserve to be discussed together, I have carried my thesis, that there is indeed a mystical trajectory in psychoanalysis.

The psychoanalytic approach to mysticism overlaps only in part with academic understandings of the phenomena. Understood psychoanalytically, mysticism begins with the unconscious systematizing function noted by Freud, that I have attributed to condensation and its secondary revision by the unconscious superego; and it proceeds through a series of increasing complexities that culminate in the integration of the psyche as a whole. The psychoanalytic understanding of mysticism includes both the assembly and construction of the self-representation over the course of development, and the internal relations of the self-representation with ego ideals that are experienced, among other manners, as personal integrity (or inauthenticity). More closely associated with the term "mysticism" in the public mind are experiences that unconsciously impose the unity of the self onto relations with other people, with the environment, and with God. Freud recognized the unitive character of these relations when in 1920 he backtracked from decades of privileging sexuality to conceptualize the essence of Eros as a drive to unity. It is not sexuality but the unitive that produces love in the dyad. It is again not sexuality but the unitive that produces morality in society. The ordinary business of psychoanalysis with "humanistic" motives and values surrounding love and work is, I suggest, precisely a concern with the mystical in the natural, secular sense of the term that I have proposed.

The first and most basic contribution of the psychoanalytic mystics was the recognition that the mystical involves a complete line of development. Because Rank, Fromm, Winnicott, and Loewald assumed that the deepest layer of the unconscious was solipsistic, they placed the infantile sources of mystical experience at the beginning of human development.

They interpreted individuation as the primary goal of both maturation and therapeutic change, and they identified failed individuation with psychopathology. Extending the same line of reasoning beyond early infancy, Kohut postulated a narcissistic line of development, which Grotstein located within a Kleinian model under the term "autochthony." Although the theory of infantile solipsism collapsed in the early 1980s, the evidence of unitive modes suggests that it is the self-representation, and not the oceanic feeling, that accounts for the mystical line of development. We can retain Ehrenzweig's notion that the mystical precedes the oral, anal, and Oedipal in the developmental layering of the unconscious, but we need to replace the oceanic feeling at its foundation with a self-representations. We need to think of self-symbolism as a category of symptoms and sublimations to be placed alongside oral, anal, and genital symbolism. Perhaps we need to think in terms of Federn's mental ego antedating the earliest demonstrable body-ego, the "primal cavity" or mouth interior of Spitz's description.

Although psychoanalytic discussions of the mystical add unconscious dimensions previously unknown to students of mysticism, the psychoanalytic mystics have simultaneously betrayed their amateurism in the academic study of religion by addressing and partly conflating five different phenomena.

(i) All of the psychoanalytic mystics have taken concern with unitive experiences, which has been my major concern in this volume.

(ii) Milner, Winnicott, Ehrenzweig, Grotstein, and Eigen discussed creative illusion, the infant's fantasizing the mother prior to discovering her in reality, the infant's similar endowment of the teddy bear with personhood, and more generally all perception, all culture, and all scientific knowledge. Limited by the universality of the illusions that we project, we cannot know the real. Where Bion was uncertain whether realism was to be preferred to idealism and limited his faith to O, it is more common to place faith in the real, whether or not one additionally places faith in a God beyond being. Whether faith or, in Winnicott's term, "belief-in," is to be counted precisely as mystical, it is presupposed by all reality-testing.

(iii) Grotstein and Eigen have invoked Otto's concept of "numinous" experience. Otto explicitly equated numinous experiences with religious experiences in general and treated mystical experiences as a subcategory. For Otto, all mystical experiences are numinous; but not all numinous experiences are mystical. Grotstein and Eigen instead reflect popular usage, which extends the term "mystical" to numinous experience in general. The merits and disadvantages of both approaches await further research. There is considerable merit, however, to Grotstein's and Eigen's view that clinical psychoanalysis should routinely inculcate the achievement of a sense of the numinous, the distinctive experience of wonderment, awe, fascination, humility, immediacy, and tranquility in the face of life's mysteries (see Merkur, 1996, 2006). At the same time, I would prefer to follow Otto and observe the terminological convention in the academic study of religion. The numinous is a different and more extensive topic than the mystical.

(iv) Ehrenzweig, Winnicott, Loewald, Bion, and Eigen have addressed the concept of undifferentiation. The organization of sense impressions into coherent perceptions involves a great deal of learning, for example, that differently colored areas within the visual field are individual objects, located at specific distances from the viewer, and so forth. Undifferentiation implies a comparative absence of ideas concerning sense impressions. It is a different phenomenon than the manifestation of a unitive mode in a mystical experience. Writing in advance of Ehrenzweig, Fromm did not use the term "undifferentiation," but he recommended its achievement when he advocated Zen Buddhist meditation and the "bare attending" procedure of Buddhist mindfulness meditation.

(v) Lastly, in their discussions of O, Bion, Grotstein, Symington, and Eigen have presented mystical theologies. For Bion, the cosmos was mental and possibly not material. God was panentheistic, being both transcendent and the substance of all existence. The other writers acknowledged the cosmos recognized by the physical sciences but differed in their accounts of God. Grotstein conceives of a transcendent God; there are, however, occasional passages where he echoed Bion's language uncritically. For Symington, God is identical with existence. For Eigen, God is paradoxical: identical with existence in theory, yet sometimes transcendent in experience. These several theological positions are speculations and they are inconsistent with each other. Each departure from methodological agnosticism has the further disadvantage of foreclosing tenable theoretical options *a priori*.

The psychoanalytic mystics have engaged precisely in explorations. Their maps show large parts of a coastline and occasional rivers leading inland, but also much *terra incognita*. They have nevertheless collectively accomplished a major repositioning of mysticism within psychoanalysis. For Rank, the mystical was "beyond psychology," and for Fromm it was "transtherapeutic." Mainstream psychoanalysis uprooted resistance, including the transference-resistance (Freud, 1914b), but it did no more. For Milner, Winnicott, and Ehrenzweig, mysticism, like artistic creativity, made a different part of the unconscious conscious. Loewald argued, however, that clinical psychoanalysis was inherently integrative; and Bion took the further step of conceptualizing psychoanalysis as a mystical regression to origin (O). Bion denied that he was himself a mystic, but his contributions made it socially viable for Grotstein, Symington, and Eigen to do so. At the same time, Loewald, Symington, and Eigen asserted that the distinction between analysis and education is a fallacy. Analysis inevitably inculcates analytic concerns with truth and integrity, empathy and moral sensitivity, and emotional experience in general. Bion, Grotstein, Symington, and Eigen further asserted that therapeutic success involves the analysand's encounter with O--an insight, a transcendent position, a vital realization, mystical experiencing. These trends compare with Klein's (1935) discovery of the depressive position and the growing appreciation, shared currently by Kleinians, British Independents, and relational psychoanalysts, that making unconscious morality conscious is integral, and not merely additional, to the core psychoanalytic project of overcoming unconscious resistance. Loewald's formulations of psychic integration repositioned mysticism vis à vis psychoanalysis, moving it from the optional adjunct that it was for Fromm, to become intrinsic to Freud's therapeutic ambitions, as Bion, Grotstein, Symington, and Eigen have appreciated. What will psychoanalysis look like when these trends have matured and developed into well understood, commnplace, and reliably duplicable procedures?

References

Abraham, Karl. (1924). A short study of the development of the libido, viewed in the light of mental disorders. In *Selected papers of Karl Abraham*, trans. Douglas Bryan & Alix Strachey (pp. 413-501). London: Hogarth Press, 1927; reprinted New York: Brunner/Mazel, n.d.

Aichhorn, August. (1925). *Wayward youth*. Revised and adapted from the second German edition, 1931. New York: Viking Press, 1935.

Alexander, Franz. (1925). A metapsychological description of the process of cure. Reprinted in *The scope of psychoanalysis 1921-1961: Selected papers of Franz Alexander* (pp. 205-24). New York: Basic Books, 1961.

_______. (1929a). The need for punishment and the death-instinct. *International Journal of Psycho-Analysis*, *10*, 256-269.

_______. (1929b). *The psychoanalysis of the total personality: The application of Freud's theory of the ego to the neuroses*, trans. Bernard Glueck & Bertram D. Lewin. New York: Nervous and Mental Disease.

_______. (1931). Buddhistic training as an artificial catatonia (The biological meaning of psychic occurrences). *Psychoanalytic Review*, *18*(2), 129-45.

_______. (1950). Analysis of the therapeutic factors in psychoanalytic treatment. Reprinted in *The scope of psychoanalysis 1921-1961* (pp. 261-75).

Alexander, Franz & French, Thomas Morton. (1946). *Psychoanalytic therapy: Principles and application*. New York: Ronald Press.

Allison, Joel. (1968). Adaptive regression and intense religious experiences. *Journal of Nervous and Mental Disease*, *145*, 452-463.

Almond, Philip C. (1982). *Mystical experience and religious doctrine: An investigation of the study of mysticism in world religions*. Berlin: Mouton.

Arieti, Silvano. (1964). The rise of creativity: From primary to tertiary process. *Contemporary Psychoanalysis*, *1*(1), 51-68.

_______. (1976). *Creativity: The magic synthesis*. New York: Basic Books.

Armstrong, A. Hilary. (1955). Plotinus's doctrine of the infinite and its significance for Christian thought. *Downside Review*, *73*, 47-58.

Austin, J. L. (1975). *How to do things with words*, 2nd ed. Ed. J. O. Urmson & Marina Sbisà. Cambridge, MA: Harvard University Press.

Bacciagaluppi, Marco. (1993). Ferenczi's influence on Fromm. In Lewis Aron & Adrienne Harris (Eds.), *The legacy of Sandor Ferenczi* (pp. 185-198). Hillsdale, NJ & London: Analytic Press.

Bachelard, Gaston. (1987). *On poetic imagination and reverie*, 2nd ed. Trans. Colette Gaudin. Dallas, TX: Spring.

Bakan, David.. (1966). Science, mysticism and psychoanalysis. *Catholic Psychological Record, 4*, 1-9.

Bakan, David; Merkur, Dan; & Weiss, David S. (2009). *Maimonides' cure of souls: Medieval precursor of psychoanalysis.* Albany: State University of New York Press.

Balint, Michael. (1932). Character analysis and new beginning. Reprinted in *Primary love and psycho-analytic technique* (pp. 159-73). London: Hogarth Press, 1952; reprinted London: Karnac Books, 1985.

_______. (1937). Early developmental states of the ego. Primary object-love. Reprinted in *Primary love and psycho-analytic technique* (pp. 90-108).

_______. (1952). *Primary love and psycho-analytic technique.* London: Hogarth Press; reprinted London: Karnac Books, 1985.

_______. (1969). *The basic fault: Therapeutic aspects of regression.* London: Tavistock; reprinted New York: Brunner/Mazel, 1979; reprinted Evanston, IL: Northwestern University Press, 1992.

Bergmann, Martin S. (2000). The Hartmann era and its contribution to psychoanalytic technique. In Martin S. Bergmann (Ed.), *The Hartmann era* (pp. 1-78). New York: Other Press, 2000.

Berke, Joseph H. & Schneider, Stanley. (2003). Repairing worlds: An exploration of the psychoanalytical and Kabbalistic concepts of reparation and *tikkun*. *Psychoanalytic Review, 90*, 723-49.

Bibring, Edward. (1937). On the theory of the therapeutic results of psychoanalysis. *International Journal of Psycho-Analysis, 18*(2-3), 170-89.

Bing, James F.; McLaughlin, Francis; & Marburg, Rudolf. (1959). The metapsychology of narcissism. *Psychoanalytic Study of the Child, 14*, 9-28.

Bion, Wilfrid R. (1961). *Experiences in groups: And other papers.* London: Tavistock; reprinted London: Routledge, 2006.

_______. (1962a). *Learning from Experience.* New York: Basic Books.

_______. (1962b). A theory of thinking. *International Journal of Psycho-Analysis, 43*, 306-310. Reprinted in *Second thoughts: Selected papers on psycho-analysis* (pp. 110-119). New York: Jason Aronson, 1967.

_______. (1963). *Elements of psycho-analysis.* London: William Heinemann; reprinted London: Karnac, 1984.

_______. (1965). *Transformations.* London: William Heinemann; reprinted London: Karnac, 1984.

_______. (1967). Notes on memory and desire. *Psychoanalytic forum* 2, 272-73, 279-80. Reprinted in Elizabeth Bott Spillius (Ed.), *Melanie Klein today: Developments in theory and practice. Volume 2: Mainly practice* (pp. 17-21). London: Routledge, 1988.

_______. (1970). *Attention and interpretation: A scientific approach to insight in psycho-analysis and groups.* New York: Basic Books; reprinted London: Karnac Books, 1984.

_______. (1978). *Four discussions with W. R. Bion.* Perthshire, UK: Clunie Press.

_______. (1980). *Bion in New York and Sao Paulo.* Perthshire, UK: Clunie Press.

_______. (1987). *Clinical seminars: Brasilia and Sao Paulo and four papers.* Ed. Francesca Bion. Abingdon, UK: Fleetwood Press.

_______. (1989). *Two papers: The grid and caesura.* London: Karnac Books.

_______. (1990). *Brazilian lectures. 1973 Sao Paulo, 1974 Rio de Janeiro/Sao Paulo.* London: Karnac Books.

_______. (1991). *A memoir of the future*, rev. ed. London: Karnac Books.

_______. (1994). *Cogitations*, 2nd ed. Ed. Francesca Bion. London: Karnac Books.

_______. (1997). *Taming wild thoughts.* Ed. Francesca Bion. London: Karnac Books.

Blaustein, Alvin B. (1975). A dream resembling the Isakower phenomenon: A brief clinical contribution. *International Journal of Psycho-Analysis*, *56*, 207-8.

Bléandonu, Gérard. (1994). *Wilfred Bion: His life and works 1897-1979.* Trans. Claire Pajaczkowska. New York: Other Press.

Boss, Medard. (1963). *Psychoanalysis and Daseinsanalysis* Trans. Ludwig B. Lefebre. New York & London: Basic Books.

Bråten, Stein. (1988). Dialogic mind: The infant and the adult in protoconversation. In Marc E. Carvallo (Ed.), *Nature, cognition and system* (Vol. 1, pp. 187-205). Dordrecht: Kluwer Academic.

Brenner, Charles. (1994). The mind as conflict and compromise formation. *Journal of Clinical Psychoanalysis*, *3*, 473-496.

Brentano, Franz. (1977). *The psychology of Aristotle: In particular his doctrine of the active intellect.* Ed. & trans. Rolf George. Berkeley: University of California Press.

Brierley, Marjorie. (1932). Some problems in the integration of women. *International Journal of Psycho-Analysis*, *13*, 433-448.

_______. (1947). Notes on psycho-analysis and integrative living. *International Journal of Psycho-Analysis*, *28*(2), 57-105.

_______. (1951). *Trends in psycho-analysis.* London: Hogarth Press & Institute of Psycho-Analysis.

Brown, Daniel P. (1977). A model for the levels of concentrative meditation. *International Journal of Clinical and Experimental Hypnosis*, *35*(4), 236-273.

Brown, Daniel P. & Engler, Jack. (1984). An outcome study of intensive mindfulness meditation. *Psychoanalytic Study of Society*, *10*, 163-225.

Buber, Martin. (1958). *I and thou*, 2nd ed. Trans. Ronald Gregor Smith. New York: Charles Scribner's Sons.

_______. (1973). *Meetings*. Ed. Maurice Friedman. La Salle, IL: Open Court.

Bucke, Richard Maurice. (1901). *Cosmic consciousness: A study in the evolution of the human mind*. Reprinted New York: E. P. Dutton, 1969.

Burrow, Trigant. (1914). Character and the neuroses. *Psychoanalytic Review, 1*(2), 121-28.

_______. (1917). The genesis and meaning of "homosexuality" and its relation to the problem of introverted mental states. *Psychoanalytic Review, 4*(3), 272-84.

_______. (1917-18a). The meaning of psychoanalysis. *Journal of Abnormal Psychology, 12*, 58-68.

_______. (1917-18b). Notes with reference to Freud, Jung and Adler. *Journal of Abnormal Psychology, 12*, 161-7.

_______. (1918). The origin of the incest-awe. *Psychoanalytic Review, 5*(3), 243-54.

_______. (1958). *A search for man's sanity: The selected letters of Trigant Burrow, with biographical notes*. Ed. William E. Galt. New York: Oxford University Press.

Burston, Daniel. (1991). *The legacy of Erich Fromm*. Cambridge, MA: Harvard University Press.

_______. (1996a). Erich Fromm: A brief biography. In Mauricio Cortina & Michael Maccoby (Eds.), *A prophetic analyst: Erich Fromm's contributions to psychoanalysis* (pp. 415-25). Northvale, NJ: Jason Aronson, 1996.

_______. (1996b). *The wing of madness: The life and work of R. D. Laing*. Cambridge, MA: Harvard University Press.

Bychowski, Gustav. (1951). From catharsis to work of art: The making of an artist. In George Wilbur B. & Werner Muensterberger (Eds.), *Psychoanalysis and culture: Essays in honor of Geza Roheim* (pp. 390-409). New York: International Universities Press, 1951.

Carver, Alfred. (1924). Primary identification and mysticism. *British Journal of Medical Psychology, 4*, 102-114.

Chasseguet-Smirgel, Janine. (1985). *The ego ideal: A psychoanalytic essay on the malady of the ideal*. Trans. Paul Barrows. New York: W. W. Norton.

Cohen, J. M. & Phipps, John-Francis. (1992). *The common experience: Signposts on the path to enlightenment*. Wheaton, IL: Quest Books/Theosophical.

Cortina, Mauricio & Maccoby, Michael (Eds.). (1996). *A prophetic analyst: Erich Fromm's contributions to psychoanalysis*. Northvale, NJ: Jason Aronson.

Curran, Charles A. (1963). *Religious values in counseling and psychotherapy*. New York: Sheed and Ward.

Danto, Arthur C. (2005). *Nietzsche as philosopher*, rev. ed. New York: Columbia University Press.

Deikman, Arthur J. (1963). Experimental meditation. *Journal of Nervous and Mental Disease, 136*, 329-73.

________. (1966a). De-automatization and the mystic experience. *Psychiatry, 29*, 324-38.

________. (1966b). Implications of experimentally induced contemplative meditation. *Journal of Nervous and Mental Disease, 142*(2), 101-116.

Deutsch, Helene. (1989). On satisfaction, happiness and ecstasy, ed. Paul Roazen. *International Journal of Psycho-Analysis, 70*, 715-23.

Devereux, George. (1957). The criterion of dual competence in psychiatric-anthropological studies. *Journal of the Hillside Hospital, 6*, 87-90.

Doblin, Rick. (1991). Pahnke's "Good Friday experiment": A long-term follow-up and methodological critique. *Journal of Transpersonal Psychology, 23*(1), 1-28.

Eagle, Morris N. (1984). *Recent developments in psychoanalysis: A critical evaluation.* Cambridge, MA: Harvard University Press.

Easson, William M. (1973). The earliest ego development, primitive memory traces, and the Isakower phenomenon. *Psychoanalytic Quarterly, 42*, 60-72.

Eckstein, Friedrich. (1936). *"Alte unnennbare Tage!": Erinnerungen aus Siebzig Lehr- und Wanderjahren.* Wien, Leipzig & Zürich: Herbert Reichner Verlag; reprinted Wien: Edition Aletlier, 1988.

Ehrenzweig, Anton. (1948-49). Unconscious form-creation in art. *British Journal of Medical Psychology, 21*, 185-214; *22*, 88-109.

________. (1949). The origin of the scientific and heroic urge (The guilt of Prometheus). *International Journal of Psycho-Analysis, 30*, 108-123.

________. (1953). *The psychoanalysis of artistic vision and hearing: An introduction to a theory of unconscious perception.* New York: Julian Press.

________. (1957). The creative surrender: A comment on "Joanna Field's" book *An experiment in leisure. American Imago, 14*, 193-210.

________. (1964). The undifferentiated matrix of artistic imagination. *Psychoanalytic Study of Society, 3*, 373-398.

________. (1967). *The hidden order of art: A study in the psychology of artistic imagination.* Berkeley: University of California Press.

Eigen, Michael. (1973). Abstinence and the schizoid ego. *International Journal of Psycho-Analysis, 54*, 493-498. Reprinted in Michael Eigen, *The electrified tightrope*, ed. Adam Phillips (pp. 1-8). Northvale, NJ: Jason Aronson, 1993.

________. (1975). Psychopathy and individuation. *Psychotherapy: Theory, Research, and Practice, 12*, 286-294. Reprinted in *The electrified tightrope* (pp. 9-20).

________. (1977). On working with 'unwanted' patients. *International Journal of Psycho-Analysis, 58*, 109-121. Reprinted in *The Electrified Tightrope* (pp. 25-41).

________. (1979). Ideal images, creativity, and the Freudian drama. *Psychocultural Review, 3*, 287-298. Reprinted in *The electrified tightrope* (pp. 95-104).

________. (1980). Instinctual fantasy and ideal images. *Contemporary Psychoanalysis, 16*, 119-137. Reprinted in *The electrified tightrope* (pp. 61-75).

_______. (1981a). The area of faith in Winnicott, Lacan and Bion. *International Journal of Psychoanalysis*, *62*, 413-433. Reprinted in *The electrified tightrope* (pp. 109-138).

_______. (1981b). Guntrip's analysis with Winnicott. *Contemporary Psychoanalysis*, *17*, 103-111. Reprinted in *The electrified tightrope* (pp. 139-146).

_______. (1982). Creativity, instinctual fantasy, and ideal images. *Psychoanalytic Review*, *69*, 317-339. Reprinted in *The electrified tightrope* (pp. 77-94).

_______. (1983). Dual union or undifferentiation? A critique of Marion Milner's view of the sense of psychic creativeness. *International Review of Psycho-Analysis*, *10*, 415-428. Reprinted in *The electrified tightrope* (pp. 157-176).

_______. (1986). *The Psychotic Core*. Northvale, NJ: Jason Aronson.

_______. (1989). Aspects of omniscience. In M. Gerard Fromm & Bruce L. Smith (Eds.), *The facilitating environment: Clinical applications of Winnicott's theory* (pp. 604-628). Madison, CT: International Universities Press. Reprinted in *The electrified tightrope* (pp. 243-257).

_______. (1992). *Coming through the whirlwind: Case studies in psychotherapy*. Wilmette, IL: Chiron.

_______. (1993). *The electrified tightrope*. Ed. Adam Phillips. Northvale, NJ: Jason Aronson.

_______. (1995). *Reshaping the self: Reflections on renewal through therapy*. Madison, CT: Psychosocial Press.

_______. (1996). *Psychic deadness*. Northvale, NJ: Jason Aronson.

_______. (1998a). *The psychoanalytic mystic*. London: Free Association Press.

_______. (1998b). Wilfred R. Bion: Infinite surfaces, explosiveness, faith. In Paul Marcus & Alan Rosenberg (Eds.), *Psychoanalytic versions of the human condition: Philosophies of life and their impact on practice* (pp. 183-205). New York: New York University Press, 1998.

_______. (1999). *Toxic nourishment*. London: Karnac.

_______. (2001a). *Damaged bonds*. London: Karnac.

_______. (2001b). *Ecstasy*. Middletown, CT: Wesleyan University Press.

_______. (2002). *Rage*. Middletown, CT: Wesleyan University Press.

_______. (2004). *The sensitive self*. Middletown, CT: Wesleyan University Press.

_______. (2005). *Emotional storm*. Middletown, CT: Wesleyan University Press.

_______. (2006a). *Age of psychopathy*. http://www.psychoanalysis-and-therapy.com/human_nature/eigen/pref.html.

_______. (2006b). *Lust*. Middletown, CT: Wesleyan University Press.

_______. (2007a). *Feeling matters: From the Yosemite god to the annihilated self*. London: Karnac.

_______. (2007b). Hidden sprouts and psyche-talk. Unpublished graduation talk, June 8, 2007. New York University Postdoctoral Program in Psychotherapy and Psychoanalysis.

Eigen, Michael & Robbins, Arthur. (1980). Object relations and expressive symbolism: Some structures and functions of expressive therapy. In Arthur Robbins (Ed.), *Expressive therapy: A creative arts approach to depth-oriented treatment* (pp. 73-94). New York: Human Sciences Press.

Elkin, Henry. (1958). On the origin of the self. *Psychoanalysis and the Psychoanalytic Review*, *45*(4), 57-76.

_______. (1972). On selfhood and the development of ego structures in infancy. *Psychoanalytic Review*, *59*, 389-416.

Erikson, Erik Homburger. (1963). *Childhood and society*, 2nd ed. New York: W. W. Norton.

Esman, Aaron H. (1972). Adolescence and the consolidation of values. In Seymour C. Post (Ed.), *Moral values and the superego concept in psychoanalysis* (pp. 87-100). New York: International Universities Press, 1972.

Fairbairn, W. R. D. (1941). A revised psychopathology of the psychoses and psychoneuroses. In *Psychoanalytic studies of the personality* (pp. 28-58). London: Routledge & Kegan Paul, 1952.

_______. (1943). The repression and the return of bad objects (with special reference to the 'war neuroses'). Reprinted in *Psychoanalytic studies of the personality* (pp. 59-81).

_______. (1944). Endopsychic structure considered in terms of object-relationships. *International Journal of Psychoanalysis* 25, 70-92. Reprinted in *Psychoanalytic studies of the personality* (pp. 82-132).

_______. (1946). Object-relationships and dynamic structure. *International Journal of Psycho-Analysis*, *27*, 30-37. Reprinted in *Psychoanalytic studies of the personality* (pp. 137-51).

_______. (1952). *Psychoanalytic studies of the personality*. London: Routledge & Kegan Paul.

_______. (1963). Synopsis of an object-relations theory of the personality. *International Journal of Psycho-Analysis*, *44*, 224-225.

_______. (1994). *From instinct to self: Selected papers of W. R. D. Fairbairn, Vol. I: Clinical and theoretical papers.* Eds. David E. Scharff & Ellinor Fairbairn Birtles. Northvale, NJ: Jason Aronson.

Farber, Leslie H. (1967). Martin Buber and psychotherapy. In Paul Arthur Schilpp & Maurice Friedman (Eds.), *The philosophy of Martin Buber* (pp. 577-601). La Salle, IL: Open Court & London: Cambridge University Press, 1967.

Fauteux, Kevin. (1994). *The recovery of self: Regression and redemption in religious experience*. New York: Paulist Press.

_______. (1997). Self-reparation in religious experience and creativity. In Charles Spezzano & Gerald J. Gargiulo (Eds.), *Soul on the couch: Spirituality, religion, and morality in contemporary psychoanalysis* (pp. 11-41). Hillsdale, NJ: Analytic Press.

Federn, Paul. (1926). Some variations in ego-feeling. *International Journal of Psycho-Analysis, 7*, 434-44.

_______. (1932). The reality of the death instinct, especially in melancholia: Remarks on Freud's book: "Civilization and Its Discontents." *Psychoanalytic Review, 19*, 129-51.

_______. (1952). *Ego psychology and the psychoses.* New York: Basic Books.

Fenichel, Otto. (1945). *The psychoanalytic theory of neurosis.* New York: W. W. Norton.

Ferenczi, Sandor. (1927). [Review] *Technik Der Psychoanalyse: I. Die Analytische Situation.* By Dr. Otto Rank. *International Journal of Psychoanalysis, 8*, 93-100.

_______. (1930). The principles of relaxation and neocatharsis. Reprinted in *Final contributions to the problems and methods of psycho-analysis*, ed. Michael Balint, trans. Eric Mosbacher and others (pp. 108-125). London: Hogarth Press, 1955; reprinted New York: Brunner/Mazel, 1980.

_______. (1932). Confusion of tongues between adults and the child. Reprinted in *Final contributions to the problems and methods of psycho-analysis* (pp. 156-67).

_______. (1933). Thalassa: A theory of genitality. *Psychoanalytic Quarterly, 2*, 361-403.

_______. (1988). *The clinical diary of Sándor Ferenczi.* Ed. Judith Dupont. Trans. Michael Balint & Nicola Zarday Jackson. Cambridge, MA: Harvard University Press.

Ferenczi, Sandor & Rank, Otto. (1924). *The development of psycho-analysis.* Trans. Caroline Newton. In Sandor Ferenczi, *Sex in psycho-analysis (Contributions to psycho-analysis)* and Sandor Ferenczi & Otto Rank, *The development of psycho-analysis*, two books bound as one. New York: Dover, 1956.

Field, Joanna (Marion Milner). (1934). *A life of one's own.* London: Chatto & Windus; reprinted London: Virago Press, 1986.

_______. (1937). *An experiment in leisure.* London: Chatto & Windus; reprinted London: Virago Press, 1986.

_______. (1957). *On not being able to paint*, 2nd edition. Los Angeles: J. P. Tarcher.

Fine, Lawrence. (2003). *Physician of the soul, healer of the cosmos: Isaac Luria and his Kabbalistic fellowship.* Stanford, CA: Stanford University Press.

Fink, Geraldine. (1967). Analysis of the Isakower phenomenon. *Journal of the American Psychoanalytic Association, 15*, 281-293.

Finn, Michael H. P. (1955). A note on a waking "blank stage" analogous to Isakower's phenomena, the dream screen, and blank dreams. *Psychoanalytic Review, 42*, 99-103.

Fisher, David James. (1976). Sigmund Freud and Romain Rolland: The terrestrial animal and his great oceanic friend. *American Imago, 33*, 1-59.

Forman, Robert K. C. (1990). Eckhart, *Gezücken*, and the ground of the soul. In Robert K. C. Forman (Ed.), *The problem of pure consciousness: Mysticism and philosophy* (pp. 98-120). New York: Oxford University Press, 1990.

Freemantle, Anne (Ed.). (1964). *The protestant mystics*. Reprinted New York: New American Library, 1965.

French, Thomas Morton. (1941). Goal, mechanism, and integrative field. *Psychosomatic Medicine, 3*(3). Reprinted in *Psychoanalytic interpretations: The selected papers of Thomas M. French* (pp. 160-197). Chicago: Quadrangle, 1970.

Freud, Anna. (1951). Obituary: August Aichhorn. *International Journal of Psycho-Analysis, 32*, 51-56.

_______. (1957). Foreword. In Joanna Field, *On not being able to paint*, 2nd ed. (pp. xiii-xv. Los Angeles: J. P. Tarcher.

_______. (1963). The concept of developmental lines. *Psychoanalytic Study of the Child, 18*, 245-265.

_______. (1966). *The ego and the mechanisms of defense*, 2nd ed. New York: International Universities Press, 1980. (Originally published in German in 1936.)

Freud, Sigmund. (1966). *The standard edition of the complete psychological works of Sigmund Freud*, 24 vols. Ed. James Strachey, with Anna Freud, Alix Strachey, & Alan Tyson. London: Hogarth Press. (Hereafter cited as *Standard edition*)

_______. (1894). The neuro-psychoses of defence. *Standard edition, 3* (pp. 45-61). London: Hogarth Press, 1962.

_______. (1900). The interpretation of dreams. *Standard edition, 4-5* (pp. 1-625). London: Hogarth Press, 1958.

_______. (1901). The psychopathology of everyday life. *Standard edition, 6* (pp. 1-279). London: Hogarth Press, 1960.

_______. (1904). On psychotherapy. *Standard edition, 7* (pp. 257-68). London: Hogarth Press, 1953.

_______. (1905). Three essays on the theory of sexuality. *Standard edition, 7* (pp. 130-243). London: Hogarth Press, 1953.

_______. (1911). Formulations on the two principles of mental functioning. *Standard edition, 12* (pp. 218-26). London: Hogarth Press, 1958.

_______. (1913). Totem and taboo: Some points of agreement between the mental lives of savages and neurotics. *Standard edition, 13* (pp. xiii-162). London: Hogarth Press, 1958.

_______. (1914a). On narcissism: an introduction. *Standard edition, 14* (pp. 78-102). London: Hogarth Press, 1957.

_______. (1914b). On the history of the psychoanalytic movement. *Standard edition, 14* (pp. 7-66). London: Hogarth Press, 1957.

_______. (1915a). Instincts and their vicissitudes. *Standard edition, 14* (pp. 117-140). London: Hogarth Press, 1957.

_______. (1915b). The unconscious. *Standard edition, 14* (pp. 166-204). London: Hogarth Press, 1957.

_______. (1916-17). Introductory lectures on psycho-analysis. *Standard edition, 15-16* (pp. 9-463). London: Hogarth Press, 1961-63.

_______. (1919). Lines of advance in psycho-analytic therapy. *Standard edition, 17* (pp. 159-68). London: Hogarth Press, 1955.

_______. (1920a). Beyond the pleasure principle. *Standard edition, 18* (pp. 7-64). London: Hogarth Press, 1955.

_______. (1920b). A note on the prehistory of the technique of analysis. *Standard edition, 18* (pp. 263-65). London: Hogarth Press, 1955.

_______. (1921). Group psychology and the analysis of the ego. *Standard edition, 18* (pp. 69-143). London: Hogarth Press, 1955.

_______. (1923a). The ego and the id. *Standard edition, 19* (pp. 12-59). London: Hogarth Press, 1961.

_______. (1923b). Remarks on the theory and practice of dream interpretation. *Standard edition, 19* (pp. 109-21). London: Hogarth Press, 1961.

_______. (1923c). Two encyclopedia articles. *Standard edition,* 18 (pp. 235-59). London: Hogarth Press, 1955.

_______. (1925). Negation. *Standard edition, 19* (pp. 235-39). London: Hogarth Press, 1961.

_______. (1926a). Inhibitions, symptoms, and anxiety. *Standard edition, 20* (pp. 87-172). London: Hogarth Press, 1959.

_______. (1926b). Psycho-analysis. *Standard edition, 20* (pp. 263-270). London: Hogarth Press, 1959.

_______. (1926c). The question of lay analysis: Conversations with an impartial person. *Standard edition, 20* (pp. 183-258). London: Hogarth Press, 1959.

_______. (1927a). The future of an illusion. *Standard edition, 21* (pp. 5-56). London: Hogarth Press, 1961.

_______. (1927b). Humour. *Standard edition, 21* (pp. 151-66). London: Hogarth Press, 1961.

_______. (1930). Civilization and its discontents. *Standard edition, 21* (pp. 64-145). London: Hogarth Press, 1961.

_______. (1933). New introductory lectures on psycho-analysis. *Standard edition, 22* (pp. 5-182). London: Hogarth Press, 1964.

_______. (1937). Analysis terminable and interminable. *Standard edition, 23* (pp. 216-53). London: Hogarth Press, 1964.

_______. (1939). Moses and monotheism: Three essays. *Standard edition, 23* (pp. 6-137). London: Hogarth Press, 1964.

_______. (1940). An outline of psycho-analysis. *Standard edition, 23* (pp. 144-207). London: Hogarth Press, 1964.

_______. (1941). Findings, ideas, problems. *Standard edition, 23* (pp. 299-300). London: Hogarth Press, 1964.

_______. (1987). *A phylogenetic fantasy: Overview of the transference neuroses.* Ed. Ilse Grubrich-Simitis. Trans. Axel Hoffer & Peter T. Hoffer. Cambridge, MA: Belknap Press of Harvard University Press.

Freud, Sigmund & Abraham, Karl. (1965). *A psycho-analytic dialogue: The letters of Sigmund Freud and Karl Abraham 1907-1926.* Ed. Hilda C. Abraham & Ernst L. Freud. Trans. Bernard Marsh & Hilda C. Abraham. New York: Basic Books.

Freud, Sigmund & Ferenczi, Sandor. (2000). *The correspondence of Sigmund Freud and Sandor Ferenczi, Volume 3, 1920-1933.* Ed. Ernest Falzeder & Eva Brabant, with Patricia Giampieri-Deutsch & André Haynal. Trans. Peter T. Hoffer. Cambridge, MA; Belknap Press of Harvard University Press.

Friedman, Maurice S. (1976). *Martin Buber: The life of dialogue*, 3rd ed. Chicago: University of Chicago Press.

_______. (1992). *Religion and psychology: A dialogical approach.* New York: Paragon House.

Fromm, Erich. (1939a). Selfishness and self-love. *Psychiatry*, *2*, 507-523.

_______. (1939b). The social philosophy of "will therapy." *Psychiatry*, *2*, 229-37.

_______. (1941). *Escape from freedom.* New York: Rinehart.

_______. (1944). Individual and social origins of neurosis. *American Sociological Review*, *9*, 380-84; reprinted in Clyde Kluckhohn & Henry A. Murray (Eds.), *Personality in nature, society, and culture* (pp. 407-413). New York: Alfred A. Knopf, 1948.

_______. (1947). *Man for himself: An inquiry into the psychology of ethics.* New York: Rinehart.

_______. (1950). *Psychoanalysis and religion.* New Haven: Yale University Press.

_______. (1951). *The forgotten language: An introduction to the understanding of dreams, fairy tales and myths.* New York: Rinehart.

_______. (1955a). Remarks on the problem of free association. *Psychiatric Research Reports of the American Psychiatric Association*, *2*, 1-6.

_______. (1955b). *The sane society.* New York: Rinehart.

_______. (1956). *The art of loving.* New York: Harper & Brothers.

_______. (1959a). The Oedipus complex and the Oedipus myth. In Ruth Nanda Anshen (Ed.), *The family: Its function and destiny*, 2nd ed. (pp. 420-448). New York: Harper & Row.

_______. (1959b). *Sigmund Freud's mission: An analysis of his personality and influence.* New York: Harper & Brothers.

_______. (1960). Psychoanalysis and Zen Buddhism. In D. T. Suzuki, Erich Fromm, & Richard De Martino, *Zen Buddhism and psychoanalysis* (pp. 77-141). New York: Harper & Brothers.

_______. (1961). *May man prevail? An inquiry into the facts and fictions of foreign policy.* Garden City, NY: Doubleday.

_______. (1962a). *Beyond the chains of illusion.* New York: Simon & Schuster.

_______. (1962b). The philosophy basic to Freud's psychoanalysis. *Pastoral Psychology, 13*(121), 26-32.

_______. (1963). *The dogma of Christ: And other essays on religion, psychology, and culture.* New York: Holt, Rinehart & Winston.

_______. (1964a). *The heart of man: Its genius for good and evil.* New York: Harper & Row.

_______. (1964b). Humanism and psychoanalysis. *Contemporary Psychoanalysis, 1*(1), 69-79.

_______. (1966). *You shall be as gods: A radical interpretation of the Old Testament and its tradition.* New York: Holt, Rinehart & Winston.

_______. (1970). *The crisis of psychoanalysis: Essays on Freud, Marx, and social psychology.* New York: Holt, Rinehart & Winston.

_______. (1973). *The anatomy of human destructiveness.* New York: Holt, Rinehard & Winston.

_______. (1976). *To have or to be?* New York: Harper & Row.

_______. (1980). *Greatness and limitations of Freud's thought.* New York: Harper & Row.

_______. (1987). Reminiscence of Shlomo Baruch Rabinkow. In Leo Jung (Ed.), *Sages and Saints* (pp. 99-105). Hoboken, NJ: Ktav Publishing House, 1987.

_______. (1991). Causes for the patient's change in analytic treatment. *Contemporary Psychoanalysis, 27*(4), 581-602.

_______. (1992a). *The art of being.* Ed. Rainer Funk. New York: Continuum.

_______. (1992b). *The revision of psychoanalysis.* Ed. Rainer Funk. Boulder, CO: Westview Press.

_______. (1994a). *The art of listening.* Ed. Rainer Funk. New York: Continuum.

_______. (1994b). *On being human.* Ed. Rainer Funk. New York: Continuum.

_______. (1997). *Love, sexuality, and matriarchy: About gender.* Ed. Rainer Funk. New York: Fromm International.

_______. (2000a). Dealing with the unconscious in psychotherapeutic practice: 3 lectures 1959. *International Forum of Psychoanalysis, 9*(3-4), 167-186.

_______. (2000b). The social determinants of psychoanalytic therapy. *International Forum of Psychoanalysis, 9*(3-4), 149-165.

Funk, Rainer. (1982). *Erich Fromm: The Courage to Be Human.* New York: Continuum.

_______. (1996). Erich Fromm's concept of social character and its relevance for clinical practice. In Mauricio Cortina & Michael Maccoby (Eds.), *A prophetic analyst: Erich Fromm's contributions to psychoanalysis* (pp. 341-60). Northvale, NJ: Jason Aronson Inc., 1996.

_______. (2000). *Erich Fromm: His Life and Ideas*. New York: Continuum.

Furst, Sidney S., Leavy, Stanley A., Lewis, Richard C., Lubin, Albert J., Ostow, Mortimer, & Zales, Michael R. (Committee on Psychiatry and Religion). (1976). *Mysticism: Spiritual quest or psychic disorder?* Group for the Advancement of Psychiatry, *9*(97), 701-825.

Gaensbauer, Theodore J. (1982). The differentiation of discrete affects: A case report. *Psychoanalytic Study of the Child*, *37*, 29-66.

Garma, Angel. (1955). Vicissitudes of the dream screen and the Isakower phenomenon. *Psychoanalytic Quarterly*, *24*, 369-382.

Garside, Bruce. (1972). Language and the interpretation of mystical experience. *International Journal of the Philosophy of Religion*, *3*, 101-2.

Ghiselin, Brewster. (1952). Introduction. In Brewster Ghiselin (Ed.), *The creative process: A symposium* (pp. 11-31). Berkeley: University of California Press; reprinted New York: New American Library, n.d.

Gill, Merton M. (1963). *Topography and systems in psychoanalytic theory*. Psychological Issues, *3*(2), Monograph 10. New York: International Universities Press.

_______. (1982). *Analysis of transference, Volume I: Theory and technique*. New York: International Universities Press.

Glover, Edward. (1927). Lectures on technique in psycho-analysis. *International Journal of Psycho-Analysis*, *8*, 311-338, 486-520.

_______. (1930). Grades of ego differentiation. *International Journal of Psycho-Analysis*, *11*, 1-11. Reprinted in *On the Early Development of Mind: Selected Papers in Psycho-Analysis, Vol. 1* (pp. 112-122). London: Imago, 1956.

_______. (1932). A psycho-analytic approach to the classification of mental disorders. *Journal of Mental Science*. Reprinted in *On the Early Development of Mind* (pp. 161-86).

_______. (1938). A note on idealization. *International Journal of Psychoanalysis*, *19*, 91-96. Reprinted in *On the Early Development of Mind* (pp. 290-306).

_______. (1943). The concept of dissociation. *International Journal of Psychoanalysis*, *24*, 7-13. Reprinted in *On the Early Development of Mind* (pp. 307-323).

_______. (1945). Examination of the Klein system of child psychology. *Psychoanalytic Study of the Child*, *1*, 75-118.

_______. (1968). *The birth of the ego: A nuclear hypothesis*. New York: International Universities Press.

Goetz, Bruno. (1975). That is all I have to say about Freud: Bruno Goetz's reminiscences of Sigmund Freud. *International Review of Psycho-Analysis*, *2*, 139-43.

Goldman, Dodi. (1993). *In search of the real: The origins and originality of D. W. Winnicott*. Northvale, NJ: Aronson.

Goleman, Daniel. (1977). *The varieties of the meditative experience.* New York: E. P. Dutton.

Greenacre, Phyllis. (1958). The family romance of the artist. *Psychoanalytic Study of the Child, 13*, 9-43. Reprinted in *Emotional growth: Psychoanalytic studies of the gifted and a great variety of other individuals*, Vol. 2 (pp. 505-32). New York: International Universities Press, 1971.

Grey, Alan. (1992). Society as destiny: Fromm's concept of social character. *Contemporary Psychoanalysis, 28*, 344-363.

Grotjahn, Martin. (1941). A child talks about pictures--Observations about the integration of fantasy into the process of thinking. *Psychoanalytic Quarterly, 10*, 385-394.

Griffiths, R. R., Richards, W. A., Johnson, M. W., McGann, U. D. & Jesse, R. (2008). Mystical-type experiences occasioned by psilocybin mediate the attribution of personal meaning and spiritual significance 14 months later. *Journal of Psychopharmacology, 22*, 621-632.

Grinberg, Leon. (1964). Two kinds of guilt--Their relations with normal and pathological aspects of mourning. *International Journal of Psycho-Analysis, 45*, 366-71.

________. (1992). *Guilt and Depression.* Trans. Christine Trollope. London: Karnac Books.

Grinker, Roy R. (1940). Reminiscences of a personal contact with Freud. *American Journal of Orthopsychiatry, 10*, 850-855. Reprinted in Hendrik M. Ruitenbeek (Ed.), *Freud as we knew him* (pp. 180-185). Detroit: Wayne State University Press, 1973.

Grotstein, James S. (1980). A proposed revision of the psychoanalytic concept of primitive mental states--Part 1. Introduction to a newer psychoanalytic metapsychology. *Contemporary Psychoanalysis, 16*, 479-546.

________. (1981a). *Splitting and projective identification.* New York: Jason Aronson.

________. (1981b). Who is the dreamer who dreams the dream and who is the dreamer who understands It? In James S. Grotstein (Ed.), *Do I dare disturb the universe? A memorial to Wilfred R. Bion* (pp. 357-416). Beverly Hills: Caesura Press, 1981.

________. (1984). Forgery of the soul: Psychogenesis of evil. In Marie Coleman Nelson & Michael Eigen (Eds.), *Evil: Self and culture* (pp. 203-226). New York: Human Sciences Press, 1984.

________. (1986). The psychology of powerlessness: Disorders of self-regulation and interactional regulation as a newer paradigm for psychopathology. *Psychoanalytic Inquiry*, *6*(1), 93-118.

_______. (1990a). The "black hole" as the basic psychotic experience. Some newer psychoanalytic and neuroscience perspectives on psychosis. *Journal of the Academy of Psychoanalysis, 18*, 29-46.

_______. (1990b). Invariants in primitive emotional disorders. In L. Bryce Boyer & Peter L. Giovacchini (Eds.), *Master clinicians on treating the regressed patient* (pp. 139-163). Northvale, NJ: Jason Aronson.

_______. (1990c). Nothingness, meaninglessness, chaos, and the "black hole" I: The importance of nothingness, meaninglessness, and chaos in psychoanalysis. *Contemporary Psychoanalysis, 26*, 257-290.

_______. (1994). "The old order changeth"--A reassessment of the basic rule of psychoanalytic technique: Commentary on John Lindon's "Gratification and provision in psychoanalysis." *Psychoanalytic Dialogues, 4*, 595-607.

_______. (1995). A reassessment of the couch in psychoanalysis. *Psychoanalytic Inquiry, 15*, 396-405.

_______. (1996). Bion's "transformation in 'O'," the "thing-in-itself," and the "real": Toward the concept of the "transcendent position." *Journal of Melanie Klein and Object Relations, 14*(2), 109-41.

_______. (1997a). Bion, the pariah of 'O.' *British Journal of Psychotherapy, 14*(1), 77-90.

_______. (1997b). Integrating one-person and two-person psychologies: Autochthony and alterity in counterpoint. *Psychoanalytic Quarterly, 66*, 403-430.

_______. (2000a). Notes on Bion's "memory and desire". *Journal of the Academy of Psychoanalysis* 28, 687-694.

_______. (2000b). *Who is the dreamer who dreams the dream? A study of psychic presences.* Hillsdale, NJ: Analytic Press.

_______. (2001). Some reflections on the psychoanalytic theory of motivation: Toward a theory of entelechy. *Psychoanalytic Inquiry, 21*(5), 572-588.

_______. (2002). One pilgrim's progress toward the psychoanalytic citadel. *Psychoanalytic Inquiry, 22*(1), 90-105.

_______. (2004a). "The light militia of the lower sky": The deeper nature of dreaming and phantasying. *Psychoanalytic Dialogues, 14*(1), 99-118.

_______. (2004b). The seventh servant: The implication of a truth drive in Bion's theory of 'O'. *Psychoanalytic Quarterly, 85*, 1081-101.

_______. (2007). *A beam of intense darkness: Wilfred Bion's legacy to psychoanalysis.* London: Karnac.

Haartman, Keith. (2001). On "unitive distortions": Toward a differential assessment of religious ecstasy. *Psychoanalytic Review, 88*(6), 811-836.

_______. (2004). *Watching and praying: Personality transformation in eighteenth century British Methodism.* Amsterdam: Rodopi.

Hamilton, Victoria. (1982). *Narcissus and Oedipus: The children of psychoanalysis.* London: Routledge & Kegan Paul.

Hammerman, Steven. (1965). Conceptions of superego development. *Journal of the American Psychoanalytic* Association, *13*, 320-55.

Harrison, Irving B. (1986). On "merging" and the fantasy of merging. *Psychoanalytic Study of the Child*, *41*, 155-70.

Hart, Henry Harper. (1950). The integrative function in creativity. *Psychiatric Quarterly*, *24*, 1-16.

Hartmann, Heinz. (1947). On rational and irrational action. Reprinted in *Essays on ego psychology: Selected problems in psychoanalytic theory* (pp. 37-68). New York: International Universities Press, 1964.

_______. (1950). Comments on the psychoanalytic theory of the ego. *Psychoanalytic Study of the Child*, *5*, 74-96. Reprinted in *Essays on ego psychology* (pp. 113-141).

_______. (1955). Notes on the theory of sublimation. *Psychoanalytic Study of the Child*, *10*, 9-29. Reprinted in *Essays on ego psychology* (pp. 215-240).

_______. (1956). The development of the ego concept in Freud's work. *International Journal of Psycho-Analysis*, *37*, 425-438. Reprinted in *Essays on ego psychology* (pp. 268-296).

_______. (1958). *Ego psychology and the problem of adaptation.* New York: International Universities Press. (Originally published in German in 1939.)

_______. (1959). Psychoanalysis as a scientific theory. Reprinted in *Essays on ego psychology* (pp. 318-350).

Hartmann, Heinz, Kris, Ernst, & Loewenstein, Rudolph M. (1946). Comments on the formation of psychic structure. *Psychoanalytic Study of the Child*, 2, 11-38. Reprinted in *Papers on psychoanalytic psychology* (pp. 27-55). (Psychological Issues, Vol. IV, No. 2, Monograph 14). New York: International Universities Press, 1964.

_______. (1949). Notes on the theory of aggression. *Psychoanalytic Study of the Child*, *3*(4), 9-36.

_______. (1951). Some psychoanalytic comments on "Culture and personality." In George B. Wilbur & Warner Muensterberger (Eds.), *Psychoanalysis and Culture* (pp. 3-31). New York: International Universities Press, 1951; reprinted in Heinz Hartmann, Ernst Kris, & Rudolph M. Loewenstein, *Papers on psychoanalytic psychology* (pp. 86-116).

Hartmann, Heinz & Loewenstein, Rudolph M. (1962). Notes on the superego. *Psychoanalytic Study of the Child*, *17*, 42-81. Reprinted in *Papers on Psychoanalytic Psychology* (pp. 144-81).

Harvey, E. Ruth. (1975). *The inward wits: Psychological theory in the middle ages and the renaissance.* London: Warburg Institute-University of London.

Hayman, Anne. (1989). What do we mean by 'phantasy'? *International Journal of Psycho-Analysis*, *70*, 105-14.

Heilbrunn, Gert. (1953). Fusion of the Isakower phenomenon with the dream screen. *Psychoanalytic Quarterly*, *22*, 200-204.

Heiler, Friedrich. (1932). *Prayer: A study in the history and psychology of religion.* Trans. Samuel McComb with J. Edgar Park. London: Oxford University Press.

Hekman, Susan. (1983). *Weber, the ideal type, and contemporary social theory.* Notre Dame: University of Notre Dame Press.

Hendrick, Ives. (1942). Instinct and the ego during infancy. *Psychoanalytic Quarterly*, *11*, 33-58.

Heschel, Abraham Joshua. (1962). *The prophets*, 2 vols. Reprinted New York: Harper, 1969.

Hoffman, Edward. (1992). *Visions of innocence: Spiritual and inspirational experiences of childhood.* Boston: Shambhala.

Hood, Jr., Ralph W. (1976). Conceptual criticisms of regressive explanations of mysticism. *Review of Religious Research*, *17*(3), 179-188.

_______. (1992). Mysticism, reality, illusion, and the Freudian critique of religion. *International Journal for the Psychology of Religion*, *2*(3), 141-159.

Horney, Karen. (1987). *Final lectures.* Ed. Douglas H. Ingram. New York: W. W. Norton.

Huxley, Aldous. (1961). Visionary experience. In John White (Ed.), *The highest state of consciousness* (pp. 34-57). Garden City, NY: Anchor Books/Doubleday, 1972.

Isaacs, Susan. (1948). The nature and function of phantasy. *International Journal of Psycho-Analysis*, *29*, 73-97. Reprinted in Melanie Klein, Paula Heimann, Susan Isaacs & Joan Riviere, *Developments in psycho-analysis.* London: Hogarth Press, 1952.

Isakower, Otto. (1938). A contribution to the psychopathology of phenomena associated with falling asleep. *International Journal of Psycho-Analysis*, *19*, 331-46.

Jacobson, Edith. (1954). The self and the object world: Vicissitudes of their infantile cathexes and their influence on ideational and affective development. *Psychoanalytic Study of the Child*, *9*, 75-127.

_______. (1964). *The self and the object world.* Journal of the American Psychoanalytic Association Monograph Series, No. 2. New York: International Universities Press.

James, William. (1890). *The principles of psychology*, 2 vols. New York: Henry Holt; reprinted New York: Dover, 1950.

_______. (1902). *The varieties of religious experience: A study in human nature.* New York: New American Library, 1958.

Jaspers, Karl. (1963). *General psychopathology.* Trans. J. Hoenig & Marian W. Hamilton. Manchester: Manchester University Press & Chicago: Chicago University Press.

Jones, Ernest. (1915). War and sublimation. Reprinted in *Psycho-myth, psychohistory: Essays on applied psychoanalysis* (Vol. I, pp. 77-87). New York: Stonehill, 1974.

_______. (1955). *The Life and Work of Sigmund Freud, Volume 2: Years of Maturity 1901-1919.* New York: Basic Books.

Jones, James W. (1992). Knowledge in transition: Toward a Winnicottian epistemology. *Psychoanalytic Review, 79*(2), 223-237.

_______. (2001). Hans Loewald: The psychoanalyst as mystic. *Psychoanalytic Review, 88*(6), 793-809.

_______. (2002). *Terror and transformation: The ambiguity of religion in psychoanalytic perspective.* Hove, UK: Brunner-Routledge/Taylor & Francis.

Josephs, Lawrence. (1989). Self psychology and the analysis of the superego. *Psychoanalytic Psychology, 6*(1), 73-86.

Jung, Carl Gustav. (1938). *The integration of the personality.* Trans. Stanley Dell. New York: Farrar & Rinehart.

Kahr, Brett. (1996). *D. W. Winnicott: A biographical portrait.* London: Karnac.

Katz, Steven T. (Ed.). (1978). *Mysticism and philosophical analysis.* London: Sheldon Press.

_______ (Ed.). (1983). *Mysticism and religious traditions.* Oxford: Oxford University Press.

Kernberg, Otto F. (1976). *Object-relations theory and clinical psychoanalysis.* New York: Jason Aronson.

_______. (1991). Some comments on early development. In Salman Akhtar & Henri Parens (Eds.), *Beyond the symbiotic orbit: Advances in separation-individuation theory. Essays in honor of Selma Kramer, M.D.* (pp. 103-120). Hillsdale, NJ: Analytic Press.

Khan, M. Masud R. (1974). *The privacy of the self: Papers on psychoanalytic theory and technique.* New York: International Universities Press.

_______. (1983). *Hidden selves: Between theory and practice in psychoanalysis.* New York: International Universities Press.

Kierkegaard, Søren. (1980). *The concept of anxiety: A simple psychologically orienting deliberation on the dogmatic issue of hereditary sin.* Trans. Reidar Thomte with Albert B. Anderson. Princeton, NJ: Princeton University Press.

King, Pearl & Riccardo Steiner. (1991). *The Freud-Klein controversies 1941-1945.* London: Tavistock Routledge.

Klein, George S. (1976). *Psychoanalytic theory: An exploration of essentials.* New York: International Universities Press, 1982.

Klein, Melanie. (1933). The early development of conscience in the child. Reprinted in *Love, guilt and reparation and other works: 1921-1945* (pp. 248-57). New York: Delacorte Press, 1975.

_______. (1935). A contribution to the psychogenesis of manic-depressive states. Reprinted in *Love, guilt and reparation and other works* (pp. 262-89).

_______. (1946). Notes on some schizoid mechanisms. Reprinted in *Envy and gratitude and other works 1946-1963* (pp. 1-24). New York: Delacorte Press, 1975; reprinted New York: Free Press-Macmillan, 1984.

_______. (1952). On observing the behaviour of young infants. Reprinted in *Envy and gratitude* (pp. 94-121).

Knowles, David. (1967). *What is mysticism?* London: Burns & Oates.

Kohut, Heinz. (1959). Introspection, empathy, and psychoanalysis: An examination of the relationship between mode of observation and theory. *Journal of the American Psychoanalytic Association, 7*, 459-483. Reprinted in *The search for the self: Selected writings of Heinz Kohut: 1950-1978*, ed. Paul H. Ornstein (Vol. 1, pp. 205-232). New York: International Universities Press, 1978.

_______. (1966). Forms and transformations of narcissism. *Journal of the American Psychoanalytic Association, 14*, 243-272. Reprinted in *The search for the self* (Vol. 1, pp. 427-460).

_______. (1971). *The analysis of the self: A systematic approach to the psychoanalytic treatment of narcissistic personality disorders.* New York: International Universities Press.

_______. (1972). Thoughts on narcissism and narcissistic rage. *Psychoanalytic Study of the Child, 27*, 360-400. Reprinted in *The search for the self: Selected writings of Heinz Kohut: 1950-1978*, ed. Paul H. Ornstein (Vol. 2, pp. 615-658). New York: International Universities Press, 1978.

_______. (1977). *The restoration of the self.* New York: International Universities Press.

_______. (1978a). "On the adolescent process as a transformation of the self" by Ernest S. Wolf, John E. Gedo, and David M. Terman. Discussion. In *The search for the self* (Vol. 2, pp. 659-662).

_______. (1978b). Narcissism as a resistance and as a driving force in psychoanalysis. In *The search for the self* (Vol. 2, pp. 547-561).

_______. (1978c). Remarks about the formation of the self: Letter to a student regarding some principles of psychoanalytic research. In *The search for the self* (Vol. 2, pp. 737-770).

_______. (1984). *How does analysis cure?* Ed. Arnold Goldberg with Paul Stepansky. Chicago: University of Chicago Press.

_______. (1985). On leadership. In Charles B. Strozier (Ed.), *Self psychology and the humanities: Reflections on a new psychoanalytic approach.* New York: W. W. Norton. Reprinted in *The search for the self: Selected writings of Heinz Ko-*

hut: 1978-1981, ed. Paul H. Ornstein (Vol. 3, pp. 103-28). Madison, CT: International Universities Press, 1990.

_______. (1990a). From the analysis of Mr. R. In *The search for the self* (Vol. 3, pp. 183-222).

_______. (1990b). Reflections on *Advances in self psychology*. In *The search for the self* (Vol. 3, pp. 261-357).

_______. (1991). Introspection, empathy, and the semicircle of mental health. In *The search for the self: Selected writings of Heinz Kohut: 1978-1981*, ed. Paul H. Ornstein (Vol. 4, pp. 537-567). Madison, CT: International Universities Press, 1991.

Kramer, Paul. (1958). Notes on one of the preoedipal roots of the superego. *Journal of the American Psychoanalytic Association*, *6*, 38-46.

Kris, Ernst. (1950). On preconscious mental processes. *Psychoanalytic Quarterly*, *19*. Reprinted in *Psychoanalytic explorations in art* (pp. 303-318). New York: International Universities Press, 1952.

_______. (1952). *Psychoanalytic exploration in art.* New York: International Universities Press.

_______. (1956). On some vicissitudes of insight in psycho-analysis. *International Journal of Psycho-Analysis*, *37*, 445-455.

Lacan, Jacques. (1982). *Feminine sexuality*. Ed. Juliet Mitchell & Jacqueline Rose; trans. Jacqueline Rose. New York: W. W Norton & Pantheon Books, 1985.

Landis, Bernard. (1971). Erich Fromm: Some biographical notes. In Bernard Landis & Edward S. Tauber (Eds.), *In the name of life: Essays in honor of Erich Fromm* (pp. x-xiv). New York: Holt, Rinehart & Winston, 1971.

_______. (2009). When you hear the word, the reality is lost. In Rainer Funk (Ed.), *The clinical Erich Fromm: Personal accounts and papers on therapeutic technique* (pp. 137-40). Amsterdam: Rodopi, 2009.

Langer, Susanne K. (1957). *Philosophy in a new key: A study in the symbolism of reason, rite, and art*, 3rd ed. Cambridge: Harvard University Press.

Lear, Jonathan. (1988). *Aristotle: The desire to understand.* Cambridge: Cambridge University Press.

Leavy, Stanley A. (1995). Roots of unitive experience. *Psychoanalytic Review*, *82*(3), 349-370.

Leijenhorst, Cees. (2005). Steiner, Rudolf. In Wouter J. Hanegraaff, with Antoine Faivre, Roelof van den Broek, & Jean-Pierre Brach (Eds.), *Dictionary of gnosis and Western esotericism* (Vol. 2, pp. 1084-1091). Leiden: E. J. Brill, 2005.

Lewin, Bertram D. (1951). *The psychoanalysis of elation.* London: Hogarth Press.

_______. (1952). Phobic symptoms and dream interpretation. *Psychoanalytic Quarterly*, *21*, 295-322.

Lichtenberg, Joseph D. (1983). *Psychoanalysis and infant research.* Hillsdale, NJ: Analytic Press.

Lieberman, E. James. (1985). *Acts of will: The life and work of Otto Rank.* New York: Free Press.

Lindblom, Johannes. (1962). *Prophecy in ancient Israel.* Philadelphia: Fortress Press.

Linn, Louis & Schwarz, Leo W. (1958). *Psychiatry and religious experience.* New York: Random House.

Lloyd, A. C. (1990). *The anatomy of Neoplatonism.* Oxford: Clarendon Press.

Loewald, Hans W. (1951). Ego and reality. *International Journal of Psychoanalysis, 32*, 10-18. Reprinted in *Papers on Psychoanalysis* (pp. 3-20). New Haven: Yale University Press, 1980.

_______. (1952). The problem of defense and the neurotic interpretation of reality. *International Journal of Psychoanalysis, 33*, 444-449. Reprinted in *Papers on psychoanalysis* (pp. 21-32).

_______. (1960). On the therapeutic action of psycho-analysis. *International Journal of Psycho-Analysis, 41*, 16-33. Reprinted in *Papers on psychoanalysis* (pp. 221-56).

_______. (1962a). Internalization, separation, mourning, and the superego. *Psychoanalytic Quarterly, 31*, 483-504. Reprinted in *Papers on psychoanalysis* (pp. 257-76).

_______. (1962b). Superego and time. *International Journal of Psycho-Analysis, 43*, 264-268. Reprinted in *Papers on psychoanalysis* (pp. 43-52).

_______. (1971a). Discussion: "The id and the regulatory principles of mental functioning," by Max Schur. In *The unconscious today: Essays in honor of Max Schur*, ed. Mark Kanzer. New York: International Universities Press, 1971; reprinted in Loewald, *Papers on psychoanalysis* (pp. 58-68).

_______. (1971b). On motivation and instinct theory. *Psychoanalytic Study of the Child, 26*, 91-128. Reprinted in *Papers on psychoanalysis* (pp. 102-37).

_______. (1971c). Some considerations on repetition and repetition compulsion. *International Journal of Psycho-Analysis, 52*, 59-66. Reprinted in *Papers on psychoanalysis* (pp. 87-101).

_______. (1972). The experience of time. *Psychoanalytic Study of the Child, 27*, 401-410. Reprinted in *Papers on psychoanalysis* (pp. 138-147).

_______. (1973). On internalization. *International Journal of Psycho-Analysis, 54*, 9-17. Reprinted in *Papers on psychoanalysis* (pp. 69-86).

_______. (1976). Perspectives on memory. In Merton M. Gill & Philip S. Holzman (Eds.). *Psychology versus metapsychology: Psychoanalytic essays in memory of George Klein.* New York: International Universities Press. Reprinted in *Papers on psychoanalysis* (pp. 148-73).

_______. (1977). Transference and countertransference: The roots of psychoanalysis. Review essay on *The Freud/Jung Letters. Psychoanalytic Quarterly, 46*, 514-527. Reprinted in *Papers on psychoanalysis* (pp. 495-18).

_______. (1978). *Psychoanalysis and the history of the individual.* New Haven: Yale University Press.

_______. (1979a). Reflections on the psychoanalytic process and its therapeutic potential. *Psychoanalytic Study of the Child, 34,* 155-167. *Reprinted in Papers on psychoanalysis* (pp. 372-83).

_______. (1979b). The waning of the Oedipus complex. *Journal of the American Psychoanalytic Association, 27,* 751-75. Reprinted in *Papers on psychoanalysis* (pp. 384-404).

_______. (1980a). Ego-organization and defense. In *Papers on psychoanalysis* (pp. 174-77).

_______. (1980b). *Papers on psychoanalysis.* New Haven: Yale University Press.

_______. (1988a). On the mode of therapeutic action of psychoanalytic psychotherapy. In Arnold Rothstein (Ed.), *How does treatment help? On the modes of therapeutic action of psychoanalytic psychotherapy* (pp. 51-59). Madison, CT: International Universities Press, 1988.

_______. (1988b). *Sublimation: Inquiries into theoretical psychoanalysis.* New Haven: Yale University Press.

Macalpine, Ida. (1950). The development of the transference. *Psychoanalytic Quarterly, 19,* 501-539.

Maccoby, Michael. (1996). The two voices of Erich Fromm: The prophetic and the analytic. In Mauricio Cortina & Michael Maccoby (Eds.), *A prophetic analyst: Erich Fromm's contributions to psychoanalysis* (pp. 415-25). Northvale, NJ: Jason Aronson, 1996.

Mahler, Margaret Schoenberger. (1979a). *The selected papers of Margaret S. Mahler. Volume one: Infantile psychosis and early contributions.* New York: Jason Aronson.

_______. (1979b). *The selected papers of Margaret S. Mahler. Volume two: Separation-individuation.* New York: Jason Aronson.

Mahler, Margaret Schoenberger, with Manuel Furer. (1968). *On human symbiosis and the vicissitudes of individuation, Volume I: Infantile psychosis.* New York: International Universities Press.

Mahler, Margaret S., Fred Pine, & Anni Bergman. (1975). *The psychological birth of the human infant: Symbiosis and individuation.* New York: Basic Books.

Maimonides, Moses. (1912). *The eight chapters of Maimonides on ethics* (Shemonah Perakim): *A psychological and ethical treatise.* Trans. Joseph I. Gorfinkle. Reprinted New York: AMS Press, 1966.

Margolies, Richard. (1996). Self development and psychotherapy in a period of rapid social change. In Mauricio Cortina & Michael Maccoby (Eds.), *A prophetic analyst: Erich Fromm's contributions to psychoanalysis* (pp. 361-401). Northvale, NJ: Jason Aronson 1996.

Maritain, Jacques. (1953). *Creative intuition in art and poetry.* Princeton, NJ: Princeton University Press; reprinted New York: New American Library, 1974.

Maroda, Karen J. (2004). *The power of counter-transference: Innovations in analytic technique*, 2nd ed. Hillsdale, NJ: Analytic Press.

Maslow, Abraham H. (1968). *Toward a psychology of being.* Reprinted New York: D. Van Nostrand & Co., n.d.

Masson, Jeffrey Moussaieff. (1984). *The assault on truth: Freud's suppression of the seduction theory.* New York: Farrar, Strauss & Giroux.

Matte-Blanco, Ignacio. (1959). On introjection and the process of psychic metabolism. *International Journal of Psycho-Analysis*, *40*, 1-5.

Meissner, W. W. (1992). *Ignatius of Loyola: The psychology of a saint.* New Haven: Yale University Press.

________. (1999). *To the greater glory--A psychological study of Ignatian spirituality.* Milwaukee, WI: Marquette University Press.

Meltzer, Donald. (1998). *The Kleinian development.* London: Clunie Press/Karnac Books.

Meltzer, Donald and Williams, Meg Harris. (1988). *The apprehension of beauty: The role of aesthetic conflict in development, violence and art.* Old Ballechin, Scotland: Clunie Press.

Menaker, Esther. (1942). The masochistic factor in the psychoanalytic situation. *Psychoanalytic Quarterly*, *11*, 171-186.

Merkur, Dan. (1985). The prophecies of Jeremiah. *American Imago*, *42*(1), 1-37.

________. (1993). Mythology into metapsychology: Freud's misappropriation of Romanticism. *Psychoanalytic Study of Society*, *18*, 345-60. Ed. L. Bryce Boyer, Ruth M. Boyer, & Stephen M. Sonnenberg. Hillsdale, NJ: Analytic Press.

________. (1996). The numinous as a category of values. In Thomas A. Idinopulos & Edward A. Yonan (Eds.), *The sacred and its scholars: Comparative methodologies for the study of primary religious data* (pp. 104-123). Leiden: E. J. Brill, 1996.

________. (1998). *The ecstatic imagination: Psychedelic experiences and the psychoanalysis of self-actualization.* Albany: State University of New York Press.

________. (1999). *Mystical moments and unitive thinking.* Albany: State University of New York Press.

________. (2001). *Unconscious wisdom: A superego function in dreams, conscience, and inspiration.* Albany: State University of New York Press.

________. (2002). Mysticism. In Neil J. Smelser & Paul B. Baltes (Eds.), *International encyclopedia of social and behavioral sciences* (pp. 10270-10273). Oxford, UK: Pergamon.

_______. (2005). *Psychoanalytic approaches to myth: Freud and the Freudians*. New York: Routledge.

_______. (2006). Interpreting numinous experiences. *Social Analysis*, *50*(2), 204-223. Reprinted in Jadran Mimica (Ed.), *Explorations in Psychoanalytic Ethnography* (pp. 204-223). New York: Berghan Books, 2007.

_______. (2007). *Crucified with Christ: Meditation on the passion, mystical death, and the medieval invention of psychotherapy*. Albany: State University of New York Press.

_______. (2009). Mysticism. *Britannica online encyclopedia*. www.britannica.com/EBchecked/topic/400861/mysticism?view=print

Merlan, Philip. (1945). Brentano and Freud. *Journal of the History of Ideas*, *6*, 375-7.

_______. (1949). Brentano and Freud--A sequel. *Journal of the History of Ideas*, *10*, 451.

Michaels, Joseph J. (1945). The concept of integration in psychoanalysis. *Journal of Nervous and Mental Disease*, *102*, 54-64.

Milner, Marion. (1987a). *Eternity's sunrise: A way of keeping a diary*. London: Virago Press.

_______. (1987b). *The suppressed madness of sane men: Forty-four years of exploring psychoanalysis*. London: Tavistock.

Modell, Arnold H. (1985). The works of Winnicott and the evolution of his thought. *Journal of the American Psychoanalytic Association*, *33*, 113-137.

_______. (1991). A confusion of tongues or whose reality is it? *Psychoanalytic Quarterly*, *60*, 227-244.

_______. (1993). *The private self*. Cambridge, MA: Harvard University Press.

_______. (2003). *Imagination and the meaningful brain*. Cambridge, MA: MIT Press.

Moxon, Cavendish. (1920). Mystical ecstasy and hysterical dream-states. *Journal of Abnormal Psychology*, *15*, 329-334.

Mueller-Vollmer, Kurt (Ed.). (1985). *The hermeneutics reader: Texts of the German tradition from the enlightenment to the present*. New York: Continuum.

Murphy, William F. (1959). Ego integration, trauma, and insight. *Psychoanalytic Quarterly*, *28*, 514-532.

Murray, Lynne. (1991). Intersubjectivity, object relations theory, and empirical evidence from mother-infant interactions. *Infant Mental Health Journal* 12/3, 219-232.

Murray, Lynne & Andrews, Liz. (2000). *The social baby: Understanding babies' communication from birth*. Richmond, UK: The Children's Project.

Nagy, Emese & Molnar, Peter. (2004). Homo imitans or homo provocans? Human imprinting model of neonatal imitation. *Infant Behavior & Development*, *27*, 54-63.

Neisser, Ulric (Ed.). (1993). *The perceived self: Ecological and interpersonal sources of self-knowledge*. Cambridge: Cambridge University Press.

Novey, Samuel. (1955). The role of the superego and ego-ideal in character formation. *International Journal of Psycho-Analysis*, *36*, 254-9.

Noy, Pinchas. (1969). A revision of the psychoanalytic theory of the primary process. *International Journal of Psycho-Analysis*, *50*, 155-78.

_______. (1979). The psychoanalytic theory of cognitive development. *Psychoanalytic Study of the Child*, *34*, 169-216.

_______. (1982). A revision of the psychoanalytic theory of affect. *Annual of Psychoanalysis*, *10*, 139-187.

_______. (1985). Originality and creativity. *Annual of Psychoanalysis*, *22-23*, 421-48.

Nunberg, Herman. (1928). Problems of therapy. *Internationale Zeitschrift für Psychoanalyse*, *14*. Translated in *Practice and Theory of Psychoanalysis* (Vol. 1, pp. 105-19). Nervous and Mental Disease Monographs, No. 74. New York: Coolidge Foundation, 1948.

_______. (1931). The synthetic function of the ego. *International Journal of Psycho-Analysis*, *12*(2), 123-140.

_______. (1955). *Principles of psychoanalysis: Their application to the neuroses.* Trans. Madlyn Kahr & Sidney Kahr. New York: International Universities Press.

Nunberg, Herman & Federn, Ernst (Eds.). (1962). *Minutes of the Vienna psychoanalytic society, Volume I: 1906-1908*, trans. M. Nunberg. New York: International Universities Press.

Oberndorf, C. P. (1950). Dr. Trigant Burrow. *International Journal of Psycho-Analysis*, *31*, 292-293.

Ogden, Thomas H. (1982). *Projective identification and psychotherapeutic technique.* Northvale, NJ: Jason Aronson.

_______. (1983). The concept of internal object relations. *International Journal of Psycho-Analysis*, *64*, 227-241.

Ortmeyer, Dale. (1995). History of the founders of interpersonal psychoanalysis. In Maryloy Lionells, John Fiscalini, Carola H. Mann, & Donnel B. Stern (Eds.), *Handbook of interpersonal psychoanalysis* (pp. 11-30). Hillsdale, NJ: Analytic Press.

Ostow, Mortimer & Scharfstein, Ben-Ami. (1954). *The need to believe: The psychology of religion.* New York: International Universities Press.

Ottenheimer, Lilly. (1959). On the nature and early development of the ego ideal. *Amererican Journal of Psychotherapy*, *9*, 612-23.

Otto, Rudolf. (1950). *The idea of the holy: An inquiry into the non-rational factor in the idea of the divine and its relation to the rational*, 2nd ed. Trans. John W. Harvey. London: Oxford University Press.

Paffard, Michael. (1973). *Inglorious Wordsworths: A study of some transcendental experiences in childhood and adolescence.* London: Hodder & Stoughton.

________. (1976). *The unattended moment: Excerpts from autobiographies with hints and guesses.* London: SCM Press.

Pahnke, Walter N. (1966). Drugs and mysticism. *International Journal of Parapsychology, 8*(1), 295-315.

Paley, William. (1819). *Natural theology; or, evidences of the existence and attributes of the deity, collected from the appearances of nature*, 16th ed. London: F. C. & J. Rivington.

Panzarella, Robert. (1980). The phenomenology of aesthetic peak experiences. *Journal of Humanistic Psychology, 20*(1), 69-85.

Pargament, Kenneth I. (1997). *The psychology of religion and coping: Theory, research, practice.* New York: Guilford Press.

Parsons, Michael. (2001). Marion Milner 1900-1998. *International Journal of Psycho-Analysis, 82*(3), 609-611.

Parsons, William B. (1999). *The enigma of the oceanic Feeling: Revisioning the psychoanalytic theory of mysticism.* New York: Oxford University Press.

Paul, Robert A. (1976). Did the primal crime take place? *Ethos, 4*:311-52.

Peto, Andrew. (1960). On the transient disintegrative effect of interpretations. *International Journal of Psycho-Analysis, 41*, 413-417.

Piaget, Jean. (1954). *The construction of reality in the child*, trans. Margaret Cook. New York: Basic Books.

Pike, Nelson. (1965). Comments. In W. H. Capitan & D. D. Merill (Eds.), *Art, mind and religion.* Pennsylvania: Univerrsity of Pittsburgh Press.

Pine, Fred. (1981). In the beginning: Contributions to a psychoanalytic developmental psychology. *International review of psycho-analysis, 8*, 15-33.

________. (1986). The "symbiotic phase" in light of current infancy research. *Bulletin of the Menninger Clinic, 50*(6), 564-569.

________. (1990). *Drive, ego, object, and self: A synthesis for clinical work.* New York: BasicBooks/HarperCollins.

Prince, Raymond. (1979-80). Religious experience and psychosis. *Journal of Altered States of Consciousness, 5*(2), 167-181.

Prince, Raymond & Savage, Charles. (1966). Mystical states and the concept of regression. *Psychedelic Review, 8*, 59-81.

Pruyser, Paul W. (1974). *Between belief and unbelief.* New York: Harper & Row.

Racker, Heinrich. (1968). *Transference and countertransference.* Madison, CT: International Universities Press.

Rado, Sandor. (1928). The problem of melancholia. *International Journal of Psycho-Analysis, 9*, 420-38.

Rangell, Leo. (1986). The executive functions of the ego: An extension of the concept of ego autonomy. *Psychoanalytic Study of the Child, 41*, 1-37.

Rank, Otto. (1927a). [Review] *Hemmung, Symptom, und Angst.* By Sigmund Freud, M.D. *Mental Hygiene, 11*, 181-186.

_______. (1927b). Psychoanalytic problems. *Psychoanalytic Review, 14*(1), 1-19.

_______. (1929a). Beyond psychoanalysis. *Psychoanalytic Review, 16*(1), 1-11.

_______. (1929b). *The trauma of birth.* London: Kegan Paul, Trench, & Trubner; reprinted New York: Dover, 1993.

_______. (1932a). *Art and the artist: Creative urge and personality development.* Trans. Charles Francis Atkinson. New York: W. W. Norton.

_______. (1932b). *Modern education: A critique of its fundamental ideas.* Trans. Mabel Moxon. New York: Alfred A. Knopf; reprinted New York: Agathon Press, 1968.

_______. (1936a). *Truth and reality.* Trans. Jessie Taft. New York: Alfred A. Knopf.

_______. (1936b). *Will therapy.* Trans. Jessie Taft. New York: Alfred A. Knopf.

_______. (1941). *Beyond psychology.* Philadelphia: E. Hauser; reprinted New York: Dover, 1958.

_______. (1996). *A psychology of difference: The American lectures.* Ed. Robert Kramer. Princeton, NJ: Princeton University Press.

_______. (1998). *Psychology and the soul: A study of the origin, conceptual evolution, and nature of the soul.* Trans. Gregory C. Richter & E. James Lieberman. Baltimore: Johns Hopkins University Press.

Rapaport, David. (1960). The theory of attention cathexis: An economic and structural attempt at the explanation of cognitive processes. Reprinted in *The collected papers of David Rapaport* (pp. 778-794). New York: Basic Books, 1967.

Rapaport, David & Gill, Merton M. (1959). The points of view and assumptions of metapsychology. *International Journal of Psycho-Analysis, 40*, 153-162. Reprinted in *The collected papers of David Rapaport* (pp. 795-811).

Read, Sir Herbert. (1951). Psycho-analysis and the problem of aesthetic value. *Psychoanalytic Quarterly, 32*, 73-82.

Read, Richard. (2002). *Art and its discontents: The early life of Adrian Stokes.* Abingdon, UK: Ashgate.

Reich, Annie. (1960). Pathologic forms of self-esteem regulations. Reprinted in *Psychoanalytic contributions* (pp. 288-311). New York: International Universities Press, 1973.

_______. (1973). *Psychoanalytic contributions.* New York: International Universities Press.

Reik, Theodor. (1933). New ways in psycho-analytic treatment. *International Journal of Psycho-Analysis, 14*, 321-334.

_______. (1936). *Surprise and the psycho-analyst: On the conjecture and comprehension of unconscious processes.* London: Kegan Paul, Trench, Trubner.

_______. (1948). *Listening with the third ear: The inner experience of psychoanalyst.* New York: Farrar, Straus & Giroux, 1983.

Reisner, Steven. (1992). Eros reclaimed: Recovering Freud's relational theory. In Neil J. Skolnick & Susan C. Warshaw (Eds.), *Relational perspectives in psychoanalysis* (pp. 281-312). Hillsdale, NJ: Analytic Press, 1992.

Ritvo, Samuel & Solnit, Albert J. (1960). The relationship of early ego identifications to superego formation. *International Journal of Psycho-Analysis, 41*, 295-300.

Rizzuto, Ana-Maria. (1979). *The birth of the living god: A psychoanalytic study.* Chicago: University of Chicago Press.

Roazen, Paul. (1975). *Freud and His Followers.* New York: Alfred A. Knopf; reprinted New York: Da Capo Press, 1991.

_______. (1996). Erich Fromm's courage. In Mauricio Cortina & Michael Maccoby (Eds.), *A prophetic analyst: Erich Fromm's contributions to psychoanalysis* (pp. 427-53). Northvale, NJ: Jason Aronson 1996.

_______. (2001). The exclusion of Erich Fromm from the I.P.A. *Contemporary Psychoanalysis, 37*(1), 5-42.

Robinson, Paul A. (1969). *The Freudian left: Wilhelm Reich, Geza Róheim, Herbert Marcuse.* New York: Harper & Row.

Róheim, Géza. (1925). *Australian totemism: A psycho-analytic study in anthropology.* New York: Humanities Press, 1971.

Rose, Gilbert J. (1964). Creative imagination in terms of ego "core" and boundaries. *International Journal of Psycho-Analysis, 45*, 75-84.

_______. (1971). Narcissistic fusion states and creativity. In Mark Kanzer (Ed.), *The unconscious today: Essays in honor of Max Schur* (pp. 495-505). New York: International Universities Press.

_______. (1972). Fusion states. In Peter L. Giovacchini (Ed.), *Tactics and techniques in psychoanalytic therapy* (pp. 170-188). New York: Science House, 1972.

_______. (1980). *The power of form: A psychoanalytic approach to aesthetic form.* Psychological Issues, Monograph 49. New York: International Universities Press.

Rycroft, Charles. (1955). On idealization, illusion, and catastrophic disillusion. *International Journal of Psycho-Analysis, 36*, 81-87. Reprinted in *Imagination and Reality* (pp. 29-41). New York: International Universities Press, 1968.

_______. (1956). Symbolism and its relationship to the primary and secondary process. *International Journal of Psycho-Analysis, 37*, 137-146. Reprinted in *Imagination and Reality* (pp. 42-60).

Sachs, Hanns. (1925). Metapsychological points of view in technique and theory. *International Journal of Psycho-Analysis, 6*, 5-12.

Sayers, Janet. (2003). *Divine therapy: Love, mysticism and psychoanalysis.* Oxford: Oxford University Press.

Schiller, Friedrich von . (1844). *The poems and ballads of Schiller.* Trans. Sir Edward Bulwer Lytton., with a Brief Sketch of the Author's Life. New York: Harper & Brothers.

Scholem, Gershom G. (1954). *Major trends in Jewish mysticism*, 3rd ed. New York: Schocken Books.

Schroeder, Theodore. (1922). Prenatal psychisms and mystical pantheism. *International Journal of Psycho-Analysis, 3*, 445-466.

Schur, Max. (1966). *The id and the regulatory principles of mental functioning.* Journal of the American Psychoanalytic Association Monograph Series Number Four. New York: International Universities Press.

Segal, Hanna. (1979). *Klein.* Glasgow: Fontana/Collins.

Shor, Ronald E. (1959). Hypnosis and the concept of the generalized reality orientation. *American Journal of Psychotherapy, 13*, 582-602.

Silberer, Herbert. (1914). *Hidden symbolism of alchemy and the occult arts.* (Originally titled: *Problems of mysticism and its symbolism*). Trans. Smith Ely Jelliffe. New York: Moffat, Yard, 1917; reprinted New York: Dover, 1971.

Skrbina, David. (2005). *Panpsychism in the west.* Cambridge, MA: MIT Press.

Socarides, Charles W. (1955). A clinical note on the Isakower phenomenon. *Psychoanalytic Review, 42*, 95-98.

Sorenson, Randall Lehmann. (2004). *Minding spirituality.* Hillsdale, NJ: Analytic Press.

Spero, Moshe Halevi. (1992). *Religious objects as psychological structures: A critical integration of object relations theory, psychotherapy, and Judaism.* Chicago: University of Chicago Press.

Spiegel, Rose. (1981). Tributes. *Contemporary Psychoanalysis*, 17, 436-440.

Spilka, Bernard; Hood, Jr., Ralph W.; Hunsberger, Bruce; & Gorsuch, Richard. (2003). *The psychology of religion: An empirical approach*, 3rd ed. New York: Guilford Press.

Spitz, René A. (1955). The primal cavity: A contribution to the genesis of perception and its role for psychoanalytic theory. *Psychoanalytic Study of the Child, 10*, 215-40.

________. (1957). *No and yes: On the genesis of human communication.* New York: International Universities Press.

________. (1958). On the genesis of superego components. *Psychoanalytic Study of the Child, 13*, 375-404.

Spitz, René A. with W. Godfrey Cobliner. (1965). *The first year of life: A psychoanalytic study of normal and deviant development of object relations.* New York: International Universities Press.

Stace, W. T. (1960). *Mysticism and philosophy.* Philadelphia: J. B. Lippincott.

Sterba, Richard. (1934). The fate of the ego in analytic therapy. *International Journal of Psycho-Analysis*, *15*(2-3), 117-26.

________. (1968). Remarks on mystic states. *American Imago*, *25*, 77-85.

________. (1978). Discussions of Sigmund Freud. *Psychoanalytic Quarterly*, *47*, 173-191.

Stern, Daniel N. (1983). The early development of schemas of self, other, and "self with other." In Joseph D. Lichtenberg & Samuel Kaplan (Eds.), *Reflections of self psychology* (pp. 49-84). Hillsdale, NJ: Analytic Press.

________. (1985). *The interpersonal world of the infant: A view from psychoanalysis and developmental psychology*. New York: BasicBooks.

Stokes, Adrian. (1955). Form in art. In Melanie Klein, Paula Heimann, & R. E. Money-Kyrle (Eds.), *New directions in psycho-analysis: The significance of infant conflict in the pattern of adult behaviour* (pp. 406-420). London: Tavistock; New York: Basic Books.

Stone, Leo. (1961). *The psychoanalytic situation: An examination of its development and essential nature*. New York: International Universities Press.

Strachey, James. (1934). The nature of the therapeutic action of psycho-analysis. *International Journal of Psycho-Analysis*, *15*, 127-59.

Strozier, Charles B. (2001). *Heinz Kohut: The making of a psychoanalyst*. New York: Farrar, Straus & Giroux.

Suttie, Ian D. (1935). *The origins of love and hate*. London: Kegan Paul, Trench, Trubner; reprinted London: Free Association Books, 1988.

Suzuki, D. T., Fromm, Erich & De Martino, Richard. (1960). *Zen Buddhism & psychoanalysis*. New York: Harper & Brothers.

Symington, Joan & Symington, Neville. (1996). *The clinical thinking of Wilfred Bion*. London: Routledge.

Symington, Neville. (1986). *The analytic experience: Lectures from the Tavistock*. London: Free Association Books.

________. (1993a). Is psychoanalysis a religion? In Ivan Ward (Ed.), *Is psychoanalysis another religion? Contemporary essays on spirit, faith and morality in psychoanalysis* (pp. 49-56). London: Freud Museum Publications, 1993.

________. (1993b). *Narcissism: A new theory*. London: Karnac Books.

________. (1994). *Emotion and spirit: Questioning the claims of psychoanalysis and religion*. London: Cassell; reprinted London: Karnac Books, 1998.

________. (2001). *The spirit of sanity*. London: Karnac.

________. (2002). *A pattern of madness*. London: Karnac.

________. (2004a). *The blind man sees: Freud's awakening and other essays*. London: Karnac.

________. (2004b). The spirituality of natural religion. *International Journal of Applied Psychoanalytic Studies*, *1*(1), 61-72.

________. (2006). *A healing conversation: How healing happens*. London: Karnac.

_______. (2007). *Becoming a person through psychoanalysis.* London: Karnac.

Tauber, Edward S. (1959). The role of immediate experience for dynamic psychiatry. A. The sense of immediacy in Fromm's conceptions. In Silvano Arieti (Ed.), *American handbook of psychiatry* (pp. 1811-1815). New York: Basic Books, 1959.

Tausk, Victor. (1933). On the origin of the "influencing machine" in schizophrenia, trans. Dorian Feigenbaum. *Psychoanalytic Quarterly* 2. Reprinted in *Sexuality, war and schizophrenia: Collected papers*, ed. Paul Roazen (pp. 185-219). New Brunswick, NJ: Transaction Publishers, 1991.

Underhill, Evelyn. (1910). *Mysticism: A study in the nature and development of man's spiritual consciousness.* Reprinted New York: New American Library, 1955.

Wain, John. (1962). *Sprightly running: Part of an autobiography.* New York: Macmillan.

Waite, Arthur Edward. (1916). Some deeper aspects of Masonic symbolism. *The Builder: A Journal for the Masonic Student*, *2*(5); reprinted as a pamphlet, Belleville, Canada: Templar Books, 1999.

Wälder, Robert. (1934). The problem of freedom in psycho-analysis and the problem of reality-testing. *International Journal of Psycho-Analysis*, *17*, 89-108.

_______. (1936). The principle of multiple function: Observations on overdetermination. *Psychoanalytic Quarterly*, *5*, 45-62.

Wallas, Graham. (1926). *The art of thought.* New York: Harcourt, Brace.

Webb, Clement C. J. (1915). *Studies in the history of natural theology.* Oxford: Clarendon Press.

Webb, James. (1976). *The occult establishment.* La Salle, IL: Open Court.

Weber, Max. (1949). *The methodology of the social sciences.* Trans. & ed. Edward A. Shils & Henry A. Finch. New York: Free Press/Macmillan.

Weiss, Joseph. (1967). The integration of defences. *International Journal of Psycho-Analysis*, *48*, 520-524.

Werman, David S. (1986). On the nature of the oceanic experience. *Journal of the American Psychoanalytic Association*, *34*, 123-39.

Whitehead, Alfred North. (1925). *Science in the modern world*, 2nd ed. New York: Mentor Books, 1952.

Williams, Meg Harris. (1997). Inspiration: A psychoanalytic and aesthetic concept. *British Journal of Psychotherapy*, *14*(1), 33-43.

_______. (2000). Keat's "Ode to Psyche." In Margaret Cohen & Alberto Hahn (Eds.), *Exploring the work of Donald Meltzer: A festschrift* (pp. 56-67). London: Karnac Books, 2000.

Willock, Brent. (2007). *Comparative-integrative psychoanalysis: A relational perspective for the discipline's second century.* New York: Analytic Press.

Winnicott, D. W. (1935). The manic defence. In *Through paediatrics to psycho-analysis: Collected papers* (pp. 129-144). 1958; reprinted New York: Brunner/Mazel, 1992.

_______. (1945). Primitive emotional development. *International Journal of Psycho-Analysis, 26*, 137-43. Reprinted in *Through paediatrics to psycho-analysis* (pp. 145-156).

_______. (1948a). Paediatrics and psychiatry. *British Journal of Medical Psychology, 21*. Reprinted in *Through paediatrics to psycho-analysis* (pp. 157-73).

_______. (1948b). Reparation in respect of mother's organized defence against depression. In *Through paediatrics to psycho-analysis* (pp. 91-96).

_______. (1950-55). Aggression in relation to emotional development. In *Through paediatrics to psycho-analysis* (pp. 204-18).

_______. (1951). Critical notice of *On not being able to paint*, by Joanna Field. *British Journal of Medical Psychology*; reprinted in *Psycho-analytic explorations*, ed. Clare Winnicott, Ray Shepherd, & Madeleine Davis (pp. 390-92). Cambridge, MA: Harvard University Press, 1989.

_______. (1952). Anxiety associated with insecurity. In *Through paediatrics to psycho-analysis* (pp. 97-100).

_______. (1953). Transitional objects and transitional phenomena: A study of the first not-me possession. *International Journal of Psycho-Analysis, 34*, 89-97. Reprinted in *Through paediatrics to psycho-analysis* (pp. 229-42).

_______. (1955a). The depressive position in normal emotional development. *British Journal of Medical Psychology, 28*. Reprinted in *Through paediatrics to psycho-analysis* (pp. 262-277).

_______. (1955b). Metapsychological and clinical aspects of regression within the psycho-analytical set-up. *International Journal of Psycho-Analysis, 36*, 16-26. Reprinted in *Through paediatrics to psycho-analysis* (pp. 278-94).

_______. (1956a). The antisocial tendency. In *Through paediatrics to psycho-analysis* (pp. 306-15).

_______. (1956b). On transference. *International Journal of Psycho-Analysis, 37*, 386-88. Reprinted in *Through paediatrics to psycho-analysis* (pp. 295-99).

_______. (1956c). Paediatrics and childhood neurosis. In *Through paediatrics to psycho-analysis* (pp. 316-21).

_______. (1958a). The capacity to be alone. *International Journal of Psycho-Analysis, 39*, 416-20. Reprinted in *The maturational processes and the facilitating environment: Studies in the theory of emotional development* (pp. 29-36). New York: International Universities Press, 1965.

_______. (1958b). Psychoanalysis and the sense of guilt. In J. D. Sutherland (Ed.), *Psychoanalysis and contemporary thought*. London: Hogarth Press; reprinted in *The maturational processes and the facilitating environment* (pp. 15-28).

_______. (1960a). Comments on "On the concept of the superego": Delivered at a Scientific Meeting of the British Psycho-Analytical Society, 7 December 1960. In *Psycho-analytic explorations* (pp. 465-73).

_______. (1960b). Counter-transference. *British Journal of Medical Psychology, 33*, 17-21. Reprinted in *The maturational processes and the facilitating environment* (pp. 158-65).

_______. (1960c). Ego distortion in terms of true and false self. In *The maturational processes and the facilitating environment* (pp. 140-152).

_______. (1960d). On the theory of the parent-infant relationship. *International Journal of Psycho-Analysis, 41*, 585-95. Reprinted in *The maturational processes and the facilitating environment* (pp. 37-55).

_______. (1962a). The aims of psycho-analytic treatment. In *The maturational processes and the facilitating environment* (pp. 166-70).

_______. (1962b). Ego integration in child development. In *The maturational processes and the facilitating environment* (pp. 56-63).

_______. (1962c). A personal view of the Kleinian contribution. In *The maturational processes and the facilitating environment* (pp. 171-78).

_______. (1963a). Communicating and not communicating leading to a study of certain opposites. In *The maturational processes and the facilitating environment* (pp. 179-92).

_______. (1963b). Dependence in infant-care, in child-care, and in the psychoanalytic setting. *International Journal of Psycho-Analysis, 44*, 339-44. Reprinted in *The maturational processes and the facilitating environment* (pp. 249-59).

_______. (1963c). From dependence towards independence in the development of the individual. In *The maturational processes and the facilitating environment* (pp. 83-92).

_______. (1963d). Morals and education. Reprinted in *The maturational processes and the facilitating environment* (pp. 93-105).

_______. (1963e). Psychotherapy of character disorders. In *The maturational processes and the facilitating environment* (pp. 203-216).

_______. (1965). *The maturational processes and the facilitating environment: Studies in the theory of emotional development*. New York: International Universities Press.

_______. (1967a). The location of cultural experience. *International Journal of Psycho-Analysis, 48*, 368-72.

_______. (1967b). Mirror-role of mother and family in child development. In P. Lomas (Ed.), *The predicament of the family: A psycho-analytical symposium*. London: Hogarth Press, 1967. Reprinted in *Playing and reality* (pp. 130-38). London: Tavistock, 1971; reprinted Harmondsworth: Penguin Books, 1974.

_______. (1969a). Obituary: James Strachey 1887-1967. *International Journal of Psycho-Analysis*, *50*, 129-32. Reprinted in *Psycho-analytic explorations* (pp. 506-510).

_______. (1969b). The use of an object and relating through identifications. *International Journal of Psycho-Analysis*, *50*, 711-16. Reprinted in *Playing and reality* (pp. 101-111).

_______. (1971). *Playing and reality.* London: Tavistock; reprinted Harmondsworth: Penguin Books, 1974.

_______. (1986). *Home is where we start from: Essays by a psychoanalyst.* Ed. Clare Winnicott, Ray Shepherd, & Madeleine Davis. New York: W. W. Norton, 1986.

_______. (1987). *The spontaneous gesture: Selected letters of D. W. Winnicott.* Ed. F. Robert Rodman. Cambridge, MA: Harvard University Press.

_______. (1988). *Human nature.* New York: Schocken Books.

_______. (1989). *Psycho-analytic explorations.* Eds. Clare Winnicott, Ray Shepherd & Madeleine Davis. Cambridge: Harvard University Press.

Winnicott, D. W. & Khan, M. Masud R. (1953). Review of *Psychoanalytic studies of the personality*, by W. R. D. Fairbairn. *International Journal of Psycho-Analysis.* Reprinted in *Psycho-analytic explorations* (pp. 413-22).

Wolfson, Harry Austryn. (1935). The internal senses in Latin, Arabic, and Hebrew philosophic texts. *Harvard Theological Review*, *28*(2), 69-133.

Wolstein, Benjamin. (1981). A historical note on Erich Fromm: 1955. *Contemporary Psychoanalysis*, *17*, 481-485.

Index

www.ingramcontent.com/pod-product-compliance
Lightning Source LLC
LaVergne TN
LVHW020650300926
849161LV00004B/883